Corporate Financial Strategy

The field of corporate finance has developed into a fairly complex one from its origins focused on a company's business and financial needs (financing, risk management, capitalization, and budgeting). *Corporate Financial Strategy* provides a critical introduction to the field and in doing so shows how organizations' financial strategies can be aligned with their overall business strategies.

Retaining the popular fundamentals of previous editions, the new edition brings things up to date with an array of new examples and cases, new pedagogical features such as learning objectives and suggested further reading, and includes new material on mergers and acquisitions, and valuations and forecasting.

Unlike other textbooks, Ruth Bender writes from the perspective of the firm rather than the investor. Combined with a structure driven by issues, the result is a textbook which is perfectly suited to those studying corporate finance and financial strategy at advanced undergraduate, postgraduate, and executive education levels.

Ruth Bender is Reader in Corporate Financial Strategy at Cranfield School of Management, UK. Prior to becoming an academic, she was a corporate finance partner with one of the UK's larger accounting firms and has also worked as a private equity manager in the City.

D1379997

Corporate Financial Strategy

Fourth Edition

Ruth Bender

Routledge
Taylor & Francis Group

LONDON AND NEW YORK

First published 2014
by Routledge
2 Park Square, Milton Park, Abingdon, Oxon OX14 4RN

and by Routledge
711 Third Avenue, New York, NY 10017

Routledge is an imprint of the Taylor & Francis Group, an informa business

British Library Cataloguing in Publication Data
A catalogue record for this book is available from the British Library

Library of Congress Cataloging-in-Publication Data
Bender, Ruth Corporate financial strategy / Ruth Bender. – Fourth Edition.
    pages cm
Includes bibliographical references and index.
ISBN 978-0-415-64039-8 (hardback) – ISBN 978-0-415-64041-1 (pbk.) –
ISBN 978-0-203-08276-8 (ebook) 1. Corporations–Finance.
2. Strategic planning. I. Title.
HG4026.W367 2013
658.15–dc23   2013014039

ISBN: 978-0-415-64039-8 (hbk)
ISBN: 978-0-415-64041-1 (pbk)
ISBN: 978-0-203-08276-8 (ebk)

Typeset in Times New Roman
by Cenveo Publisher Services

Printed and bound in Great Britain by
TJ International Ltd, Padstow, Cornwall

Contents

Figures

Tables

Case Studies

Working Insights

Preface to fourth edition

Although this is a fourth edition, it is the first edition of the book to be authored by 'Bender' rather than 'Bender and Ward'. However, the change in authorship has not led to any major amendments to the fundamental nature of the book. Keith Ward and I worked together and wrote together, and previous editions have reflected our common approach. Readers of previous editions will recognize the structure of the book and the models in use. Given that, now that Keith has retired from the project it seemed a little presumptuous to claim sole authorship of words originally written by both of us, and so in much of this preface, and throughout the book, the authorship is generally described as 'we' rather than 'I'.

The book focuses on the practical aspects of corporate finance. It shows how an appropriate financial strategy can be designed to complement corporate strategy and add value to an organization. While considering relevant theories of corporate finance, the main thrust is to show how they can be applied in the real world.

The material for the book is based upon our many years' experience as practitioners and consultants in, and teachers of, corporate finance. It has been refined and tested by use on advanced MBA courses at Cranfield School of Management and in programmes held for senior managers and financiers around the world. To bring it to life we include a number of real-company Case Studies, together with a wide range of illustrative examples. We link together various parts of financial theory and try to explain numerically how financial markets really work.

This is not a core financial management textbook. We have made no attempt to reproduce the many existing textbooks on financial theory, although the requisite theories are briefly summarized and explained. The objective is to go much further in placing the theory into a usable context, which should enable practising managers to understand more fully the potential value added by the best financial strategy available to them.

The structure of the book has been designed to make it of value even if not read from cover to cover. It is divided into four parts.

In Part 1 we give an overview of financial strategy and its role within the overall corporate strategy of the business. Set in the context of shareholder value, we examine what the share price tells us about the market's expectations of the business and how this can affect both corporate and financial strategies. We build up a model examining how these expectations and the financial drivers change over the life cycle of the company, and demonstrate what this means for a company's financial choices. We also examine how and why governance requirements of the business change as it develops through different stages of ownership.

Part 2 considers in much more detail the various components of the financial strategies which are appropriate to each stage of the company's development. We consider how the company's strategy will adapt to its changing circumstances, look at the changing sources of business risk, and explain how dividend policies and funding sources match the organization's needs.

In Part 3 we move away from the life cycle model to examine different types of financial instrument. The choice of financial instruments is fundamental to designing a financial strategy, and we deconstruct the key features of a variety of securities, setting them out in terms of the basic risk–return relationship that underlies pretty much everything in finance. Within this section we also examine companies' dividend and buy-back choices.

We have entitled Part 4 'Transactions and operating issues'. We start with a new chapter on valuations and forecasting, as these underlie most financial transactions and fundraising. Then we consider the major transactions that a company might encounter – flotation, acquisitions, restructuring. We also examine the role of the private equity industry in business today, and show how and why these investors can create value for their participants. Finally, we examine some issues fundamental to the running of a business – international considerations and working capital management.

We have relegated underlying detail to the Appendices, not because it is unimportant, but because our readership will either have studied it in detail (degree courses) or will perhaps be less interested in it (executives). Here you will find a brief overview of all of the theories of corporate finance needed to understand our approach in this book.

Very deliberately the illustrative examples and real Case Studies used throughout the book have been analysed using relatively simple mathematics; the simplifying assumptions do not destroy the underlying reasoning behind the analysis. The objective is to convey the conceptual logic behind financial strategy rather than to confuse with spuriously accurate mathematics and excessively complex formulae.

Changes in this edition

The third edition of this book was published in 2009, at a time when the financial world had just tipped into what the media were calling 'the credit crunch'. Since then, times have become darker for many people in the western economies, less so for the developing economies. But, in updating the text, I found that the principles and commentary remain valid today. That is why there are no significant changes to the structure of this text. However, the world's knowledge of finance has progressed, as has my own, and the updates that have been made reflect this.

The major changes made in this edition include:

Revision to the structure of 'linking corporate and financial strategies'	Chapter 4 of the third edition covered everything on how one should link corporate and financial strategies. While I kept stating that this was necessary, my students argued that it was far too long. That chapter has now been split into two, with Chapter 4 dealing with the explanation of financial strategy, and Chapter 5 covering the life cycle model.
Revised sections on corporate governance	The importance of corporate governance to corporate finance was emphasized in the third edition, with separate chapters on governance and on executive compensation. In this edition the work on executive compensation has been reduced, and is incorporated into the one governance chapter.
New chapter on valuations and forecasting	Few corporate finance textbooks explain valuation in a manner that reflects common practice and is easily understandable for readers without a technical background. Chapter 14 of this edition tries to remedy that, and also includes the material on forecasting that had previously been in an appendix.
Spreadsheets	The website accompanying the book now contains downloadable spreadsheets to demonstrate some of the concepts and calculations.
Index of companies	The vignettes used throughout the book provide insight into live corporate finance issues. To make them easier to find, there is now a separate index of companies.

We have also updated many of the Case Studies and Working Insights, and made textual alterations to most chapters.

In addition to changes to the material, we have made some changes to the layout of each chapter, as requested by our readers. Chapters now start with Learning objectives. Perhaps more significantly, we have included Suggested further reading at the end of each chapter, and tried to ensure where possible that this is material that is easily accessible (and, where possible, freely downloadable), so that all readers can use it. Within chapters, we have also added references to support the material, although we have tried to maintain the flavour of the earlier editions, and not to turn this into an academic treatise.

Companion website

The website that accompanies the book (www.routledge.com/9780415640398) has been extended to make it more useful to readers. As previously, it contains all of the Figures and Tables used in the book. Downloadable spreadsheets have also been included, to demonstrate, for example, valuations, acquisition synergies, and private equity structures.

The website also includes some key references and internet sites that I regularly use in my own work. And I have a fondness for some of the older Case Studies that were in previous editions but had to be deleted this time around, they too are on the website in case you were missing them.

Acknowledgements

I have received input from many sources in preparing this fourth edition. I am grateful to generations of MBA students and executives, and to colleagues and past colleagues at Cranfield, all of whom have given feedback and ideas. However, I started this preface by pointing out that the development of this book was a joint venture. Accordingly, I dedicate this edition, with thanks, to Keith Ward.

Ruth Bender

Part 1

Putting financial strategy into context

1 Corporate financial strategy

Setting the context

Learning objectives

After reading this chapter you should be able to:

1. Understand what financial strategy is, and how it can add value.
2. Explain why shareholder value is created by investments with a positive net present value.
3. Appreciate how the relationship between perceived risk and required return governs companies and investors.
4. Differentiate the different models of measuring shareholder value.
5. Explain why share price is not necessarily a good proxy for company value.
6. Outline how agency theory is relevant to corporate finance.
7. Identify the impact of different stakeholders on financial strategy and shareholder value.

Introduction

The main focus of a financial strategy is on the financial aspects of strategic decisions. Inevitably, this implies a close linkage with the interests of shareholders and hence with capital markets. However, a sound financial strategy must, like the best corporate and competitive strategies, take account of all the external and internal stakeholders in the business.

Capital market theories and research are mainly concerned with the macro economic level, whereas financial strategies are specific and tailored to the needs of the individual company and, in some cases, even to subdivisions within that company. Therefore the working definition of financial strategy which will be used throughout the book tries to take account of the need to focus on these interrelationships at the micro level of individual business organizations.

Financial strategy has two components:

(1)   Raising the funds needed by an organization in the most appropriate manner.
(2)   Managing the employment of those funds within the organization.

When we discuss the most appropriate manner for raising funds, we take account both of the overall strategy of the organization and the combined weighted requirements of its key stakeholders. It is important to realize that 'most appropriate' might not mean 'at the lowest cost': a major objective of financial strategy should be to add value, which may not always be achieved by attempting to minimize costs. And when we discuss the employment of funds, we include within that the decision to reinvest or distribute any profit generated by the organization.

A major objective for commercial organizations is to develop a sustainable competitive advantage in order to achieve a more than acceptable, risk adjusted rate of return for the key stakeholders. Therefore, a logical way to judge the success of a financial strategy is by reference to the contribution made to such an overall objective.

Financial strategy and standard financial theory

Let us state our case immediately – if you worship at the altar of the efficient market hypothesis; if you consider that the market value of a company really reflects the discounted value of its future cash flows; if you believe implicitly the work of Modigliani and Miller (as an absolute rather than as a guide to theory development), then some of what you read in this book is going to make you uncomfortable.[1]

However, if you have ever wondered why it is that intelligent and well-qualified finance directors and their advisers seem to be prepared to spend large amounts of their time and their shareholders' money devising complex schemes to do things which, according to financial theory, are either completely unproductive or actually counterproductive in terms of increasing shareholder wealth … read on.

There is a large body of research evidence which indicates that financial markets are quite efficient at identifying and allowing for some relatively simple accounting tricks, such as changes in inventory valuation or depreciation policies. The research shows that such

---

1   Having said that, if you have no idea about the concepts mentioned in this paragraph, it would be well worth your while to explore them in one of the standard financial textbooks.

accounting manoeuvres do not increase company value, as the markets see through them. However, as will be illustrated by the real examples used throughout the book, many reputable companies employ sophisticated 'creative' accounting presentations to disguise the effects of their (presumably widely understood) transactions. A major thrust of this book is therefore to try to bridge this gap between the academic theorists, who profess to believe that financial markets are becoming ever more efficient and perfect, and the practising financial managers, who ignore the financial theory and rely on what they see as working in practice.

A fundamental proposition behind this book is that financial theory fulfils a very useful conceptual role in providing an analytical framework with which to dissect and understand actual, individual corporate finance transactions. It is also a major contention of ours that people are wrong to interpret financial theory as suggesting that shareholder value cannot be significantly improved by the implementation of the most appropriate financial strategy for each particular business. Value, as we shall see, is a function of the relationship between perceived risk and required return. Shareholders, and other key stakeholders, do not all perceive risks in the same way, nor do they have the same desired relationship between risk and return. Thus value can be created in the cracks between the different perceptions, and it is here that financial strategy can blossom.

Risk and return: a fundamental of finance

A fundamental principle underlying financial theory is that investors will demand a return commensurate with the risk characteristics that they perceive in their investment. This is illustrated in Figure 1.1.

The diagram in Figure 1.1 is known colloquially as the 'risk–return line' and shows the required return for any given level of risk. Although the axes are often referred to as 'risk' and 'return', it is important to appreciate that their full descriptions are 'perceived risk' and 'required return'. If you do not understand the full extent of the risks that you are taking on an investment, you might settle for a lower required return than another investor with a better appreciation. Alternatively, a sophisticated investor with a great understanding of the low probability of a particularly adverse outcome might settle for a lower return than a naïve investor who runs scared of the downside. What is important is each investor's *perception* of the risk; it is in the gaps between their different views that a tailored financial strategy can often add value.

In a similar fashion the vertical axis in Figure 1.1, often referred to as 'return', is actually *required* return. The very fact that an investment carries a level of risk means that there is no

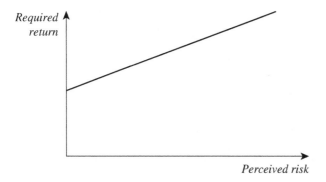

Figure 1.1 The relationship between risk and return.

guarantee of its final outcome (risk is generally defined in finance as the volatility of expected outcomes);[2] the graph shows what the investor would need in order to match the market expectations.

Financial strategy

We must start this section with a disclaimer: although we will use some strategic models, this is not a book on competitive strategy. Many excellent tomes discuss that subject, setting out the whys and wherefores of determining and pursuing appropriate strategies. This book is about corporate financial strategy and it is in this context that strategy is discussed. However, because we make this distinction, we have to define our terms very clearly, so that you, our readers, are left in no doubt about our purpose.

Consider the representation of a company in Figure 1.2.

To most people, a company is seen as an end in its own right. It serves markets, manufactures products (in this book, for simplicity we use 'product' to include service provision), employs staff, and its strategy should be about selecting the most appropriate markets, production facilities, or employees in which to invest. Corporate growth and success – often measured financially in terms of turnover or profit, or by non-financial stakeholders in terms of inputs and outputs – are what's seen as important, and the business develops a momentum of its own. But Figure 1.2 shows that the investment process does in fact extend over two stages: investors choose the companies in which they want to invest, and the companies choose how to apply those funds to their activities.

For example, as investors we can choose to invest our funds in the UK or elsewhere in the world. We can opt to put our money into the pharmaceutical sector, or into printing or food production or any other sector we choose. And if we do care to be exposed to UK pharmaceutical companies, we can decide specifically, for example, to buy shares in very different companies such as GlaxoSmithKline or Oxford BioMedica. The top process in Figure 1.2 relates to this investor decision.

The lower process shows how the company (acting through its directors' decisions) decides that yes, it does want to be in the pharmaceuticals sector; that it will apply this strategy

Figure 1.2 The two-stage investment process.

---

2   Although financiers model risk in terms of volatility, to most of us it is the downside volatility that is the issue, profits or cash flows being too low rather than too high. Stulz suggests that the goal for corporate risk management should be the 'elimination of costly lower-tail outcomes', reducing the costs of financial distress while preserving the ability to benefit from upside volatility. Stulz, R. M. (1996), 'Rethinking Risk Management', *Journal of Applied Corporate Finance*, 9(3): 8–25.

Working Insight 1.1

Definitions of value

Investor value: Reflects the required returns of the capital markets, and is mirrored in the financial value placed on the company's securities by the markets.

Corporate value: Is the present value of the expected returns from a combination of the current business strategies and future investment programmes.

---

by developing its own drugs (or perhaps by buying the results of others' research, or perhaps by producing generics); or that it will sell in various specific geographical markets but not others. The 'projects' referred to in the lower box in Figure 1.2 refer to how the company configures its assets, ranging from how many staff it chooses to employ, through to whether it should develop a new product, acquire a competitor, or move into a different sector.

The energies of most business people tend to be applied to the lower box, to improving the investment in the project portfolio, to 'making it a better business'. But in corporate financial strategy our aim is different: we are trying to improve matters in the top box, to make it a better investment for shareholders, to create shareholder value.

This leads us to two definitions, one for each of the processes shown in Figure 1.2.

The two definitions of value shown in Working Insight 1.1 correspond to the two-stage investment model. Investor value is about creating value in the top box, for investors. Corporate value, the one with which most business people are more familiar, is about configuring the company to be a 'better' business. It is a prime role of management to ensure that the shareholder value properly reflects the corporate value; this is one of the roles of financial strategy. Further, as we will discuss later, our working definition of 'investor value' comes down to 'value for shareholders', focusing on a specific category of investor.

It is possible for a business to generate value in one box, but not the other. In analysing a company, there are four questions to ask: Is it a good product? Is it a good business? Is it a good company? Is it a good investment? Working Insight 1.2 illustrates this.

Valuing investments

Any financial investment can be valued by reference to the present value of the future cash flows which it is expected to generate. It is intuitively obvious that a future cash inflow is not worth as much as the same sum of money received immediately, due to the waiting period involved. Even if we know for certain that we will get this money, there is still the 'time value' of the delay. And in the real business world, little is certain; there is also the risk that these expected future cash flows will not actually be realized. Furthermore, inflation might erode the value of monies to be received in the future. These are three good reasons why we prefer money now rather than in the future.

Using a well-developed technique, known as discounted cash flow, or DCF,[3] expected future cash flows can be converted to their present value equivalents by multiplying them by

---

3 Readers unfamiliar with the technique will find it fully covered in any of the standard finance textbooks.

Working Insight 1.2

Is it good?

A good **Product** is one that is fit for purpose.

It is possible to have a good Product that is not in a good **Business**. This is clearly demonstrated by the many social networking companies with millions of users which have yet to work out a model for monetizing their potential asset. But even having a good product and an income stream does not in itself create a good business: in the 1980s poor management and some bad business decisions led to Apple's Mac losing the market to the PC, to which it was technically superior.

It is possible to have a good Business, but not a good **Company**. What we mean by this is that a sound business can be crippled by the wrong financial strategy. A classic example of a good Business in a bad Company was Eurotunnel, which took on too much gearing in its early years, and struggled until its financial strategy was eventually changed in a reconstruction that swapped debt for equity.

Finally, it is possible to have a good Company that is a bad **Investment**. Shareholders invest in order to make a return that more than reflects their perceived risk, and that return comes from dividends and growth in the share price. If a share is already overvalued, such growth is unlikely. This point is discussed continually throughout the book.

---

an appropriate discount factor, using a discount rate that takes account of the pure time value of money, the associated risk, and likely inflation. Applying such a discount rate to all the future cash flows makes the resulting present values directly comparable. Using these DCF techniques, we can determine a present value for each of the cash flow streams from an investment, and add them together to arrive at a net present value (NPV). An example is shown in Working Insight 1.3. Tables of discount factors are included at the back of this book.

The outcomes of Working Insight 1.3 are shown graphically in Figure 1.3.

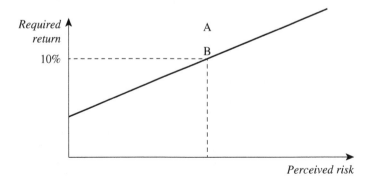

Figure 1.3 Value creation in discounting example.

Project A has made a return of £64 more than the required 10%, putting it above the risk–return line, showing that it generates value. Project B produces an NPV of zero – it is exactly on the line.

Working Insight 1.3

Illustrating discounting

DisCo has the opportunity to invest in one of two, four-year projects. Each involves spending £1,000 immediately. In Project A, it will receive a return of £300 in Year 1, then £350 for each of the next three years. In Project B the return is higher, but delayed: £30 in the first year, then £300, then £400 and then £620 in the final year. DisCo requires a rate of return of 10% for investments of this risk level.

The formula for calculating the discount factor is $1 \div (1+i)^n$

Where i is the required rate of return, and n is the number of years.

Thus the discount factors for a 10% required rate of return are calculated as follows:

	Year 0	Year 1	Year 2	Year 3	Year 4
Formula	$1 \div (1.1)^0$	$1 \div (1.1)^1$	$1 \div (1.1)^2$	$1 \div (1.1)^3$	$1 \div (1.1)^4$
Discount factor	1.000	0.909	0.826	0.751	0.683

The streams of cash flows is discounted as follows:

	Year 0	Year 1	Year 2	Year 3	Year 4
Project A cash flows	(1,000)	300	350	350	350
Discount factor	1.000	0.909	0.826	0.751	0.683
Present value	(1,000)	273	289	263	239
Net Present Value	**64**				
Project B cash flows	(1,000)	30	300	400	620
Discount factor	1.000	0.909	0.826	0.751	0.683
Present value	(1,000)	27	248	301	424
Net Present Value	**0**				

Summing the present values of each project gives its NPV. From this, we see that DisCo would be better off taking project A. Its NPV is +£64, meaning that the return exceeds the 10% requirement by £64. Project B, with its NPV of zero, means that they would have worked at the project for four years and ended up no better off than with any alternative investment of a similar risk level.

Applying this technique to any investment immediately highlights a key element in increasing shareholder value; shareholder value is increased only if the discounted present value of the expected future cash flows generated by any investment is greater than the current cost of that investment. In Working Insight 1.3, by taking Project A, DisCo has increased shareholder value by £64. It is not good enough merely to generate the 'market' (risk-adjusted) return, as DisCo does in Project B – we have to exceed it.

Why is it not good enough merely to satisfy shareholders' requirements? The answer to that is that the risk–return line shows what the market requires for a particular level of risk. Any competitor company should deliver that on average – it's the norm. Providing value means being better than the market, otherwise what reason is there for the shareholder to invest in one company rather than another? Merely generating the rate of return required by the investor creates no value at all: it would be the equivalent of paying £1,000 to receive, immediately, the sum of £1,000 – value is not destroyed in such a transaction, but there is no real reason for bothering to undertake it. In a zero NPV transaction investors are merely swapping current sums of money for their equivalent in future cash flows. This is perhaps obvious, but absolutely critical to appreciate.

Creating shareholder value

In a perfectly competitive market, market forces would dictate that all investments receive only their risk-adjusted required rates of return. Consequently, no shareholder value would be created. Accordingly, it stands to reason that shareholder value is only increased by exploiting imperfections in the marketplace.

The greatest imperfections arise in product markets, i.e. the actual marketplaces in which specific products are sold to customers. Companies can increase shareholder value by creating a sustainable competitive advantage through selecting and implementing an appropriate competitive strategy. For example, they can create barriers to entry into an industry to keep out competitors and thus prevent the rules of perfect competition from applying in that industry. As a result, new companies cannot economically afford to enter the industry even though the financial returns available are above normal levels. This restriction on potential new competition enables the existing players in the industry to enjoy an apparently excessive financial return on their investments.[4]

More importantly from our point of view, investment can be related to the two-stage process illustrated in Figure 1.2, in which investments in specific product–market interfaces form the second stage. Initially a group of investors (shareholders, banks, etc.) put funds into a company, and the company subsequently invests these funds in a range of specific projects in particular markets. The optimum relative mix of these investors in any particular company, the way in which they perceive the risks involved in the investment and the alternative methods of giving them their required financial return, can also create a super-normal return and are the principal aspects of financial strategy. Consequently this book concentrates primarily on this first stage of raising the funds required by the business and on the methods of managing these funds within the company. Financial strategy is about raising the funds required by the organization in the manner most appropriate to its overall corporate and competitive strategies, and also managing the use of those funds within the organization.

In the theoretical world of perfectly competitive markets, the overall portfolio of projects which makes up each company can only achieve exactly the risk-adjusted return required by the investors in the company. As explained in Appendix 1 on financial theory, investors can diversify, and hence reduce their overall risks by holding an appropriate portfolio of different investments. Thus their dependence upon the financial performance of any single company can be lowered by diversification strategies. Consequently in an efficient financial market the return received from any such single company investment should be driven only by the specific risk associated with that investment, when considered relative to the total available investment opportunities.

---

4   However, in reality, creating an effective barrier to entry normally requires substantial additional financial investment; for example, in very strong branding through heavy marketing expenditure, or by achieving material cost advantages through developing significant economies of scale, etc. Consequently this apparently excessive financial return can initially be regarded as providing the normal required return on this additional investment. Any remaining excess financial return represents the true 'value added' for shareholders.

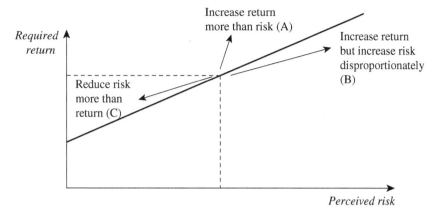

Figure 1.4 Value-creating alternatives.

This investor-based view of portfolio management suggests that if companies invest in an inappropriate range of projects which, when combined directly together, compound the overall risk of the business, they will reduce investor value rather than increase it. Sophisticated investors could build their own investment portfolios so as to achieve an equivalent overall return, but without incurring the increased business risk associated with this combined business. Consequently they demand a higher return to compensate for the higher risk, and this is achieved by giving the investment in such a combined business a lower value. It is not the high risk of any individual project which destroys investor value, as the high-risk project should have a correspondingly high required return to offset the risk. However, if the overall risk of the portfolio is greater than the sum of its parts, the total portfolio (i.e. the company) will be worth less to an investor.

Interestingly, companies which try to reduce risks by investing in a well-diversified range of products can destroy shareholder value rather than enhance it. If significant costs are incurred by the company (such as the classic conglomerate) in creating and managing such a diversified portfolio of businesses, the investor might be substantially worse off. Intelligent investors can achieve this reduced investment risk at much lower cost by setting up their own, similarly diversified investment portfolio. Consequently in an efficient and rational financial market, they will penalize, rather than reward, companies for incurring these unnecessary management costs which do not add value.[5] Indeed in the real world, with its inherent imperfections, this illustrates the ways in which shareholder value can be created. As shown in Figure 1.4, any strategic move above the risk–return line creates shareholder value, whereas anything which results in a position below the line destroys value. Therefore it is not simply a question of increasing return or reducing risk, but of the level of increased return compared to the increased perception of risk.

In Figure 1.4, any strategy which moves below the shareholders' risk–return line will destroy shareholder value. Thus, strategy A is obviously value-enhancing, increasing returns

---

5 One explanation for the conglomerate discount is that analysts following a conglomerate cannot be specialists in all of its business areas, and their sentiment and [lack of] knowledge can be drivers of the discount. Research on conglomerate discounts suggests that they vary between countries and do not always exist. There is also a suggestion that the perceived discount actually arises due to errors in research techniques: Villalonga, B. (2004), 'Diversification Discount or Premium? New Evidence from the Business Information Tracking Series', *Journal of Finance*, 59(2): 479–506.

to far more than the associated risk profile. Similarly, strategy B is obviously value-destroying; although returns have increased, the disproportionate rise in risk moves the value below the line. (For strategy B, markets might be fooled for a short time by the increase in profits, but as soon as the risk-increasing nature of the strategy changes is realized, share prices will fall.)

Strategy C in Figure 1.4 is interesting. Although it is obvious that C should add value, as it is an 'above the line' move, many people have difficulty with the concept of a company deliberately reducing profitability and yet still adding value. However, this is a perfectly legitimate, and common, tactic – any time a company buys an insurance policy it is reducing profits in order to safeguard against risk.

It should, however, be noted that there is potentially a difference between the risk–return perceptions of the senior managers of the company and its investors, and that this could cause a conflict in their objectives. The theoretical assumption is that everyone has the same perception of risk, but this is most unlikely to be true. As already stated, professionally managed investment institutions can develop sophisticated investment portfolios which substantially diversify their investors' risk away from any particular company. It is much more difficult for the full-time managers within a particular company to diversify their perceived risks, e.g. the risk of losing their jobs, which may be associated with any specific high-risk business strategy (particularly if the failure of such a high-risk strategy could lead to the total financial collapse of the company). Senior managers can, and often do, attempt to achieve some degree of risk reduction either by implementing a less risky strategy or by diversifying into other areas of operation. As the risk of corporate collapse, or of high volatility in profits, is the key driver to this managerially led diversification strategy, the business is likely to invest in less risky projects or in areas of operation which are counter-cyclical to the current main business focus.

Such a perceived need to reduce overall risk may well become more important to these key managers as they become older, particularly if they have very long periods of employment in a single company. These long-serving managers may only have the normal linear positive correlation between risk and return at the lower end of the risk spectrum. However, they may demand an almost exponentially increasing return in order to compensate them for taking on what they would otherwise consider as an unacceptably high-risk strategy. This is graphically illustrated in Figure 1.5, which also shows the well-diversified institutionally-based investor, who has a linear risk–return expectation across the whole range of potential investment risks.

A type of investor with yet another different potential perception of risk is also shown in Figure 1.5: the venture capitalist. Venture capitalists are only interested in relatively high-risk and high-return investments. This is their chosen investment territory, which means that they would consider most large diversified businesses as not being worth their consideration. They demand a relatively high minimum return from any project they take on (represented by the horizontal portion of their line in Figure 1.5). Inevitably this tends to force them to focus on higher-risk projects as only these can supply the type of return which they consider acceptable.

In determining a suitable financial and corporate strategy for a business, it is important to understand the drivers of the key stakeholders. A venture capital-backed business run by a risk-averse senior manager may be an uncomfortable place to be, as there will be a clash in their objectives: the minimum return demanded by the venture capitalist may be greater than the return associated with the highest-risk project which is acceptable to the manager.[6]

---

6   And, while avoiding the financial risk of investment, the manager might be courting the risk of dismissal if s/he fails to satisfy the backers.

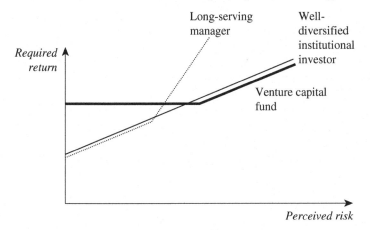

Figure 1.5 Risk profiles of different stakeholder groups.

The well-diversified investor takes a linear view of the risk–return relationship. This contrasts with the long-serving manager, who becomes very risk-averse above a certain level of risk. The venture capital fund demands too high a return to invest in low-risk opportunities, but becomes interested at higher-risk levels. Although the venture capital required return could be synchronous with that of other investors, it is shown here as being slightly lower, for illustrative purposes.

Sustainable competitive advantage

The overriding financial reason for the existence of most commercial organizations is to achieve a more than acceptable return for the investors and other key stakeholders in the business. As demonstrated in Figure 1.1, this return must be assessed in the context of the particular risks associated with any business, as it is a fundamental economic principle that increased risks must be compensated for with higher potential for returns.

It is also fundamental that this economic corporate objective is described as achieving a 'more than acceptable' return (i.e. a positive net present value). However, in some ways this may appear to contradict modern financial theory, which suggests that it is impossible for investors consistently to achieve an abnormally large risk-adjusted return on their investments. In a perfectly competitive market this is undoubtedly true, as these perfect competition forces will drive down all returns to the 'normal' level required by the market.

For example, if a particular investment were to show a return above the normal market level, investors in the perfect market would all try to buy this investment. Inevitably this buying pressure would increase the price of the investment and reduce the rate of return to the normal market level, when it would no longer be exceptionally attractive. Conversely, an investment showing a lower than normal return is unattractive, with existing investors looking to sell but other potential investors having no incentive to buy. This will force the price of the investment to fall, until its return has increased to the normal market level.

In the real world, it is impossible to find any long-term investment which can truly be regarded as risk-free. This has been very forcibly demonstrated to many investors in recent years with the dramatic collapses of very large companies, financial institutions and even governments. But even a government-backed security issued in a financially sound and politically stable economy can only be regarded as truly risk-free if it is a very short-term investment. Over the longer term, such a government security has risks regarding the relative purchasing power of the funds which are received back at the final maturity of the investment; higher-than-expected inflation could significantly reduce the real value of these funds. Also such investments normally pay interest during their lifetime, and the total expected return over the life of the investment would have been based on reinvesting these periodic interest receipts at the market rate of return until the final maturity date. If prevailing interest rates decline during the period of the investment, the total funds available on final termination may be lower than originally forecast. Such differences introduce a risk into this guaranteed investment.

Much greater uncertainties and risk are inevitable facts of life in the commercial world, where future returns are not guaranteed, nor even known with any degree of certainty, and where the competitive situation can change dramatically in a very short period of time. Consequently the ability to manage in such an environment is a critical component of any organization's business strategy, as will be made clear throughout the book. In fact it is true to say that a business can only achieve its desired aim of a 'more than satisfactory return' for investors by identifying and exploiting imperfections in the markets in which it operates (which can be done by successfully investing in R&D, or branding, or creating other strategic assets). Thus a major objective of corporate and competitive strategies is to develop a sustainable competitive advantage, which enables the business to achieve and maintain a return in excess of that which would be allowed in a perfectly competitive market. This process is essential to increasing long-term shareholder value, which itself is a key objective for nearly all the large companies, particularly those which are publicly quoted, which today dominate the major economies of the world.

Managing and measuring shareholder value

Thus far, we have defined shareholder value in terms of the investors' achievement of a positive net present value – a return that more than compensates for the perceived risks. This was illustrated in Figure 1.4 as being an 'above the line' return. In this section we examine three different (but linked) ways of measuring shareholder value, and demonstrate how they might be used in practice to create that value. The three metrics under consideration are:

1   Shareholder Value Added
2   Economic profit
3   Total shareholder return.

Shareholder Value Added

The Shareholder Value Added (SVA) approach set out by Alfred Rappaport[7] estimates the value of an investment by discounting forecast cash flows by the cost of capital. Rappaport stated that the value of a company is dependent on seven drivers of value, as shown in Working Insight 1.4.

Management can use their knowledge of current sales levels and forecasts of the first five drivers in order to prepare cash flow forecasts for a suitable period. Such a period would be defined based on the likely time-span for the company's competitive advantage – driver six. Discounting these at the cost of capital (driver seven) leads to an enterprise value for operations; this can easily be translated into a value for equity. This technique is most effectively applied to individual business units within a company, whose separate values can be cumulated to arrive at the value of a business, or to create alternate scenarios.

We have introduced the drivers of value briefly here, but this is a very useful model, and you will see us refer to it over and again in this book. The model reflects the methodology

---

7   Rappaport, A. (1998), *Creating Shareholder Value* (New York: Free Press).

Working Insight 1.4

Seven drivers of value

1 Increase sales growth
2 Increase operating profit margin
3 Reduce cash tax rate
4 Reduce incremental investment in capital expenditure
5 Reduce investment in working capital
6 Increase time period of competitive advantage
7 Reduce cost of capital

underlying most corporate valuations (Chapter 14). Furthermore, it is a useful way to explore sensitivity analysis and to evaluate synergies in acquisitions (Chapter 16).

Unlike the two metrics discussed below, SVA can be difficult to use as a one-period tool. Positive free cash flow in a period is not necessarily good; negative free cash flow might not be bad. The metric is mainly used for valuation and planning rather than as a periodic measure of performance.

Economic profit

Economic profit (sometimes known as 'residual income') is a generic name that covers many of the different variants of profit-based measures of shareholder value. This is the surplus earned by a business in a period after deducting all expenses including the cost of capital. It can be calculated in two ways, as shown in Working Insight 1.5.

Working Insight 1.5

Calculation of economic profit

Operating profit after tax	£2,400
Capital employed	£20,000
Cost of capital	10%

Therefore, the Return on Investment is 2,400 ÷ 20,000 = 12%

Calculation 1	
Operating profit after tax	2,400
less: cost of capital (20,000 @ 10%)	2,000
Economic profit	£400

Calculation 2	
Economic profit = Capital employed × Spread	
Spread = Return on Investment less Cost of Capital	
Economic profit = 20,000 × (12% − 10%) =	£400

Economic profit (EP) is primarily used for performance measurement. It has the advantage that it teaches managers a great respect for capital – it is no longer seen as 'free' – and encourages them to run their businesses so as to minimize capital employed.[8] In many instances this behavioural change is beneficial to the business, although some would argue that EP is a single-period measure, and taking it to extremes can lead to capital-starved businesses, limiting growth, and reducing the utility of other stakeholders.

There is of course a relationship between SVA and economic profit. It can be shown that the discounted value of the projected future economic profits of a business will equate to the SVA. Perhaps more intuitively, whereas SVA shows the value of a business over its lifetime, economic profit shows whether the company is creating value in any single period.

Total shareholder return

Both SVA and economic profit are 'internal' measures of shareholder value: in terms of the two-decision model introduced in Figure 1.2 they show how well the company is implementing its competitive strategy to create value from the product–market mix and funding arrangements it has chosen. Total shareholder return (TSR) is an 'external' measure – it looks at the value created for shareholders, the top box in Figure 1.2.

TSR represents the total return to the shareholders in a period: the increase in share price, plus any dividends paid during the period (see Working Insight 1.6). This performance measure is very commonly used in directors' long-term incentive plans, often calculated over a three-year period.

From the point of view of the shareholders, TSR is probably the most accurate measure of value – it shows exactly what they have received from the company in the period. However, as a measure of managers' performance the metric has limitations. Share prices (as we will discuss in Chapter 2) reflect market expectations rather than corporate performance. Adequate performance from a company expected to do poorly might increase share price far more than superb performance from one that was already a market favourite. A company could be doing well, but be in an out-of-favour sector and thus see its share price fall. Alternatively, a poor company could see its price rise for reasons unconnected with underlying performance. When used as a

---

Working Insight 1.6

Total shareholder return

Share price at 1 January	100
Share price at 31 December	110
Capital gain in the year	10
Dividend paid in the year	5
Total return	15
Total Shareholder Return (TSR)	15%

---

8   Economic profit is a generic version of Economic Value Added, EVA™, a measure promoted by the consultancy firm Stern Stewart. In EVA calculations, both the operating profit and the capital employed are adjusted to remove some of the distorting effects of accounting adjustments.

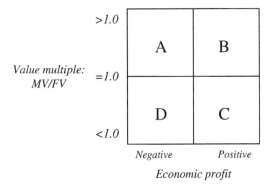

Figure 1.6 The value matrix.

measure of directors' performance, TSR is generally benchmarked relative to similar companies, which helps eliminate some – but by no means all – of these difficulties.[9]

Some reflections on shareholder value

Earlier, we stated that shareholder value should properly reflect corporate value. It is now appropriate to explore that statement in more depth.

Figure 1.6 sets out the dimensions of a company's value in a two-by-two matrix. Assume that you, as a very skilled financier, have calculated the exact price at which the company's shares should trade. This is the *fundamental value* (FV) of the share. The value multiple on the vertical axis represents the actual market value (MV) divided by this fundamental value. If the share is trading at its fundamental value, this will be 1.0.

The horizontal axis of the matrix represents economic profit or any similar measure of 'is this a good company?'. A positive economic profit implies a business that is doing well; negative economic profit indicates a poor business. (It should be noted that this last definition is quite restrictive as, in practice, a good business might make an economic loss if in any one year it were to invest heavily for the future. However, the principles hold.)

Our company can fall into any of the four segments shown in the matrix, labelled A to D for convenience. So, in which segment do you want to be?

We have asked this question of many different groups of MBA students and executives, with interesting results. Almost invariably the majority of respondents chose to be in segment B, a good company with a high share price – overvalued by the markets. But there is always a minority who would prefer to be in C, and the occasional choice of A, or even D. Further questioning reveals that each of the different responses comes about because the respondents have, without consciously realizing it, taken on a different point of view.

For a company situated in quadrants A or B, i.e. with a value multiple greater than 1, the implication is that the market is overvaluing its shares. The only real issue then becomes: how long can we continue to fool the market? In practice, companies might remain overvalued for many years, but ultimately reality will catch up with them and the share price will

9   The TSR calculation can be made considerably more sophisticated than suggested in Working Insight 1.6. For example, average share prices over a period can be used rather than spot prices on particular dates. Or, the dividend can be assumed to be reinvested in the company's shares rather than paid as cash.

fall. So, A or B are good positions to be in if you are about to sell your shares, but probably not otherwise. As managers about to exercise our share options we would like to see the company in B: we could sell the shares quickly, but still remain with a fundamentally good business. As outgoing managers we may have less interest in the strength of the business, so quadrant A would also be a reasonable place – provided that we can escape quickly with our money and reputation intact!

Undervalued companies, with a value multiple of less than 1, sit in quadrants C or D. Who would want their company to be undervalued? Well, those same managers who were happy to exercise their share options while sitting in quadrant B might be very pleased to be granted those options while the company was sitting in C: they could make money on the share options simply by persuading the market to reassess its false view of the company's prospects, causing an automatic share price rise.[10]

There is of course a danger to being in quadrant C or D. The company in C is a takeover target. It is a valuable asset, well run, and not appreciated by the market. Almost anyone could buy it at this undervalue, and make a profit. The company in D is less attractive: it is an undervalued asset but it is also underperforming. But to a purchaser in the same industry, who would know how to turn it around, it could be an attractive buy. And although as existing shareholders a position in C or D would fail to please us, as prospective shareholders, we might choose to buy into C or D in the hope that they attract a takeover which will return us a swift profit.[11]

There are two key lessons to be learned from an analysis of the value matrix. The first is that the different groups of stakeholders have different interests in the company and its activities, and that these interests may conflict. The shareholder's keen anticipation of a takeover may not be shared by the incumbent management and employees who could lose their jobs. Prospective shareholders seek an undervalued company; existing shareholders want to sell on a high. This stakeholder analysis leads into agency theory, which exposes the different motivations of directors and shareholders. Both stakeholder analysis and agency theory are discussed later in this chapter.

The second key lesson is that in the long term there is only one place to be that is fair to all of the stakeholders, existing and prospective, and that is to be trading at the fundamental value; a company which is fairly valued by the market such that its share price reflects its worth. (We hope that it goes without saying that one would want the company to be on the right-hand side of the matrix, in 'good company' territory.)

It is interesting to note that Warren Buffett, the legendary investor who runs Berkshire Hathaway, effectively states this in his 'Owner's Manual' for shareholders. He sets out thirteen principles, and adds a fourteenth: that the share price should accurately reflect, as far as possible, the fundamental (intrinsic) value of the company. Case Study 1.1 quotes this in full.

---

10 Aboody, D. and Kasznik, R. (2000), 'CEO Stock Options and the Timing of Corporate Voluntary Disclosures', *Journal of Accounting and Economic*, 29(1): 73–100, found that chief executive officers (CEOs) manage share prices around option award dates by delaying good news and rushing forward bad news.

11 Before you lose money by following this investment strategy, we should point out that although in the long run the prices of shares in quadrants C or D will rise, this will only happen as the market reassesses its views of the company. In other words, you can make money by buying the whole of a company in quadrant C, but if you are just buying a small stake, value will only be realized once the market has reappraised the company. And, as the economist John Maynard Keynes warned, 'the markets can remain irrational for longer than you can remain solvent'.

Case Study 1.1

Berkshire Hathaway

To the extent possible, we would like each Berkshire shareholder to record a gain or loss in market value during his period of ownership that is proportional to the gain or loss in per-share intrinsic value recorded by the company during that holding period. For this to come about, the relationship between the intrinsic value and the market price of a Berkshire share would need to remain constant, and by our preferences at 1-to-1. As that implies, we would rather see Berkshire's stock price at a fair level than a high level. Obviously, Charlie and I can't control Berkshire's price. But by our policies and communications, we can encourage informed, rational behavior by owners that, in turn, will tend to produce a stock price that is also rational. Our it's-as-bad-to-be-overvalued-as-to-be-undervalued approach may disappoint some shareholders. We believe, however, that it affords Berkshire the best prospect of attracting long-term investors who seek to profit from the progress of the company rather than from the investment mistakes of their partners.

Source: www.berkshirehathaway.com/owners.html

Reasons that market value might differ from fundamental value

Having stated that a company's market value might (indeed, probably will) differ from its fundamental value, it is worth considering why this should be. One obvious reason is that the share price of a company reflects a view of its future prospects, and an asymmetry of information might lead the market to have different views to the executives and board. Other possible reasons are given in Working Insight 1.7.

Who are the shareholders?

We ought here to highlight a dilemma faced by the directors of many public companies. We speak in this book about creating value for 'shareholders', as if shareholders were an amorphous mass, who all had the same objectives and were all interested in the long-term value of the company. Alas, this is no longer the case. Shareholders holding a majority might have different desires from minority shareholders seeking investment performance. Some shareholders will remain as owners of the shares for many years; others will hold them for a matter of months, days or perhaps just seconds. Some will be content to wait for the business growth to be reflected in the share price; others may want immediate cash pay-outs. The growth in high-frequency trading means that a company's shareholder base can change from one second to the next: algorithm-driven trades take no account of long-term value.

Market statistics show that the average holding period for UK equities had fallen from about five years in the mid-1960s to about 7.5 months by 2007. This mirrors trends in the USA, Tokyo, and other major exchanges.[12]

Furthermore, share ownership is often decoupled from voting rights, which causes more problems for conscientious directors wishing to run the business for the long term. It is possible

12 Data are taken from a speech given by Andrew Haldane, an executive director of the Bank of England, in September 2010. www.bankofengland.co.uk/publications/Documents/speeches/2010/speech445.pdf

---

Working Insight 1.7

Reasons for market value to diverge from fundamental value

- The company's strategy, profitability, or risk might not be communicated properly to the markets.
- Supply and demand for the share might be in imbalance. For example, some companies undertaking an Initial Public Offering deliberately restrict the number of available shares, in order to increase the price. (See Chapter 15.) Another example would be a company that moved into the FTSE 100 index, where some tracker funds would have to own it, thus boosting demand.
- For a share with low liquidity (i.e. few shares traded/available), even small purchases or sales can increase volatility in prices.
- Takeover expectations might raise the share price.
- Governance issues can influence perceptions of risk, and therefore price.
- Shares followed by few analysts can have greater volatility, as less information is available.
- The market sometimes applies a 'conglomerate discount' to groups containing companies with dissimilar activities.
- Behavioural finance biases such as Anchoring can explain some share price movements.

One further point worth mentioning is that the share price reflects the price of the last trade, *not* the price at which the whole company could be acquired. Generally, the last trade reflects the transfer of only a small percentage of the company's issued capital. Thus, there is no good theoretical reason why this market value should reflect the fundamental value – most of the shareholders chose *not* to sell at this price.

---

for investors to sell short or to enter into derivative contracts whereby they will gain if a company's share price falls. It is further possible for those same investors to borrow shares; when this happens, the lender of the shares retains the economic ownership but the borrower can use the votes. Thus, companies can find themselves in a position whereby their business strategies, for example, regarding acquisitions, are being voted upon by 'investors' whose interests will be served if the companies fail rather than succeed.[13] In the absence of regulation, one can only sympathize with boards having to deal with this ludicrous conflict of interest.

Our interest in this book – and, we hope, the interest of those running our public companies – is in creating value on a sustainable basis for those who will hold the shares for a reasonable length of time. In this manner, it is more likely that value will be created for all stakeholders, and for the overall economy.

Other stakeholders

There are two issues to consider about stakeholders: who are the stakeholders of a company, and why does financial strategy seek to maximize shareholder value rather than the value to any other stakeholder group?

---

13 A discussion of this, with examples, is contained in Hu, H. T. C. and Black, B. S. (2006), 'The New Vote Buying: Empty Voting and Hidden (Morphable) Ownership', *Southern California Law Review*, 79(4): 811–908. http://ssrn.com/abstract=904004

Working Insight 1.8

Examples of stakeholders

Internal stakeholders	Board of directors
	Management
	Employees
Stakeholders with a direct relationship	Company pension fund and pensioners
	Shareholders
	Lenders
	Customers
	Suppliers
	Landlords
Regulatory stakeholders	Government departments and regulators
	Tax authorities
Stakeholders with wider relationships	Unions
	Local communities
	Environmental and social bodies and other non-governmental organizations
	Public at large
	Media

There are many stakeholders who might have an interest in a company's performance and may influence its activities, as illustrated in Working Insight 1.8.

Strategic business decisions are taken in the light of pressures from a host of internal and external stakeholders. The degree of interest in, and influence on, any particular decision will vary dramatically for each stakeholder group in each circumstance. Strategic business decisions are taken in the light of pressures from a host of internal and external stakeholders. The degree of interest in and influence on any particular decision will vary dramatically for each stakeholder group in each circumstance, as evidenced in the way that French car manufacturers face political and union pressure if they try to close down French car factories, but can expect less interest when they take similar actions with their plants elsewhere in the world. Other examples of stakeholder interest are seen in the pressure that labour rights activists put on companies like Apple or Nike about the practices along their supply chains, and the actions those companies have taken in response.

Companies should make decisions in the light of these influences; that is just good business sense. Although 'shareholder value' has received a bad press, being seen as the pursuit of short-term profits, in its original form it is decidedly a long-term concept. When we consider the seven drivers of value, one of the most important is the timescale over which the company can maintain its competitive advantage: companies that upset any of their major constituencies are in danger of damaging their legitimacy, and thus their long-term value.

It would be possible to find examples of stakeholder power for each of the groups set out in Working Insight 1.8. This being the case, why does financial theory (and Anglo-American financial practice) dictate that shareholder value is the appropriate corporate aim? There are various responses given to this question, for example, that the shareholders are the owners of the company, or that it needs to keep them satisfied in order to protect access to future funds. The answer that we find most persuasive is that the shareholders are the only direct stakeholder group who do not have a contractual relationship with the company.

A supplier of the company will supply product and receive payment in return. A customer will hand over money and receive the agreed goods or services. Employees know that if they give the specified number of labour hours they will receive an agreed wage at the end of the week or month. Lenders receive interest, governments collect tax. Each stakeholder knows what their relationship with the company will produce. Shareholders on the other hand invest their money in the hope of receiving dividends and capital gains, in order to make an above-market return. However, there is no requirement for the directors to declare a dividend, and there is no guarantee that the share price will rise. Accordingly, shareholders are bearing the ultimate risk, and so the company has an obligation to play fair with them by managing its activities to create value for this group of stakeholders.

The fact that creating long-term shareholder value is seen as the most important task of the company does not mean that creating value for other stakeholders is unimportant. If a business neglects customer value, it will soon not have any customers; poor treatment of employees will lead to them leaving, denuding the company of their skills; neglecting broader concerns such as environmental or human rights issues can lead to consumer protest, as demonstrated in the ongoing anti-globalization campaigns against high-profile companies for their sourcing practices in less-developed countries. All of these constituencies are important to a company, but the long-term shareholder interest has the highest priority.

This common-sense practice was incorporated into the UK's Companies Act 2006, which reflects the principles of *enlightened shareholder value*, and states that the directors should work to promote the success of the company for the benefit of the shareholders, having regard to the interest of other stakeholders. (The problem with this, as with many aspects of stakeholder analysis, is that the Act gives no guidance as to how to prioritize if the interests of two groups of stakeholders conflict. This is another good reason to set the interests of shareholders above others – it helps to determine priorities.)

We consider the position of stakeholders again in Chapter 6, on the financial strategy implications of corporate governance.

Agency theory

Agency theory informs the discussion at several stages in this book. An agency relationship exists when one party (the principal) employs another (the agent) to perform a task that involves an element of the agent's discretion.[14] Given that the parties are unlikely to have totally congruent interests, there is an incentive for the agent to act in a way that is to his benefit, but which could produce a lesser outcome for the principal. For example, they

---

14   This definition and discussion rely on the work of Jensen, M. C. and Meckling, W. H. (1976), 'Theory of the Firm: Managerial Behavior, Agency Costs and Ownership Structure', *Journal of Financial Economics*, 3(4): 305–60.

might take pay or perks at higher levels than justified, or make investments in areas that interest them rather than those that create value. In order to prevent this, agency costs are incurred in, for example, monitoring the agent's behaviour or designing incentive contracts to align their interests. Agency theory is discussed further in Chapter 6.

Agency theory is relevant to an understanding of corporate finance. In a company under the control of a majority shareholder, that shareholder would find it worthwhile to divert company resources to activities advantageous to themselves, knowing that they would receive 100 per cent of the benefit but that part of the cost, reflected in lower profits and share price, would ultimately be paid by the minority shareholders. Or, in a company substantially financed by debt, there is an incentive for the shareholder-manager to take substantial risks in the business, knowing that the upside would be shown in the share price, but the downside would be partly borne by the debt-holders in a liquidation. There could also be a problem in that executives, with one, undiversified job, might be reluctant to take business risks that would be preferred by the diversified shareholder base. Corporate laws and regulations aim to curtail these examples of agency problems.

Different types of shareholding structure can reflect other agency problems. In many countries around the world, the potential conflict of interest arises not between directors and shareholders, but between block-holding shareholders and the minority. Here, the issue is to ensure that minority investors have sufficient protection from decisions that might prejudice their interests.

Agency theory can be extended further, to consider the double agency relationship. When we talk about the potential conflict between executives and shareholders, we are referring to those who hold the shares, mostly large investment houses and pension funds. But these institutions are holding the investments for the benefit of their investors and employees or pensioners, and the second part of the agency relationship is the conflict between the institutions and their ultimate investors. This conflict is evidenced in short-term decisions by the institutions, which can boost their short-term portfolio returns but be less than beneficial in the longer term. For example, a pension fund manager gets ranked on performance every quarter, whereas the pensioners need them to consider investment returns for the next decade and beyond. The impact of this on financial strategy is seen in the way some fund managers prefer short-term dividends and buy-backs to longer-term potential growth.

The importance of accounting results

Corporate value is created by increasing the discounted value of future cash flows. Academic research suggests that manipulation of accounting policies is ignored by the market, which sees through the final profit figures to the health of the underlying business. However, companies and their advisers sometimes appear to be obsessed with accounting results and, in particular, earnings per share (eps), the profit earned in a year for each ordinary share.

As a significant part of this book discusses how companies can use financial strategy to manipulate eps, we feel obliged to defend our position on this matter. We believe that eps is, in practice, important; some of our colleagues suggest that markets ignore accounting practices – who is right? In our defence we cite two recent examples of how changes to accounting practices influenced corporate practice.

Case Study 1.2

Impact of accounting standards on financial practice

IFRS

The introduction of International Financial Reporting Standards meant that some financial instruments such as preference shares were reclassified from equity to debt in the financial statements.[15] The cash flows arising from these financial instruments were not changed at all, nor were the organization's obligations. However, research showed that following the change in accounting presentation, many companies chose to buy back their preference shares or alter their characteristics so as to maintain them as equity on the balance sheet.[16]

SFAS123R – Share options

A change in accounting standards which meant that an expense for issuing share options had to be recognized in a company's income statement led to a decrease in the use of share options, with other forms of incentive being used instead. Brown and Lee state, 'Collectively, our evidence suggests that [executive share options'] favorable accounting treatment prior to SFAS 123R provided firms with incentives to make compensation decisions that minimized accounting expense but did not maximize firm value.'[17]

Theory tells us that cash flow is what matters in company valuation. However, the reported actions of finance directors and the investment community indicate that it may be some time before we can structure transactions ignoring the effects of eps movements.[18]

Behavioural finance

In the course of this book we are likely to make some assertions that appear illogical to the casual reader (although all are supported by evidence in companies and markets). The problem is that people do act illogically. As individuals, our investment decisions are biased by experience and environment rather than a rational understanding of the facts of the case. Thus we welcome the growth in studies of behavioural finance (also known as behavioural economics), which discusses how and why people and markets experience irrational behaviour. Some of the key propositions are set out in Chapter 14, which deals with forecasting.

Key messages

- Financial strategy concerns how companies raise and deploy their funds.
- The investors' required return can be mapped against their perceived risk. Delivering value for shareholders – which is the main financial objective of a company – means giving them an above-the-line return.

---

15 Characteristics of different financial instruments are discussed in Chapters 11 and 12.
16 de Jong, A., Rosellon, M. A., and Verwijmeren, P. (2006), 'The Economic Consequences of IFRS: The Impact of IAS 32 on Preference Shares in the Netherlands', *European Accounting Review*, 3(1): 169–85.
17 Brown, L. D. and Lee, Y.-J. (2011), 'Changes in Option-Based Compensation Around the Issuance of SFAS 123R', *Journal of Business Finance & Accounting*, 38(9–10): 1053–95
18 A useful paper that contrasts various research papers and sets out current practice is Koller, T., Raj, R. and Saxena, A. (2013), 'Avoiding the Consensus Earnings Trap', *McKinsey Quarterly*, 1: 20–3.

- A company can be valued by discounting its expected future cash flows at an appropriate cost of capital. Value arises from creating competitive advantage through successful business strategy, in combination with a successful financial strategy, to increase those cash flows and reduce the cost of capital.
- Markets are not perfect, nor totally efficient. Often, they are not rational. Companies and investors can create value in the market imperfections.
- Ideally, a company's market value should reflect its fundamental value. If this is not the case, one or more groups of stakeholders will suffer.
- Shareholder value can be calculated using various methods, each of which measures different attributes.
- Agency theory, which discusses the difference in objectives between managers and owners, can be used to explain many aspects of corporate finance.
- Stakeholder management is an important part of long-term shareholder value creation.
- Although accounting results are not necessarily an indicator of shareholder value, companies spend much time and effort on ensuring that the accounting results look good, sometimes to the detriment of long-term value.

Suggested further reading

Finance textbooks

There are many textbooks that cover corporate finance; here are two that I have found useful. The first one has extensive coverage, the second is a bit shorter.

Vernimmen, P., Quiry, P., Dallochio, M., Le Fur, Y and Salvi, A. (2011), *Corporate Finance Theory and Practice* 3rd edn, Chichester: Wiley.

Business Finance: A Value-Based Approach (2004), Neale and McElroy, New York: FT Prentice-Hall.

Shareholder value

Rappaport, A. (1998), *Creating Shareholder Value*, 2nd edn, New York: Free Press.
This is the classic text on shareholder value, and is still well worth reading.

Agency theory

Goergen, M. (2012), *International Corporate Governance*, Harlow/New York: Pearson.
This book focuses on corporate governance and its links with corporate finance, and sets out a useful discussion of agency theory.

Stakeholders and sustainability

Rappaport, A. (2012), *Saving Capitalism from Short-Termism: How to Build Long-Term Value and Take Back Our Financial Future*, New York: McGraw-Hill.
One of the doyens of the shareholder value movement analyses the rise and impact of corporate short-termism, and suggests ways in which the system could change.

Grayson, D. and Exeter, N. (eds), *Cranfield on Corporate Sustainability* (2012), Bedford: Greenleaf Publishing.
A useful publication, which contains chapters on all aspects of incorporating sustainability into business, written by faculty of Cranfield School of Management. (Declaration of interest – I wrote the chapter on reporting sustainability performance.)

The Doughty Centre for Corporate Responsibility at Cranfield School of Management produces regular (free) publications on how to incorporate sustainable practices into business. www.doughtycentre.info

2 What does the share price tell us?

Learning objectives

After reading this chapter you should be able to:

1. Understand how the P/E ratio should change with market expectations of growth and risk.
2. Distinguish between different versions of the P/E ratio and determine which is most relevant for your needs.
3. Appreciate how the theoretical construct of steady state is derived from the dividend growth model.
4. Calculate and interpret the present value of growth opportunities (PVGO) inherent in a company's share price.
5. Calculate the expected eps growth built into a company's share price.

Introduction

A company's business and financial strategies must operate in tandem to deliver the value demanded by shareholders. In order to accomplish this, it is useful for its directors and advisers to understand how the shareholders expect to achieve that value, as expressed through its price/earnings (P/E) ratio. Many naïve directors and investors see a high P/E ratio as an indicator of a good company; in fact, it is more like a treadmill – the higher the P/E, the harder the directors have to work to achieve the implied growth.

Calculation of the price/earnings ratio

Price/earnings ratios for many companies can be obtained from the tables of share price information published daily by most good newspapers, or from finance sites on the internet. However, rather than just relying on these sources, we need to understand how the ratio is calculated.

The price/earnings ratio for a company is determined by dividing its current share price by its earnings per share (eps). This equation can be rearranged, and so doing explains, at least partially, a popular misconception about share prices.

$$P/E = \text{share price} \div \text{eps} \tag{1}$$

Then

$$\text{Share price} = P/E \times \text{eps} \tag{2}$$

So far, there is no problem with this rearrangement. The problem arises when people assume that this second equation implies a causality: that the share price is a function of P/E and eps rather than P/E being itself a function of the share price.

Why does this matter? Well, if directors believe this causality, they could come to the conclusion that in order to increase the share price, all that needs to be done is to increase the eps. Under this logic, the P/E of the company will remain unchanged, so any increase in eps will translate directly into a higher price. Such reasoning is at least partially to blame for the unnatural focus on earnings per share mentioned in Chapter 1. However, as we shall see in this chapter, the P/E is complex and unlikely to remain constant over a period.

Which earnings figure should be used?

In calculating the P/E we often use the eps from the last financial statements, calculating the *historic* P/E. However, share prices reflect the market's views of the future, and it is also appropriate to calculate a *prospective* P/E based on the analysts' consensus eps, or some other forecast eps.

In looking at the financial statements you will often see different versions of eps displayed: basic eps, diluted eps, and sometimes adjusted eps. To know which of these figures to use, it helps to understand why they have been calculated. Working Insight 2.1 explains.

If a company is making losses, it will not have a P/E ratio that makes any sense, as the earnings figure is negative. Chapter 14 discusses how a company is valued in these circumstances. For the calculations in this chapter, a judgement needs to be made in each case, after understanding what has caused the losses and how future profitability may develop.

Working Insight 2.1

Different versions of earnings per share

Basic eps	This is calculated based on the net income for the year and the average number of shares in issue during the year. This is the default figure for calculations.
Diluted eps	If the company has shares which contractually it might have to issue (for example, due to share options, or convertibles), then it has also to display a diluted eps figure, which allows for the additional shares as if they had all been issued, and the proceeds received. Generally, diluted eps is lower than basic eps, but often the difference is insignificant to the calculations in this chapter.
	If diluted eps differs significantly from basic eps, then you need to understand the reasons for the dilution and how likely it is to take place. For example, if the potential dilution relates to options that are underwater, these are unlikely to be exercised and so the diluted figure can be ignored for these calculations. If the new shares are likely to be issued (or if they relate to earnings for which we have already taken credit, such as the deferred consideration on an acquisition), then it is appropriate to use the diluted eps.
Adjusted eps	It is common for companies to display 'adjusted' earnings in addition to their earnings under the accounting standards. This is done in order to separate out items that distort this year's results but are not expected to continue. It is also done to take out the impact of accounting treatments that are necessary under the standards, but that the company believes to be confusing.
	It is important to realize that there is no standard definition of 'adjusted' and companies can make any adjustments they choose.[1] In deciding whether to use adjusted eps in your calculations, you need to establish exactly what the adjustments are, and take a view on how each should be treated.

What does the price/earnings ratio mean?

A company's price/earnings ratio first reflects the market's perceptions of its future eps growth, as illustrated in Figure 2.1.

Figure 2.1 shows two companies. High plc is a company with a high P/E ratio, and Low plc has a low P/E ratio. At the time of analysis, both companies have the same level of eps. However, the markets believe that High will grow eps rapidly over a period, and so give it a high share price and thus a high P/E ratio. They cannot foresee such rapid growth prospects for Low, hence its low multiple.

Before we examine the mathematics behind the illustration in Figure 2.1, it is important to note that the P/E multiple for a company reflects the expected future growth in earnings per share *which is already incorporated into the share price*. Hence the share price will only move due to changes in this expected growth, or if the actual performance shows greater or

---

1 Non-GAAP (or non-IFRS) measures are often valid, but some companies do use them to manipulate perceptions of performance. A classic example was the use by Groupon in its IPO filing of a novel measure, ACSOI (adjusted consolidated segment operating income), which was basically profit before marketing expenses. This was later withdrawn.

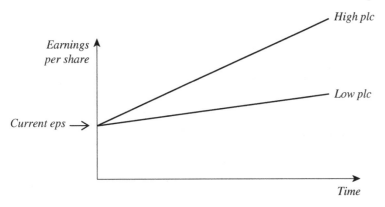

Figure 2.1 P/E ratio and market perceptions of growth.

lower growth than has already been paid for by current investors in the existing share price. Merely achieving some growth in earnings per share is no guarantee of a rising share price; particularly for a high P/E company.

An exposition of some of the key points in financial theory is set out in Appendix 1. However, in order to explain the meaning of the P/E ratio we need at this point to introduce one of the underlying theoretical models, the dividend growth model (DGM).[2] This, very broadly, sets out the shareholders' required return on their investment in terms of the ways in which it is achieved, a mixture of dividend yield and capital gain.

One explanation: using the dividend growth model without alteration

The dividend growth model states that

$$Ke = (D_1 \div P) + g \tag{3}$$

Where Ke is the cost of equity (the shareholders' required return); D_1 is the prospective dividend; P is the current share price; and g is the anticipated growth rate.

Equation 3 states:[3]

Shareholders' required return = dividend yield plus capital growth

Equation 3 can be rewritten, to give:

$$P = D_1 \times 1 \div (Ke - g) \tag{4}$$

We can take the relationship expressed in equation 4 and analyse it in two separate ways. For the first of these, we divide each side of the equation by the earnings per share. Thus:

$$(P \div eps) = (D_1 \div eps) \times 1 \div (Ke - g) \tag{5}$$

---

2 Also known as the dividend discount model and as the Gordon growth model.
3 Yes, we know that this is only an approximation of what the equation states, but it is a useful approximation and serves the purpose well.

Working Insight 2.2

An estimate of expected growth using the dividend growth model

Expansion plc has a share price of 250p. Its earnings per share are 10p, out of which it is expected to pay a dividend of 2p per share. The cost of equity has been calculated at 10%.

Price/earnings ratio = share price ÷ eps = 250 ÷ 10 = 25 times
Pay-out ratio = dividend per share ÷ eps = 2 ÷ 10 = 20%

Using the equation from (5)

P/E = (D_1 ÷ eps) × 1÷(Ke – g)
25 = 20% × 1÷(10% – g)
g = 9.2%

The directors of Expansion plc now have to determine whether 9.2% compound growth is a target that they can achieve, and how they might be able to attain it. Should they not be able to realize this growth, the share price will fall, and shareholders who bought shares anticipating this growth level will fail to make their required return.

The left-hand side of this equation, P ÷ eps, is our price/earnings ratio. The right-hand side contains two expressions of which one, D_1 ÷ eps, represents the prospective pay-out ratio. Thus, equation 5 states:

P/E ratio = pay-out ratio × 1 ÷ (Ke – g)

Given this relationship, an analyst (or indeed, the directors of the company) can feed in estimates of the company's cost of equity (Ke), its prospective dividends and its growth prospects, and determine the P/E ratio at which the company should be trading. Alternately – and perhaps more significantly – they can analyse the existing P/E ratio (a known number) and pay-out ratio (a known number) and cost of equity (Appendix 1 explains how to calculate this) to determine what level of growth the market expects. Working Insight 2.2 gives an example of such a calculation, and Table 2.1 sets out a sensitivity analysis using different levels of P/E ratio.

The P/E ratio and risk

A second aspect of the P/E ratio is reflected in Table 2.1. Not only does it reflect the market's views of the company's growth prospects, it also indicates the market's views of its risk profile. Equation 5 was rewritten to show that:

P/E ratio = pay-out ratio × 1 ÷ (Ke – g)

This means that the P/E ratio is affected both by the forecast growth (g) and also by the cost of equity (Ke). If g rises, the P/E goes up. But if Ke rises, the P/E goes down. To put it another way, if the market perception of the company's risk increases, the discounted value of its future cash flows will be lower, and thus its price will fall; this being the case, it will trade on a lower P/E ratio. This is an important relationship to remember: an increase in the eps which was driven by taking on excessive risk could actually cause the share price (and the P/E ratio) to fall rather than rise.

Table 2.1 Impact of P/E changes on growth assumptions

The data table shows, for Expansion plc, how changes to the P/E ratio affect the required growth.

		P/E ratio						
		15	17.5	20	22.5	25	27.5	30
	6%	4.7%	4.9%	5.0%	5.1%	5.2%	5.3%	5.3%
	7%	5.7%	5.9%	6.0%	6.1%	6.2%	6.3%	6.3%
	8%	6.7%	6.9%	7.0%	7.1%	7.2%	7.3%	7.3%
Cost of	9%	7.7%	7.9%	8.0%	8.1%	8.2%	8.3%	8.3%
equity	10%	8.7%	8.9%	9.0%	9.1%	9.2%	9.3%	9.3%
	11%	9.7%	9.9%	10.0%	10.1%	10.2%	10.3%	10.3%
	12%	10.7%	10.9%	11.0%	11.1%	11.2%	11.3%	11.3%

The highlighted growth of 9.2% reflects the numbers used for Expansion plc. The reason that its growth figures appear demanding is that shareholders in Expansion require a return of 10%, but only 2% of that comes from yield. If the yield were increased, growth requirements would change accordingly (although the growth itself might become less attainable with more limited resources). Similarly, a reduction in perceived risk causing Ke to fall would reduce the growth requirement.

The book's website contains the spreadsheet underlying this table.

The P/E ratio and dividends

One further misconception that follows from equation 5 is that the dividend pay-out ratio can be used to manipulate the share price. Look again at the equation:

$$(P \div eps) = (D_1 \div eps) \times 1 \div (Ke - g) \tag{5}$$

At first sight, it might appear that the P/E ratio – and thus the share price – could be increased merely by increasing the dividend pay-out ratio; paying a higher percentage of profits out to the shareholders would have a direct impact on prices. This argument is flawed. The company generates funds which can be used either to pay out dividends or to reinvest in the future growth of the business. If the company were to increase the dividend pay-out ratio, fewer funds would be available for reinvestment and so (presumably) future growth would be less than otherwise anticipated. Thus although the function $(D_1 \div eps)$ in equation 5 would increase, the denominator $(Ke - g)$ would also increase as g fell.[4] Accordingly, there is not necessarily a simple arithmetical relationship between changes in the dividend pay-out ratio and changes in the share price.[5]

There are several different methods of demonstrating what the P/E ratio means in terms of corporate growth, and generally they arrive at different answers, depending on the assumptions made. We have set out this simplistic technique as an illustration of what can be done. However, the slightly more sophisticated technique that follows is the one to be used in the rest of this book.

---

4 Chapter 20 sets out an equation linking sustainable growth to the retention ratio.
5 In periods when interest rates are low, increasing a dividend can improve the share price by attracting investors who seek yield, but this is just supply and demand, nothing to do with the intrinsic value of the company. Chapter 13 discusses further instances where increasing dividends will increase share price.

A second explanation: introducing 'steady state'

Steady state is a theoretical construct that we use to consider a company with a growth rate of zero. It must be emphasized that steady state is a theoretical state; the model is developed in order to build up an argument – in practice there is no such animal as a company in steady state, as even mature companies always have an element of growth or decline.

In order to define steady state we have to make two main assumptions, necessary in order to maintain over time the constant real levels of profit which are essential to the only rational financial definition of 'steady state'. First, depreciation would need to be based on true replacement cost accounting and the annual depreciation expense would have to be reinvested in the business; if this were done, the business would be capable of producing the same physical level of output over time. Second, all of the constant real profits achieved after charging this replacement cost depreciation must be paid out as dividends. If any of the profits were reinvested, the business should grow, whereas if the dividends paid out were greater than the profits earned the business would get smaller over time: therefore, a 100 per cent dividend pay out ratio is essential. (Obviously there are some other more general assumptions required such as either the absence of inflation, or the maintenance of real net profit margins and a neutral influence on net working capital.)

The result of these assumptions is that we can determine both a company's P/E and its cost of equity at steady state, as shown in Working Insight 2.3. Either of these can be used in a valuation.

As can be seen from Working Insight 2.3, for a steady state company the appropriate P/E multiple equals the inverse of the company's cost of equity capital (Ke_{ss}). *It cannot be emphasized too greatly that this relationship only holds for a steady state company.* Occasionally, we read articles suggesting that a company's cost of capital is its 'earnings/price ratio', the inverse of its P/E. In most cases, this is wrong. For a growth company, the P/E multiple will be greater than this inverse of the cost of equity capital, whereas for a declining company the P/E multiple would be lower, reflecting the expected decline in the future potential stream of earnings and dividends. Hence this very simple relationship provides a very powerful reference base for assessing both the risk profile and the future expectations signalled by any P/E multiple given to a company by the financial markets. It must be remembered that, in reality, the P/E multiple is mathematically calculated by dividing the share price by the current or expected eps, rather than the computation being the other way round; hence it is more correct to say that the share price drives the P/E multiple.

How can this relationship be used to analyse the price/earnings ratio (and thus the share price) of a company? To do this, we have to consider what the risk profile of the company might look like in this mythical steady state.

We know from Chapter 1 that the return required by investors bears a direct relationship to the perceived risk they are taking. Thus investors in high-risk companies demand a high return; as risk reduces, so does that required return. Risk, to a financier, is the volatility of expected returns: by definition in steady state the results of the company will be stable, so there is less risk (although overall market risk will still affect the share price). Accordingly, the cost of equity should be lower for a company in steady state than for a growth company. So if we know the current cost of equity, we can establish that the steady state cost of equity, Ke_{ss}, is lower than this figure.

Working Insight 2.3

Valuation of a steady state company

The dividend growth model was set out in equation (4) as:

$$P = D_1 \times 1 \div (Ke - g)$$

As shown in Appendix 1, the derivation of this equation is that the share price reflects the discounted value of all future dividends to be received by the shareholder. Dividends are forecast to grow at the rate g, and the discount rate applied is the shareholders' cost of equity, Ke.

Thus, the dividend growth model is derived from solving the progression:

$$P = D_1 \div (1+Ke) + D_2 \div (1+Ke)^2 + D_3 \div (1+Ke)^3 + \ldots Dt \div (1+Ke)^t \qquad (6)$$

But for a steady state company, defined as having zero growth, the dividend stream will be constant. This means that

$$D_1 = D_2 = D_3 \ldots = Dt$$

Thus the shareholder's income stream is a perpetuity of the dividend payment.

Furthermore, as there is no requirement for reinvestment, the pay-out ratio will be 100%. Therefore dividends will equal earnings per share. Thus the income stream that the shareholder receives will be a perpetuity of the company's earnings per share. To calculate the value of a perpetuity, we simply divide the perpetual payment by the relevant cost of capital.

Thus for a steady state company equation (6) can be simplified to:

$$P = eps \div Ke \qquad (7)$$

Dividing through by eps gives:

$$P/E = 1 \div Ke \qquad (8)$$

Again, we emphasize that this relationship only holds at the theoretical point of steady state. Accordingly, we rewrite equation 8 as:

$$P/E_{ss} = 1 \div Ke_{ss} \qquad (9)$$

The steady state cost of equity will be driven, using the Capital Asset Pricing Model (CAPM) described in Appendix 1, by the risk-free interest rate, the market premium, and the company's beta:

$$Ke = Rf + \beta (Rm - Rf) \qquad (10)$$

As neither the risk-free rate nor the market premium will be affected by a company moving into steady state, the only variable to change will be the company's beta. Accordingly, at steady state, equation 10 may be expressed as:

$$Ke_{ss} = Rf + \beta_{ss} (Rm - Rf) \qquad (11)$$

Where β_{ss} must be lower than the company's current beta.

Although β_{ss} will be lower than the company's current beta, it need not be 1.0. A beta of 1.0 implies a company whose risk exactly mirrors that of the market as a whole. Although our steady state company has shed all of its share price volatility due to growth, it will still reflect the volatility of its industry. For example, a construction company will always reflect the economic cycle even if it is not growing over the cycle; it will inherently have a beta higher than, say, a water company.

Working Insight 2.3 set out the theory behind the steady state model of price/earnings ratios. Working Insight 2.4 applies this theory to the numbers for Expansion plc.

As explained in Figure 2.1, it is useful to think of the P/E multiple as being a signalling device by current and prospective shareholders (the capital market) to the company, giving a clear indication of their expectations regarding growth in earnings per share, adjusted for risk. High P/Es indicate high growth expectations; low P/Es indicate an expectation of little growth, or high perceived risk. These signals can be compared to the signals sent out by the company's managers to the financial markets regarding their own views on future growth prospects, which will be considered further throughout the book.

One of the problems encountered in the financial strategies of major publicly quoted companies is that senior managers, and especially chief executives and chairpersons, do not seem to accept the inevitability of a declining P/E multiple as their company matures. This overwhelming desire to maintain over time, if not to increase, an already high P/E multiple can become the dominant driver of the corporate and competitive strategy of the business, often leading the company to diversify into new areas of potential growth even though the organization has absolutely no competitive advantage in this new sector.

Working Insight 2.4

An estimate of expected share price using the steady state model

Expansion plc has a share price of 250p. Its eps are 10p, out of which it is expected to pay a dividend of 2p per share. The cost of equity has been calculated at 10%, based on a risk-free rate of 4%, a market premium of 5% and a beta of 1.2.

In this example we assume that the industry in which Expansion operates carries an inherent level of risk, such that the steady state beta will be 1.1 (i.e. lower than the current beta but higher than 1.0).

Therefore, using the CAPM per equation (11), the steady state cost of equity will be:

$$Ke_{ss} = Rf + \beta_{ss} (Rm - Rf)$$
$$Ke_{ss} = 4\% + (1.1 \times 5\%)$$
$$= 9.5\%$$

On this basis, the price/earnings ratio of the company at steady state will be, per equation (9):

$$P/E_{ss} = 1 \div Ke_{ss}$$
$$P/E_{ss} = 1 \div 9.5\%$$
$$= 10.526 \text{ times}$$

(The steady state P/E has been shown to three decimal places solely to facilitate later explanations.)

Working Insight 2.5

Steady state value of a company

Let the annual (constant) dividend paid to shareholders be D

Shareholders' cost of capital is Ke_{ss}

Therefore, the value of the company is $D \div Ke_{ss}$

Looking at this problem with a financier's hat on, we can see that if the company chases growth by diversifying into non-related activities, in which it has no competitive advantage, this is likely to increase its risk profile. Increasing the risk profile will, if the market understands what is going on, reduce the share price and thus the P/E ratio.

Growth included in the share price

Consider the mythical steady state company. Its profits are the same year after year; its dividends represent a 100 per cent pay-out of these profits. A stream of income that is the same year after year into the infinite future is a perpetuity, and its value can be easily calculated. Working Insight 2.5 shows the value of a company in steady state.

If we know the value of a company at steady state, we can compare this with the current market value to determine how much growth the market is pricing into the share. The easiest way to explain this is by means of an example, and Working Insight 2.6 returns to Expansion plc to illustrate.

The implication of the calculations in Working Insight 2.6 is that if Expansion were to announce to the market that the directors see no further prospects of growth and it has become a steady state company, its share price would drop to about 105p from the current level of 250p. Thus we can say that 145p of the current share price, i.e. almost 60 per cent of the value of the share, represents growth anticipated by the market.

This is a fundamental point to appreciate in understanding how shareholder value is created. Most of the share price relates to activities that the company has not yet achieved. Only 40 per cent of Expansion's share price is justified on its current earnings; the rest represents the Present Value of Growth Opportunities (PVGO) which the market assumes that the management can generate.

At this point, as we are considering a company's need for growth, it is useful to bring in one of the classic models in strategy, the Ansoff matrix. Figure 2.2[6]

Igor Ansoff's simple, but very powerful insight was that growth can come in four ways. A company can sell more of the same product to the same market (quadrant 1); it can sell new products into the same markets (2), existing products into new markets (3) or it can take the high-risk strategy of diversifying totally (4).

The directors of a company can use the Ansoff matrix in conjunction with their PVGO analysis to analyse how the company can achieve the growth implicit in its current share price. Figure 2.3 illustrates this.

---

6 Ansoff, H. I. (1965), *Corporate Strategy. An Analytic Approach to Business Policy for Growth and Expansion*, New York: McGraw-Hill.

Working Insight 2.6

Growth inherent in the share price

Expansion plc has a share price of 250p and earnings per share of 10p. Its current cost of equity is 10%, but we have established (Working Insight 2.4) that its steady state cost of equity is about 9.5%.

If Expansion were to become overnight a steady state company, the income stream of 10p per share would continue effectively for ever and would be paid out as dividend. Thus the steady state share price of the company, using the perpetuity formula is:

$$P_{ss} = D \div Ke_{ss}$$
$$= 10 \div 0.095$$
$$= 105.26p$$

Looked at another way, the share price at steady state would be the eps at steady state multiplied by the P/E ratio at steady state:

$$P_{ss} = eps \times P/E_{ss}$$
$$= 10 \times 10.526$$
$$= 105.26p$$

In Figure 2.3 the left axis of the diagram represents the eps and the right axis represents the share price. If the company continues to make its current eps, E_1, then it will only be worth a price of P_0, representing the perpetuity value of E_1. In order to justify the current share price of P_1 the company has to increase earnings to reflect the PVGO. The increase in earnings will come, depending on the company's strategy and prospects, from developing its products and/or markets, with different associated levels of risk.

Should the management fail to generate growth that meets the market's expectations, the company's value will fall, reflecting the lower growth. Thus although a high P/E ratio, which implies high market expectations of growth, is seen by many as a sign of a strong company, it is also in some ways a curse for management: the more the market believes they can achieve, the faster they have to grow to justify the rating. (Ultimately, of course, growth to infinity is mathematically impossible, and companies eventually fail to meet the ever-increasing market expectations. At this point the share price is re-based to something more

		Products	
		Existing	*New*
	Existing	(1) Market penetration	(2) Product development
Markets			
	New	(3) Market development	(4) Diversification

Figure 2.2 Strategies for growth: the Ansoff matrix.

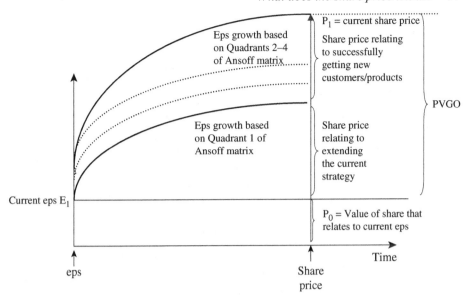

Figure 2.3 PVGO and strategies for achieving the required growth.

realistic. This makes perfect financial sense, but is understandably traumatic for the management and shareholders at the time.)

PVGO and growth expectations

The mathematics underlying the growth expectations in share prices can be taken one stage further, to consider the compound annual growth that a company needs to deliver in order to achieve the value for which shareholders have paid by buying its shares.

As a simple illustration, let us look once again at Expansion plc. Let us assume (on a totally arbitrary basis) that the company will reach steady state in ten years' time. Working Insight 2.7 demonstrates the consequences of this.

Working Insight 2.7 makes some heroic assumptions about the future for Expansion plc, and draws some interesting conclusions. Let us first examine the conclusions.

1 If the P/E ratio of the company is going to fall, the rate of growth in eps must exceed the required rate of growth in the share price.
2 For the share price to reflect a fair value for the company, the directors must understand the high level of eps growth anticipated by the market, and have a strategy in place to achieve this.

The assumptions behind Working Insight 2.7 are of course unrealistic. We are assuming that (1) the company will reach steady state; and (2) that it will do so in ten years. As we have stated earlier, steady state is a concept that does not actually exist, hence assumption (1) is false. And assumption (2) is somewhat arbitrary – calculate what happens to the required growth if instead you substitute a period of five or fifteen years. (A further unrealistic assumption, although one that is slightly more esoteric, is that the required growth in share price remains at 9.2 per cent, which takes no account of either the reduced risk of the company over the

Working Insight 2.7

Growth in eps required as the company falls to steady state

Expansion plc has a share price of 250p. Its eps is 10p, out of which it is expected to pay a dividend of 2p per share. The current cost of equity has been calculated at 10%. The steady state cost of equity is 9.5%, giving a P/E at steady state of 10.5 times.

Shareholders require a return of 10% on their investment. The dividend yield for Expansion is 0.8% ($^2/_{250}$), which implies that they expect a 9.2% per annum cumulative capital gain.

If the P/E multiple were to remain constant over the company's life, a 9.2% per annum capital gain would equate to a growth in eps of 9.2% per annum.

However, if Expansion falls to steady state in 10 years:

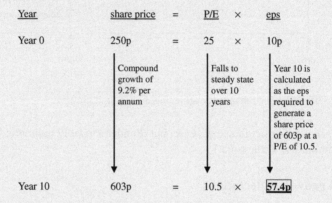

Year	share price	=	P/E	×	eps
Year 0	250p	=	25	×	10p
	Compound growth of 9.2% per annum		Falls to steady state over 10 years		Year 10 is calculated as the eps required to generate a share price of 603p at a P/E of 10.5.
Year 10	603p	=	10.5	×	57.4p

Thus, to increase the share price by 9.2% per annum over the period, eps has to grow at a compound rate of 19%.

---

period or changes to its dividend yield over the period. Remember, we're dealing here with illustrative concepts, not facts to be taken literally.)

If we relax the key assumptions in Working Insight 2.7 we can obtain a more realistic analysis. The company will not fall to steady state. However, the logic of a falling P/E still holds. Working Insight 2.8 indicates the growth in eps required should the P/E fall to say, 20, in seven years' time.

It can thus be seen that any drop in the P/E will have a potentially significant effect on the company's growth requirements over the period.[7]

It must further be remembered that achieving the growth illustrated in Working Insight 2.8 is, from the shareholders' point of view, no big deal. Based on these assumptions, a shareholder buying today at 250p *expects* a price of 463p in seven years' time. Achieving this, delivers a return exactly in line with the market which, as we established in Chapter 1, neither adds to nor reduces shareholder value. Shareholder value will only be created if the company beats this growth target.

---

7 This proposition is illustrated for Google and Amazon by Estrada, J. (2012), 'Blinded by Growth', *Journal of Applied Corporate Finance*, 24(3): 19–25. He shows that substantial earnings growth between 2006 and 2010 produced inadequate investor returns due to the large falls in the companies' P/E ratios.

Working Insight 2.8

Growth in eps required for a drop in P/E ratio

If Expansion's P/E of 25 drops to 20 in seven years' time, all other matters remain the same.
  Shareholders require a return of 10% on their investment. The dividend yield for Expansion is 0.8%, which implies that they expect a 9.2% per annum cumulative capital gain.

Year	share price	=	P/E	×	eps
Year 0	250p	=	25	×	10p

	Compound growth of 9.2% per annum	Falls to 20 as per assumption	Year 7 is calculated as the eps required to generate a share price of 463p at a P/E of 20.

| Year 7 | 463p | = | 20 | × | **23.1p** |

Thus, to increase the share price by 9.2% per annum over the period, eps has to grow at a compound rate of just under 13%.

One further exercise would be to take the projected eps from the calculations (e.g. 23.1p in Working Insight 2.8) and use this to calculate what that implies for profit in the final year, and then determine what sort of sales level that indicates. The sales level can then be compared to the product market, to see if it is feasible, given what we know of the company and its industry.

What does a negative PVGO mean?

Occasionally, particularly in periods when cost of capital is low, one finds a company whose PVGO is negative, such as is illustrated in Working Insight 2.9.

  There are three possible reasons for a negative PVGO. First, the market expects profits to fall, which means that the determination of steady state based on current eps is wrong. Second, it could mean that the market perceives the risk of the company as being very high – in which case the cost of equity calculated under CAPM is not representing market thought, and needs to be reconsidered. Or, the third and final answer is that the market has got it wrong – the share is undervalued and at some point in the future there could be a price correction.

Some problems with share prices

All of the above assumes that the share price represents the market's evaluation of the value of the underlying company. This is not necessarily true. Over the last decade the average

---

Working Insight 2.9

Illustrating negative PVGO

Dipsy has a share price of 213p, and earnings per share of 22p. The risk-free rate is 3%, the market premium is 5% and the company's beta is estimated at 0.9.

Using CAPM, Dipsy's cost of equity is 7.5%.
At steady state, the beta would be lower, say 0.85. So, the cost of equity at steady state would be 7.25%.
With eps of 22p, that implies a steady state valuation of the company at 303p.

The current share price is 213p, which means that PVGO is *negative*, at 90p.

---

holding period for shares has decreased considerably, and shares are seen as an asset for trading rather than holding. In conjunction with this there have been major developments in high-frequency trading (HFT). Broadly, this involves the trading of shares using high-speed, sophisticated computer programs driven by algorithms, based on market signals and with no human interaction in the trading strategy. Although HFT can make profits for those who use it, it can also distort markets. Furthermore, it might be difficult for a company differentiated on fundamentals to stand out in circumstances where HFT is prevalent. Given that it is suggested that HFT represents over 30 per cent of volume in the UK market and perhaps double that in USA, there are significant implications for pricing.[8]

Overall, rather than being an indication of the quality of earnings, a high share price can reflect an expectation that the stock will become popular rather than the fact that the owner believes the underlying company to be valuable. The economist John Maynard Keynes likened this to a beauty contest saying, 'it is not a case of choosing those which, to the best of one's judgment are really the prettiest, nor even those which average opinion genuinely thinks the prettiest. We have reached the third degree where we devote our intelligences to anticipating what average opinion expects the average opinion to be.'[9]

A final thought on share price

Having shown you how to deconstruct a share price, in this book we spend a fair amount of time pointing out that the share price is not necessarily a good representation of the value of the company. Nevertheless, managers and directors can often be obsessed with it. Working Insight 2.10 sets out some reasons why in practice the share price matters.

---

8   A detailed analysis of high frequency trading can be found in a report commissioned by the UK's Department for Business, Innovation & Skills: *The Future of Computer Trading in Financial Markets: An International Perspective* (2012). Available at www.bis.gov.uk/assets/foresight/docs/computer-trading/12-1086-future-of-computer-trading-in-financial-markets-report.pdf
9   *The General Theory of Employment, Interest and Money* (1936), London/New York: Macmillan.

Working Insight 2.10

Some reasons why the share price matters

- A high price is seen as a sign of success.
- A high price is seen as a sign of the strength of the underlying business.
- Share price is often used as a proxy for performance.
- A high share price is the best protection against takeover.
- Raising future capital becomes easier if the price is high, as fewer shares have to be issued, and the existing investors are well disposed to the company already.
- Shareholders expect a growing share price.
- Share price is often used as a metric for calculating management bonuses.
- Management have share options, which only have value if the share price rises.
- A high share price improves morale, particularly if employees own shares.
- There is a strong correlation between power, influence, and company size.

Key messages

- A company's share price reflects the market's risk-adjusted expectations of its future performance, thus it varies with changes in perceived risk and growth. The higher the share price relative to current earnings (as measured by the P/E ratio), the harder the management will have to work to achieve the growth inherent in the share price.
- One way of calculating the expected growth uses the dividend growth model, taking the cost of equity as calculated by the Capital Asset Pricing Model, and feeding in the known dividend and share price.
- Merely achieving the growth inherent in the share price does not generate shareholder value; value is created when the growth requirement is exceeded.
- Because companies cannot grow at a high rate for ever, P/E ratios will reduce over time. This means that eps growth has to exceed the required share price growth in order to generate the expected return.
- Steady state – a theoretical concept – can be used to calculate what the company's share price would be if it were to remain at the same profit level for ever. The difference between the current share price and the steady state price reflects the Present Value of Growth Opportunities (PVGO).

Suggested further reading

Nolen Foushee, S., Koller, T., and Mehta, A. (2012), 'Why Bad Multiples Happen to Good Companies', *McKinsey Quarterly*, 3 (May): 23–5.
Discusses the P/E multiple and enterprise value multiples (which are covered in Chapter 14 of this book). States that value creation is more important than high multiples.
Estrada, J. (2012), 'Blinded by Growth', *Journal of Applied Corporate Finance*, 24(3): 19–25.
Discusses economic growth and uses arithmetic examples to show how growth relates to equity returns. Illustrated using data from Google and Amazon as well as the 'world market'.

3 Executive summary
Linking corporate and financial strategies

Introduction

This chapter provides an executive summary of the core model set out in Chapters 4 and 5, which links corporate and financial strategies. No learning objectives are provided for this chapter, as these are covered in the main work.

Chapters 4 and 5 are detailed. The model they describe underlies much of our thinking, and we felt it important to explain it fully. Any theoretical model is only a partial representation of reality, and we always encourage our students and clients to treat models cautiously – use them when they make sense, and change them to suit the circumstances. But to make meaningful adaptations, you need to understand the thinking behind the model, to know what to change, all of which is set out in detail in those chapters. However, we do appreciate that this makes the length rather daunting, so this short piece will give you a quick idea of the concepts, to see what's coming.

In this chapter we set out an executive summary of the core model underlying much of the rest of this book. Reading this chapter is sufficient to give you a good view of *what* the model is, but not necessarily *why* it is.

The four decisions in financial strategy

Financial strategy is about the choices a company makes in raising and deploying its finances. There are four strategic decisions to be made:

1   How large should the asset base be, and in what assets?
2   How much of the finance should be debt, and how much in equity?

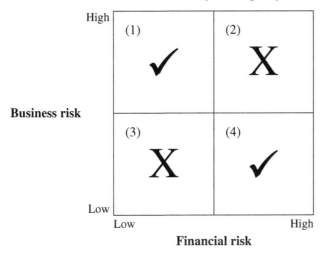

Figure 3.1 Matrix of business and financial risk.

3   How much profit should be paid out in dividend, and how much retained?
4   Should new equity be issued?

An understanding of how shareholder value is created can help answer all of these questions.

Balancing business and financial risk

The basic principle is really simple. Businesses need to take risk – without risk there is no opportunity and no reward. But taking too much risk can destroy the organization. Risk comes from business activities as well as financial strategy, and therefore the decision on how much financial risk to take will depend fundamentally on the characteristics of the business. Figure 3.1 illustrates this.

Figure 3.1 shows that a combination of high business risk and high financial risk (i.e. borrowing too much) would be foolhardy and is not recommended: Quadrant 2 is to be avoided. Likewise, in most circumstances, Quadrant 3 is to be avoided: low-risk businesses could and should reduce their cost of capital by taking on more borrowing. Quadrants 1 and 4 are both good places to be, balancing the business and financial risks.

The life cycle model

In order to evaluate business risk we use a model based on the product life cycle, adapting it to companies and their divisions. The basic life cycle model used by marketers often shows just how sales change as a company develops. The model is expanded upon in Figure 3.2.

Figure 3.2 represents the annual levels of sales, profits and cash flows in a typical business over its life cycle. In its early life it is likely to be loss-making and cash-negative. As it goes through the growth stage, it will turn profitable, but could still be cash-negative due to the required investment in working capital and fixed assets needed to support this rapid growth. It is only when the business becomes mature that the cash flows reflect the profitability. Once the

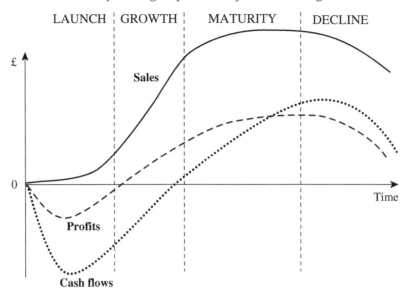

Figure 3.2 Life cycle model.

business goes into managed decline, sales fall, as do profits. In this stage, cash flows will remain positive, as little ongoing investment is needed.

Debt or equity? Integrating business risk and the life cycle model to develop a financing strategy

Early-stage businesses are risky, as there are too many unknowns. This being the case, it would be foolish to attempt to finance them with debt, which would both increase their overall risk, and lead to outflows of cash from companies that are already cash-negative. Thus, businesses at the launch stage should be financed with equity that is prepared to accept a high risk, such as venture capital.

At the growth stage, the business is still risky: managing rapid growth is hard work, and many companies fail to make the transition successfully. Accordingly, debt is generally not a good idea for growth companies either – their finance should mostly be equity, often taken from the capital markets. However, once the business has stabilized and reached maturity, its business risk reduces. At this point it can – and should – reduce its overall cost of capital by taking on cheap debt to replace the expensive equity. And once the business goes into managed decline, its risk (the volatility of expected results) is low – we *know* what is going to happen – and so the financial risk can increase and the company should borrow.

Dividend strategy over the life cycle

An early-stage company would be foolish to pay dividends to its shareholders, even assuming it had the profits out of which to declare a dividend. First, it needs its money as a buffer against the risks it faces. Second, it is cash-negative, so any cash paid out to shareholders would only have to be replaced by having them invest more equity, which would be a particularly pointless exercise. And the third reason why such a company should not pay dividends is that its growth prospects are exciting, and the investors stand to make more money by reinvesting in that business than they would by taking their money out by way of dividend.

Similar arguments apply to growth companies, which often pay no dividends. However, in some cases the arguments against a growth company paying dividends are tempered by a desire to give a little something back to the investors, as a signal of better things to come. Accordingly, some growth companies will make a nominal dividend pay-out.

Mature companies are in a different position. They are less risky, but also need much less investment. Having fewer growth opportunities, they need less working capital and less investment in new plant, etc. Accordingly, with fewer business opportunities, their money is not working as hard in the business. Thus is should be repaid to shareholders, and the dividend should increase significantly, to form a substantial part of profits.

For the company in managed decline, there are no investment opportunities and little point in reinvestment: dividends should represent the maximum that is safely payable.

P/E ratio and share price over the life cycle

A company's P/E ratio represents, in part, the market's expectations of its future growth potential. It stands to reason that the growth potential decreases over the life cycle: so will the P/E. The earnings per share will be negative at the start of the cycle, turning positive and growing with the company's profits. Thus the combination of these factors, the share price, will vary dependent on how investors see the future prospects. In early days, the company's share price will be volatile, reflecting changed expectations of risk and of profit potential; as the company matures, expectations stabilize and so does the share price.

Putting it all together

Combining all of these points, our basic exposition of a company's financial strategy is shown in Figure 3.3.

GROWTH	LAUNCH
Business risk high	Business risk very high
Financial risk low	Financial risk very low
Funding equity	Funding equity
Dividend pay-out nominal	Dividend pay-out nil
Growth high	Growth very high
P/E high	P/E very high
Eps low	Eps nominal
Share price growing and volatile	Share price growing and highly volatile
MATURITY	**DECLINE**
Business risk medium	Business risk low
Financial risk medium	Financial risk high
Funding debt	Funding debt
Dividend pay-out high	Dividend pay-out total
Growth medium/low	Growth negative
P/E medium	P/E low
Eps high	Eps declining
Share price stable with limited volatility	Share price declining and volatile

Figure 3.3 Financial strategy over the life cycle.

Key messages

- Financial risk must be managed against the business risk, in order to produce the most effective risk profile out of which to create value.
- Risk changes over the company's life cycle, as should the financing strategy and the dividend pay-out strategy.
- If you have read this chapter, you have *read* the basic model but you have not learned enough to *understand* it or manipulate it.[1] Chapters 4 and 5 give you the underlying rationale.

---

1 Or to pass an exam!

4 Linking corporate and financial strategies

Learning objectives

After reading this chapter you should be able to:

1   Distinguish between business risk and financial risk, and explain why there should be an inverse relationship between them.
2   Explain the different elements of financial strategy.
3   Assess how risky a particular business is, with a view to understanding how it should be financed.
4   Understand the seven drivers of value, and how they can be related to business strategy in order to increase value.
5   Discuss how the elements of financial strategy might apply differently to public and privately owned companies.

Introduction

Business risk is the inherent risk associated with the underlying nature of the particular business and the specific competitive strategy that is being implemented. It covers everything except the risk from the financing structure. Financial strategy includes a company's choice of sources of finance and its dividend policy, and should relate to the business risks that a company faces. In this chapter we consider the two types of risk and develop thoughts about how a business should be financed. It is inappropriate for a company with high business risk to adopt a financial strategy involving high financial risk. Similarly, for public companies it is unwise for a low-risk business to use mostly equity, which is low-risk finance.

Assessing business risk

Businesses take risks, they have to: without risk there is little chance of a reward. One of the characteristics that distinguishes successful businesses from those that fail is the way in which they understand and manage the risks they face, both business and financial. Accordingly, an understanding of financial strategy involves first a clear appreciation of business risk. Once the business risk is analysed, the financial strategy can be designed to complement it. If the financial strategy is appropriately designed and properly implemented it can enhance shareholder value but, even more dramatically, when an inappropriate financial strategy is applied the entire business can be placed in jeopardy.

Accordingly, we start by considering business risk.

Business risk describes the inherent risk associated with both the underlying nature of the particular business and the specific competitive strategy which is being implemented. Thus a very new, focused, single-product, high-technology company (such as a business developing a specific aspect of biogenetic engineering or a new style of super-computer) would have a very high intrinsic business risk. At the opposite end of the risk spectrum would be a very well-established, highly diversified (both geographically and industrially) conglomerate-style group, which has a relatively low overall business risk. It must be remembered that, of itself, neither a high nor a low business risk is better; as long as the relative level of return matches the level of associated risk, either is acceptable.

Business risk often has little to do with risk as discussed by financiers, calculated as β in the Capital Asset Pricing Model (see Appendix 1). Company-specific risks are irrelevant in a diversified investment portfolio, and all that matters is correlation with markets. However, here we are concerned with *corporate* financial strategy, not investment strategy, and business risk does matter.

The simplest way to consider business risk is that it relates to all of the risks that the company faces, other than those which relate directly to financing decisions. It thus deals with the volatility of the operating cash flows. Such volatility might arise from sources external to the organization, for example: changes in legislation or in fashions or public opinion; the actions of competitors; or the general economic climate. Businesses that have cash flow streams in different currencies also face business risks, as exchange rate changes can lead to volatility. Internal risks also need to be considered, for example: the risks associated with a particular manufacturing process; or the ways in which an organization communicates with its key stakeholders; or its cost structure. Internal risks are often easier to control than external risks, but all potential risks need to be considered.

An embarrassingly simple model for a preliminary analysis of business risk is shown in Figure 4.1

In Figure 4.1 the constituents of profitability are broken down to facilitate analysis. As business risk relates to variability in operating results, it seems reasonable to examine the

Figure 4.1 Analysis of business risks.

factors making up these operating results, which takes us back to the basic accounting model: Sales less Costs = Profits. We can then begin to see what affects each of these items for our particular company. For sales, it might be appropriate to examine what affects our selling price and the volumes we sell; or an analysis of products and markets may be more useful; probably both should be used. For cost analysis, a preliminary approach may be to determine the *operating leverage*, the relative level of fixed to variable costs, on the basis that companies with high levels of fixed costs may have difficulty achieving break-even if sales fall. The level of committed costs may also be important; a business with a high commitment to forward expenditure is more vulnerable (i.e. riskier) than one with no such commitments.

For each business the specific risk factors will differ. Working Insight 4.1 illustrates some examples of issues to consider in analysing business risk.

Also of importance is the company's attitude to risk, its 'risk appetite'. This will be reflected in the culture of the organization, as promoted from the top by the board, and evidenced in its behaviour and attitudes. Organizations will display different levels of tolerance to different risks, either because they clearly understand them and know how to deal with them (which is good) or because they don't understand them at all (which is rather less so).[1]

Strategic analysis

As we stated earlier, this is not a book about corporate strategy, but if we are to match financial strategy with business strategy it is important to have at least some understanding of some of the key tools of the latter. Accordingly, before we dive into financial strategy, let us have a quick look at some useful strategic tools which can inform our analysis of business risks and opportunities.

Porter's five forces

In a widely known model, Michael Porter set out five forces that drive industrial competition: the relative bargaining power of buyers, that of suppliers, the threat of new entrants, the

---

1 An analysis of risk culture is outside the scope of this book, but useful guidance can be found in *Risk Culture Under the Microscope: Guidance for Boards*, published by the Institute of Risk Management (2012) (available through www.theirm.org).

Working Insight 4.1

Some examples of issues to consider in analysing business risk

---

Demand volatility
- market factors
- changes in tastes
- short product lives
- competitors' actions

Input cost volatility
- number and strength of suppliers
- efficiency
- relative level of fixed costs
- reliance on commodity markets
- level of committed costs in terms of volume and price

Growth drivers
- ability to develop new products
- ability to acquire sufficient resources for expansion: skilled employees, materials, new sites on which to expand
- ability of existing management to take the company to the next stage of development

Selling price volatility
- market factors
- price wars
- economic conditions
- prices of substitutes and complements
- oversupply (or shortages)

Expense volatility
- reliance on key suppliers
- relative level of fixed costs
- how significant is the level of expenses relative to the size of the business?
- level of committed costs (e.g. leases)

Other issues to consider
- industry analysis – relative strengths of rivals, suppliers, and customers; likelihood of new industry entrants; availability of substitutes
- analysis of political, environmental, social, technological, legal, and economic developments that may affect future business
- working capital needs
- exposure to currency risks
- corporate governance failure

Once business risks have been analysed, the company may find it appropriate to develop strategies to mitigate some of its key risks.

---

threat of substitute products, and the degree of rivalry among existing firms in the industry. Although this model no longer takes pride of place in strategy courses,[2] the analysis is still useful: the relative strengths of these forces indicate the attractiveness of an industry to a particular player, and suggest where they might wish to compete.

The five forces model can also inform the analysis of business risk. By rating the threat posed by each of the five areas, a quick picture of industry attractiveness can be obtained. Attention can be focused on the key forces, and business strategies determined to preserve advantage or mitigate threats.

2　The model is described in Porter, M. (2004), *Competitive Strategy* (New York: Free Press). However, academic research suggests that its explanatory power is relatively low – see for example, McNamara, G. Aime, F., and Vaaler, P. (2005), 'Is Performance Driven by Industry or Firm Specific Factors?', *Strategic Management Journal*, 26(11): 1075–81.

PESTLE analysis

In analysing a company's competitive position, it is essential to understand how changes will affect it. Some of the key drivers of change are:

Political
Economic
Social
Technological
Legal; and
Environmental issues.

A PESTLE analysis considers how these factors are likely to affect the company and the industry in which it operates. The business strategy and risk assessment then need to take these into account.

Resource-based theory

Whereas the five forces analysis takes the approach that competitive advantage lies in industry characteristics, the resource-based view of competitive advantage is that it lies in the company's own unique set of assets. In other words – what is this company particularly good at, which enables it to compete successfully? It has been argued that any assets that an organization has which can confer competitive advantage must have the following characteristics and be:[3]

Valuable
Rare
Imperfectly imitable; and
Non-substitutable.

The rather unwieldy acronym VRIN is used to describe such strategic assets. An assessment of business risk should consider these assets and identify what needs to be done to preserve and enhance them. This is particularly relevant in mergers and acquisitions, where the acquirer needs to understand the nature of the strategic assets before integrating the acquired business, or they could accidentally destroy them.

Linking corporate and financial strategies to enhance shareholder value

Before we go into a detailed discussion of how to tailor a financial strategy, it is worth taking time to see how these strategic models interact with the value drivers discussed in Chapter 2, and with the company's value in the stock market. Figure 4.2 sets out a model of this.

The organizational aim is to create shareholder value. This is done by selecting a business strategy that it is believed will be successful, and that business strategy is derived from analysis

---

3 Barney, J. (1991), 'Firm Resources and Sustained Competitive Advantage', *Journal of Management*, 17(1): 99–120.

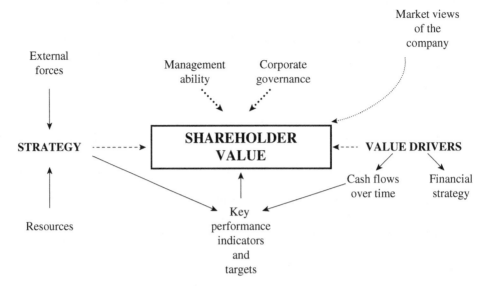

Figure 4.2 Developing strategies to enhance shareholder value.

of external forces (for example using the Porter model and a PESTLE analysis) and of the company's internal resources and capabilities (VRIN). However, the strategy so determined should link to what is seen to drive value in the business, using the seven drivers of value introduced in Chapter 1. These are explained in Working Insight 4.2.

Figure 4.2 shows that the strategy developed by internal and external analysis should also reflect the relative worth of the seven value drivers. If this is done, and if the appropriate performance measures designed, with targets that are stretching but achievable, value should be created.

Alas, it's not quite that simple. The upper part of Figure 4.2 shows that the value created is also, fundamentally, a function of management ability – the best strategy in the world is useless unless it is implemented well. And, as we discuss in Chapter 6, corporate governance in its widest sense also has a part to play, both in managing the company, and in shaping market perceptions. Finally, shareholder value in the short and medium term is dependent on the market itself, which is not necessarily rational: we discussed in Chapter 2 the fact that the market price rarely reflects fundamental value.

Constituents of financial strategy

Business risk was defined as representing the risks to the company's operating results and cash flows. Financial risk is the risk inherent in the company's choice of financing structure. At this juncture it is worth considering the key decisions to be made in determining a financial strategy, and the associated risks.

Think about the flows of funds through a company.[4] It will use its asset base to generate profits, of which some will be paid out to shareholders as dividends, and the rest will be retained for future growth. Although the level of those profits will depend partly on its operating

4   This explanation is based on work originally published in *Building Value with Capital-Structure Strategies* by
   H. A. Davis and W. W. Sihler (1998), Financial Executives Research Foundation Inc.

Working Insight 4.2

Creating value with the seven drivers

1 Increase sales growth
2 Increase operating profit margin
3 Reduce cash tax rate
4 Reduce incremental investment in capital expenditure
5 Reduce investment in working capital
6 Increase time period of competitive advantage
7 Reduce cost of capital

The drivers are not all to be treated equally – in different businesses, different drivers will be important. For example, in a hotel, with a high fixed cost base, the most important driver is sales, as measured by the occupancy rate. Increasing the sale of room nights by 10% is likely to have far more of an impact on value than increasing margins, and the strategic focus should be on increasing the number of bed-nights sold. This is a totally different model from, say, a bank lending to corporate customers, where profits arise from a slim margin between the rate at which the bank borrows and that at which it lends. Here, more value will be created by improving interest margins and by reducing operating costs than can be derived from increasing the volume of business: in such a bank, the cost–income ratio is an important measure of performance.

The seventh value driver is the cost of capital. As we have stated elsewhere in this book, managing financial strategy well can enhance the value of a company, but financial strategy on its own is not a key driver of value for most businesses outside the financial services industries.

---

efficiency, the ultimate level of profit available to shareholders will depend on the interest burden that the company is carrying – which itself depends on the level of debt it takes on. Thus initially the directors have three decisions to make:

1 How large do we want (or need) the asset base to be, and in what assets?
2 How much of the company's finance should be as debt (and therefore how much as equity)?
3 How much of the profit should be paid out in dividend (and therefore how much should be retained for future growth)?

These decisions are closely linked. If the directors see attractive growth opportunities, they may wish to retain the funds rather than pay them out in dividend (the practicalities of this action will be discussed in Chapter 13). If they feel obliged to pay out dividends, then the expansion could be financed by increasing the company's debt levels. Should the directors feel that such an action would be unwise, then perhaps they should not increase the asset base at all.

The three decisions above describe a relatively closed system. There is, however, a fourth decision for the directors to make:

4 Should we issue new equity?

Issuing new equity expands the company's funding. If it has a target debt-to-equity ratio (something which appears to be rather more common in academic textbooks than it is in practice), then increasing the equity base also means that it can take on more debt.

Table 4.1 Risk from different perspectives

	Debt	Equity
Features for issuer (*the company*)	Interest must be paid Repayments must be made The lender may have the right to repossess assets A HIGH-RISK INSTRUMENT	Can choose whether to pay dividends No repayment obligation A LOW-RISK INSTRUMENT
Features for investor	Interest is contractual Repayment is contractual The lender may obtain security A LOW-RISK INSTRUMENT	Dividends are at the discretion of the company No right to receive capital back A HIGH-RISK INSTRUMENT

Putting it very simplistically, these are the only four decisions that need to be taken in financial strategy.[5]

Financial risk

Financial risk relates to the level of debt a company is carrying (its gearing, or leverage). In assessing the riskiness of debt and equity it is essential to specify the perspective from which the analysis is being made. This is illustrated with respect to debt and equity funding in Table 4.1.

Any commercial lender such as a bank will try to reduce its financial risk by a whole series of actions. These include ensuring that it has priority in terms of both repayment of principal and payment of interest, possibly by taking security over specific assets, and by insisting on covenants in its loan agreements, which can entitle it to demand early and immediate repayment if the financial position of the borrower appears to deteriorate. Clearly these steps transfer a large part of the financial risk to the company, as any breach of the loan agreement conditions can place the continued existence of the company in jeopardy.

Conversely the financial rights of the same company's shareholders are minimal and hence their financial risk is higher. The company has discretion over whether or not to pay a dividend, even if it has sufficient distributable profits, whereas the payment of interest is effectively committed and mandatory. Ordinary shareholders cannot demand from the company the repayment of their investment even if no dividends are paid over a long period, except by placing the company into liquidation; in which case they are last in the queue and do not receive any distribution until all the company's creditors have been paid in full. They seek a large part of their return in the form of a capital gain in the share price – which is by no means guaranteed to them, even if the company prospers.

Balancing this lack of control and higher level of risk on the part of the shareholders, of course, are the potentially unlimited returns which they can achieve if the share price rises. The lender, taking lower risks, receives a more certain but much lower maximum return in the form of interest and the repayment of principal.

We deal above with 'plain vanilla' debt and equity. Many years ago, when we first became involved in corporate finance, most financing options could quite easily be categorized as

---

5 Pedants sometimes argue that a share buy-back could be a fifth decision, but we see that merely as an extension of decision 3, or the reverse of decision 4.

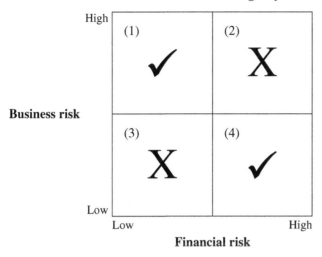

Figure 4.3 Matrix of business and financial risk.

either debt or equity; nowadays there is a continuum between secured term lending at one extreme and ordinary, permanent shares at the other. Many of the categories in between are discussed in Chapters 11 and 12 of this book.

For the purposes of this discussion of business and financial risk, our perspective is that of the company raising funds and investing them. Although the shareholders' risk associated with investing in equity is quite high, the financial risk of using predominantly equity financing from the company's perspective is much lower than if a high proportion of debt funding were used.

Balancing business and financial risk

Financial risk should complement the business risk profile, in order to develop logical alternative financial strategies for different types of business. Combining a high business risk strategy with a high financial risk strategy (such as would be achieved by borrowing to fund a start up bio-tech company) gives a very, very high total risk profile: such a company may succeed spectacularly but it is much more likely to fail completely and disappear. Thus, as illustrated in Figure 4.3, the combination of strategies in Quadrant 2 is not a logical, long-term basis for creating a successful business.

However, when the differing risk–return profiles of various stakeholders are taken into account, this type of strategy can be seen to be potentially very attractive to risk-taking entrepreneurs. If most of the required funding can be raised in the form of debt, the entrepreneurs have to inject very little of their own money. If the business turns out to be successful, they will get the vast majority of these upside gains: the return to the lenders of the debt financing being fixed. However, if the high-risk business fails, as it probably will, they can only lose the small amount of equity which they have injected. From their perspective this appears to be the ultimate combination of 'you take all the risk and we'll take all the return!'.[6]

---

6 Yes, you are right. This does appear to have been the business model followed by many companies and financial institutions in the run-up to the financial crash of 2008.

Unfortunately for these entrepreneurs, smart lenders do not see this as an acceptable combination of risk and return. It is now well established that very high business risk enterprises should be funded with equity which the investors know is potentially at risk (i.e. venture capital). Where it has proved possible to raise large amounts of inappropriate debt capital for such high business risk investments, the fault lies with the lender far more than with the borrower, because the lender is committing what can be regarded as the most heinous sin of corporate finance: accepting a debt-type return while taking equity-type risk.

In our opinion, funding should only be regarded as 'true' debt when there is an alternative way out, i.e. if the lender can still recover the balance outstanding even if the business or project concerned fails to perform as originally expected. Normally this alternative exit route would be provided by realizing the underlying value of certain assets owned by the business or pledged as security for the loan by a guarantor. If no such realizable assets exist, the true risk associated with the funding is that of an equity investor. Hence, if the lenders settle for an interest-based return, they are not matching their real risk profile to the return being achieved. There is nothing wrong in taking on a high-risk equity investment, as long as the expected return is commensurately high; otherwise it is an unacceptable risk–return relationship.

Referring to Figure 4.3, this means that high business risk companies should use low-risk financing, i.e. equity venture capital, and should keep their cost bases as variable and discretionary as possible (Quadrant 1). This logic is now fairly well understood and accepted by the capital markets, even to the extent that venture capital is primarily provided by a relatively small number of specialist finance organizations. They understand the high business risks involved and aim to manage these risks by demanding a very high level of return on their investment and using portfolio management techniques, which allow for a proportion of their investments failing completely.

The greater problems at this very simple level of financial strategy tend to be encountered with the lower business risk companies. In general, business risk tends to reduce as companies mature; not least because the unsuccessful ones will fail and cease to exist. For example, the earlier examples of high-technology start-up companies have a very high business risk, but the surviving equivalent high-tech start ups of 100 years or 50 years ago are now the well-established major corporations of today, with much lower business risk profiles. Not only does the business risk decline, but, as the company matures, the cash flow tends to become heavily positive, having been significantly negative during the development and launch stage. Therefore, if the initial finance was raised as equity, which would be appropriate, the financial structure of this more mature company can easily stay predominantly equity based, due to a lack of need for substantial external funding once the cash flow becomes significantly positive.

Unfortunately, this can result in a disastrous combination of a low business risk strategy and an even lower financial risk; i.e. Quadrant 3 of Figure 4.3. Not only is this unsatisfactory for shareholders, but it can lead to a hostile takeover bid for the company, as this incredibly low-risk strategy has led to the company being undervalued by the capital markets. Successful corporate raiders do not always change the business strategies of the companies they buy, but they do alter their financial strategies; normally by dramatically increasing the financial risk profile by raising the debt-to-equity ratio.[7]

The result of this simple analysis is that there should be an inverse correlation between the business risk of a company and its financial risk profile. Normally the business risk

---

7   These highly leveraged takeover deals should be focused on relatively mature, low business risk companies with strongly positive cash flows, which would enable the company to service and repay the increased borrowings.

reduces over time as the company's core business matures or it diversifies into other areas, and therefore the financial risk should be correspondingly increased. However, changes in the external environment or in the internal competitive strategy can lead to quite sudden increases in the level of business risk. When this happens managers may well be advised to restore the overall risk perception for their company by reducing the level of financial risk; such as could be achieved by making an equity rights issue and using the funds raised to repay some of the outstanding debt of the company. Consequently, although the most common direction of strategic movement would be from Quadrants 1 to 4 of Figure 4.3 – i.e. moving from high to low business risk and from low to high financial risk – it is possible and logical for companies to move in the opposite direction.

Risk management as part of financial strategy

Risk management is fundamentally important to business. A detailed discussion is outside the scope of this book, although some suggested readings are given at the end of this chapter and in Chapter 6 on corporate governance. However, one aspect of risk management is very relevant to financial strategy: by changing the business risk profile of the business it is possible to change its financial strategy.

If business risks are high, this implies high volatility of profits and cash flows, which in turn means that lenders will be reluctant to lend, other than at high rates, and the company should not wish to borrow a lot. Given that debt is cheaper than equity, this can result in a high-cost capital structure. By adopting risk management tools such as hedging currency flows, or insuring against adverse conditions, or buying/selling forward commodities to protect prices, a company can reduce the variability of profits and cash flow. In doing so, it opens up opportunities to replace equity with debt, or replace expensive debt with cheaper debt.

Looked at this way, equity and good risk management can be seen as alternatives to each other. Simple choices about risk management can be reflected in financing alternatives, resulting in an overall more efficient business.

Privately held companies are different

At this point we should point out that although much of what we say in this book is relevant to all companies, the issues raised in the preceding paragraphs need not be applied by the owner/managers of private companies.

In a listed company, as we discussed in Chapter 1, although the shareholders own the company, the directors run it. There is thus a potential agency conflict. Furthermore, most listed companies have thousands of shareholders, and it would be impossible for the directors to determine the individual goals of these shareholders, so the generic 'shareholder value' is assumed as the company's target. Added to this is the threat of takeover if a listed company's share price fails to perform.

The situation in a private company is very different. The directors are often the owners, and even if they are not, there is likely to be a strong link between the two. Accordingly, the directors can ask the shareholders directly what they want from the company. The answer may not be 'shareholder value': in many private companies the chief objectives are financial security for the family shareholders, and the creation of a business to pass down to future generations. Accordingly, shareholders in private companies may be reluctant to take on any debt, despite it being an excellent idea in theory, if it means that they could lose sleep over it. And as private companies cannot suffer the threat of a hostile takeover, there is no need

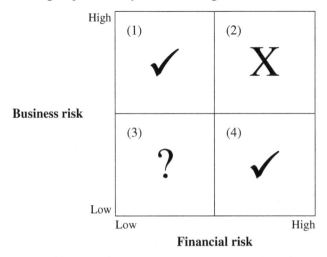

Figure 4.4 Matrix of business and financial risk for a private company.

for them to follow the prescribed strategy of gearing up a low risk business. Thus for a private company we can redraw the risk matrix as Figure 4.4.

Pecking order theory

One final thought about the choice of finance is relevant. Although debt is cheaper than equity, and although there are 'rules' as to what finance might be appropriate, managers tend to finance their businesses according to a 'pecking order' that prefers fundraising with low information asymmetry, and also reflects how easy it is to access the funds.

Information asymmetry is an important concept. It is realistic for a potential investor to assume that companies would only wish to issue shares if their share price were high rather than low, because they would raise more money or suffer less dilution. The corollary of that is that investors expect equity to be overpriced. As they are at the wrong end of the information gap with the company's managers, they demand a lower price than might otherwise be hoped, to compensate: this is a cost to the company of raising external finance, to which have to be added any intermediation costs of raising that money. Similarly, a company raising external debt will find that potential lenders see themselves (correctly) at an information disadvantage, and so impose conditions and costs on the loan. Internal funds, however, are readily available and appear cost-free.[8]

Managers thus have a pecking order of preferences, which suggests that if the company has internal resources available it will use these first as they involve no information asymmetry and can be accessed easily. Once available internal resources have been used up, the next easiest form of finance is generally to raise debt. And raising equity is time-consuming and expensive, as well as leading to dilution of control, so that is seen as the last resort for fundraising. Those companies where the asymmetry is the strongest are the most likely to display the pecking order in their financial choices, even if that does not always fit in with the suggestions in the rest of this book.

---

8   Internal funds do of course represent equity and so are not really free.

Key messages

- Risk relates to the volatility of expected results. It can arise from the characteristics of the business, or the chosen financial strategy.
- Financial strategy covers four decisions: How much shall we invest in assets? How shall we finance the business? What dividend policy is appropriate? Shall we raise new equity?
- A company's choice of financial strategy must relate to its business strategy, its business risk, and the cash flows it is expected to generate. Companies with high business risk should adopt a low-risk financial strategy, and vice versa.
- The appropriate business strategy takes account of strategic analysis in the light of the seven drivers of value.
- Companies often follow a pecking order of funding, preferring sources with lower information asymmetry (i.e. internal funds, then debt) over expensive equity.

Suggested further reading

The Institute of Risk Management calls itself 'the world's leading enterprise-wide risk education institute'. Its website, www.theirm.org, gives access to a menu of publications and reports about risk and how companies approach risk management. If you are interested in the subject, it is worth browsing.

Aswath Damodaran, Professor of Finance at New York University Stern School of Business, produced a long working paper in 2010, entitled *Risk Management: A Corporate Governance Manual*. Comprising very short chapters, this focuses more on behavioural issues and the financial management of risks than their assessment, but is a very interesting read. It is available at http://ssrn.com/abstract=1681017

5 Financial strategies over the life cycle

Learning objectives

After reading this chapter you should be able to:

1   Understand and apply a model that relates business risks and financial strategy to the business life cycle.
2   Evaluate the appropriateness of a company's gearing and dividend policies.
3   Appreciate the inevitability of a declining P/E multiple and understand how this affects shareholder returns as a company matures.

Understanding the life cycle

Products can follow a well-established life cycle, with trends in sales values, in real terms, rationally explained by reference to the current stage of development. The basic practical problem associated with the life cycle is that it is much easier to use the technique to explain why sales moved as they did (used as an *ex-post* analysis), than it is to use it to predict what sales will be in the future (in an *ex-ante* role). However, if the life cycle is broken into several stages, as shown in Figure 5.1, it does become possible to understand what the long-term future trend in sales levels might be and to make strategic decisions accordingly.

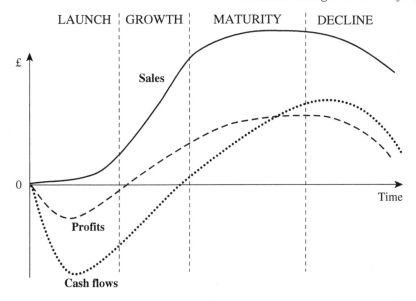

Figure 5.1 Life cycle model.

The traditional 'S curve' focuses on the level of sales over the life cycle. As we are more interested in the company's financial position, Figure 5.1 also illustrates what the related profits and cash-flows profiles could be.

In the launch stage, both profit and cash flow are likely to be negative, reflecting the investment made in developing the product and the market. The progression through the life cycle sees both profit and cash flow becoming positive (there is little point in starting if this is not likely to happen). The stage at which each stops being a drain on the organization will depend on the characteristics of the enterprise; in Figure 5.1 it is assumed that capitalization of costs will mean that profits turn the corner sooner than cash flows.

Clearly the initial sales levels during the launch phase of any product will be low; at this stage there is a significant business risk that sales will never increase and may disappear altogether if the product does not work properly, or is not accepted by the market. Should these initial risks be overcome so that the product becomes accepted by the critical mass of the important opinion-forming segment of potential customers, sales levels in the market as a whole should start to increase significantly. This period of dramatic sales growth cannot continue for ever, as the total demand for any product is finite. Inevitably the increase in sales starts to slow down as all the potential customers for the product come into the market and establish their normal rate of usage for the product.

It is very common to find that this period of fast growth in demand attracts a number of late entrants into the market; the apparent risk associated with the product has reduced since it is now accepted by the customers, but the continuing growth indicates an opportunity to make an attractive financial return. Obviously these new entrants will increase the total capacity for the product, but the existing players are also trying to increase their shares of this growing market. This can cause a significant increase in total industry capacity, even though the demand for the product is starting to stabilize (further business risks relate to the problems of accurately forecasting the change-over points in the product life cycle). As a result many businesses in the industry will have spare new capacity, which can cause fierce price competition until a more stable equilibrium position is established. This overcapacity

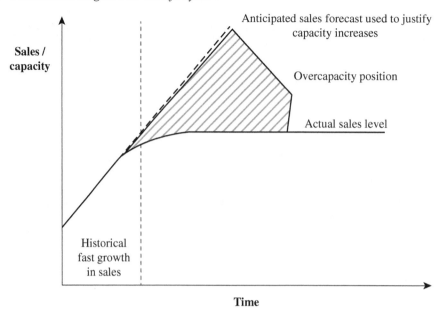

Figure 5.2 Shake-out period.

is diagrammatically shown in Figure 5.2, and the maturity stage of the life cycle cannot be properly started until this position is resolved.

In the maturity stage, demand and supply are much more in balance, so that the remaining efficient producers can expect to make stable profits on their substantial sales volumes. Unfortunately, this happy state of affairs eventually ends when demand for the product starts to die away. This can be caused by saturation of the market or by the launch of a better replacement product which rapidly attracts away most of the current mature product's users.

An important element highlighted by the product life cycle is the concept of changes in market share for the competitors in any particular industry. It is quite straightforward to distinguish between the different stages of development in terms of the key strategic thrusts of the business and to relate these to the relative associated business risks at each stage. This can be most easily demonstrated by applying the Boston Consulting Group's portfolio matrix, albeit in a slightly different manner to its traditional use.

The Boston matrix

Figure 5.3 shows the product life cycle in a diagrammatic representation developed by the Boston Consulting Group to explain the concept of product portfolio management to senior managers of large groups.

The two axes represent two key business success factors: relative market share and the rate of growth of the particular markets. (The research underlying the model also identified the level of product profitability as a third factor.) If the product life cycle is added into the discussion, they can be related to the key strategic thrusts of the business and to the most appropriate management style. In Figure 5.3 the horizontal axis shows the relative market share of the company, i.e. its share compared to its largest competitor. This *relative* measure

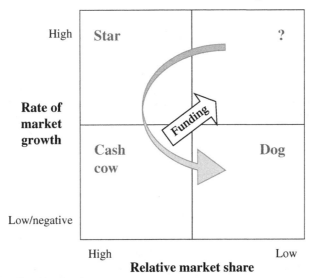

(Based on Boston Consulting Group)

Figure 5.3 Portfolio matrix, incorporating product life cycle.

is vitally important because a 20 per cent market share may sound impressive, but if a single competitor has most of the other 80 per cent, the company's competitive position is relatively weak. The vertical axis represents the rate of growth in sales volumes for the market in total, and hence goes from highly positive at the top to significantly negative at the bottom; thus replicating the product life cycle's S curve.

The four boxes of the Boston matrix can be matched – approximately – to the four stages of the product life cycle. The question mark represents the launch stage; growth is the star; the mature company is used as a cash cow (and the original Boston matrix saw this as funding more new launches and stars); and the low-growth, low-share dog can be seen as the decline stage of the life cycle, when perhaps the product should be put out of its misery.

Business risk and cash flows over the life cycle

Having set out our basic model, what we now need to do is show how business risk maps onto each stage of the product life cycle, as this will help determine the appropriate financial strategy. Table 5.1 illustrates how the level of knowledge increases as time progresses.

The analysis in Table 5.1, which is expanded upon in the rest of this section, is summarized in Figure 5.4, which shows the business risk profile of the company at each stage of development.

During the development and launch stage we have many assumptions, but little knowledge. Any forecasts we prepare to show the business's future are speculative. The product may not work properly or, even if it does work, the market research indications may prove to be wrong, with the eventual demand being too small to justify financially the total required investment. The key strategic thrust at this stage is to focus on product development and market research. It may be important to be first to market, to blunt the attack of potential competitors. At this stage, the business risk is very high. Cash flows are likely to be negative,

Table 5.1 Unknowns decrease over the life cycle

LAUNCH	GROWTH	MATURITY	DECLINE
Product risk			
Market acceptance			
Market share	Market share		
Size of market at maturity	Size of market at maturity		
Length of maturity period	Length of maturity period	Length of maturity period	
Maintenance of market share	Maintenance of market share	Maintenance of market share	
Rate of eventual decline	Rate of eventual decline	Rate of eventual decline	Rate of eventual decline

reflecting a significant investment in research and development, market research, and fixed assets, with minimal, if any, sales income. Depending on the industry, this stage could last for weeks, months, or even years.

Should the product launch prove successful and the sales volumes start to grow, the strategic thrust changes to market development, particularly market share development.

It is much easier for a company to increase its market share while the market is growing rapidly than it is in a static market. In a growth market, even if one company grows faster than the market, others can still increase their sales volumes quite rapidly on a year-on-year basis, and might not even notice that their market share is declining. Even if they do, they may be capacity or capital constrained from increasing their output sufficiently rapidly to maintain their previous shares. If a similar market share growth objective were set for a mature, very low-growth product, the competitive response would probably be much more severe, as the increased sales volumes would almost all have to be achieved at the expense of lower sales volumes on the part of competitors. Consequently it is a sound business strategy to try to achieve the maximum desired market share before the market itself reaches its maximum size. This requires a clear focus on market share development, but a leading company in a

Growth	Launch
High	Very high
Maturity	**Decline**
Medium	Low

Figure 5.4 Business risk.

high-growth industry should also invest in ensuring that the market matures at as large a size as is financially justifiable.[1]

Such a concentrated strategic focus on market development and sales growth requires a shift in management style to 'marketing-led' management, where the emphasis is not necessarily on continually changing the product, unless that is required to achieve a competitive advantage in the marketplace. Some management teams seem to be capable of operating successfully in both entrepreneurial and marketing-led modes, whereas others have been unable to change their style, with a corresponding detrimental impact on the business.

The business risk profile during this rapid growth phase has declined somewhat from the very high level of the launch stage but is still high. Managing a rapidly growing business brings its own challenges, in terms of the style and capability of the executives. The main unknowns at this stage relate to the ultimate market share achieved by the company and the length of this period of sustained growth which together dictate the sales volumes which will be achieved during the maturity stage of the life cycle.

Cash flow at the growth stage could be neutral, or could remain negative. In some industries, the growing sales income will provide sufficient funding to cover all of the outflows. However, companies with a high working capital requirement will find that the inflow from sales is devoured by the increases in inventories and receivables (see Chapter 20 for more about working capital management). Other businesses may need capacity increases that require investment in fixed assets.

Eventually, the sales growth will slow and the product will enter its mature phase. Here, sales have stabilized, the competition is identified and understood, the cost base is known and controlled. There should be no need for working capital increases, and cash flows should be positive. Business risk has decreased, and is mainly focused around the need to maintain this cash cow position for as long as possible.

If the company has been successful in implementing its marketing strategy during the period of rapid growth, it should enter the maturity stage with a very high relative market share of a large total market. This is important because it is during this stage that the company recoups the investments made during the earlier stages. As shown in Figure 5.5, the net cash flows in the launch phase are heavily negative and might stay negative during the high growth stage, although they should end it as reasonably balanced, depending on the rate of growth and need for additional investment in fixed assets or working capital. Once the rate of growth slows, this cash outflow reduces, while the cash produced from sales revenues increases (high sales volumes at a good profit per unit) resulting in a strong positive net cash flow.

Clearly this move into the maturity stage of the life cycle represents a very significant change in the strategic thrust of the business. As previously mentioned, any attempt now to grow market share is likely to be fiercely resisted by competitors, particularly where the cost structure of the industry is substantially fixed and committed on a long-term basis. (In other words, if significant exit barriers from the industry have been erected, there may well be intense competition to maintain market share.)

The most appropriate management style during this phase can be described as 'controller' mode, because the business should be maximizing the return which can be generated over

1 Financial expenditure on market development – increasing the size of the overall market, rather than increasing the company's own share of this market – is very difficult to justify if the company has a small share of the market. If only a 10 per cent share is held by the company, 90 per cent of any general market development expenditure can be argued as being to the benefit of competitors.

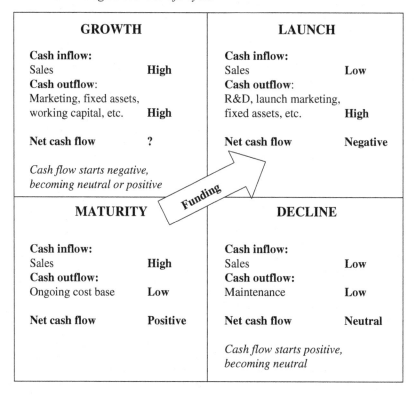

Figure 5.5 Net cash flows at different stages of development.

this mature stage of the life cycle. It is important that the business does not switch suddenly from its marketing-led growth strategy to a cost-cutting, short-term profit maximization mindset. This type of change could lead to a rapid decline in market share and a dramatic shortening of the period over which high profits and strong positive cash flows can be generated. The key objective is to maintain market share as long as the total market demand justifies the required level of marketing support, but at the same time to look for efficiency gains which can improve the overall return on investment. This fundamental change from a growth management focus to a profit improvement emphasis is difficult for many management teams to accept and implement, with the result that many businesses try to grow when market conditions and competitive pressures make this financially very unattractive. If such growth is impossible in their original business, they may turn to a diversification strategy by investing in new product areas.

Once again this move along the product life cycle reduces the level of business risk as, in the maturity stage, the main risk relates to the length of this period of stable sales volumes and high total profit levels. From the economic viewpoint of the shareholder, this cash-positive phase is the justification for the initial investment in the development and launch of the product. Indeed financially rational investors would like the company to move as rapidly as possible around the product life cycle until the maturity stage is reached, and then the company should stay in this cash-generating phase for as long as possible. Unfortunately the earlier styles of innovation and growth tend to be more attractive to many managers, who can find the appropriate controller style of the maturity phase quite boring.

Nothing good lasts for ever, and during the final decline stage of the life cycle, cash inflows and outflows both fall. As the investment in working capital decreases, the business may be cash positive, but the net cash flow must be at least neutral, as otherwise the product should be culled instantly. (No company should be a net investor on a long-term basis in a dying product.) This overall position often causes management to invest in new growth opportunities, with funding moving in the direction indicated by the arrow in Figure 5.5. However, as is argued later in this chapter such a reinvestment is neither inevitable nor, in many cases, desirable.

In fact, for some groups of managers the declining stage of the product life cycle may be more exciting, as the dominant style now becomes 'cost cutter' in order to ensure that the cash flows do remain at least neutral. The product is now dying, although the process may take many years and some spin-off ideas may be relaunched as new products in their own right. However, even in the move from the maturity stage to the declining phase, the business risk can still be argued as reducing. The only remaining business risk associated with the product is how long it will take to die. No dramatic positive cash inflows are expected from this phase and, if no further cost savings can be made to keep the cash flow slightly positive or neutral, the product may be closed down by the company before the market demand completely disappears. One major practical problem, caused by the failure to change managers during the progression of a product through its life cycle, is that it can be very difficult for managers who have developed, launched, grown and then maintained a product to accept that it is now time to kill it. Far too often, products are kept going too long in the vain hope that the market will pick up or that a way will be found to cut costs still further.

Changing the financing strategy over the life cycle

Having looked at business risks and cash flows, we can develop the appropriate financial strategy for each stage of the life cycle. Two, related, matters need to be considered:

- The business should make the best use of its available cash; and
- Business risk and financial risk should be inversely correlated (as shown in Figure 4.3).

Let us remind ourselves of the key characteristics of debt and equity, from the point of view of the company being funded. Debt is high risk, and involves cash outflows in interest and repayments. Equity is low risk, with no contractual cash outflow, although the board may choose to declare a dividend. Thus, a company in the high-risk launch and growth stages, needing to invest in assets and development, would be foolish to let cash leak out of the business to service debt (even if a lender could be found with such a poor appreciation of risk that they would fund it). In maturity, with a lower business risk and less need for cash for investment, it is altogether appropriate to make use of debt as a low-cost source of funding.

Coupled with this is the inverse correlation of business and financial risk. Since the business risk decreases as the product moves through its life cycle, it is logical that the financial risk can be correspondingly increased without creating a completely unacceptable combined risk for the shareholders and other stakeholders in the company. This is illustrated in Figure 5.6 and leads to the obvious question of what impact this changing risk profile has on the financial strategy of the business.

Growth	Launch
Business risk high	*Business risk very high*
Financial risk low	Financial risk very low
Maturity	**Decline**
Business risk medium	*Business risk low*
Financial risk medium	Financial risk high

Figure 5.6 Financial risk.

As is illustrated in Figure 5.6, the financial risk profile should be very low during the very high-risk stage of product development and launch.[2] In essence, an investment at this early stage is made on the strength of a product concept, with possibly some prototypes and some market research, and a business plan indicating the future prospects for the eventual product. It is desirable at this stage to use low-risk equity sources of funding, raising capital from venture capital, specialist investors who understand the high business risk associated with the company.

Once the product is launched and initial sales growth can be demonstrated together with substantial future growth prospects, a much larger body of potential investors becomes available to the company. This is just as well, because the growth stage will demand more funding. This can be combined with providing an exit for the venture capital company, as illustrated in Figure 5.7.

The best way of achieving this type of exit route for venture capital initial funding is through an Initial Public Offering (IPO), where a much broader range of equity investors can be attracted to buy shares in the company. Such an IPO is not normally possible for a start-up company as, by definition, the business has no track record which can be used to indicate its existing success or its realistic prospects for the future.

The changing source of funding over the whole life cycle is illustrated in Figure 5.8, and this indicates the fundamental change which can occur when the product matures. This maturity stage carries less business risk so that a medium level of financial risk can now be taken on by the company. The cash flow from the product has also turned significantly

---

2   The weighting of these business risks and financial risks is by no means equal. For most companies, the importance of the business risk profile is greater than the financial risk element. After all, an unsound business strategy cannot be made successful by clever financing; if the fundamental business is doomed, the best financial strategy can only delay its inevitable collapse.

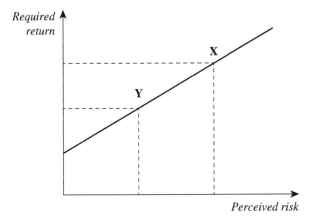

Figure 5.7 The changing risk profile of equity investment.

At the very high-risk launch stage, the required return is X. Equity funding is provided by venture capital. As the business moves into the growth stage it needs further funding, but the risks have decreased such that the appropriate return is only Y. This is not attractive to the venture capitalist, but equity can be found on the capital markets, by means of a flotation. The flotation has the added advantage of providing an exit for the venture capitalist.

positive at this time and this combination allows the company to borrow, rather than only using the equity sources of funding which have been accessed so far in its development.

It is also important to consider the business from the perspective of the rational investor, who quite rightly regards this cash positive, mature stage as the most attractive phase of the life cycle. So far equity funding has been injected into the business to develop and launch the product and then to increase both the total market size and the company's share of that market. If more equity funding is required during the maturity stage, this investment starts to look a lot like a financial black hole: money keeps going in, but nothing ever comes out.

Growth	**Launch**
Business risk high	*Business risk very high*
Financial risk low	*Financial risk very low*
Equity	Equity
(growth investors)	(venture capital)
Maturity	**Decline**
Business risk medium	*Business risk low*
Financial risk medium	*Financial risk high*
Debt and equity	Debt
(retained earnings)	

Figure 5.8 Changing sources of funding.

Therefore the only logical source of additional equity funding during this maturity stage is for some of the profits being made by the company to be reinvested into the business. Additional financing can be raised through borrowing money. This is now practical because the positive cash flow of the business provides the source of servicing the debt, paying the interest and repaying the principal. If debt financing had been used at the earlier stages of the life cycle, the absence of such positive cash flow would mean that the repayments could only be made by rolling over the original loans or by raising equity to repay the debt funding.

This is a reminder of a key issue regarding the use of debt and equity funding: a lender's risk is lower than an equity investor's risk, due to the security taken and legally granted priority on full repayment. (Remember that the risk ranking is reversed when viewed from the perspective of the company, i.e. the user of the funding.) Risk and return are positively correlated, so that the return required on debt funding should always be less than that required on equity financing for the same company; i.e. debt is cheaper for the company. This is completely logical from the company's perspective because, as debt is higher-risk funding for the company, the company should demand a cost saving to justify incurring the extra risk.

Therefore, as long as increasing the financial risk through borrowing does not lead to an unacceptable total combined risk, the cheaper debt funding will increase the residual profits achieved by the company. Thus the profits generated by the mature company, which uses some debt financing, will be enhanced and the return on equity will look even better, as less equity is required to fund the business.

This is even more important when the product moves into the decline phase of the life cycle, and it becomes clear that the product is dying. As debt is cheaper than equity, it is financially beneficial to the shareholders to extract their equity investment from the dying business as early as possible, replacing it with debt. Clearly it should not be acceptable to a lender to take on an unacceptable, equity-type risk, but it can be practical to borrow against the residual value of those assets which are, of necessity, tied up in the business until it is finally liquidated. These funds can then be distributed to shareholders, effectively representing a repayment of capital. In this way the present value of the shareholders' investment is increased, without adversely affecting the position of the lender who is suitably secured on the residual value of the assets, and who receives a risk-related rate of interest. Consequently the principal source of funding for the declining business is debt finance with its associated high financial risk, partially offsetting the low business risk associated with this final stage of development.

Debt profile

In considering the balance between debt and equity in a company's financial strategy, one other issue should be mentioned: of the debt, how much should be borrowed short-term and how much long-term?

The answer to this question depends, unsurprisingly, on the company's business, its assets and the structure of its operations. Broadly, the company's debt portfolio should attempt to match long-term assets with long-term finance, and short-term assets with short-term funding sources. So, the acquisition of a building would best be financed through long-term debt (if, indeed, debt is the best solution); additional inventories should be funded using short-term facilities such as an overdraft or revolving credit line. However, if a company has permanent working capital, this should be regarded as part of long-term needs. (This is discussed further in Chapter 20.)

The advantage to a company of using long-term rather than short-term debt finance is that once the loan has been agreed, the company can be confident that it cannot be taken away.[3] Short-term debt needs to be refinanced at regular intervals and, if the company's financial situation has deteriorated or the credit markets tightened, this may become a problem.

Exceptions do exist to this broad rule about using long-term funding for long-term needs. If short-term interest rates are considerably lower than long-term ones, and the company believes that long-term rates will fall, it may be worth using short-term finance to start, with the intention of refinancing at a later date, in a more favourable environment. This strategy does, of course, carry obvious risks. The point here is that the *policy* would be for long-term debt, the issue is one of *timing*.[4]

A logical dividend policy

Throughout this discussion on increasing levels of financial risk, the issue of how investors receive their required financial return has been critical. Ordinary shareholders can only receive this return in two ways: either the company pays a dividend, or the value of their shares increases so that they can sell and achieve a capital gain. Obviously, the total return can take the form of a combination of dividend yield and capital appreciation but, theoretically, the shareholder should be indifferent as to whether the company pays a dividend or not. This is because, if the company does not pay a dividend, the value of the shares should increase to reflect the present value of the future cash flows which should be generated by the reinvestment of these profits which were available to be paid out as dividends. Clearly this argument is based on heroic assumptions regarding the availability of attractive reinvestment opportunities, the complete absence of tax considerations, and a rational stock market with perfect understanding. The tax and perfect market assumptions are obviously not true; the assumption of an infinite number of attractive reinvestment projects is not relevant if the company is restricted to one product, which progresses through its life cycle.

Hence for the current structured analysis, it is possible to indicate a logical dividend policy for a company at each stage of development, and this is diagrammatically shown in Figure 5.9. During the cash-negative launch phase it is completely illogical for shareholders to expect a dividend from the company. They are supplying all the funding and therefore, if the company were to pay a dividend, they would have to increase their investment in order to pay part of it back to themselves! Consequently a nil dividend pay-out ratio is appropriate for these start-up, venture capital-funded businesses; all of the high required return being in the form of capital growth.

There is also a very simple practical restraint on many such companies paying dividends. In order to pay dividends, companies require both cash and distributable profits, i.e. profits after tax generated either in the current year or retained from past years. During the launch phase, the business could well be generating accounting losses and therefore might have no distributable profits from which it could declare a dividend.

Even when the company has moved into the high growth stage of the life cycle, the cash flow is still, at best, only neutral and the source of funding is still equity. Thus a high dividend pay-out policy is still illogical and this is made even clearer when the key strategic thrust at this stage is considered. The business is trying to increase its market share while the market is still growing strongly: a logical investor would want the company to take advantage of these attractive growth

---

3 Subject of course to the company's continuing to meet its obligations under the loan agreement.

4 This is one reasons why a gearing calculation should be based on net debt, including both long- and short-term debt, net of cash. Some textbooks state that only long-term debt should be included in the gearing calculation, or that cash should be ignored. However, a company's treasury strategy may be such that the exact configuration of the elements at any point in time differs from their longer-term strategy, and it can be misleading just to consider a snapshot position of long-term debt.

Growth	Launch
Business risk high *Financial risk low* *Funding equity* Nominal dividend pay-out ratio	*Business risk very high* *Financial risk very low* *Funding equity* Nil dividend pay-out ratio
Maturity	**Decline**
Business risk medium *Financial risk medium* *Funding debt* High dividend pay-out ratio	*Business risk low* *Financial risk high* *Funding debt* Total dividend pay-out ratio

Figure 5.9 Dividend policy: pay-out ratio.

opportunities while they exist and this could be constrained if cash were paid out as dividends. As new investors are being attracted into the company during this stage in order to replace the existing venture capitalists and to finance the rapid growth, it may be necessary to pay a nominal dividend out of the increasing profit stream. However, most of the required investor return would still come from capital growth in the value of the shares in the company.

Once the maturity stage of the life cycle is reached, the dividend policy should change, for a number of reasons. The cash flow from the business is now strongly positive and debt financing is now a practical and sensible alternative source of funding. Accounting profits should now be high and relatively stable so that a high dividend pay-out can be properly supported. More fundamentally, it is important that the dividend pay-out ratio is increased as there will be restricted opportunities for reinvesting the whole of the current profit stream in the existing business. There is a strong possibility of the law of diminishing returns setting in on incremental levels of reinvestment. If a company cannot reinvest funds at the rate of return demanded by its shareholders, it destroys shareholder value by retaining these funds.

Consequently, as profitable reinvestment opportunities reduce due to the lack of growth in the now mature business, shareholder value can be maximized by paying out these surplus funds as dividends. Furthermore, as the company matures, the opportunities for the shareholders to make a substantial capital gain must be limited, as the high-growth period is in the past. Accordingly, in order to provide shareholder return the dividend yield would be expected to increase, to compensate for the decline in potential capital gain.

This required change in dividend policy represents yet another of the potential conflicts discussed in agency theory, because senior managers will normally prefer to retain these surplus funds within the company. These funds provide them with operational flexibility should an attractive opportunity be identified in the future and they also act as a buffer in case there is an unforeseen economic downturn or adverse change in the competitive environment. Furthermore, paying dividends might decrease both earnings per share and share price, both of which are metrics commonly used for management incentives. None of these arguments is based on the concept of maximizing shareholder wealth; they are more closely focused on a concept of increasing managerial utility.

Inevitably the strong cash flows and high profits will die away as the product starts to decline: Figure 5.9 then advocates a total dividend pay-out ratio. In this context, 'total' means all the free cash flow generated by the business which, during this declining stage, is likely to be in excess of the profits reported by the company.

During the maturity phase, the company produces high profits and high net cash flows, out of which it should pay a high proportion as dividend. As illustrated in Working Insight 5.1, this dividend yield will represent a substantial proportion of the total return expected by the shareholders, because future prospects for capital growth are now relatively low. However, once the product starts to decline, this future growth becomes negative with the result that the company may not want to reinvest to maintain the existing scale of business. This means that the depreciation expense (which is, of course, a non-cash operating expense charged in arriving at post-tax profits) may not necessarily be reinvested in replacing the assets which are being used up. This would increase the level of free cash flow generated by the business which could be paid out as dividends to shareholders.

The dividends could be further increased if the residual value of essential assets were funded by borrowing, and the cash distributed to shareholders, as suggested earlier. This clearly highlights that part of the high dividends paid by declining companies really represents a repayment of shareholders' capital.

This changing picture of the dividend pay-out ratio and its offsetting relationship with expected capital growth in the share value must always be considered in the context of a decreasing overall risk profile for the company as it matures. The reducing risk profile means that investors demand a lower total rate of return; the sort of relationships which can apply between dividend yields and capital growth are illustrated in Working Insight 5.1.

The impact on the price/earnings multiple

Working Insight 5.1 shows that the capital growth component of the total expected shareholder return reduces as the product passes through its life cycle. This is logical because the future

---

Working Insight 5.1

Illustrative example of changes in total shareholder return and its component elements

Stage of maturity	Total annual required return (i.e. Ke)		Dividend yield	+	Capital growth
			Generated by		
Launch	40%	=	0		40%
Growth	25%	=	2%		23%
Maturity	15%	=	12%		3%
Decline	12%	=	18%		−6%

These total required returns are illustrative only. Tax is ignored, but does not affect the logic of the analysis. However, the different tax positions of various groups of shareholders may make companies in particular stages of maturity more or less attractive to them.

Growth	**Launch**
Business risk high *Financial risk low* *Funding equity* *Dividend pay-out nominal* High growth	*Business risk very high* *Financial risk very low* *Funding equity* *Dividend pay-out nil* Very high growth
Maturity	**Decline**
Business risk medium *Financial risk medium* *Funding debt* *Dividend pay-out high* Medium/low growth	*Business risk low* *Financial risk high* *Funding debt* *Dividend pay-out total* Negative growth

Figure 5.10 Future growth prospects.

growth prospects for the product start off very high and reduce as these prospects are actually achieved. The development of future growth prospects over the life cycle is illustrated in Figure 5.10, which highlights that the future growth of a mature product is relatively low and that a declining product will experience negative growth in the future.

As discussed in Chapter 2, a company's price/earnings (P/E) ratio reflects its expected future growth prospects: the higher the growth expectations, the higher the P/E. Accordingly, the P/E ratio might be expected to fall over the company's life cycle. Figure 5.11 shows this.

Growth	**Launch**
Business risk high *Financial risk low* *Funding equity* *Dividend pay-out nominal* *Growth high* High P/E	*Business risk very high* *Financial risk very low* *Funding equity* *Dividend pay-out nil* *Growth very high* Very high P/E
Maturity	**Decline**
Business risk medium *Financial risk medium* *Funding debt* *Dividend pay-out high* *Growth medium/low* Medium/low P/E	*Business risk low* *Financial risk high* *Funding debt* *Dividend pay-out total* *Growth negative* Low P/E

Figure 5.11 Price/earnings multiple.

Working Insight 5.2

The impact on required eps of a declining P/E multiple

	(1)	(2)	(3)
Stage of maturity	*Appropriate P/E multiple*	*Required eps*	*Market price of share*
Launch	40	2.5p	100p
Growth	20	5p	100p
Maturity	10	10p	100p
Steady state	7	14.3p	100p
Decline	4	12.5p	50p

(1) The P/E multiples are illustrative, not calculated.[5]
(2) Eps in column (2) is calculated using the required market price in column (3) divided by the P/E ratio in column (1)
(3) The market price is held constant in column (3). This shows that in order to deliver value from the current share price, eps must rise. It falls in the decline stage, which reflects the negative capital gain illustrated in Working Insight 5.1.

We can now expand upon the analysis in Chapter 2 to show how a company's earnings per share (eps) will need to increase over its life cycle due to the decreasing P/E ratio. Working Insight 5.2 demonstrates the rising levels of eps needed to justify a share price of 100p.

In Working Insight 5.2 the share price does not rise above the initial 100p paid by the shareholders. Of course, were this to happen in practice the shareholders would be most dissatisfied with the company's performance. This illustrates an important point: the very high real growth in eps already included in the share price when a very high P/E multiple is applied to the company. The delivery of this expected growth will not make the share price increase, because it has already been taken account of in the current share price. The share price will only rise if the company can actually exceed this expected and paid-for rate of growth, or continue to grow at this rate for longer than expected. However, in the first three stages of the life cycle it is quite possible for the company to deliver strongly growing eps.

This continued period of rapidly increasing eps is very important from the shareholders' point of view because, as was made clear in Working Insight 5.1, during the launch and growth stages almost all of their financial return is generated from capital growth in the value of their share, the company having a very low dividend pay-out policy at this time. Consequently, generating only that rate of growth in eps which merely maintains the existing share price would be considered a very poor performance by the company. The eps growth during the launch and growth periods should drive up the share price so that an acceptable overall annual rate of return is achieved by the shareholders. This needs to take account both of the declining P/E multiple which will be applied to these earnings as they grow, and of the

5 In practice, of course, a P/E multiple of 40 would imply considerable growth expectations from the market, particularly in the light of the high cost of equity used to illustrate the differences between the stages in this and in Working Insight 5.1.

Working Insight 5.3

Uphill struggle

Stage of maturity	(1) Illustrative length of stage (in years)	(2) Appropriate annual capital gain required through share price (from Working Insight 5.1)	(3) Compound factor (based on column 2)^t	(4) Required share price at start of each stage (see note)	(5) Future growth-related P/E multiple (from Working Insight 5.2)	(6) Desired eps by start of each stage
Initial value at time of first external investment – 100p						
Launch	2	40%	1.960 ×	100p ↓	40	2.5p
Growth	5	23%	2.815 ×	196p ↓	20	9.8p
Maturity	10	3%	1.344 ×	552p ↓	10	55.2p
Steady state	N/A	Nil	1 ×	742p	7	106p

Thus in the 17 years that this product takes to reach a steady state position the growth in eps is from 2.5p to 106p. If the company were only to achieve the eps of 14.3p shown in Working Insight 5.2, the share price would not increase to the level required by investors.

At the final steady state position, the eps of 106p will be paid out annually as dividend. Based on the share price of 742p this gives a dividend yield of 14.3%. This return represents the full cost of capital to shareholders (consistent with the inverse of the steady state P/E ratio of 7 times).

Note to column (4): The required share price at the beginning of each subsequent stage is calculated by multiplying the opening share price for the previous stage by the compound factor required for that stage, as shown by the × and ↓ in the figure.

changing dividend pay-out ratio which should reduce expectations of future growth as the company matures.

The dramatic impact which this additional requirement for share value growth has on the need to generate eps growth is mathematically illustrated in Working Insight 5.3.

Working Insight 5.3 builds on the discussion in Chapter 2 about the need for eps to grow at a faster rate than the share price. It shows that for a particular, relatively short life cycle the growth in share price which is required to give shareholders their expected total annual return, including the capital gain element, is itself quite dramatic (from 100p to 742p over the seventeen-year life cycle period to the steady state stage as shown in column 4). However, due to the declining P/E multiple which is applied as the product matures, the required increase in eps needed to generate this final share price is even greater (an incredible growth from 2.5p to 106p, as shown in column 6).

The underlying assumptions for these illustrations are slightly exaggerated, and have been deliberately kept consistent so that the scale of the changes can be seen quite clearly as the analysis is made more comprehensive.[6] We can now complete the overall financial strategy

---

6   A real-life example of this is illustrated by Estrada, J. (2012). He shows that substantial earnings growth of Google and Amazon between 2006 and 2010 produced inadequate investor returns due to the large falls in the companies' P/E ratios.

GROWTH	LAUNCH
Business risk high	*Business risk very high*
Financial risk low	*Financial risk very low*
Funding equity	*Funding equity*
Dividend pay-out nominal	*Dividend pay-out nil*
Growth high	*Growth very high*
P/E high	*P/E very high*
Eps low	*Eps nominal*
Share price growing and volatile	Share price growing and highly volatile
MATURITY	**DECLINE**
Business risk medium	*Business risk low*
Financial risk medium	*Financial risk high*
Funding debt	*Funding debt*
Dividend pay-out high	*Dividend pay-out total*
Growth medium/low	*Growth negative*
P/E medium	*P/E low*
Eps high	*Eps declining*
Share price stable with limited volatility	Share price declining and volatile

Figure 5.12 Share price and volatility.

analysis to be completed by adding in the share price of the company over the product life cycle, as is done in Figure 5.12.

This figure shows both the movement in the actual share price over the life cycle and the associated volatility. The share price is obviously the result of multiplying the P/E multiple and the eps level, and its required trend over time depends on the proportion of the total shareholders' return which must be delivered through capital growth. As highlighted in Working Insight 5.3, the share price should be increasing during the launch and growth stages, and then stabilizing during maturity, before declining during the product's final phase of its life cycle.

During the very early period of the launch stage, any financial valuation exercise is very speculative as nominal (or even negative) earnings are being multiplied by the very high P/E multiple which reflects the expectations of strong future growth. As already discussed, this stage of investment is really an area for sophisticated professionals who appreciate the high associated risks and, potentially, commensurately high financial returns. The considerable potential for complete business failure or outstanding success results in very high volatility in share prices during this stage of the life cycle.

Once the product moves into the growth phase, this volatility will decline somewhat but will still be high due to the continued expectations of significant future growth in share values, eps, market share, and the total size of the market. Failure of any of these factors (which are of course interlinked) can lead to a rapid decline in share values, while unpredicted favourable developments can create quite spectacular growth in share prices. However, during the maturity stage, when the major element of shareholders' return comes from dividend yield, the share price should become much less volatile. This is because the strong positive cash flow and ability to use debt financing should enable the company to maintain the expected dividend payments even through normal economic cycles, so that the share price is consistently supported by this stable dividend stream. It is also much easier to value this type of income-generating share by reference to equivalent risk-adjusted interest-earning alternative investments; thus prices of high dividend-paying shares tend to move very directly as a result of any changes in interest rates which affect the yields on corporate bonds and other such investments.

This period of relatively low volatility comes to an end as the single-product company moves into the final phase of its life cycle because the volatility of the now declining share price increases again. In spite of the reducing business risk, the share price is now controlled by a total dividend pay-out policy and the investors' view on the length of time for which such payments can be maintained. Consequently, small external influences on the rate of decline of the product and its consequent cash generation capability can have very significant impacts on the share value, thus increasing the volatility.

Impact of a diversification strategy

Analysis so far has related to single-product companies as they and their products progress through the life cycle. As mentioned earlier, the inevitable result of the ultimate decline and death of such companies is not an attractive proposition for the senior managers and some of the other stakeholders. The analysis does, however, highlight that this inevitable liquidation of the company is not necessarily of great concern to shareholders in the company, although these shareholders are likely to change over time as the relative balance in the form of their financial return between capital gain and dividend yield changes.

Clearly, rational shareholders may be unconcerned about the forthcoming decline and death of any one investment from which they are currently receiving very high dividends (which partially represent a repayment of their invested capital). If they wish to preserve the value of their total investments, they can reinvest this capital repayment in other companies. Indeed it is fairly obvious that rational investors can generate any desired mix of capital gain and divided yield by investing in a suitable portfolio of companies. Similarly they can create a portfolio with any desired overall risk profile by suitably weighting the different types of available investments. Thus no sensible investor is forced to accept the reducing risk profile and increasing dividend yield which should be offered by a maturing company. A readjustment to the overall portfolio can be made either by reinvesting this increasing income stream in higher-risk, higher-growth companies, or, more rapidly, by actually selling some shares in the now mature business.

The costs of these changes to the investors' portfolios are normally very small and, more importantly, such changes should be easily planned well in advance if the company and the capital markets are using the appropriate signalling procedures. Therefore, from a shareholder's perspective there is no obvious need for a company to implement a diversification strategy when the growth prospects from the original core business reduce due to the product's maturity. However, such corporate strategies of utilizing the strong positive cash flow from the successful, but now mature, core businesses to invest in new higher-growth potential products, lie at the very heart of the Boston matrix.

As demonstrated in Figure 5.5, the growth and decline stages of the life cycle can both be broadly neutral in terms of net cash flow. The strong positive net cash flows of the maturity stage, which are not required for reinvestment in the core business, are therefore often used to fund the launch of other new products, which are at the beginning of their life cycles. Inevitably, over time, such a cross-subsidization reinvestment strategy will create a diversified conglomerate-style group which, due to its continued high level of reinvestment, should be considerably bigger than an originally similar, but still focused business which had followed

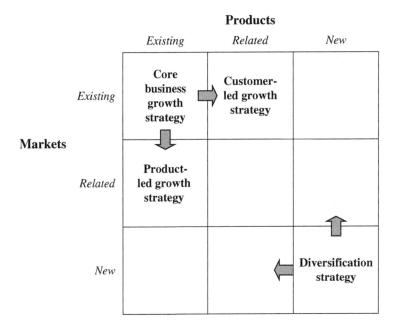

Figure 5.13 Modified Ansoff matrix.

a financial strategy of increasing its dividend pay-out ratio over the same period. The question is whether shareholder value has been increased or destroyed by the diversification alternative strategy.

In Chapter 1 we emphasized that shareholder value is increased by developing and maintaining a sustainable competitive advantage. It is therefore critical that the business can develop such a competitive advantage in these new areas of commercial endeavour. Obviously it may be that the new products utilize some technological breakthrough which was developed in the core business, and thus the company is not truly diversifying. Similarly the new areas of investment may build on an existing strength of the business so as to increase the overall competitive advantage held by the company. This can be diagrammatically illustrated by using a variation of the Ansoff matrix, as is shown in Figure 5.13.

If a key competitive strength of the existing business is built on the current product attributes or strong branding which have created very loyal customers, a strategic thrust for continued growth could be based on umbrella branding of new products with comparable attributes. This would utilize the major intangible asset of the company: its loyal customers. Such a customer-based competitive strategy has been implemented by many retailers, highlighted by the development of retailer brands. Alternatively the existing product may have reached maturity in its current markets but other markets may be less fully developed, and so may represent additional growth opportunities. Once again this growth strategy is based on an existing competitive advantage of the business: its ability to manage the launch and growth stages of a product, as demonstrated in its original market. However, if doing this, the managers need to be very careful to modify their previous strategy to reflect a different competitive environment.

These growth strategies can be successfully developed from an existing competitive advantage but, as with the case of the growth strategy focused on the original core business, the external business environment must be consistent with the strategy selected. Thus for growth of the core business to be financially successful the product must be at the right stage of development. Similarly, for the customer-led strategy any new products must have similar attributes so that they appeal to existing loyal customers and any umbrella branding is appropriate. For the market development strategy, the dynamics of the new markets must be sufficiently similar to enable the company to make use of its existing competitive advantage developed in its more mature home market; there are many examples of very expensive failures from this type of product globalization strategy and far fewer examples of success. However Figure 5.13 also shows where genuine diversification strategies fit and why they are unlikely to create increased shareholder value. Rather than building on existing competitive advantages, diversification goes to the other extreme and can be somewhat cynically described as 'selling products you don't have to people you don't know'.

It is very interesting that most companies regard diversification as a risk-reduction exercise. For the shareholder, it is clear that investing in a portfolio of shares spreads, and hence reduces, the risk associated with any one share. However, from the company's perspective, it can mean moving into areas where it has little or no experience and thus there is no particular reason why the company should achieve an above-normal rate of return. Of course if the risk profile is reduced, then a lower rate of return may still create shareholder value.

This highlights another major problem with basing a diversification strategy on a successful mature, cash positive business. As was shown in Figure 5.13, the mature stage of the life cycle should have the lowest volatility in share prices. Volatility is a good indicator of risk in assessing any financial investment, as a 'guaranteed' level of return represents a low risk to the investor. Hence, if a company diversifies into launch and growth products, the associated risk will increase from the perception of the investor; thus an increased return will be demanded to compensate for this increased risk. As the company has no significant competitive advantage it might not be possible to deliver such an increased return, with a consequent reduction in shareholder value.

Further it is clearly much more difficult for a diversified company, with businesses at all the different stages of the life cycle, to communicate a clear, focused financial strategy to the financial markets via its dividend policy or its debt-to-equity ratio. Theoretically such a conglomerate should be valued by the financial markets at a minimum of the weighted average P/E multiple of its component businesses; the excess valuation over this minimum representing the value created by the existence of the conglomerate group. In reality the share price of many such groups is often at a discount to this theoretical minimum, either due to the reasons above, or because analysts do not understand all the diverse businesses. This explains why so many of these companies have been the target of corporate raiders. If successful, the raider often changes the financial strategy of the group rather than the competitive strategies of the component parts.

Application internally to the divisions of a group

As the threat of takeover and break-up is potentially on the horizon for many large diversified groups, it is important that this analysis of appropriate financial strategies is applied internally by them to their individual operating divisions. In other words, the target financial return set for each division should be based on an assessment of the associated risk; thus a start-up division would be treated as effectively having venture capital funding, with a consequently high requirement for financial return. Also the form of that financial return would be dictated by the stage of development of the particular business so that cash (dividends

Case Study 5.1

Henkel: cost of capital in a divisional structure

German-based multinational Henkel has three divisions: laundry & home care; cosmetics & toiletries; and adhesive technologies. The laundry and cosmetics businesses sell items in daily use by consumers; the adhesive technologies business mostly operates business to business, producing adhesives for, for example, the global automotive and construction industries.

The 2012 financial statements of Henkel set out the calculation of the company's weighted average cost of capital (WACC). They then state, 'We apply different WACC rates depending on the business sector involved.' They go on to explain that the WACC used for the consumer-facing businesses is lower than that for adhesives, reflecting the relative risks of these businesses, reflected in industry betas.

Source: www.henkel.com

paid by the division to head office as the only shareholder) would only be extracted from mature divisions, where the opportunities for reinvestment were less attractive.

Companies rarely publish their internal costs of capital. However, the case of Henkel, in Case Study 5.1, a German-based multinational, is instructive.

The establishment of very clear, specific, tailored financial targets for each division of a large group can greatly help to focus the attention of divisional managers on those objectives which can create the maximum impact on the value of the total group. This would not be achieved if all the divisions tried to maximize short-term profits or cash flow, or even used some form of return on investment as the principal measure of divisional performance. Unfortunately, in many large groups, this level of financial sophistication is still not being applied today. In some, the hurdle rate for financial investments throughout the group is taken to be the weighted average cost of capital for the group and almost all divisions are expected to contribute towards the overall dividends paid out by the group to its shareholders. The almost inevitable result of this type of control system is that the divisions themselves start to develop a portfolio of businesses which are in different stages of development, so that they can then manage their financial resources across their own portfolio!

A caveat

Together with Chapter 4, this chapter has set out the model we will use in discussing financing strategy throughout the rest of the book. We now wish to make a caveat on how you should use it.

Models are useful to guide your thinking; they are not a substitute for that thinking. Throughout these chapters we have made generalizations about how organizations operate, for example, we have said that launch businesses are cash-hungry, that growth businesses need to fund inventory, and so on. But we could provide you with many examples of companies and industries where these axioms do not hold true, and where growth has successfully been debt-financed, without any adverse effects. Our advice is: get to grips with the models, and understand what they are telling you, and why. Once you understand these underlying assumptions, don't follow them blindly – feel free to adapt the model to your own circumstances. Just remember that financial risk and business risk should be inversely correlated; that debt is cheaper than equity; and that the most important thing is not to run out of cash.

Key messages

- The life cycle model shows how business risk is likely to change as a company develops, and, accordingly, how financial strategy should develop.
- Start-ups and growth companies are usually high-risk businesses strapped for cash, and should adopt low-risk financing structures, primarily equity-based. Dividends should not be paid.
- Mature companies are generally cash-generative low-risk businesses, which can improve their return to shareholders by increasing their financing risk, taking on debt and paying dividends.
- Businesses in managed decline, where the cash flows are clearly understood, should pay out as much in dividend and borrow as much as they are able.
- As a business progresses through the life cycle, its P/E ratio should fall, meaning that eps needs to rise, to provide the investors' required return.

Suggested further reading

Estrada, J. (2012), 'Blinded by Growth', *Journal of Applied Corporate Finance* 24(3): 19–25. Uses arithmetic examples to show how growth relates to equity returns, and how the shareholder returns from Google and Amazon were insufficient, despite a high level of growth in earnings, because of the fall in P/E as they moved along the life cycle.

Readings on risk management can be downloaded from the Institute of Risk Management at www. theirm.org

6 Corporate governance and financial strategy

Learning objectives

After reading this chapter you should be able to:

1   Apply a model to determine which aspects of corporate governance are most relevant at different stages of a company's life cycle.
2   Recognize the limitations of different types of executive remuneration plan, and evaluate how their performance measures link to the creation of value.
3   Understand and explain how differences in corporate governance regimes can affect the financing strategies of companies in those jurisdictions.
4   Contrast the different mechanisms by which block-holders can control a company, and explain the impact, positive and negative, that this can have.
5   Explain why stakeholders merit consideration in a discussion of financial strategy.

Introduction

In Chapter 1 we stated that financial strategy was about raising funds and managing their employment in the organization. Corporate governance, which relates to the way in which companies are directed and controlled, has ramifications for both of these. A discussion of corporate governance would describe companies' responsibilities to their key stakeholders, in particular those stakeholders who provide funding. It would include internal control mechanisms such as the accounting systems and the way in which investment decisions are made. Corporate governance is a means by which risk can be reduced – both for the company itself, and for its funders. Given that an important aspect of financial strategy is the matching of perceived risk with required return, consideration of corporate governance is fundamental to an analysis of corporate financial strategy.

It is not the function of this chapter to review all aspects of governance; there are several excellent readings in this field, some suggested at the end of this chapter. Nor do we intend to give you details of the governance regimes in any particular jurisdictions; these would probably change as soon as the book went to press. What we seek to do is examine several broad aspects of governance that are specifically relevant to financial strategy. We refer back to agency theory when looking at the different motivations of management and shareholders. We look at internal control, the implementation of systems to ensure that assets are safeguarded, liabilities controlled, risks managed, and transactions correctly processed. We consider how the way in which executives are paid drives the financial and business strategies they adopt. We discuss the implications of different forms of ownership, and different legal systems. And we develop a model that illustrates how governance requirements change over the business life cycle. We do this in very general terms, with the aim of giving our readers sufficient insight to be able to analyse their own situations.

The corporate governance life cycle

The life cycle model used throughout this book takes the company through the stages of launch, growth, maturity, and eventual decline. It would have been nice to fit our analysis of governance into those same categories, but unfortunately it didn't work out that way.[1] An underlying theme in governance, followed by regulators and academics, is agency theory, which considers the differences in motivation between principals (shareholders) and their agents (executives). Accordingly, our analysis begins by following the development of the agency relationship as ownership changes over the life cycle, which does not necessarily directly mirror the commercial stages.

The ownership cycle includes some or all of the following steps:

1   Sole trader
2   Partnership
3   Company with equity funding from the management
4   Company with equity funding from close associates (e.g. family)
5   Company with funding from private equity
6   Company with funding from the public (including institutional investors).

---

1   It is painful for any business school lecturer to have to admit that not everything in life fits neatly into a two-by-two matrix.

In each stage the company will also have funding from lenders – either negotiated finance from banks and similar organizations, or spontaneous funding from trade creditors. The protection of these lenders' positions is also an aspect of governance to consider.

Of course, the stages we describe need not happen in sequence – some organizations might never progress beyond Stage 3; others could start at Stage 4; some might move from Stage 6 back to Stage 5 by way of a buy-out. However, this is a convenient peg from which to hang the analysis.

The model we are using to describe governance characteristics over the ownership life cycle is set out in Table 6.1.

The model in Table 6.1 reflects how investors' risks grow as management and ownership become increasingly separated. Given that the cost of funding reflects the investor's or lender's perceived risk, one important function of corporate governance is to reduce this. Mechanisms of risk reduction can broadly be categorized as 'monitoring' or 'control'. Monitoring involves the disclosure of information by the company to the stakeholder, which allows that stakeholder to evaluate management's activities. Control gives the stakeholder the ability to prevent management from undertaking certain activities, or to oblige them to take others. Both types of mechanism have their place, and increase in intensity as we move from left to right across Table 6.1.

Internal control and financial reporting over the life cycle

Governance regulations in different jurisdictions define internal control in various ways. Here, when we talk about internal control we mean all controls, financial and otherwise, implemented by the organization in order to safeguard its assets, control its liabilities, manage its risks, and ensure that transactions are conducted and recorded properly.

For the sole trader with no employees, the main function of internal control is to keep track of the money. Accounting records are needed, at a minimum, to manage the cash, and to facilitate the preparation of tax returns. Forecasts of activity and cash requirements are needed to ensure that obligations can be met. A canny owner will set up more sophisticated accounting systems to provide information on product or customer profitability.

Once the trader takes on employees, internal control systems are also needed to monitor and coordinate their activities.

If the sole trader takes a partner, moving to Stage 2, the need for formal internal controls becomes more important. Partners have a responsibility to each other (and in some jurisdictions all are equally liable for partnership debts), and so there is a need for good records. Also, with several people involved in management, coordination is important, and good record-keeping and internal control can facilitate this.

The move from Stage 2 to the corporate form in Stage 3 is significant: the company is a legal entity distinct from its owners. It is important that business transactions are kept separate from those of the managers and owners, and properly accounted for; there is an obligation for better record-keeping and systems. In some jurisdictions there may be a requirement for the company's records to be independently audited; in others, this obligation applies only to companies above a certain size.[2]

In terms of agency theory there is a significant leap from Stage 3 to Stage 4. For the first time, there are owners of the company who are not involved in its day-to-day management. These equity providers may be family members, or outsiders such as business angels. In order

---

2   Some smaller organizations might still choose to have an audit, or to introduce an internal audit function, as an
    assurance for management and the owners that things are being done properly.

Table 6.1 Indicative changing role of corporate governance over the ownership life cycle

	Sole trader	Partnership	Limited company, owned by management	Limited company, owned by management and close associates (e.g. family and friends)	Limited company, with private equity investment	Limited company, owned by the public (inc. institutions)
Agency problems	**(1)** None	**(2)**	**(3)** None, until the business becomes so big that the management function is delegated.	**(4)** Some, but close contact between management and shareholder(s) can reduce this.	**(5)** Some, but private equity investors maintain close contact with the business, and share with management the desire for a profitable exit.	**(6)** Growing agency problems, as management is separate from the dispersed ownership.
Internal control and internal reporting	Make sure everything gets invoiced and nothing gets lost. As the business grows, need to ensure employees are acting properly. Regular reporting of profits, cash, and balance sheet position.		Division of duties and clarity of delegated activities. Formalized internal control and risk management systems. As the business grows, the internal control system becomes more critical. Outside shareholders may also demand that the organization has an internal audit function. Regular reporting of profits, cash, and balance sheet position, including more sophisticated systems to be able to answer investors' and analysts' legitimate queries.			
External reporting (excluding tax requirements)	Not required	Not required	May be a legal need to file financial statements.	Need to report the company's performance and financial position to investors. Might also be a regulatory need for external reporting	Need to report the company's performance and financial position to investors. Might also be a regulatory need for external reporting	Probably a requirement for extensive reporting on a regular basis. To include financial and non-financial information.
External audit	No need	Optional	Compulsory in many regimes, depending on size of company.	Compulsory in many regimes, depending on size of company. May be demanded by the shareholders.	Compulsory in many regimes, depending on size of company. Will be demanded by the investors.	Compulsory

Management and direction of the business	Self	Partners	Directors	Management, and investors if they choose.	Management, with a strong steer from the private equity investors, who will have board seats and a veto on certain decisions	Bring in outsiders for advice and resources, and also for independent action. Board committees needed in line with regulation.
Management compensation	To suit self and business needs.	To suit partners and business needs.	To suit owners and business needs.	Agree with external investors to suit the business strategy and goals.	Agree with private equity investors. Will include a large capital-related element, to encourage growth and exit.	Agree with external investors and governance regulation. Format of compensation will vary as to salary, bonus, and long-term incentive dependent on the corporate objectives and life cycle stage.

to reduce their risk – actual and perceived – it is important that they receive regular communication about the business, in the form of financial statements. A narrative analysis of the business position and prospects is likely to be appreciated, and will reduce risk perception still further. The shareholders will also probably request an independent audit, and might require a representative position on the board, or the appointment of a non-executive director.

The move from Stage 3 to Stage 4 often coincides with the growth phase of the business's life cycle. Elsewhere in this book we discuss the business risks involved in rapid growth; here we merely point out the need for good management information and control systems to manage an expanding business, with a larger workforce, and perhaps addressing different geographical areas and markets. Case Study 6.1 shows how a failure in internal controls affected Groupon, a listed company that should have had better systems.

Stage 5 companies also have outside investors, professional private equity firms. The internal control requirements are the same, but are likely to be enforced more rigorously.

As part of their internal controls, companies should have in place good mechanisms for risk management to guard against errors like those seen in Groupon. Registers to list and classify business risks have their place, but are often just prepared and then filed rather than actively used. For example, Indian computer services company Satyam was the subject of a major corporate fraud, discovered in 2009, which resulted from inadequate internal controls. However, the company's audit committee charter, published in its SEC filings, specifically noted that part of the committee's role was a review of the adequacy of internal controls and internal audit. The risk was appreciated, but inadequately addressed.

As companies grow and have more resources put into them by a wider body of investors, the role of accounting communication expands. Companies listed on stock markets are generally required to follow very detailed rules and codes, and make extensive disclosures.

Case Study 6.1

Groupon – offering up excuses

Groupon, an internet voucher company, was forced to restate its quarterly figures in April 2012 because of material weaknesses in its financial and control systems. The company had to refile figures with the SEC, increasing the quarter's losses from just under $43m to over $65m.

The company was forced to admit that it 'did not maintain financial close process and procedures that were adequately designed, documented and executed to support the accurate and timely reporting of our financial results'.

The company's UK joint managing director was reported in the press as saying that the 'young company in a completely new industry' had sometimes 'not been able to put all the checks and balances in place'. The errors had arisen due to the company's failing to understand how many rebates it would be required to give on a new line of business, which implies that this internal control weakness affected management processes and decisions, as well as their external financial reporting.

Groupon's management systems had also failed in other respects, for example, it was found to have made substantial breaches of UK consumer protection laws in the way it conducted its advertising.

Groupon, had floated on NASDAQ in autumn 2011, about three years after it started business. The stock market's rules require that its systems should have been robust by the time it floated. The share price dropped 7% on release of the restatement to the market.

The CEO of Groupon was fired by the board in February 2013.

Source: www.guardian.co.uk and www.sec.gov

Markets also demand that their accounting and control systems can stand up to scrutiny, and this will be verified through the report of an independent auditor.[3] Again, this is done to reduce the perceived and actual risk of investors, and also to raise the profile of the particular stock exchange, positioning it as attractive to investors. Of course, this protection of investors can come at a cost to the companies, and there are some frustrating aspects of governance regulation; there is a trade-off between corporate performance and conformance to the rules.

In this context it is interesting to note the implications of a significant body of research on voluntary disclosures and on governance requirements. Many academics and interested parties have tried to capture the financial impact of 'good' governance. To summarize an extensive body of work in a couple of sentences, the overall conclusion is that well-governed companies attract a pricing premium in poorly governed regimes, as they stand out as lower risk for investors.[4] However, the impact of good governance, although still there, is less obvious in regimes which have an institutional context that supports good governance.

Management and direction of the business

The good thing about being a sole trader is that you can make all your own decisions, with no reference to anyone else. The bad thing is that this also applies to making your own mistakes. The wise sole trader takes counsel when needed, but has the ultimate right to choose what s/he wants.

In a partnership, the management structure differs. For a partnership of just a few people, it might be that all partners have equal rights, and decisions are taken jointly. But once the number of partners grows, some sort of executive structure is essential for the day-to-day running of the business. However, the choice of structure is entirely up to the partners themselves.

Once a business incorporates, directors are appointed to run it. (Here, we follow UK terminology, referring to all the main board members as 'directors' and differentiating 'non-executives' (NEDs) from those with executive responsibility.) Corporate governance regulations will set out who can appoint these directors, who can remove them, and what powers they have. Control over board membership is a useful protection for the investors.

Non-executive directors can have some ties with the company, such as being past employees, family members, or representatives of significant investors. Alternatively, the NEDs can be independent, and such independence is seen as the pinnacle of corporate governance. For example, the UK Corporate Governance Code ('UK Code'), which governs the behaviour of companies listed on the London Stock Exchange, states that large listed companies should have on their boards at least three *independent* NEDs, who will sit on the various board committees relating to audit and remuneration.

Definitions of independence vary between jurisdictions. Working Insight 6.1 sets out some criteria that may be considered. The reasoning behind this is to avoid the possibility of a conflict of interest between these independent directors and the shareholders, and to reduce the likelihood of 'capture' of the NEDs by the executives.

As students of governance, we appreciate the need for independent non-executives on the board, and value the role they play. However, having been involved in the running of businesses, it does rather amuse us that a strict adherence to the need for independence could lead to a board comprising individuals who had had no contact with the business and did not actually understand it! For example, the UK Code suggests that any NED who has served for

---

3 In the USA the provisions of s. 404 of the Sarbanes–Oxley Act of 2002 have led to many millions of dollars being spent on demonstrating that internal controls are adequate.

4 For a detailed discussion of the impact of governance regimes, we recommend Goergen, *International Corporate Governance*.

Working Insight 6.1

Examples of criteria indicating that directors are not independent

The following criteria are used, in various jurisdictions, as indicators that a director is *not* independent:

- Has been an employee or executive of the company or a related company in the past X years.
- Is a close family member of a director of the company or a related company.
- Has had a significant business relationship with the company in the past Y years.
- Is a professional adviser to the company, or has some other business relationship.
- Represents a block shareholder or a major lender to the company, or has significant business transactions with same.
- Holds cross-directorships with other members of the company's board.
- Participates in the company's pension scheme or share option scheme.
- Has served on the board continuously for more than Z years

---

more than nine years can no longer be considered independent, as they may be too closely aligned to the management. The other way of looking at this is that, given the limited time that NEDs spend with their companies, it is only after several years that they might be embedded enough to make useful suggestions on strategy. The role of the NED is a sometimes uneasy balance between ensuring *conformance* with governance regulation and assisting corporate *performance*.

In this respect we note the work of Filatotchev and Wright, who differentiate between the role of governance in different stages of the business life cycle.[5] They see a *value creation* role in early-stage businesses, leading to a *value protection role* in the larger companies where an agency conflict is more likely. It is that value protection role that leads to demands for a stricter set of criteria for independence.

Executive directors' pay and shareholder value

Executive pay is a contentious area in governance, and much has been written on the subject. In this section we consider how the structure of executive director pay can impact on the financial and business strategies adopted in a company, and how this relates to shareholder value.

We must start, yet again, with agency theory. Not because agency theory is necessarily the best way to approach governance, but because it is the most common way, and is the theory underlying much of current regulation. If there is indeed a conflict of interest between the directors and shareholders, then one way to resolve it is through setting remuneration contracts that encourage the directors to act for the benefit of the company, ultimately reflecting benefit to its shareholders. Hence the demand for 'pay for performance'. There are only two problems with this – how to define 'pay' and how to define 'performance'.

Performance measures

We shall start with performance. If our objective is long-term shareholder value, then directors' performance should be benchmarked over the long term – a whole business cycle – preferably

---

5 Filatotchev, I. and Wright, M. (2005), 'The Corporate Governance Life Cycle', in *The Life Cycle of Corporate Governance* ed. Filatotchev, I., and Wright, M. (Cheltenham: Edward Elgar).

Working Insight 6.2

Advantages and disadvantages of using eps as a performance measure for executive pay

Advantages

> Eps is based on audited numbers, has a consistent definition, and is understood by all stakeholders. Furthermore, eps is a measure of profit, and profit is essential for the long-term survival of a business.

Disadvantages

> As an accounting measure, it is considerably affected by the choice of accounting policies.
> It takes no account of risk.
> It takes no account of the cost of capital employed to generate the eps.
> It is easy to manipulate in the short term.[6]
> It can be increased by undertaking a share buy-back, regardless of whether this is good financial practice.

> Some of these disadvantages are peculiar to eps; most relate to all accounting-based measures of performance.

---

by examination of a model such as Rappaport's SVA discussed in Chapter 1. We would see if the appropriate drivers were in place and how they had been used, and draw conclusions as to how effective that had been in creating value.

Unfortunately, individuals' timescales are not at the moment sufficiently long to take this approach, and anyway, good as SVA is, it is tricky to use it as a performance measure because it reflects expected forecasts, not achieved results. Accordingly, the last few decades have seen directors rewarded with annual bonuses, and with 'long-term' awards that mostly last for three years. The performance measures used have varied, but in the majority of cases have included eps growth and total shareholder return (TSR).

In Chapter 1 we stated that we don't think eps growth is a particularly good performance measure. Working Insight 6.2 lists the reasons.

The other reason that attaining eps growth need not be an indicator of value is that the targets set for such growth are often inadequate. Although this is gradually changing, for years the most widely used target was that bonus should start to be earned if eps growth over a three-year period exceeded inflation plus 3 per cent. Figure 6.1 illustrates why there should not be a universal target.

A universal eps target cannot be right for every company, and may not be right for any. If eps is to be used as a performance target, then a more appropriate calculation would be to start with the share price and use it to determine the growth that shareholders expect from the business, basing targets around that.

---

6 Research shows that the level of 'abnormal accruals' – accounting adjustments – increases significantly at the inflection points of companies' bonus plans – when profits are just at the level where a bonus can be earned, or just at the point where the maximum bonus is being earned and so there is no advantage in reporting higher results. For example, Bergstresser, D. and Philippon, T. (2006), 'CEO Incentives and Earnings Management', *Journal of Financial Economics*, 80(3): 511–29.

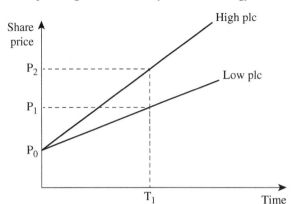

Figure 6.1 Eps growth as a target in different growth scenarios.

Referring back to High plc and Low plc, who we encountered in Chapter 2, the market expects High plc to grow its share price rapidly; lower expectations are held for Low plc. Both companies start the period with the price at P_0, and are expected to rise to P_2 and P_1 respectively. That being so, it is reasonable to assume that their profit growth is expected to be different, with High being more profitable, more quickly. If both companies reward directors for growing eps at inflation plus 3%, then either Low plc is setting outrageously aggressive targets (which may not motivate), or High plc is setting targets that are so low that achieving them will not generate any value at all for shareholders.

The other commonly used performance measure for executive pay is total shareholder return (TSR), which is widely adopted in long-term incentive plans. TSR, as discussed in Chapter 1, represents the return to the shareholders over the period, generally calculated based on the increase in share price and the dividends paid over the period, assuming those dividends are then reinvested in the company's shares. TSR is measured as a percentage return.

A percentage return to shareholders, on its own, is not a good measure of directors' performance, because company share prices reflect market movements. An investment returning 10 per cent might be seen as excellent during an economic downturn, but inadequate in a boom. Accordingly, relative TSR is used: the company's TSR is benchmarked against the equivalently calculated TSRs for a group of peer companies, and the incentive is only earned once the company exceeds their median.

Shareholders like TSR as a performance measure, arguing that it reflects what they get. However, as corporate financiers we argue that the share price does not represent what the company achieved, but what the markets expect it yet to achieve. As we said in earlier chapters, a high share price is a rod for the directors' backs, as they have to work hard to achieve the underlying earnings. And as we also said, market imperfections mean that share prices rarely reflect the value of the company. Furthermore, they are easily manipulated by the judicious timing of disclosures of good or bad news to the markets. So, even without going into the arguments about the difficulties of establishing a consistent peer group, of determining the measurement dates, or of motivating individuals with over-complex schemes, TSR has significant flaws.[7]

There is an academic paper with a wonderful title – 'On the Folly of Rewarding A, While Hoping for B'[8] – which demonstrates that you get what you pay for, and that setting poor measures and targets will not result in good outcomes. The two main measures used for

---

7   Much as I would like to go into those arguments, this is a corporate finance book and they add little to that central theme.
8   Kerr, S. (1995), 'On the Folly of Rewarding A, While Hoping for B', *Academy of Management Executive*, 9(1): 7–14.

executive pay, eps growth, and TSR, might have advantages, but neither is designed to align with the generation of shareholder value.

Methods of payment

Although executive pay can take many forms, in terms of the impact on financial strategy in the context of this book we only wish to consider share options. Executive share options are call options, generally granted at-the-money, and normally with a vesting period of between three and ten years. There might or might not be performance conditions attached to the vesting; in the USA this is not common, but it is compulsory in the UK, where the performance condition one sees most frequently is eps growth.[9]

Share options are discussed in Chapters 11 and 12, and in Appendix 2. There, we discuss the factors affecting the value of an option, one of which is volatility. The directors stand to make a gain if the share price rises, because they can then exercise the option and sell the newly acquired shares. Conversely, they do not need to exercise their options if the share price has fallen. They thus have all the benefit of upside volatility and none of the downside. It may be a coincidence, but academic research shows that companies in which the executives hold a lot of share options tend to conduct themselves such that the volatility of their results increases, for example by undertaking more acquisition activity.[10]

Executive share options can also influence companies' decisions on whether or not to pay a dividend or to do a share repurchase, or to issue shares or debt. These matters are discussed at relevant points in the book.

The position of minority shareholders

In this section we examine governance in a different way, considering the nature of ownership. In particular, we look at the rights of minority owners, how these play out in different jurisdictions, and what this means in terms of investors' and lenders' perceived risk and thus the company's finance-raising ability.

In a widely owned company with no controlling shareholder and no block-holder, there is clearly the potential for an agency problem between investors and management. Management have the ability to give themselves an easy life, should they so wish. Shareholders would need to band together to prevent them from, for example, increasing executive pay or perks, undertaking pet projects, or reducing their risk by rejecting potentially profitable projects or having too little debt in the capital structure.

This differs from a company where there is a block-holder with both an interest in the business and the power to do something about it, a situation that is very common in many parts of the world.[11] There is less of an agency problem between the management and shareholders, as

---

9 Which measure, of course, does not necessarily relate to increased shareholder wealth, although if the option exercise price were indexed to reflect shareholders' required return, it would help.

10 For example, Becher, D. A., Juergens, J. L., and Vogel, J. (2012), 'Do Acquirer CEO Incentives Impact Mergers?', available at http://ssrn.com/abstract=2117397, which suggests that CEOs with share options behave differently to those without, and that: 'CEOs with high option holdings may be motivated more by agency conflicts than acting in shareholder interests.'

11 Although listed companies in the UK and USA are widely held, this is not the norm in many other jurisdictions, partly for historical reasons and in part because of the lack of minority protections discussed in this chapter. Goergen (2012) sets out a table in chapter 4 which shows for about fifty countries the legal protection for investors and creditors and the levels of ownership of the three largest shareholders. In over half the countries, the block-holders control more than 40 per cent of the shares.

Working Insight 6.3

Some control enhancement mechanisms

CEMs which work by giving block-holders enhanced voting rights[12]

> Shares with multiple voting rights
> Non-voting shares
> Pyramid structures

CEMS which lock in control

> Priority shares with veto rights over certain decisions
> Voting rights ceilings (which limit voting power regardless of how many shares are owned)
> Ownership ceilings (which prevent transfer of shares to owners if they would take the holding above a certain percentage)
> Golden shares (often used by governments in sensitive privatized companies)

Source: Report on the Proportionality Principle in the European Union Available via http://ec.europa.eu/internal_market/company/shareholders/indexb_en.htm

---

the shareholders – or at least some of them – are in a better position to control the managers' actions. This can be very beneficial to the minority (non-block-holder) shareholders, as there is a powerful party with the desire to create value for the company. However, it is also possible for the block-holders to act in their own interests to the detriment of other shareholders.

We are deliberately vague in our definition of block-holder. Many academic papers take a shareholding of around 5 per cent as being 'controlling'. That is fine for research purposes, but in terms of practical corporate finance it is a bit limiting. Our concept of a block-holder ranges along a continuum between the shareholder (or shareholders working in concert) who has sufficient votes to make management pay attention, through to a level of voting power such that they can pass resolutions with minimal consideration for the desires of other shareholders. Examples of such block shareholders could include a founding family, a holding company, or the state.

The block-holder's controlling power can come about in through, for example, having classes of shares with different rights, or through setting up corporate ownership structures such as pyramids that give control over several entities. In 2007 an EU investigation into 'control enhancement measures' (CEMs) listed out some of those found, as set out in Working Insight 6.3.

Case Study 6.2 sets out some examples of companies where the block-holders maintain their power through enhanced voting powers using different classes of share.

As we explain in Chapter 11, ownership of a share gives rights over capital appreciation and dividends, and – sometimes – gives voting rights which can guide the direction of the business.

---

12   At the time of writing, the EU is considering giving additional voting rights and dividends to investors holding shares for a period of years, with the aim of encouraging long-term investment.

Case Study 6.2

Maintaining block-holder power through different classes of share

Henkel, the German multinational, has two classes of share – ordinary and preferred.[13] The main difference between the shares is that ordinary shares carry the entitlement to vote, but preferred shares do not. There are more ordinary shares than preferred, but a majority of the ordinary shares are in the hands of the Henkel family, which has committed to retaining ownership until 2016, thus protecting the company from a takeover and encouraging a longer-term view.

Although there is Henkel family representation on the supervisory board, no family members take part in the running of the company. This differs from the American family-controlled company, **Ford**. Members of the Ford family own shares which carry multiple voting rights, giving their 2% of shares 40% of the overall vote. The Ford family has at various times taken the decision to make a family member the company's CEO.

This differs again from the extreme examples of block-holder activity that can be seen in **Google**, and some other internet companies. These companies are recently formed, unlike Ford where the multiple classes of share date back a long time.

When it floated in 2004, **Google** created a dual-class share structure whereby the founding management team could retain control by owning Class B shares with 10 votes each, compared to other shareholders' single-vote Class A shares. This gave the management voting control, with 61.4% of the voting power. However, in 2012 they decided that this was inadequate to protect their voting control against future issues of shares (which would increase the number of A shares, thus gradually diluting them). Accordingly, Google created a new class of non-voting shares, which could be used for future capital increases. They explained the supposed benefit to investors as follows: 'we have set up a corporate structure that will make it harder for outside parties to take over or influence Google. This structure will also make it easier for our management team to follow the long term, innovative approach.'

It is difficult to argue with the success that Google has had while under the control of its founders. However, times change, people change, and there may come a time when these individuals are no longer the most appropriate people to run Google.[14] At this point, there will be little that other shareholders can do about that.

Sources: www.henkel.com, http://corporate.ford.com, http://investor.google.com

Even without the use of separate share classes, a block-holder can control the votes without actually having economic ownership. This can happen where the shareholding is structured through a series of partly owned holding companies. Figure 6.2 gives two illustrations of this.

A problem with these types of structure is that the Target company's operations and financial policies can be structured for the benefit of the controlling shareholder, even though that shareholder should only be entitled to a minority of the company's cash flows: their voting interest is greater than their shareholding would suggest. Although in many instances such a structure is all above board, and can indeed be beneficial, examples can be found where it has been used to expropriate assets from the Target business. This is known as the 'tunnelling' of funds. Case Study 6.3 gives an example of such a corporate structure.

13 The preferred shares carry an additional dividend.
14 Those who dispute that might consider the example of Jerry Yang, the founder of Yahoo!, who built and grew the company but made some bad decisions later in its life. When Yang eventually left Yahoo!, the share price rose on the news.

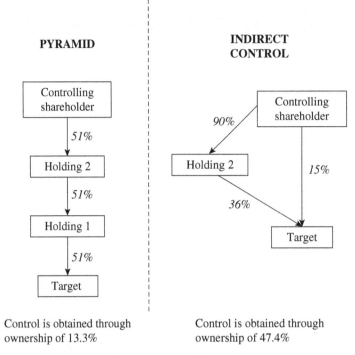

Figure 6.2 Illustrating structures of control.

In the Pyramid example, technically, the controlling shareholder only owns 13.3% of the target company. However, they control Holding 2, which controls Holding 1, which itself controls Target. Therefore, the controlling shareholder has effective control over Target.

In the example of Indirect control, the controlling shareholder owns only 47.4% of the Target, but has voting control through its subsidiary's holding together with its own.

Although these examples show substantial holdings, in practice a much lower shareholding may be sufficient to give effective control, depending on the distribution and interest of the other shareholders.

Case Study 6.3

Hollinger – a study in complexity

In 2004 a special committee of the board of Hollinger International published a report giving the background to legal actions for fraud against Conrad Black, its former CEO, and David Radler, the former COO. A diagram of the corporate structure showed that Black and Radler owned 79.2% of a company that itself owned 78.2% of a company that in turn owned 30.3% of Hollinger. The net economic entitlement of Black and Radler to 18.8% of Hollinger's profits was outweighed by their ability to set up management charges up to the top company, diverting its profits.

Source: Report accessed from www.sec.gov/Archives/edgar/
data/868512/000095012304010413/y01437exv99w2.htm

Case Study 6.4

Newscorp – shareholders take action against a controlling owner's use of corporate funds

In summer 2011 a group of minority shareholders in News Corporation commenced legal action against Rupert Murdoch, its founder, Chairman, CEO and controlling shareholder, and various of his associates. Among the many charges made, one related to the group's $615m acquisition of Shine Group, a company owned by Murdoch's daughter. The shareholder action stated that this acquisition was at 'an artificially inflated price', had no 'valid strategic purpose' and was an improper use of company money for personal motives.

Source: The shareholder action in the Court of Chancery in the State of Delaware can be downloaded via http://newsandinsight.thomsonreuters.com/uploadedFiles/ Reuters_Content/2011/07_-_July/News%20Corp%20Page%20Complaint.pdf

Tunnelling can take various forms. At an extreme, the controlling shareholder can just order the transfer of assets at an undervalue from the controlled company to the holding companies, or to another business that it owns. This could be in the form of outright asset sales, or in excessive management charges or dubious transfer prices. Even if none of these takes place, the very existence of the controlling shareholder will make the company more vulnerable to such activities and can therefore increase the other shareholders' perceived risk and thus their cost of capital. It may also leave them without protection in the event that the controlling shareholder chooses to make a bid for the whole of the share capital: they may see no realistic alternative to selling out. Case Study 6.4 gives information on a court case where a major company was accused of using company funds to suit private needs.

To summarize this section, block-holders can be a powerful force in a company. They can operate for the benefit of the business and its external investors, or to their detriment. The way in which they act is not necessarily a function of the regulatory regime, but of the individuals concerned. Nevertheless, the regime is important, and it is to this that we move in the next section.

Corporate governance impact on raising funds

The nature of the governance regime can have a significant effect on the financial strategies followed in different jurisdictions.

There is a direct relationship between the risk perceived by a funder and the return they require. The rules and regulations in force in different countries can themselves be favourable towards the rights of the funder, thus reducing their risk, or could be tilted towards protecting the interests of management, which can be seen to make the investment riskier. Likewise, regimes where all investors are treated equally are seen to be less risky for minority shareholders than are those where block-holders are favoured. More generally, the impact of a country's legal and governance regime can be seen clearly in the development of private equity, in particular venture capital. Countries with strong laws to protect intellectual capital and shareholder's rights tend to have developed their private equity markets far in advance of countries where rights are flawed.

Working Insight 6.4 sets out some indicators of shareholder rights, and devices which indicate that investments may be riskier.

Working Insight 6.4

Corporate governance mechanisms and the minority shareholder

Reducing risk for minority shareholders	*Increasing risk for minority shareholders*
• Ability to vote on all resolutions, including voting directors onto or off the board • Ease of voting • Legal mechanisms for minority shareholders to take action against oppression by the majority or against expropriations by management • Laws or codes protecting the minority during a takeover • Laws protecting against insider trading • Requirement for independent non-executive directors on the board • Requirement for high levels of relevant financial and non-financial disclosures, for example details of transactions with related parties	• Control enhancement mechanisms (CEMs) such as certain shares carrying multiple votes, or no votes, or ceilings on voting rights, or vetoes in certain situations

In addition, factors affecting the perception of risk include the overall corruption rating of the country, the standards of accounting and auditing, and the rigour, or otherwise, with which laws are enforced. For listed companies, the regulations of each particular stock exchange regarding such matters as insider trading will also be relevant, as strong regulation means that investors should be less vulnerable to losses due to information asymmetry. In addition, an active market for corporate control will reassure investors.

In general these risk-reduction governance mechanisms have led to a positive relationship between the strength of protection of minority shareholders and the number of market partici- pants in a country. In countries where there are fewer investor protections, corporate owner- ship is often concentrated into the hands of block-holders. This has implications for companies in such regimes which wish to raise equity and extend their share ownership. Often they overcome some of the disadvantages by choosing to list their shares on a stock exchange in a country where governance is stronger. This can give access to equity at a lower cost.

Lenders too have to consider their risk–return relationship. Working Insight 6.5 sets out some characteristics that may be perceived as more or less favourable to creditors.

In the same manner as for shareholders, a background level of good corporate governance in a regime, with low corruption, good accounting and corporate reporting, and strong enforcement of the law will lead to a perception of lower risk and more enthusiasm to lend money.[15]

---

15   *The OECD Principles of Corporate Governance* (2004), which have been agreed by all thirty OECD member countries, set out some common elements underlying good governance in different regimes. They can be down- loaded from www.ecgi.org or www.oecd.org

Working Insight 6.5

Corporate governance mechanisms and the lender

Reducing risk for lenders	*Increasing risk for lenders*
• Ease of ability of a lender to enforce their security to repossess assets if loan terms are breached • Strong legal protection over property rights, including intellectual property rights (so that the company's assets cannot be expropriated)	• Bankruptcy laws that leave the existing executives in control of the company rather than letting creditors put in their own management • Bankruptcy laws that enable management to protect the company against creditor claims • Priority of social or government claims over the rights of secured lenders

The role of the investor in governance

Corporate governance is not just a matter for the company and its management; the investors also have their part to play. In Chapter 1 we referred to the difficulties faced by directors trying to reconcile the needs of the business with the interests of a variety of shareholders with different interests, some of which would actually benefit if the company were to fail rather than grow. Rather than repeat that discussion, here we refer in particular to institutional ownership of large listed companies.

A fundamental problem for investors in public companies, which have an extensive share register, is the *free rider* problem. Any investor choosing to spend time dealing with a company's issues in performance and governance should – if they are doing it correctly – be enhancing the value of their investment. However, their stake in the company might only be about 3 per cent of the shares – which means that the holders of the other 97 per cent of the shares have seen the value of their own investments rise, without having taken any action themselves. They are free riders.

Nonetheless, in recent years a growing number of investing institutions have become more active (or 'activist'), devoting time and resources to improving corporate governance and social responsibility in the companies in which they invest. The current view of regulators and media is that this is beneficial, and that investors should take a more active stewardship role in their investee companies.

Corporate governance and stakeholders

Corporate governance is one aspect of a wider movement of corporate responsibility (CR). In order to set the tone for this section, we borrow a definition from Tomorrow's Company to explain what we mean. They bring together shareholder value and sustainability to define the purpose of 'tomorrow's global company':

Table 6.2 How corporate responsibility can help to create shareholder value

Driver of value	*Some examples of driving performance through sustainability*
Grow sales faster	Innovative products to meet sustainability needs. Attract customers by corporate responsibility stance.
Increase operating profit margin	Better workforce efficiency by treating people better: attract better people, more training, less absenteeism, lower staff turnover. Efficiencies due to energy and waste management.
Reduce cash tax rate	Possibly take advantage of incentives.
Fewer fixed assets	Improved efficiencies.
Less working capital	Reduced waste leading to reduced inventory. Better supply chain practices as companies work in coordination.
Increase the period for which the organization has a competitive advantage	Increased brand equity in the sustainable company. Compliance leads to legitimacy which extends the 'licence to operate'.
Lower cost of capital	Investors perceive lower risk in companies that are compliant with 'best practice' governance regulations.

To provide ever better goods and services in a way that is profitable, ethical and respects the environment, individuals and the communities within which it operates.[16]

This corporate purpose reflects the ideas of 'enlightened shareholder value' mentioned earlier, as well as the 'triple bottom line' criteria of financial, environmental, and social performance. Thus, corporate decisions have to consider a wider constituency than long-term profitability. So, for example, decisions on sourcing should take account of labour conditions in the supplier countries. Perhaps of most relevance to financial strategy is the need to think about the ethical implications of a highly geared capital structure: while this reduces the weighted average cost of capital for the diversified investors, it does mean that the company is taking on higher levels of risk, which may be unacceptable to the non-diversified employees.

Looking more broadly at corporate responsibility, there is of course no reason why these principles should be in direct conflict with the creation of shareholder value. Table 6.2 sets out some ways in which following a CR agenda can lead directly to the creation of value for shareholders as well as benefiting other stakeholders.

Key messages

- Corporate governance relates to accounting and management systems, as well as to the composition of the board. It can be a means of reducing business risk.
- The ownership life cycle takes a business from sole trader through to various forms of corporate ownership and direction. As an organization moves through this cycle, different aspects of governance become more important.
- An investor's or lender's perception of the governance regime under which a company operates will significantly affect their perception of risk, and thus their required cost of capital.

16 www.tomorrowscompany.com

- Companies need to pay attention to stakeholder requirements as well as those of their shareholders.
- Institutional investors may choose to play an active part in the governance of listed companies.
- Executive remuneration strategies should relate to the company's corporate and financial strategy. Performance measures such as eps or TSR have limitations and where used, the targets should be based on expected performance and not universal norms. The use of share options can encourage strategies that drive volatility.
- Block-holders can operate for the benefit of the company as a whole, but it is possible that they will attempt to gain unfair advantage over other shareholders.

Suggested further reading

Goergen, M. (2012), *International Corporate Governance*, Harlow: Pearson.
   An interesting and very relevant book. Professor Goergen has a background in teaching finance, and the book reflects this, with chapters on governance as it relates to acquisitions, IPOs, private equity, and other relevant topics.
Corporate Governance for Main Market and AIM Companies (2012), London Stock Exchange.
   Published by the London Stock Exchange, and written by leading practitioners, this guide covers regulation and practice. It also contrasts the UK environment with USA and Hong Kong exchanges. Downloadable free from www.londonstockexchange.com
Weight, C. (2012), *Directors' Remuneration Handbook*, London: Bloomsbury Professional.
   The book, written by a remuneration consultant, describes the UK legal aspects of directors' remuneration and the main players, and provides an extensive guide to how remuneration plans should be structured and implemented.
Readers wishing to know more about corporate governance in specific parts of the world should consider a series of books written by Chris Pierce, CEO of Global Governance Services Ltd.
My own websites contain my writings on corporate governance and corporate finance. www.cranfield.ac.uk and uk.linkedin.com/in/ruthbender1
A useful examination of the corporate responsibility debate, with many downloadable publications and videos, can be found in Cranfield's Doughty Centre for Corporate Responsibility, www.doughtycentre.info

Part 2

Financial strategy and the corporate life cycle

7 Start-up businesses and venture capital

Learning objectives

After reading this chapter you should be able to:

1   Explain how the life cycle model is applied to the start-up stage of a business.
2   Contrast the different ways that companies use to account for high business risk.
3   Prepare or appraise a venture capital term sheet, and explain the potential impact of some common investor protection clauses.
4   Distinguish the various different forms of early-stage financing and comment on their strengths and weaknesses.

Summary: applying the overall model to start-up companies

The start-up stage of the business life cycle clearly represents the highest level of business risk. There are compounding risks associated with whether the new product will work effectively; if it works, whether the product will be accepted by its prospective customers; if it is accepted, whether the market will grow to a sufficient size given the development and launch

---

Working Insight 7.1

Financial strategy parameters: start-up businesses

Business risk	Very high
Financial risk	Very low
Source of outside funding	Venture capital
Dividend policy	Nil pay-out ratio
Future growth prospects	Very high
Price/earnings multiple	Very high
Current profitability, i.e. eps	Nominal or negative
Share price	Rapidly growing but highly volatile

---

costs involved; and, even if all this succeeds, whether the company will gain an adequate market share to justify its involvement in the industry.

This high level of business risk means that the associated financial risk should be kept as low as possible during the launch period. Thus equity funding is most appropriate. In most businesses this will come from the entrepreneurs themselves, or friends and family, but where larger sums are needed, outside investment will be sought. However, the high overall risk of the company will attract only certain investors, such as venture capital companies, and they will require a correspondingly high return. This high return will come in the form of capital gains to the investors because the negative cash flow of the business makes it impractical to pay dividends during this start-up stage. These issues are illustrated in Working Insight 7.1.

This dominance of capital gains creates a key concern on the part of the venture capital investors in such high-risk businesses. How do they realize the capital gain that is created if the company is successful? They do not wish to be locked in until the business becomes cash positive and can start to pay dividends. Hence buyers need to be found for this equity at its increased value, once the company has proved that the product works and that its market potential makes the investment financially attractive.

It is in the interest of all parties that this exit should take place, because venture capitalists require very high rates of return on their investment portfolio. As the total risk of the company reduces over its transition from launch to growth, the returns on new capital will inevitably decline. Accordingly the original venture capitalists might not be interested in several further funding rounds, for which they would have to pay higher and higher prices. Ideally, they want the chance to exit early, to realize their gains and to reinvest the proceeds in further high-risk investments. This initial funding can be replaced by equity investors who require a lower rate of return, even though they are still primarily interested in investing for capital growth.

Two possible exit routes for venture capitalists are a trade sale, or the public flotation of the company on a stock exchange. These have very different implications for the parties, with managers possibly preferring the float, and investors the trade sale. In a flotation, the management keep their jobs; a trade acquirer may wish to replace them. However, a trade sale tends to be better for the venture capital investor because they can exit completely, with no lock-up clause and often at a higher price. It is important that entrepreneurs and venture capitalists understand each other's needs at the start of the investment process: the nightmare for a venture capitalist is to have funds tied up in a successful company for which the owner/ directors have no desire to create an exit: until that exit is achieved, the return is not realized.[1]

In many cases, a start-up business will either be very successful or will fail completely; there may be no middle ground. (As a rule of thumb, half of start-up businesses fail within five years.)[2] For management, their fate is tied to the company's outcome. However, venture capitalists can diversify their investment risk by investing in a portfolio of start-up businesses, rather than in one company only. They demand very high returns on their investments, in the knowledge that some of the investee companies will fail, but hoping that some will be stars, and that their portfolio returns overall will realistically reflect the level of risk taken.

Having set out an overview of financial strategy in the start-up phase, the rest of this chapter explores the subject in more detail.

Very high level of business risk

Figure 7.1 illustrates a possible sequence of activities undertaken in a start-up business which has little more than a concept. It illustrates why investment in start-ups is risky: there are many stages where the whole project might fail.

The first stage for many start-ups is an investment in research and development in order to try to identify new product concepts which may be worthy of closer investigation. This is the pre-launch stage of the business, and funding at this stage is often referred to as *seed capital*. This stage will extend to the production of prototypes, to prove the viability of the concept. Alternatively, the product concept might already be proven, but this first business stage will require expenditure on market research to determine whether there is truly a valuable commercial opportunity.

If the product opportunity still appears financially attractive after these investments have been made, there is normally considerable additional expenditure required for operating facilities, support facilities, and initial sales and marketing activities before the product can actually be launched. For most products, these early stages of launch and sales development are periods of net cash outflow. The inflows from sales revenues are not only small but delayed, while the cash outflows still include high levels of one-off launch-associated costs as well as the normal ongoing operating expenses.

Capital invested at this stage, slightly less of a gamble than seed capital but still enormously risky, is known as *start-up capital*. Some venture capital companies (and some of their individual counterparts, known as *business angels*) have a preference for investing only at the seed stage, others only invest in start-ups.[3]

---

1 Academic research suggests that venture capital firms 'bribe' entrepreneurs into trade sales: Broughman, B. J. and Fried, J. M. (2013), *Carrots & Sticks: How VCs Induce Entrepreneurial Teams to Sell Startups*, http://ssrn. com/abstract=2221033. Another way in which VC investors might choose to ensure an exit is to write a clause into the shareholders' agreement which states that if the company has not floated or been sold within a specific period, the venture capitalists are entitled to an increasing percentage of profits each year as a special dividend. This focuses the management's attention on the need to achieve an exit, and at least gives the venture capitalist a running yield while they await exit.
2 An interesting piece of research shows that companies starting up in tough economic times have a higher survival rate than those begun in more benign climates, possibly because they have to work harder at the start. Burke, A. and Hussels, S. (2013), 'How Competition Strengthens Start-ups', *Harvard Business Review*, 91(3): 24.
3 Still others, who sometimes call themselves venture capitalists, only invest in large, safe deals such as management buyouts or development capital for established companies. These investors provide private equity, but the term 'venture capital' should really be restricted to use in high-risk situations. The mechanics of buyout deals, which use very high levels of debt in a relatively low business risk environment, are discussed in Chapter 18.

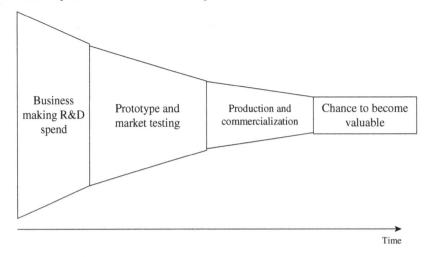

Figure 7.1 Stages in a start-up.

The length of each stage depend on the industry and business model.

The number of successful entities decreases at each stage.

Seed and start-up funds are invested in the hope of the successful development of the product and the resulting high ultimate net cash inflows when the sales volumes finally mature. Clearly there are very significant business risks associated with this start-up strategy. Each subsequent stage is dependent on the successful completion of the earlier stages, as illustrated in Figure 7.1. The Figure ends after the very early stages of the project are completed; this, fairly obviously, does not imply that all projects that pass that stage become commercial successes, but one hopes that the resulting business can then be developed through the growth and maturity stages of the life cycle.

Correspondingly high level of return?

The compounding sequential risks lead to the conclusion that the start-up phase is a very high-risk stage of the life cycle; therefore logically a correspondingly high return should be required. This is intuitively self-evident. However, it is not at first sight in accordance with financial theory.

If the rationale of the Capital Asset Pricing Model (CAPM) were strictly applied, the increase in required return would only be related to the level of market (or systematic) risk incurred by the company; i.e. the degree to which the company's total return is affected by changes in the return of the market. The specific sales opportunity and, particularly, the required solution of a technical problem may be almost completely unrelated to any changes in the overall market, so that their appropriate beta factor would be zero. Only once the company has become established might the ultimate level of sales and the subsequent cash inflows be much more affected by changes in the market as a whole, so that the beta of these later cash flows would be higher. Under the CAPM, the beta drives the required premium return over the risk-free rate, so a CAPM analysis would seem to indicate that the required rate of return could start relatively low but would need to increase over the life of the product. This is counter-intuitive to the trend of business risk.

The argument of the pure theorist is that the very high business risk at the start of the product's life cycle is almost exclusively caused by the unique risk associated with the product. Therefore this can be diversified away by rational investors, who would always incorporate this high risk investment into an efficiently constructed portfolio. (This does not mean that the *company* can only undertake such start-up product investments as part of a widely diversified portfolio of products. As has already been discussed, since investors can themselves easily diversify away unique company risk they will not pay extra for companies to do this for them.)

The dramatic implication of the CAPM theory is that a start-up business does not need to offer significantly enhanced rates of return to investors to compensate for the high business risk because this is mainly unique, diversifiable risk. Yet in practice the returns demanded by investors in new business start-ups are significantly higher than for more mature companies. Does this represent an inefficiency in the market, a breakdown in the theory, or both?

The answer is no to all the above questions, because the apparently relatively low return expected by these rational diversified investors under the theory would be based on the probability-adjusted expected value of the cash flows of the company.

For a start-up business the range of its expected cash flows is going to be very wide, due to all of the volatilities discussed earlier. As explained, the high standard deviation (volatility) of these future cash flows can be regarded as being caused primarily by the unique or unsystematic risk of the company, and therefore it does not lead to an increased expected return. However, the true expected value of the resulting cash flows is going to be depressed due to the sequential probabilities which need to be applied to each subsequent stage of the project. As illustrated in Working Insight 7.2, the investments required in the very early years of the product's development are much more certain than the subsequent cash flows, which depend on the successful conclusion of all the earlier stages; thus the expected values of these later cash flows are significantly affected by the cumulative probability factors which need to be applied.

The application of the (subjective) probability factors results in the less certain cash inflows being reduced in both expected value terms and in present value, not by having an extremely high discount factor applied to them directly, but by being assessed as expected values before being discounted.

(A similar effect could be obtained by developing multiple cash-flow scenarios for a project, both good and bad, and then calculating an average cash flow to be discounted at a 'normal' cost of capital. This has some similarities to Monte Carlo analysis, discussed in Chapter 14.)

By using probability-weighted expected cash flows the unique risk of the investment has already been taken into account so that only the market-related risk remains. In Working Insight 7.3, net present values are compared for two sets of calculations: if the original cash flow estimates given in Working Insight 7.2 are discounted at 35 per cent p.a. (a high-risk discount rate) and if the probability-adjusted expected cash flows are discounted at 12 per cent (a more normal company cost of capital rate).

From Working insight 7.3 we can see that although the approaches are similar, they give different results.[4] The use of probability-adjusted expected cash flows is greatly to be preferred over the alternative use of a much higher discount rate. It is theoretically more sound, if only for the reason that the discount factor is applied to all cash flows, whereas normally it is only the cash *inflows* that are uncertain – costs can often be forecast with reasonable accuracy, but the emergent market is an unknown. Working Insight 7.3 shows the 35 per cent

4 For this particular stream of cash flows, applying a discount rate of 32.8 per cent to the unadjusted cash flows would give the same NPV as using 12 per cent on the probability-adjusted numbers. But of course, this would not apply to any other cash-flow profile.

Working Insight 7.2

Use of expected values in start-up business cash projections

A new business estimates that the annual expenditures shown below are needed to develop and launch a new product. If successful, the *expected* annual cash inflows are also shown. At the end of each year, the business can review the project and cancel all subsequent expenditures if insufficient progress has been made; therefore probability forecasts of success at each individual stage are also given, together with the appropriate cumulative probabilities.

Year	Forecast annual cash flow (£millions)	Probability of success of previous stage	Cumulative probability factor	Probability-adjusted expected annual cash flow (£millions)
1	(3)	N/A	1	(3)
2	(4)	0.5	0.5	(2)
3	(4)	0.6	0.3	(1.2)
4	(6)	0.8	0.24	(1.44)
5–15	10	0.8	0.192	1.92

Explanation of final column figures:

£3 million will be spent in Year 1. The expenditure of £4 million in Year 2 is dependent on the success of the development activity in Year 1. As this success has only a 50% cent probability, it is not certain that £4 million will be spent in Year 2; hence the expected value of £2 million (£4 million at a probability of 50%). As each successive stage is conditional on the success of *all* the preceding stages, the cumulative probability factor is the product of all these probabilities. Thus there is less than a 20% chance that the £10 million annual cash flow will be received from years 5–15.

Working Insight 7.3

Comparison of net present value calculations

Year	Probability-adjusted cash flows			Unadjusted cash flows		
	Expected annual cash flows (£m)	Discount factor @ 12%	Present value	Original annual cash flows (£m)	Discount factor @ 35%	Present value
1	(3)	0.893	(2.68)	(3)	0.741	(2.22)
2	(2)	0.797	(1.59)	(4)	0.549	(2.20)
3	(1.2)	0.712	(0.85)	(4)	0.406	(1.62)
4	(1.44)	0.636	(0.92)	(6)	0.301	(1.81)
5–15	1.92	3.774	7.25	10	0.828	8.28
	Net present value		+1.21	Net present value		+0.43

rate applied to all the cash flows including the very early expenditures which are relatively certain (e.g. the £3 million investment in Year 1 is guaranteed to be incurred, and the £4 million expenditure in Year 2 has a 50 per cent probability). Instead, the use of expected cash flows highlights the rapidly increasing value of the project as a successful outcome becomes progressively more likely.

(We should, however, point out that, as in many similar cases in finance, theoretical soundness tends to lose out to ease and accepted practice. Most companies and investors apply higher discount rates in these situations rather than using probability-weighted expected values for the cash flows together with a lower discount rate. Similar examples can be cited of net present value and residual income being conceptually superior to internal rate of return and return on investment respectively, yet in practice the latter methods are more widely used.)

In Working Insight 7.4, the present values under the two methods have been recalculated as if the expenditure in Year 1 has now been successfully completed. This now increases significantly the probability of receiving the £10 million cash inflows and therefore the net present value is also increased dramatically, even though the same discount rate of 12 per cent is applied. In order to reflect the higher probability of success under the other method,

---

Working Insight 7.4

Increasing present values as project success becomes more likely

The first investment stage (Year 1) has now been successfully completed on budget. No other estimates have been changed and the same discount factors have been appropriately applied to the expected remaining future cash flows.

Year	Annual cash flow (£m)	Probability of success of previous stage	Cumulative probability factor	Probability-adjusted expected annual cash flow
1	(4)	N/A	1	(4)
2	(4)	0.6	0.6	(2.4)
3	(6)	0.8	0.48	(2.88)
4–14	10	0.8	0.384	3.84

Year	Probability-adjusted cash flows			Unadjusted cash flows		
	Expected annual cash flows (£m)	Discount factor @ 12%	Present value	Original annual cash flows (£m)	Discount factor @ 35%	Present value
1	(4)	0.893	(3.57)	(4)	0.741	(2.96)
2	(2.4)	0.797	(1.91)	(4)	0.549	(2.20)
3	(2.88)	0.712	(2.05)	(6)	0.406	(2.44)
4–14	3.84	4.226	16.23	10	1.118	11.18
	Net present value		+8.69	Net present value		+3.58

In order to generate the same net present value as given by the probability-adjusted flows, the discount factor used on the gross expected cash flows would have to be reduced to approximately 27%.

the risk-related discount rate should be reduced as each stage of the project is completed. Unfortunately in practice it is very difficult to develop meaningful risk measures for such discrete elements within a total business project.

One further point is worth mentioning. We use NPV to evaluate these new projects because it is a sound financial tool. But other tools might also be appropriate, and it is only fair to point out that companies aiming for radical innovation might be better off avoiding NPV, given that the sales forecasts underlying the technique will be difficult to project with any accuracy.[5]

Real options

Most forecasts turn out to be wrong. This is not necessarily a problem: much of the value of the forecasts lies in the act of preparing them, and the considerable thought and analysis that goes into the underlying business assumptions and sensitivity analysis. However, circumstances change, and there is value in being able to adapt to this.

Options give you the right to do something, but do not require you to do it. We discuss financial options in Chapter 11, and expand upon them in Appendix 2. Here, we consider the practical and strategic implications of conducting a business so as to create real options. This is a relatively new branch of finance,[6] which considers the value of flexibility and having the option to change plans, or to develop a larger business from an initial pilot study.

Working Insight 7.4 showed that if the project did not fulfil early expectations, the managers would terminate it rather than continue making losses and destroying shareholder value. If stage 1 were unsuccessful, the company would not invest another £4 million in stage 2. This highlights an interesting aspect of discounted cash-flow analysis. The way that we set out forecasts in DCF analysis, and calculate the expected probabilities of success, indicates a static position. It implies that this is what will happen, and ignores the flexibility that a change in circumstances could bring.

This can be misleading. For example, a forecast to support a ten-year investment in rental property will assume that the building is sold at the end of Year 10. But if property prices have crashed during that final year, there is value in the investor's ability to defer the sale decision until the market rebounds: there is no compelling reason to stick to the original forecast and sell at a loss. Likewise, faced with a property market that had tripled in value over a five-year period, the investor might just decide to take advantage of the bubble, and sell out at a high – there is no requirement to keep the investment for the period originally planned.

Working Insight 7.5 gives some examples of where flexibility can add value to a business.

The financial techniques behind the evaluation of real options are varied, and include a proxy for the Black–Scholes equation used in financial options, the use of binomial tree models, or Monte Carlo analysis. These techniques are beyond the remit of this book. What is important to us is how real options fit into corporate financial strategy.

---

5 The suggested reading at the end of this chapter includes two pieces by Goffin and Mitchell relevant to this.
6 Stewart Myers wrote about real options in 1977. We take the view that that is relatively recent. 'Determinants of Corporate Borrowing', *Journal of Financial Economics*, 5(2): 147–75.

Working Insight 7.5

Some examples of the value of flexibility

Multi-stage projects

If a project can be split into stages, rather than investing in the whole thing up front, then it can be assessed at each stage to see if it is still worth proceeding. This minimizes the risk, and also reduces the amount of cash needed at the start of the cycle. Working Insight 7.2 gives an example of a multi-stage project: the investment is made over a series of years rather than all at the start. In other words, at the end of each year there is a call option to undertake the next stage. This gives a chance to abandon it if the financials become unattractive.

Timing flexibility

If an investment can safely be delayed without handing over a strategic advantage to competitors, then there can be an advantage in delaying it to learn more about the potential market and pitfalls. Again, there is a call option on the investment. This reduces risk and delays cash outflows (although, of course, it may also delay the associated cash inflows).

Alternative uses

An investment in assets becomes more valuable if those assets have more than one possible use. This applies both to tangible assets and to intangibles. For example, a conference hall with fixed seating is potentially less valuable than one where the seating can be removed to accommodate a broader range of activities. Alternative sourcing is also valuable – a power plant that can use either oil or gas has advantages over a single-source operation. This situation reflects both a put and a call.

Growth potential

Sometimes it is worth undertaking a small project, with no profit potential, in order to gain entry to a potentially larger market. The cost of the small project (its negative NPV) can be seen as the price paid for the call option to grab the later market opportunity should that arise. For example, a company might make a strategic decision to bid for an unprofitable contract, solely to establish itself as a capable player in a particular market. The loss on the contract is a price worth paying in order to gain future, profitable business.

Exit option

The ability to terminate a loss-making venture has great value. For example, a business committed to paying high rents on an unbreakable 20-year lease might regret not having paid a small premium up front to negotiate a break clause, a put option on the rest of the lease.

Real options represent a different way of looking at the present value of growth opportunities (PVGO), introduced in Chapter 2. The value of a company represents the value of its assets-in-place plus the NPV of its future activities; the real options are what give the company some of that PVGO. This being the case, it is obvious that companies should conduct themselves in such a way as to maximize their strategic options, thus creating several paths for value-generation in the future.

Later in this chapter we will discuss corporate venturing. This is a good example of real options in practice. The large corporates put money into small start-up businesses on the assumption that although many will fail, some will develop valuable intellectual property and become commercial successes. The sums invested by these corporate venturing arms are the cost of the call option – worth making because of the potential payoffs, which might ultimately be realized in the form of an acquisition of the venture partner in order to acquire technology, or its sale, making a capital gain, or in another way, as yet unforeseen.

Portfolio returns

As we have already explained, the required returns on start-up investments are very high, to compensate for the very high risk. But these returns are not always made – venture capital investors need each investment to promise the potential of very high returns in order to compensate for those that fail completely.[7]

Overall a portfolio of such venture capital investments should produce an acceptable return over time. In the example given, the increase in net present value of the successful investment of £3 million in Year 1 would balance the cost incurred by another similar scale project which was aborted at the end of Year 1 because of lack of success in its development activity. The portfolio impact of making several investments is to deliver, overall, something like the original return expected at the outset.

The conclusions that can be drawn from this analysis are that the very high business risk associated with new start-ups is taken into account in the return expected by investors applying the CAPM theory, but not by directly increasing the discount rate to include the unique risk of the company.

On a practical basis, this has very important implications for companies trying to raise start-up capital and for venture capital fund managers. The very high rates of return required by most venture capital fund managers to evaluate potential start-up investments must be applied to the expected cash flows which assume a successful outcome. If the cash flows have been adjusted to reflect probability weightings of success, then the much lower beta-driven rates of return should be used.

It is vitally important that the cash-flow projections resulting from the business plans of prospective start-ups are compiled with in a manner totally consistent with the way in which they will subsequently be valued by the venture capitalist. Unfortunately, it is not uncommon to find entrepreneurs preparing their plans on a very prudent basis and incorporating decision trees and probabilities to produce the adjusted best estimate expected cash flow, and then for this to be discounted by the venture capitalists at their very high, risk-inclusive, required rates of return. Not surprisingly the resulting investment valuation will not normally look too appealing to either party.

This argument can be even more important when the start-up project is within an existing large group. Most large groups now use increased discount rates to evaluate investment projects which appear to have higher than normal levels of risk. However, this risk assessment normally includes all the aspects of risk associated with the new project, whether these are unique to the project or reflect the systematic risk. More critically, the resulting high, risk-inclusive discount rate is often applied to project cash flows which have already been

---

7   Chapter 18 sets out the other ways in which the VC companies make their return, including fees.

subjected to the application of sequential, cumulative probability factor weightings. Consequently, the major element of the project risk is included in the evaluation twice, and these large groups can find it very difficult to approve investments in new products or in any area with higher than normal risk levels.

Need for low financial risk

Start-up businesses have very high business risk, so, following the logic of Chapter 4, they should have low financial risk, i.e. they should be funded by equity, preferably with no debt financing at all. Is that conclusion supported by the relevant finance theory? In a perfect market, there would be no added value from different capital structures, but the effects of taxation and costs of financial distress discussed in Appendix 1 do mean that capital structure is important.

These two market imperfections highlight why start-up companies cannot gain from the use of debt financing. If having any level of debt in a company increases the risk of default, investors will reduce the value of the investment by at least the expected value of any costs associated with such default or earlier stage of financial distress. Therefore a key factor in assessing the importance of potential financial distress is the relative level of costs which are likely to be incurred in the event of such financial distress. Where the underlying assets of the business are relatively discrete with clearly established, high realizable values, the costs of financial distress are likely to be quite low. However, for most start-up companies the current investment value is created by the present value of the expected future cash flows which will result from the successful development, launch, and growth of the product. Thus the assets underlying the business are intangible, without any easily established discrete realizable values; this means that the costs of financial distress are likely to be very high for a start-up business.

The other key component determining the total impact of the risk of default is the likelihood of it occurring. This obviously increases with the relative proportion of debt financing used by the business, but for a start-up company the risk can be high if even a small proportion of debt funding is raised. The high risk of complete business failure means that no cash inflows may actually be generated, so that any level of outstanding debt would lead to a state of severe financial distress.

A high probability of occurrence combined with a high cost if it occurs makes the risk premium required for potential financial distress very high; thus making debt financing unattractive from this perspective.

At the other end of the capital structure analysis was the benefit created by the tax shield effect of debt financing. However, the start-up business may well be making accounting losses or very nominal profits in its early years of operations so that there is no tax advantage to be gained from debt financing either.

Quite apart from the issues of risk correlation and financial theory, there is a practical reason why start-up businesses should not be financed using debt. Start-up companies have a large and growing demand for cash flow. Taking on debt involves making regular cash outgoings to service the interest and repayments; that cash would be better used within the company to drive the growth.

(We should point out that in practice we have known businesses started up on the back of the entrepreneurs' credit cards, due to their inability to convince financiers of the validity of their arguments. Some of these have worked; others have not. Our thesis is that this compounding of risk is not a good idea – not that it never happens.)

Nil dividend pay-out policy

This leads to consideration of another aspect of finance theory: dividend policy. In theory, investors should be indifferent as to whether they receive dividends or achieve their return through capital gains; yet the recommended dividend policy for a start-up company is to pay no dividends at all.

The cash flow of a newly formed business is normally highly negative and new funds are needed for the investment opportunities available to the company. If debt financing is inappropriate, this funding has to be by equity, which means that if investors require a dividend they would have to invest more money into the business to pay for this dividend. In a perfect capital market this would be perfectly acceptable and, indeed, many finance textbooks go to great lengths to demonstrate how it doesn't make any difference to the investors. This is, of course, fairly obvious if there are no taxes and no transaction costs. Unfortunately, in the real world both exist and the transaction costs associated with raising new equity funding are considerable for high-risk start-up businesses. Not only are the costs high but they are relatively fixed, which means that to raise small amounts of equity is exorbitantly expensive. These costs cover the legal and professional fees charged, where the work involved does not vary in accordance with the amount of money being raised. Hence it is not logical to pay dividends and replace the funding by raising new equity investments.

Further constraints include the tax and legal positions on dividends. Dividends are not a tax-deductible expense for the company but are taxable on the investor, so there is a tax penalty involved. Also the company may not legally be able to pay dividends as it must have distributable reserves (principally undistributed post-tax profits) out of which to declare dividends. Many loss-making new businesses will have no such accumulated profits and so cannot legally declare dividends.

Venture capital investors

The ideal equity investors for start-up companies must appreciate the risks involved, including the potential for a total loss of their investment, and must want to receive their financial return in the form of capital gains. These venture capitalists are normally professional investment firms who attempt to compensate for the high risks associated with any specific investment by developing a portfolio comprising similarly high-risk individual investments. They hope that the complete failure of some investments in the portfolio will be offset by the outstanding success of others. Many venture capital investors specialize in particular industry sectors, such as information technology or bio-technology, but hold a portfolio of investments in the sector, taking the view that the sector will produce winners, but spreading the risk on the individual companies.

Using the logic developed earlier in this chapter, such a focused portfolio would clearly deserve the beta for the particular industry sector. This should enable a risk-adjusted discount factor to be developed, incorporating the appropriate level of market-related risk premium, but the unique project risks must still be included by the use of probability-weighted expected cash flows. The argument used by many such focused, yet portfolio-diversified venture capital fund managers is that they are confident that the particular industry (say, bio-technology) will generate some major new companies in the future, but they are less confident of their ability to pick out these specific companies at this very early stage. Hence by investing in a broad range of the high-potential growth companies in this industry, it is hoped that the venture capital fund participates in the success of the few, even at the expense of making many more unsuccessful investments.

Further, contrary to common perceptions, venture capitalists generally act in a risk-averse manner, inasmuch as they manage their risks by limiting their investment portfolios to businesses they understand. Often, venture capital firms will only invest in certain sectors, or will not invest in others. Their industry specialism gives them a greater knowledge of the issues, thus reducing their investment risk. Other firms will limit their investment portfolio to a particular geographical area, or to a particular size of investment, with which they have experience. Venture capital is about making investments with the potential to generate high returns; it is not about taking unnecessary risks.

There is also the problem that, even for the successful investments, there may be a long time gap between the development of the new technology and the cash positive maturity stage of the resulting products. This factor proved particularly interesting during the dot.com boom of the late 1990s, during which many 'incubator' firms were formed to invest in and nurture very early-stage investment opportunities. These incubators mostly had a fundamental flaw in their own financial strategies: the funds outflow to the investee company occurred immediately; if exits were not possible through the anticipated early flotation, the incubator still had to find cash flow to support its own level of expenses. Many of the incubators, including some high-profile ones, followed their investee companies into liquidation.

Many venture capitalists have a relatively short investment time horizon. This is logical as they wish to focus on investing during the high-risk start-up period of a business; if it succeeds, they want to realize their resulting capital gain and reinvest this in more new start-up investments. Therefore, being locked into any particular company, no matter how successful it is, is not an attractive proposition for the investor. It should not be regarded as attractive by the company either, unless the venture capitalist is prepared to accept a reducing level of return as the associated risk is reduced. This is not usually the case, so that it is mutually beneficial to find new equity investors who are willing to buy out the venture capitalists well before the company has become cash positive and dividend paying. This refinancing issue is discussed as part of the transition from start-up to growth stage in Chapter 8.[8]

Business angels

As mentioned earlier, individuals who invest in venture capital opportunities are known as business angels. Often these individuals have made money in their own enterprises and are seeking the excitement and the financial reward of investing in another's business. A fundamental difference between angel investors and venture capital firms is that the angels are investing their own money, whereas the VC firms are acting as intermediaries, raising funds and then investing them. As a result of this, business angel investment is often more informal than that from specialist venture capital companies: the documentation is much simpler, and the deal can be done more quickly due to the individuals being satisfied with doing less due diligence.

Angels' decision criteria for investment include having a favourable impression of the management team, a familiarity with the sector, projected financial rewards, and a synergy with their own skills.

---

8 It is also fair to point out that not all venture capitalists always have a short time horizon – it depends on the investment. For example, Kleiner Perkins and Sequoia Capital owned shares in Google for about five years before its IPO but did not sell any of their investment when it floated, choosing to retain the shares for their future growth.

Companies which have used angel investment report both good and bad experiences with it. On the positive side, angels will often rush in where venture capital firms fear to tread, and will provide finance for investment opportunities that have been unable to attract it otherwise. Angels will invest much lower amounts than traditional venture capitalists (which they can afford to do, as their fixed costs per deal are much less than those of the venture capital companies). Also, they may be a lot more flexible in their approach, prepared to invest for the longer term, and are able to provide management skills which the entrepreneur may lack. However, the negatives of angel investment include the fact that they rarely have 'deep pockets' and so cannot always invest in second- and third-round financing. Also, individuals who have made money in their own companies might have a 'Midas complex', believing that their judgement is infallible, or may be seeking to 'buy a job' by using a redundancy package to buy into another company.

The poetic collective nouns for heavenly angels include 'choir' and 'flight'. More prosaically, a collection of business angels is referred to as a syndicate or a network. Such bodies are very common. They provide better access to deal flow, because entrepreneurs know where to find them. Also, they allow the angels to share resources in performing due diligence, and to syndicate larger investments between themselves.

Crowdfunding

A relatively new phenomenon in start-up finance is crowdfunding: raising small amounts of money from a large number of people, generally through a dedicated website. The investors might be doing this for a potential monetary gain, but frequently there is no monetary reward, and instead, particularly for investments in creative businesses, they receive special privileges or merchandise.

Crowdfunding has had some success in raising money for interesting and exciting projects, but is as yet unproven as a business model. In the USA, the JOBS Act of 2012 facilitated crowdfunding. In the UK, the first platform, Crowdcube, received regulatory approval in 2012.

Corporate venturing

An alternative to traditional venture capital, or even to angel capital, is to accept funding from a large corporate. Many businesses, such as Cisco, and Siemens, have corporate venturing arms, the aim of which is twofold. First, these companies invest in promising new ventures in order to exploit their ideas, to obtain the benefit of their new technologies and gain an edge on the market (interestingly, the USA Department of Defense also does this, for the same reasons).[9] Second, corporate venturing can prove profitable for these companies, in the same way that it provides a good return for professional venture capitalists. Case Study 7.1 illustrates how two corporate venturers operate.

Accepting investment from a corporate venturer can provide useful financial support, and give access to a wide range of useful business contacts. If the venturer has a portfolio of investments, there might also be synergies between the different businesses. If it is in a related industry, there can be a lot of spin-off benefits. And, as with high-profile venture capital investors, having a significant investor can add to a company's profile in the business and investment communities.

9 www.darpa.mil

Case Study 7.1

Some examples of corporate venturing

Car manufacturer **BMW** operates a corporate venturing unit to provide funding for early and mid-stage investments with high potential in mobility services and clean tech. The company provides incubator space for promising businesses whose product or service might fit the BMW brand.

Whereas BMW focuses on very early stage businesses, **Samsung**'s corporate venturing arm has a much broader remit, and will invest in a wide range of industries (as befits the group's corporate span), and at all stages of the business life up to pre-IPO.

Sources: www.bmw-i.co.uk/en_gb/i-ventures and www.samsungventures.com

---

However, there are three main issues to consider before accepting funding from a corporate venturer.

1   Does each party understand the other's motivation? In particular, it is important to understand whether the venturer is expecting to buy out the investee business once it has developed its products and grown. (In this vein, it is also vital to understand the shareholder agreement with the venturer – often these contain 'first refusal' clauses that can prevent the investee company selling out to another party should the opportunity arise.)
2   Is a reciprocal arrangement planned whereby the venturer will provide business advice and contacts (similar in some ways to an incubator)? If so, does the venturer have a good track record in this area? Often the planned advice and contacts fail to materialize, at least to the extent promised at the start of the deal.
3   How important is the investee business to the venturer? Many companies moved into corporate venturing at the heart of the dot.com boom, only to retreat again once the bubble burst, leaving their investee companies without recourse to the anticipated further funds.

Terms of venture capital deals

This section relates to the *term sheet*, the document setting out the agreement between the venture capitalist(s) and entrepreneur, listing the types and amounts of securities to be issued, and their rights and obligations.

One fundamental reason that early-stage investment differs from investment in later stage enterprises is the level of uncertainty about the likely success of the business. As corporate financiers, we would be reluctant to describe start-up valuations as 'guesswork', but, let's face it, that is what they often are. Because of this, the terms surrounding such investment tend to differ from more established businesses, and it is worth spending a few paragraphs outlining just how.

A start-up company might need £100,000, with the entrepreneur agreeing that the venture capitalist will receive 25 per cent of the business for her money.[10] If £100,000 bought 25 per cent of the enlarged company, this implies that the business was worth £300,000 before the investment was made. The calculations and formula for this are shown in Working Insight 7.6.

---

10 The entrepreneur will probably, very grudgingly, refer to this as 'giving away' 25 per cent of the company. She should be reminded that she is not giving it away, she is selling it for £100,000!

Working Insight 7.6

Pre- and post-money valuation calculations

Let the value of the business before the investment be x
Therefore the value of the business after the investment must be $x + £100,000$
Therefore VC company has an investment worth 25% $(x + £100,000)$
The VC company put in £100,000
So, 25% $(x + £100,000)$ is worth £100,000
Solving this, x is £300,000

The pre-money value of the company is £300,000.
The post-money value of the company is £300,000 + £100,000 = £400,000

Another way to calculate the post-money value is to take the price per share paid by the VC and multiply this by the total number of shares in issue post deal. So, if the VC bought 100,000 shares at £1, the post-money value would be £1 x 400,000, i.e. £400,000. If the VC had paid £2 per share, their 50,000 shares would still represent 25% of the equity, so the total number of share in issue would be 200,000. 200,000 shares at £2 again gives a post-money value of £400,000.

Readers trying to determine why the company is worth £300,000 pre-money will be disappointed: there is not necessarily any logic behind this number. Case Study 7.2 illustrates this with some large numbers.

Although venture capital is seen as high-risk investment, venture capital companies take every opportunity to reduce the risks they face, and have developed a series of mechanisms to protect their position. Broadly, these mechanisms ensure that the venture capitalists can exit the investment when the opportunity presents itself, and that they do not suffer too much if the investee company does not perform as originally expected.

One way of managing this is to issue different classes of share to the different parties. For example, the entrepreneur might have founders shares, the first venture capital investor(s) could be issued with series A shares, the second VCs with series B shares, and so on. The plan is that the value of the investment will grow each year, with each round of venture capital

Case Study 7.2

Pre-money valuation – think of a number

In 1986, Steve Jobs conducted a fundraising exercise for NeXT, a new computer company. His initial proposal to venture capital companies offered a 10% stake in NeXT for $3 million, i.e. a pre-money valuation of $27m. Jobs's biographer states that this was, 'a number that Jobs had pulled out of thin air. Less than $7 million had gone into the company thus far, and there was little to show for it other than a neat logo and some fancy offices.' The venture capitalists all turned this down.

Jobs then offered a stake in NeXT to the investor and businessman Ross Perot. The agreed deal was that Jobs would inject $5m into the company and then Perot would put in $20m for a 16% share. That gave a post-money valuation of about $125m, and thus a pre-money value of about $100m.

Source: Isaacson, W. (2011), *Steve Jobs: The Exclusive Biography*, New York: Little, Brown.

Working Insight 7.7

Venture capital deal structure as planned

The entrepreneur who founded Venco raised £100,000 from a venture capital company (VC1), selling them 100,000 shares at £1 each. She held 300,000 shares, which gave VC1 a 25% stake in the business.

(This implied a pre-money value of £300,000 and a post-money value of £400,000.)

A year later, more funding was needed. VC1 invested a further £50,000 and another investor, VC2, came in with £200,000. The pre-money value of the business at this point was agreed to be £1,000,000, which meant that the new money, £250,000 in total, would comprise 20% of the enlarged company [$^{250}/_{(1000 + 250)} = 20\%$]. Given that the existing capital comprised 400,000 shares, as Series B shareholders needed 20% of the enlarged company, 100,000 Series B shares should be issued, at £2.50 each.

At this point the share capital comprised 500,00 shares, as follows:

Entrepreneur		
Founder shares	300,000	*60%*
VC1		
Series A shares	100,000	
Series B shares	20,000	*24%*
VC2		
Series B shares	80,000	*16%*
Total number of shares	500,000	*100%*

The post-money value is £1.25m (500,000 shares in issue, at the latest issue price of £2.50).

At the point of sale of the business, all the different share types would convert to Ordinary shares. The Founder would receive 60% of the sales proceeds, and VC1 and VC2 receive 24% and 16% respectively. Everyone would be happy (assuming the sales proceeds exceed £1.25m).

---

investors paying a higher per-share price and then the whole business being sold or floated at a profit. When this happens it is customary for the different classes of share capital all to convert into ordinary shares at the point of sale, with proceeds being allocated accordingly. This is illustrated in Working Insight 7.7

The use of different financial instruments enables some sophisticated deal structuring if the scenario does not work out so happily. For example, VC1 might insist on an *anti-dilution clause* in their agreement. Most start-up companies need several rounds of finance, and the expectation is that each round will be at a higher share price (an *up-round*), because the business has become more valuable. However, should the business suffer a setback, the issue price might go down (a *down-round*). In normal circumstances this would mean that the existing investors would be diluted by the new, cheaper shares. The anti-dilution protection means that in the event of a down-round some or all of the venture capitalist's existing shares will be re-priced as if they had been issued at this lower price, thus increasing the number of shares and minimizing the dilution.[11] Working Insight 7.8 gives a simple example

---

11 We are hoping to be able to apply this type of provision in our own lives, being able to improve prices retrospectively every time we make a purchasing error. As yet, most retailers are unwilling to cooperate.

of how this might work (different types of anti-dilution clause contain different levels of complexity).

Although anti-dilution clauses are common, they might not always be used. Often, the Series B investor will insist that the Series A waive their anti-dilution rights, as otherwise the incentives of the founders are reduced unacceptably.

Anti-dilution clauses are just one mechanism used by venture capitalists to protect their investment position against poor future performance. Another such is the *liquidation*

Working Insight 7.8

Anti-dilution clauses in venture capital agreements

The entrepreneur who founded Venco raised £100,000 from a venture capital company (VC1), selling them 100,000 shares at £1 each. She held 300,000 shares, which gave VC1 a 25% stake in the business.

(This implies a pre-money value of £300,000 and a post-money value of £400,000.)

The situation now differs from Working Insight 7.7 in that the business failed to perform to expectations, and more funding was needed to develop it. They needed another £100,000 which, for convenience, we will assume all comes from a new investor, VC2. However, the pre-money value of the company was now assessed at only £300,000. This would mean a post-money value of £400,000, and VC2 receiving 25% of the business (133,333 shares) for his £100,000. The share price for the Series B shares would be 75p. If this were to happen, the shareholding structure would have developed as follows:

	Pre-money value is £300,000		Post-money value is £400,000	
	Number of shares '000	%	Number of shares '000	%
Entrepreneur	300	75%	300	56%
VC1 (invested £100,000 @ 100p)	100	25%	100	19%
VC2 (invested £100,000 @ 75p)	–	–	133	25%
Total	400	100%	533	100%

For VC1 this is a bit of a disaster. The fact that their percentage of the company has fallen from 25% to 19% implies that their initial investment decision was poor: either they should not have invested, or they should have demanded a lower investment price.

The purpose of the anti-dilution clause is to put VC1 in the same position they would have been in if they paid the 'right' price originally, maintaining their percentage share of the company. The way this is achieved is to alter the conversion rights for their Series A shares such that, on the ultimate sale of the business, they don't convert at 1:1, but at a rate that will give VC1 25% of the business, just as they originally planned.

But if VC1 gets 25% of the business, who suffers a reduction? It's not going to be VC2 – they have bought 25% and that's the end of their story. The additional percentage to VC1 comes from the Entrepreneur's share – her stake will fall to 50% to allow VC1's to rise to 25%. (Anti-dilution clauses are slightly misnamed – they are anti-dilution for the venture capitalist, but most definitely dilutive for the founders.)

On the final sale of the business, in order for the percentage stakes to give the desired effect, the conversion rate from Series A shares into Ordinary shares (which are equivalent to the Founder shares) is 1.5:1; i.e. for 100,000 Series A shares VC1 will receive 150,000 Ordinary shares. VC2 will convert Series B shares into Ordinaries at 1.125:1, meaning that their 133,333 shares turn into 150,000 Ordinaries. The final table of values looks like this.

	£'000 invested (1)	Original number of shares ('000) (2)	Required final % (3)	Final number of shares (4)	Conversion ratio (5) = (4) ÷ (2)
Entrepreneur	300	300	50%	300	1:1
VC1 Series A	100	100	25%	150	1.5:1
VC2 Series B	100	133	25%	150	1.125:1
Total	£500k	533	100%	600	

Note: column (4) is calculated by assuming that entrepreneur shares convert at par, and so her 300,000 shares represent 50% of the total. That gives total Ordinary shares of 600,000, from which the other shareholdings can be determined.[12]

preference. A liquidation preference (which relates to any disposal of the business) works to ensure that the venture capitalist receives back at least the sum they invested in the company, even if future values are lower than expected. This is illustrated in Working Insight 7.9.

Another way in which the VC might try to protect their position could be evidenced in the treatment of the share options to be issued to future employees. Some venture capitalists insist that the shares for any future option pool come from the entrepreneur's shareholding rather than their own. However, VCs often accept that the employee incentivization will benefit all shareholders and that they should take some of the pain.

Of course, there is no requirement on the entrepreneur to accept an anti-dilution clause or liquidation preference or anything else in the term sheet, and many will argue strongly against it, but be willing to concede terms in other areas. A term sheet should be considered in its entirety rather than as a series of separate clauses, and the overall position of entrepreneur and investor should be assessed with each change.

In addition to these specific types of clause, companies accepting venture capital investment should expect to sign term sheets which give the investors board seats, a veto over capital expenditure and budgets and significant transactions, and other control or voting rights. Other clauses are also common. For example, *drag-along rights* apply if an offer is made for a company. They give the majority shareholder who wishes to sell, the right to force the minority to join in the sale, on the same terms. This prevents minority shareholders from stopping the deal taking place. The corollary to drag along is *tag-along* rights, which provide that an offer made to one shareholder, or group of shareholders, has to be made to

12 And just to check the maths, the original purchase price of Series B, after the conversion, will become 75p ÷ 1.125, i.e. 66.67p. There will be 600,000 shares in issue, and multiplying these gives the expected post-money value of £400,000.

Working Insight 7.9

An example of liquidation preference

The founder of LiquiCo raised £150,000 venture capital to start his company, for which the venture capital company received 40% of the shares. The VC has a liquidation preference clause, which states that on a disposal, it will get back at least the original £150,000. The tables below show how disposal proceeds of various levels could be split between the parties.
OPTION 1 – WITH NO 'CATCH-UP'

All figures in £'000	£100k proceeds	£200k proceeds	£600k proceeds
If there had been no LP the VC would have received 40%, i.e.	40	80	240
With the LP, the VC receives the first £150k of proceeds and then 40% of the balance	100	150 + (40% x 50) = 170	150 + (40% x 450) = 330
	VC receives all of the proceeds: not sufficient to repay the initial investment, but all that is available	*VC recovers the initial investment and an additional 40% of the remainder*	

OPTION 2 – WITH 'CATCH-UP'

All figures in £'000	£100k proceeds	£200k proceeds	£600k proceeds
If there had been no LP the VC would have received 40%, i.e.	40	80	240
With the LP, the VC receives the first £150k of proceeds, and then the return is balanced between the parties in the correct proportion.	100	150	150 + (40% x (600 – 150 – 225)) = 240
	VC receives all of the proceeds: not sufficient to repay the initial investment, but all that is available	*VC receives their 150k, then the entrepreneur receives the rest, which contributes towards the 60% that they would have received had there been no LP*	*VC receives the first 150k. Entrepreneur receives the next 225k (the 60% equivalent of the VC's 40%). The balance is split in the proportion 40:60*

The terms of a liquidation preference really are important to understand – the catch-up provision is fairer to the entrepreneur, who benefits considerably at larger disposals values.

If there have been several rounds of investment, it is likely that the Series C liquidation preference will take priority over the Series B, which will be at an advantage to the Series A.

The Working Insight illustrates what is known as a 1 x liquidation preference, which means that the VC company gets back the sum it put in. However, it is very common to see liquidation preference of 2x or 3x or more, which weight the odds in favour of the VC company. Case Study 7.3 shows an extract from the financial statements of a UK company backed by private equity.

Case Study 7.3

Extract from financial statements of a UK company with a liquidation preference

£

Issued and fully paid:
35,857 shares, consisting of:
- A shares   18,555
- B shares   7,088
- ordinary shares   10,214

    35,857

The A shares and B shares have specific rights (prior to distribution amongst all shareholders) to recover their original investments up to certain levels upon sale or liquidation of the entire share capital of the company. The A shareholders hold this right until they have received, in aggregate, four times their original investment. The B shareholders hold this right until they have received, in aggregate, two and a half times their original investment.

The company has a venture capital investment in the form of A and B shares, plus ordinary shares owned by the Founders. The A shares, which would have been issued in the first round, have a 4x liquidation preference and the B shares carry a 2.5x liquidation preference. The founding entrepreneur and his colleagues only participate once these are paid.

Mechanisms for obtaining return		Mechanisms for risk – reduction (avoiding losses)
Yield	**Capital gain**	
Dividend: a fixed amount, or dependent on profits, or related to a specific transaction. Dividend can be for all shareholders or just the venture capitalists.	Proceeds on sale of the shares: based on market prices or a pre-agreed multiple of the investment, or a mixture.	Ratchets (see Chapter 18). Liquidation preference. Anti-dilution. Drag-along and tag-along rights. Voting rights, veto rights. The right to appoint a director to the board. Covenants.

Figure 7.2 Characteristics of financial instruments in venture capital.

the other shareholders too. Tag-along is a mechanism to prevent one shareholder from selling out on very good terms which are not available to the others. Figure 7.2 sets out some common ways in which venture capital investors obtain their return, or reduce their risk of losses.

Key messages

- Start-ups carry a high business risk and so their financial strategy should be low risk. This means equity finance, by venture capital investors, with no dividend pay-out but seeking a high capital gain.

- In evaluating risky investments, probability-adjusted cash flows can be discounted at a 'normal' cost of capital. Failing this, the base forecast cash flows should be discounted at a cost of capital that has been increased to allow for the risk. Although this latter method is the most common, the former is intellectually more attractive and leads to fewer errors.
- Venture capital can come from specialist investment funds, from commercial companies in the form of corporate venturing, or from individuals, known as business angels.
- Companies raising venture capital can expect to have to give special protections to their investors, via the share agreement. Such protections include anti-dilution and liquidation preference clauses. The term sheet should be negotiated to balance investors' protections with the entrepreneur's ability to make a fair return.

Suggested further reading

Metrick, A. and Yasuda, A. (2011), *Venture Capital & the Finance of Innovation* (2nd edn, Chichester: Wiley).
   This gives a good explanation of the VC industry, going in to great detail on term sheet and deal terms, how to value early-stage businesses, and real options.
Davies, R., Goedhart, M., and Koller, T. (2012), 'Avoiding a Risk Premium That Unnecessarily Kills Your Project', *McKinsey Online Journal*, available at http://www.mckinsey.com/insights/corporate_finance/avoiding_a_risk_premium_that_unnecessarily_kills_your_project.
   This article demonstrates that using too high a discount rate to allow for risk is unproductive, and suggests developing multiple cash-flow scenarios, valued at the company's cost of capital, and then averaged.
Goffin, K. and Mitchell, R. (2006), 'Learning to Avoid the Net Present Value Trap', *Financial Times Mastering Management*, 26 May.
   This article points out the difficulties of applying net present value to innovative projects, and suggests instead a scoring system with an iterative forecasting process, in which the prediction of value develops and improves over time.
Goffin, K. and Mitchell, R. (2005), *Innovation Management: Strategy and Implementation: Using the Pentathlon Framework* (Basingstoke: Palgrave Macmillan).
   Sets out a framework for assessing and managing innovative projects.
Christensen, C. M., Kaufman, S. P., and Shih, W. C. (2008), 'Innovation Killers: How Financial Tools Destroy Your Capacity to Do New Things', *Harvard Business Review*, 86(1): 98–105.
   The financial tools in question are discounted cash flow, the treatment of sunk costs in investment analysis, and the undue emphasis on earnings per share as a driver of value.
OECD (2011), *Financing High-Growth Firms: The Role of Angel Investors*, OECD Publishing, www.oecdbookshop.org/oecd/display.asp?sf1=identifiers&st1=9789264118782
   Reports the results of an OECD project on high-growth financing. Covers thirty-two countries. Available for purchase or to read online.
Damodaran, A. (2010), *Risk Management: A Corporate Governance Manual*, http://ssrn.com/abstract=1681017
   Chapter 8 of this manual deals with real options.
National Venture Capital Association (USA) has useful resources on its website www.nvca.org, including model deal documentation, and reports on the industry.
Examples of term sheets can be downloaded from the European site http://seedsummit.org/legal-docs

8 Growth companies

Learning objectives

After reading this chapter you should be able to:

1   Explain how the life cycle model relates to a company in the growth stages of its life.
2   Critique the financial strategy adopted by a growth company, making a decision as to which aspects of the life cycle model are relevant to its circumstances, and why.
3   Appreciate some of the assumptions behind the Capital Asset Pricing Model, and their flaws.
4   Calculate the theoretical impact of rights issues, bonus issues, and share splits, and understand their likely effect on corporate value.

Summary of the life cycle model relating to growth companies

Once the new product has been successfully launched into its marketplace, sales volumes should start to grow rapidly. This represents a reduction in the overall business risk associated with the product, and also suggests that the strategic thrust of the company should change. The key emphasis of the competitive strategy should now be placed on marketing activities in order to ensure both that the total growth of sales is satisfactory and that the company increases its share of an expanding market.

Although reduced, the business risk is still high during the period of rapid sales growth. Thus the source of funding must be designed to keep the financial risk profile low; this indicates continued use of equity funding. However, an important aspect of managing the transition from start-up to growth is that the initial venture capitalist investors will be keen to realize their capital gains in order to enable them to reinvest in other start-up businesses. This means that new equity investors need to be identified to replace the original venture capital and to provide for any continued funding needs during this period of high growth. The most attractive source of such funding is often from a public flotation of the company.

The higher sales volumes (which should now be generating reasonable profit margins) will generate much stronger cash flows than during the start-up stage. However, increasing operating capacity will demand more investment in working capital and fixed assets. That, together with the need to invest in overall market development and market share development, will burn cash. Consequently, the cash generated is required for reinvestment in the business, with the result that the dividend pay-out ratio will remain very low. This should not be a problem for the new equity investors because they will have been attracted primarily by the prospects of high future growth.

These growth prospects should be reflected in a share price that shows a high price/earnings multiple applied to the low earnings per share of the company. As the dividend yield is very small, the bulk of the investors' expected return has to be generated as capital gains, by increases in the share price. This means that the company has to produce substantial growth in earnings per share during this stage of development; this could be achieved by winning a dominant market share in the rapidly growing market. These issues are illustrated in Working Insight 8.1.

The rest of this chapter fleshes out this summary, and discusses various aspects of finance that might be relevant to the growing company.

Continuing high business risk

During the growth stage the business continues to develop its competitive advantage while driving strong growth, preferably at a rate faster than the overall market is growing, so that

---

Working Insight 8.1

Financial strategy parameters

Growth business

Business risk	High
Financial risk	Low
Source of funding	Growth equity investors
Dividend policy	Nominal pay-out ratio
Future growth prospects	High
Price/earnings multiple	High
Current profitability, i.e. eps	Low
Share price	Growing but volatile

it will become a significant player. Its strategies for this might include developing strong brands, achieving significant economies of scale, or reducing costs through moving down the learning curve. There are significant risks associated with any of these strategies, and they all require considerable up-front investment.

Thus for these companies the level of business risk remains high. The risks of managing growth must be considered alongside the risks that the anticipated growth in demand will not fully materialize.

Another reason that the business risk of the growth phase is still high is that the transition from start-up to growth requires a number of changes to be implemented by the company. Change always implies risk as, if the change is not managed properly, it can hurt the future performance of the business. Where the required changes are significant and wide-reaching, the level of increased risk that results is also greater. An obvious area of change is in the strategic thrust of the company. During their start-up periods, most businesses would have concentrated on research and development, either in order to exploit an identified market opportunity or in the hopes of creating one through a technological breakthrough. Even in its latter stages where the product was being prepared for launch, the main emphasis would have been on problem-solving as quickly as possible. Delays in getting the product into the marketplace can prove extremely expensive if, as a consequence, a competitor is able to establish its product first, or if the window of opportunity has simply been closed during the period of delay.

Once the product has been successfully launched, the company should concentrate its efforts on building market share (and, if it is a market leader, the total market). This requires a marketing focus on the part of senior managers rather than the R&D or technology focus which might have been more appropriate during its earlier years. A fundamental change in management focus is not easy to achieve (without changing the managers) and so the scale of the required change is important in terms of the risk associated with this transition. If the company's original product development strategy was very market-oriented, the change may not be that great. However, for many high-technology businesses the requirement to focus on the needs of customers rather than solving stimulating intellectual problems has proved difficult to manage.

In addition to the change in business focus, the growth stage brings with it the need for different business processes. Small organizations can thrive on informal systems, but as the scale of operations grows, and the number of employees and divisions increases, there is a need for more structure. Managing this transition is another contributor to the level of business risk.

As mentioned in the previous chapter, there also needs to be a fundamental change in the investor profile during the transition from start-up to rapid growth. The venture capitalist was the ideal shareholder for the newly formed very high-risk company, but it is not appropriate for the company to retain this investor base as it moves through the growth stage. However, the continuing high business risk associated with most rapidly growing companies means that low-risk financing is still appropriate. This requires finding new equity investors who are prepared not only to buy out the original venture capital shareholders but also to provide any funding needed during this period of rapid growth.

These new investors are taking on a lower-risk investment than did the venture capitalists, because the product is normally now proven and has some sales. Also the company is now much more substantial than the business plan and product concept which it may have comprised when initial financing was being raised. Hence it is possible to look to raise this new equity funding from a broader potential base of investors, possibly including the general public.

Raising funds from the public carries a particular risk–return trade-off. Most countries have strict rules to control companies wishing to raise funds from the general public. The objective of this is to try to safeguard the less sophisticated investor and to maintain the confidence of investors in general in the financial markets. Clearly, if the confidence of investors were undermined they would either cease to invest altogether or would demand significantly increased returns to compensate for their higher risk perceptions. Thus, a high risk to the investor can be costly to the company. However, implementing tighter controls carries the downside to the company of higher costs. These relate, for example, to being listed on a stock exchange, having share price information included in major newspapers and other information services, communicating with existing and potential investors, introducing rigorous systems, and complying with the rules of the various bodies of which the company becomes a member.

Many of these costs can be minimized if this second phase of equity funding is raised by private placement. Private placements involve issuing shares without seeking a stock exchange listing or inviting the public at large to invest in the company. Instead, investors are invited to participate, so membership is more tightly controlled than a listing, generally comprising private equity and other institutional investors, and accredited high net worth individuals. Such investors would still expect a (limited) prospectus to be available, and a sound and well-controlled business, but the regulatory and communication costs would be significantly reduced, as is the cost of external scrutiny of the business. In times when listed markets have dried up and it is difficult to float a company, the private placement route is very useful.

Private placements are a popular investment with eligible investors, and many institutions have portfolios including pre-IPO companies, which have raised private funding at a stage of development prior to flotation. However, investors in private placements must accept that part of their funds might go, not to the company itself, but to buy out part of the stake of existing venture capital shareholders or employees. The remainder of the investment does go into the company and is used to finance its rapid growth. Thus the major financial return to these new investors will take the form of capital gains on their shares.[1]

Unless these investors are going to stay in the company until it eventually does become mature, cash positive, and dividend paying, they too will require other new investors to buy their shares in due course. This is a key problem caused by continuing to use private sources of equity finance: it provides initial funding to the company but it does not create an easy exit route for those investors who wish to sell some shares and realize part of their capital gain.

The best way of achieving this exit is for the company to be quoted on a stock exchange so that prices for its shares are known. Equally importantly, financial traders stand ready to buy and sell the shares at all times, thus providing a ready exit route for current shareholders. IPOs are discussed in more detail in Chapter 15. Much of the remainder of this chapter considers financial strategy issues from the perspective of companies that are already listed on a public stock exchange.

---

1   The capital gains are a lot more uncertain than for a listed company, as there is no immediate liquid market on which to sell the shares (although private secondary markets do exist).

Calculating the cost of equity

Prospective investors in a newly floated company will compare the return on this company as a potential investment against all their similar existing available opportunities. This means that they will need to assess their required return from the new company. Two main methods are available to conduct this calculation. Of these, the Capital Asset Pricing Model is by far the most common, and is discussed below. The dividend growth model is also used sometimes, and this is considered briefly later in the chapter. Fuller detail of these models is given in Appendix 1.[2]

Capital Asset Pricing Model (CAPM)

$$K_e = R_f + \beta(R_m - R_f)$$

Where K_e is the shareholder's required return, R_f is the risk-free rate, β is the sensitivity of the share price to market movements, and $(R_m - R_f)$ is the market premium.

Using CAPM, the cost of equity (i.e. the shareholders' required return) is dictated by the beta factor of the company. The problem is that to calculate the beta, the volatility of the company's return relative to the total market should be measured. It is difficult to do this for unquoted shares because the data do not yet exist. This makes an assessment of market sensitivity particularly fraught for unquoted high-growth companies, where capital growth is a major component of the investors' return. One way round the problem is to try to identify similar companies that are publicly quoted and to use some sort of adjusted average of their beta factors.

However, even if such a compromise proves possible, several complexities remain. Beta calculations reflect what has happened in the past; investors' required return is based on their expectation of future volatility. In a rapidly changing company, these are likely to differ, and so any historically-based estimate of beta must be treated with caution.

There are statistical techniques which assist in this assessment of risk. Any calculation of the beta from actual data is subject to an estimating range, which can itself be calculated. If it is assumed that the actual measurements are normally distributed about the mean (i.e. the individual measurements are randomly distributed rather than being skewed by some estimating bias or flaw in the method of calculation), it is possible to be 95 per cent confident that the true beta lies within 1.96 standard deviations (in either direction) of the estimated value. This gives a range for the expected value of the beta for any particular company, which appears to be helpful, particularly since beta calculations are available for the major shares in many stock markets from, for example, interested stockbrokers, investment banks, and some business schools. Unfortunately, the standard deviations for most high-growth companies are very large, due to frequent violent swings in returns experienced during the periods used in the calculations. This high level of movement in return should not come as a surprise due to the high level of business risk during this period.

This high level of total business risk now includes an increasing component of market or systematic risk, because high-growth businesses can be significantly affected by changes in external environmental factors. Obviously there is still a substantial element of unique risk associated with high-growth businesses, relating to the development of the particular product

2 Other models are available, some of which are considered better than CAPM, but they are not as widely used in practice, and are outside the scope of this book.

Working Insight 8.2

A range for β leads to a wide variation in cost of equity

Risk-free debt has an expected return of 4%. The equity risk premium is estimated to be 5% and the calculated beta factor for a particular high-growth company is 1.5. The standard error for this company is calculated to be 0.25.

Using the CAPM on the base data gives

$$K_e = R_f + \beta(R_m - R_f)$$
$$= 4\% + (1.5 \times 5\%)$$
$$= 11.5\%$$

However, the standard error means that the 95% confidence limit for the beta factor is given by

95% confidence range = estimated value + 1.96 standard errors (say two)

$$= 1.5 \pm 0.5$$
$$= 1 \text{ to } 2$$

Therefore the cost of equity for this company is between

$$K_e = 4\% + (1 \times 5\%) = 9\%$$

And

$$K_e = 4\% + (2 \times 5\%) = 14\%$$

---

and the marketing success of the company in building its share of the market. This unique risk can be taken into account by using cumulative probability factors to adjust the expected values of the future returns, as explained in Chapter 7, but the higher market-related risk may lead to an increase in the discount rate applied to these adjusted expected cash flows.

If the estimated beta for a particular high-growth company is 1.5, and the standard deviation is 0.25, the confidence range for the beta factor is between one and two. As illustrated in Working Insight 8.2 this can give an estimated cost of capital between 9 per cent and 14 per cent for the company, which is too broad a range to be of much use in assessing the attractiveness of the investment. Many investors appear to rank companies on their expected returns calculated using the arithmetic mean of the factor computations, but with such high ranges this is a somewhat dangerous practice.

Although we have focused on beta, CAPM also suffers from inaccuracies in the calculation of the market risk premium $(R_m - R_f)$. Estimates can vary by several percentage points, depending on the method of calculation.[3] Opinions also vary as to which risk-free debt to use in the calculation, as this will vary depending on whether short-, medium- or long-term debt

---

3 An idea of the potential for confusion is given in the following working paper: *Market Risk Premium Used in 82 Countries in 2012: A Survey with 7,192 Answers*, by Fernandez *et al.* (2012), http://ssrn.com/abstract=2084213

is chosen. And, at the time of writing, when yields on government debt are artificially low, CAPM becomes even more susceptible to error.

Dividend growth model

$$P = D_1 \div (K_e - g)$$

Where P is the share price, D_1 is the next dividend, K_e is the shareholder's required return, and g is the future compound growth in dividends.

Another method of determining the cost of equity is to use the dividend growth model (DGM). The principles behind the DGM calculation differ radically from the CAPM: the latter uses solely market-based data, whereas the DGM uses company-specific data.

Our own preference is to use CAPM to calculate the investors' required return, despite all of its flaws. Being based on market information, CAPM is less susceptible to the idiosyncrasies of a particular company's results. The DGM, being dependent on a dividend growth rate, is particularly unreliable for companies which have no dividends, or have very high or very low growth rates. For a company in the launch or growth stages of its life cycle, this is an obvious drawback. The fact that a company has grown profits at, say 25 per cent per year for the last three years does not (indeed, cannot) mean that it will continue to grow at that pace, and does not imply that its cost of equity must be in excess of that 25 per cent.

Nevertheless, we do like to use the DGM as a sanity check of the company's share price. We do this by calculating the cost of equity using CAPM, and then feeding this back into the DGM model to see what underlying growth rates are implied. Working Insight 8.3 gives an illustration of this.

Reinvestment projects

Growth companies tend to be developed with minimal or no dividend paid out, and reinvest post-tax profits to finance their high-growth objectives. Such growth can come from taking

Working Insight 8.3

Using the dividend growth model as a sanity check of the share price

The company's cost of equity, calculated using CAPM, is 11.5%. Its share price is £1, and the dividend due to be paid next month is 3p.

Using the dividend growth model:

$$P = D_1 \div (Ke - g)$$
$$100p = 3p \div (11.5\% - g)$$
$$g = 8.5\%$$

Attention would now focus on whether, and for how long, the company's current strategy could deliver growth of 8.5% compound.

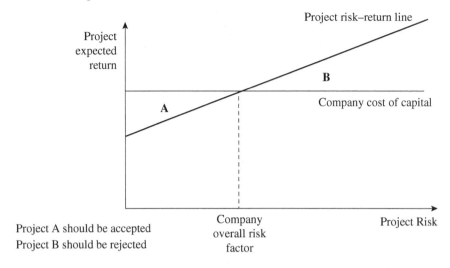

Figure 8.1 Project risk–return.

on projects with a very similar risk profile to the existing business, or taking on projects with a different risk profile.

If growth is through new projects with a similar risk profile to the existing business, and if shareholder wealth is to be enhanced not destroyed, the return on reinvestment must be at least equal to the investors' required return on equity.

However, many businesses expand in different directions, and it is not true that all their projects face the same level of risk. So, should all reinvestment projects be expected to make a return greater than the company's cost of capital?

It should be immediately clear that this would be illogical; if a project has a lower risk than the average risk of the company, it should be expected to make a lower return. As long as the expected return from the project is greater than its risk-adjusted cost of capital, the project is financially acceptable. If all projects are required to earn more than the company's average cost of capital, the business runs the risk of rejecting many financially attractive, low-risk projects while accepting some unattractive higher-risk projects. This is clearly illustrated in Figure 8.1.

Unfortunately, this concept is not applied by many leading companies. In many cases the company's cost of capital (which should be related to its *overall* risk level) is taken as a minimum required rate of return for individual reinvestment projects, with extra return requirements being added for above-average risk projects. This leads to the position shown in Figure 8.2, where low-risk investment opportunities are rejected because their return is below the company's cost of capital.

In some companies, the use of an average cost of capital as a hurdle is a deliberate strategy rather than being based on ignorance or misunderstanding of the financial theory. One financially very astute chairman of a very large UK-based group justified this strategy because 'our investors would not understand why we should reinvest their money at lower rates of return than they demanded'. In other words this chairman did not believe that the risk profile of the group would be adjusted to reflect its new overall weighting, including the lower-risk/lower-return projects.[4]

---

4 This might indeed be true. Markets do not always know best.

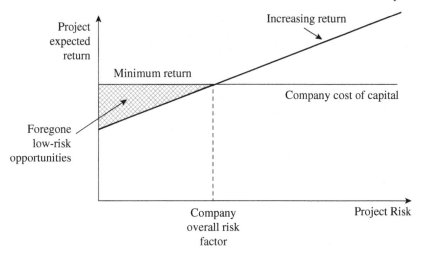

Figure 8.2 Particular reinvestment return requirements.

Unfortunately, this group also tried to reflect all of the project-associated risk through the discount rate. It would have been more effective to use probability weighting factors to take account of the unique risk of each project. This would leave only the market-related risk to be reflected in the discount factor (applied to adjusted cash flows). This part of the project risk can be much more logically compared to the company's overall cost of capital, which will be linked to the company's beta. The problem that this causes is that the project beta has to be estimated, which raises all the issues already discussed in respect of the company itself. However, there is no way of avoiding assessing the risks associated with an investment project and this method at least forces the company to focus separately on the unique risks of the project (which can be managed or diversified) and the impact of the project on the systematic risk of the company.

For most high-growth companies, as we have already discussed, the dominant source of funding will be equity. Therefore the company's cost of capital is the cost of equity. However, when this reinvestment analysis is applied to more mature businesses, the impact of capital structure also needs to be taken into account. In general the company's weighted average cost of capital is normally used but this is not appropriate if the funding for a particular project should differ from the average of the group, or where this project leads to a change in the group funding strategy. Thus, if a mature group with a relatively high debt-to-equity ratio is considering a reinvestment project in a new high-growth or even start-up area of activity, the project should be regarded as being funded appropriately to its risk profile, i.e. with equity funding rather than using a high proportion of debt.

Rights issues – concepts and practice

So far, there has been an implicit assumption that these high-growth companies can finance growth by their IPO proceeds, and then with a high retention ratio applied to growing profits. However, the desired growth rate might be such that even retaining 100 per cent of profits will provide insufficient funding.

Case Study 8.1

Marconi plc: an unfortunate financial strategy

The GEC group was a UK-based defence and electronics company, which produced strong operating performance from a series of growing and mature businesses. The operating results meant that the business was strongly cash positive. Indeed, during the 1980s and early 1990s GEC was criticized by the markets for its excessive cash holdings; well in excess of £2 billion.[5] This cash mountain was not required to fund the company's growth, and the City's view was that it should be returned to shareholders.

In 1996 the management of the company changed, as did its strategy. Over the next few years a number of the company's businesses were sold, including its defence interests. Acquisitions were made to reposition the company in the fast-growing telecoms sector, and in 1999 GEC was renamed 'Marconi' to reflect this.

The serial acquisitions were paid for out of the company's cash pile, and in addition debt was taken on to meet their financing needs. By 2001 the company had net debt of about £3 billion.

Although initially investors approved the change in strategy from a cash-rich, low-risk defence company to a highly geared telecoms business, changes in market conditions in the telecoms sector led to the collapse of the company's markets, its share price, and its credit rating. Ultimately, shareholders lost all of their money.

With hindsight, it is apparent that while it was wrong for the mature defence businesses to be financed using equity, it was also wrong for the high-growth telecoms business – with its considerable business risk – to be funded mainly with debt. The Marconi story appears to be a case of total mismatch of business and financial strategies. However, whereas GEC's over-reliance on equity merely irritated its shareholders, Marconi's over-gearing destroyed the value of their investment.

Consequently, there may be a need for additional fundraising exercises from time to time. These should again be in the form of equity because of the continuing high level of business risk. A publicly quoted company can raise this through a direct offer to outside investors of new shares in the company to be issued at the current market price: this is known as a Secondary Public Offering (SPO). Ideally, an SPO should be made at the full current market price, as otherwise the existing shareholders are giving away a subsidy to these new investors. (Once issued, the new shares are indistinguishable from the already issued existing shares, and the new total value of the company is simply divided by the new total number of shares in order to arrive at a new price per share; any differential in issue price would therefore represent a wealth transfer from one shareholder to another.)

It is not very practical to attempt to issue these new shares at a premium to the existing share price, because a rational new investor would prefer to buy existing shares directly in the market rather than more expensive new ones from the company. Equally, it is normally difficult to make a substantial new issue of shares at the prevailing market price; if lots of potential investors wanted shares at this price, there should be substantial buying pressure in the market but, by definition, at the current market price supply and demand are balanced. A significant and sudden increase in the supply of any commodity normally leads to a decline in its price, even if only temporarily.

---

5   This was in the days when £2bn was a lot of money

Working Insight 8.4

What price for rights?

Satellite Television Audiovisual Recordings plc (STAR) wishes to increase its equity base to fund its continuing high growth rate and an exciting product development programme. It wants to raise over £100m in new equity through a rights issue. Its existing issued share base of 1,000m shares are currently trading at 50p, giving a market capitalization of £500m. Current earnings per share are 2.5p and dividends per share are 0.5p.

The company's financial advisers have suggested a rights issue of one for four at 45p per share, which would raise £112.5m, excluding issue costs.

Analysis

This company is currently positioned as a growth company because it has a P/E multiple of 20 [50p ÷ 2.5p] and a dividend yield of only 1% [0.5p ÷ 50p], indicating that existing investors are buying the shares in the expectation of capital growth. This growth expectation seems reasonable as the company is at present retaining 80% of its profits for reinvestment; i.e. 2p out of 2.5p.

Thus the company must consider making the new issue at a discount to the current market price, but to do so would be to rob existing shareholders. This can be avoided if the existing shareholders are given a pre-emption right to buy the discounted shares in proportion to their existing shareholdings; hence the name 'rights issue'. These issues are normally described by reference to how many new shares can be bought for a number of existing shares owned; e.g. a one for five rights issue means that for every five shares owned the shareholder gets the right (i.e. opportunity) to buy one of the new shares being offered. The company cannot force its existing shareholders to buy any more shares in the company; hence it is granting them a call option to buy these new shares. As the new shares are being issued at a lower price than the current market price of the existing shares, this option should have a value and can be sold if the current shareholder does not want to take it up.[6]

These points can be most clearly illustrated by a numerical example and one is presented in Working Insight 8.4. The rights issue is proposed at a small discount of 10 per cent to the current share price (45p compared to 50p); the discount may be higher in volatile markets, as illustrated in Case Study 15.4. It is important to understand what should, in theory, happen and what, in practice, normally does happen as a result of these types of rights issue.

On the announcement of a rights issue, the stock market receives two separate pieces of new information; it is told that the company wishes to raise new equity and it is also told what the company intends to do with that money. The stock market analyses this information and adjusts the share price accordingly, depending on whether it believes that the new issue will lead to

6 Rights issues have clear advantages to existing shareholders, in that by giving them first refusal, new shares cannot be issued to dilute them. However, although pre-emption rights are common in the UK, they are not used in many other jurisdictions, including the US. An argument used there is that having pre-emption rights would slow down the finance-raising process, as approval of existing shareholders is required for a capital-raising. In a market where rights issues are not common, this is possibly a valid argument, but custom and practice in the UK do show that shareholders are flexible, and issues can proceed quickly if need be. (Although UK regulations generally permit companies to place new shares directly, provided the new issue is less than 5 per cent of the capital.) A secondary offer where the rights cannot be sold on is referred to as an *open offer*.

substantially enhanced future cash flows. In other words the information elements of the announcement are separately incorporated into the share price. If the proposed investment looks financially attractive, the share price may rise to reflect this new opportunity; if the proposed source of funding, equity, is also considered sensible, this may enhance the value still further.

However, initially the company has issued new shares in exchange for an explicit amount of cash. The share price will immediately move to reflect this new situation before then taking into account the longer-term impact of the investment of these funds. This immediate reaction is shown in Working Insight 8.5.

It can be seen that the post-rights share price now reflects the weighted average of the original share price and the rights offer price, so that the discount in the rights offer has been spread over all the shares. The share price has fallen accordingly, but this does not automatically make existing shareholders worse off. They have been given a right to buy a share at 45p, which will now be worth 49p when the right is taken up. If they do not wish to invest 45p more in the company, they can sell the right for 4p which recoups the 4p (4 × 1p) which they have lost on their existing shareholding. This impact is balanced no matter how large the original shareholding and irrespective of whether the rights are taken up or sold, as shown in Working Insight 8.6.

It is by no means certain that the share price will move to 49p, but the final actual price will be affected by the stock market's reaction to the new investment opportunity and by the company's decision to use equity to fund it, as well as any other new information which affects the company or share prices in general. However, any such movement is not caused by the specific details of the rights issue, which produces no gain and no loss whether the rights are taken up or sold.

As it has been shown that the discount on a rights issue confers no advantage or disadvantage to existing shareholders, the terms of a rights issue should make no difference to its attractiveness to the existing shareholders. However, launching a narrow (i.e. small) discount

---

Working Insight 8.5

Immediate price adjustments on rights issue announcements

STAR plc – one for four rights issue at 45p per share

	No. of shares (m)	Price (p)		Market Cap'n (£m)	
Existing position	1,000 shares	@	50p	⇒	500.0
Rights issue (one for four)	250 shares	@	45p	⇒	112.5
Immediate position post-announcement	1,250 shares	⇒	49p*	⇐	612.5
The shareholder is given the right to buy shares at					45p
The post-rights price of all shares (everything else being equal) should be					49p
Therefore rights value per right (ignoring the time value of money impact caused by different settlement dates)					4p

*The 49p is calculated as 612.5 ÷ 1,250

Working Insight 8.6

Impact of rights issues on shareholders

STAR plc – alternatives for holder of 100m shares.

This shareholder receives rights to buy 25m new shares at 45p and has two alternatives: either take up the rights or sell them.

Take up rights

Existing investment	100m	@ 50p	=	£50.00m
Pay for rights	25m	@ 45p	=	£11.25m
Shareholder now owns	125m shares			
but should have an				
investment worth				£61.25m

If share price moves to 49p, this is true because 125m shares @ 49p gives £61.25m Therefore there is no gain and no loss.

Sell rights

Existing investment	100m	@ 50 p	=	£50m
Receive from sale of rights	25m	@ 4 p	=	£1m
Leaving a net investment of	100m	worth		£49m

This will be true if share price moves to 49p as it should. Therefore, again, there is no gain and no loss.

rights issue introduces a risk for the company, in that it may not receive its desired new funding.

A rights issue has to be available for a specified period of time in order for shareholders to decide what to do and to send in their cheques or sell their rights in the market (the normal period is around three weeks). During this period, the rights exercise price is fixed but the share price will fluctuate, so that the gap between the two will change. In the case of a high-growth share with a high beta, small movements in the total market can result in larger movements in the particular share price. If the share price rises, the value of the rights offer increases and the rights become more attractive to investors. However, if the share price falls, the converse is true. Should the share price go below the rights offer price there is no reason for anyone to want to buy these new shares (i.e. take up the rights). In the example already given, it would be illogical for an investor to pay 45p to exercise their rights if the market price of STAR plc's shares had fallen below this level. Equally there is no reason for any outsider to want to buy these rights in order to take them up.

Thus an unexpected fall in the share price could mean that the proposed rights issue would fail, with the result that the company would not receive the required new funding. This could leave the company unable to implement its now publicly stated strategy and so it needs to have an insurance policy. It can remove this risk of funding failure by underwriting the rights issue through an investment bank or similar institution.

An underwriting contract is a guarantee to take up, at the issue price, any of the new shares which are not bought by either existing shareholders or buyers of their rights in the market. Obviously this transfers the risk of any fall in the share price to the underwriters because it is only likely that they will have to buy the shares if the exercise price is below the market value of the shares at the end of the rights offer period. The company has to pay an underwriting premium in order to buy what is really a put option on the underwriters for all the shares, exercisable at the rights offer price. An important driver of option values (discussed in Appendix 2) is the option exercise price (i.e. the rights offer price) relative to the current asset value. Accordingly, the smaller the discount offered on the rights issue, the greater the value of the put option and hence the higher the insurance premium needs to be.

Arranging underwriting provides insurance to the company, but comes at a cost. As we have established that the discount on a rights issue should have no impact on shareholder wealth, this should be an incentive for companies to offer rights issues at much greater discounts; the larger discount would reduce the guarantee costs incurred. This incentive should be dramatically increased because all the analysis and comparisons of actual underwriting fees and their equivalent put option valuations shows that underwriting fees are excessively high; it is therefore a very inefficient market. However, many companies still prefer to make narrow discount rights issues, presumably at least partly because 'that is what successful companies do'. (Deep discount rights issues are discussed in Chapter 10.)

The discussion on the movements in rights values and share prices may have indicated a short-term investment strategy which could be of interest to a high-risk speculator. Suppose such a speculator had £196,000 to invest in STAR plc at the time of its rights issue, as is shown in Working Insight 8.7; this investment could be made as 400,000 shares at the post-rights price of 49p, or instead the speculator could purchase 4,900,000 short-term rights to buy shares.

Working Insight 8.7

Using rights issues as a leveraged positively skewed speculative investment

STAR plc has offered a one for four rights issue at 45p compared to its original market price of 50p. Post-rights weighted average share price should be 49p. The rights value should be 4p per share.

The speculator could invest £196,000 in 400,000 shares of STAR or in buying 4,900,000 rights to STAR shares to be issued at 45p (fixed offer price for rights).

If the share price rises by 10p during the rights offer period, the value of the rights should also rise 10p (ignoring the time value of money). However, if the share price falls by 10p, the rights value cannot go below zero; hence the outcome is positively skewed. The higher volume investment in rights multiplies the change in return for the same change in share price in the same way as using borrowed funds increases volatility (i.e. leverages up the return).

		Impact of ± 10p in share price
Equity investment	400,000 shares	± £40 000
Rights investment	4,900,000 Rights	+£490 000 – £196 000

If the share price is volatile during the period before the rights are actually taken up, these movements will be reflected in the rights value because the exercise price (45p) of the rights offer is fixed. Thus the increased volume of rights which can be acquired multiplies up the impact of any particular movement in the share price. If this increased impact is the same whether prices go up or down, a similar effect could be obtained by borrowing funds so as to buy 4.9 million shares (leveraging up the investment). However, the value of the rights cannot become negative, so the maximum loss is the 4p purchase price whereas the upside potential is not similarly constrained; thus the return is skewed as well as multiplied. The speculator has really acquired a low-valued, short-dated call option on the shares with an exercise price of 45p.

These option markets in rights issues are actively traded during the offer periods, and arbitrageurs help to ensure the gap between the actual share price and the rights exercise price is always equal to the value of the rights. If this kind of option trading can be done, it may be possible for the underwriters of the rights issue to reduce their risk during the life of their insurance contract. The underwriting risk can, of course, be split into the normal two components, market risk and unique risk. The systematic risk element can be triggered if the whole market collapses during the rights period, with the result that the company exercises its put option and leaves the underwriter sitting on a large capital loss. This risk can be hedged if part of the underwriting premium is used to buy a similarly structured put option, but on the whole market (e.g. the stock market index) rather than on the specific share. If the market does collapse, the gains on this put option will offset the loss on the underwriting contract.

(These examples of the underwriters wanting to hedge their market risk and the speculator wanting to multiply up their potential gain illustrate the critical strengths of option markets and option trading strategies. Players with completely opposite aims and objectives can all be attracted to use options in their different forms as part of their financing and investment strategies.)

There remains the risk that the overall market is stable or goes up, but the share price of the company collapses. It is much more difficult to hedge this risk specifically but it can partly be achieved if a suitably designed portfolio is used as the basis of the option hedge rather than the total market index. This can at least take account of key industry factors or major risk items which may affect the company's share price more violently than the stock market. Of course, in a perfectly efficient market the costs involved in designing the perfect hedge would exactly equal the premium received for undertaking the underwriting contract. Fortunately, life is not that boring, as the markets are not that perfectly efficient.

Bonus issues and share splits

A rights issue can be regarded as a sale of the shares at full price, together with a bonus issue of free shares representing the discount in the rights price. This is mathematically illustrated in Working Insight 8.8.

A bonus issue is an issue of shares made from the company's retained profits. Effectively, the retained profits are capitalized, and moved in the balance sheet from the 'reserves' category to the 'share capital' category. Shareholders receive the relevant number of shares (based on their existing shareholdings) for free, leaving them with proportionately the same percentage of the company as they owned previously.

A transaction often compared to a bonus issue is a share split, for example, one £1 share being split into two 50p shares. The difference is that in a share split the nominal value of

> **Working Insight 8.8**
>
> **Rights issues as a sale at full price plus a bonus issue of the discount element**
>
> *STAR plc*
>
> | | |
> |---|---|
> | Rights issue of 250m shares @ 45p generating | £112.5m in cash |
> | This cash inflow could have been achieved by selling 225m shares @ 50p = | £112.5m |
>
> The remaining 25m shares therefore represent a free bonus issue distribution to the existing shareholders.
>
> This is how companies actually account for rights issues. They adjust prior years' figures to take account of this bonus element, as this would otherwise represent dilution in earnings per share due to the increase in the number of issued shares.

each share is reduced, so that the value of share capital on the balance sheet is unchanged, whereas in the bonus issue the nominal value of the shares remains the same as reserves are capitalized. Working Insight 8.9 illustrates the different transactions.

As can be seen, in neither case is there a cash flow impact to these balance sheet rearrangements. Bonus issues and share splits should not affect share values because they do not change the expected future cash flows which will be generated by the business. If the number of issued shares is doubled by a bonus issue or split, the price per share should halve. However, this does not always seem to happen in practice. Furthermore, companies obviously believe that share splits have some value as they are very common, yet they actually cost the company money in advisers' fees to implement them.

There are several explanations suggested for any supposed increase in total market capitalization resulting from a bonus issue or share split:

1 Restriction of future dividends, thus strengthening the balance sheet.
2 A sign of management's confidence in the future.
3 A signal of increased dividends.[7]

The first suggested explanation is that the capitalization of reserves which occurs in a bonus issue (albeit not in a share split) removes the possibility that these reserves can be paid out as dividends and hence reduces the perception of financial risk on the part of lenders to the company. Any value from such a change should be observable through lower-interest rates being charged to the company or by a move towards a higher proportion of debt financing; neither has been observed empirically after a bonus issue.

A more popular explanation for the relative increase in price is that the share split reflects a feeling of confidence on the part of the managers of the company. Therefore a bonus issue or share split may communicate useful information to investors regarding this improved level of confidence which can then get reflected in an increased share price. This can be expressed as, 'successful companies make bonus issues'. (The converse can also be seen in

---

7 Yes, we are aware that 1 and 3 conflict.

Working Insight 8.9

A bonus issue and a share split

	BonusCo	*SplitCo*
Capital structure prior to transaction:		
Share capital		
100,000 shares @ £1 par value	100,000	100,000
Retained profits	250,000	250,000
	£350,000	£350,000
After a bonus issue of one for four shares:		
Share capital		
125,000 shares @ £1 par value	125,000	
Retained profits	225,000	
	£350,000	
After an 1.25 for one share split:		
Share capital		
125,000 shares @ 80p par value		100,000
Retained profits		250,000
		£350,000

that companies listed on the New York Stock Exchange lose their listing if their share price falls below $1: directors who fear that this might occur undertake share consolidations, which are the opposite of share splits, in order to prevent this happening.)

Another explanation is that many companies maintain their dividend per share payments after a bonus issue or stock split. Logically, doubling the number of shares should halve the dividend per share. However, often the dividend is reduced by less than 50 per cent. This means that the dividend pay-out ratio is increased, unless earnings are expected suddenly to rise following the transaction. (The implication of this explanation is that shareholders prefer dividends to reinvestment by this company. This might well be true, but it is not logical for a high-growth company which should be pursuing a high reinvestment strategy.)

Two further arguments are put forward as to why companies undertake share splits. The first relates to companies that encourage employees to hold shares in the business; if the share price rises to too high a level, this may make employee share ownership more difficult, or may discourage them from buying shares.

The final argument appears particularly relevant to the UK stock market, where companies seem to worry if their share prices are too high in absolute terms, as this might make them less attractive. (Relatively few shares trade on the London Stock Exchange over £20 per share, while in the USA companies trade at more than $100 per share with no detectable decrease in demand.) There is no theoretical logic to this argument because it is the proportionate share of the earnings stream which is important and doubling the physical number of issued shares doesn't change the proportion of the company owned by any individual shareholder. However, if the absolute share price is lower, it is supposed to attract more investors to buy shares in the company, thus forcing the price up and increasing the total market capitalization of the company. There is no empirical evidence to support an argument that lower valued shares show greater gains over time which might justify such an investor preference

---

Case Study 8.2

Coca-Cola splits

The Board of Directors of the Coca-Cola Company today voted to recommend a two-for-one stock split to shareowners. The split would be the eleventh in the stock's 92-year history and the first in 16 years.

> 'Our recommended two-for-one stock split reflects the Board of Directors' continued confidence in the long-term growth and financial performance of our Company', said Muhtar Kent, Chairman and CEO of the Coca-Cola Company. 'Our system's 2020 Vision to double our revenues over this decade provides a clear roadmap for creating value for our consumers, customers, bottling partners and shareowners. A stock split reflects our desire to share value with an ever-growing number of people and organizations around the world.'

The announcement went on to discuss the mechanics for the share split, saying:

> These matters will be voted on at a special shareowners meeting anticipated to be held on July 10, 2012. If approved, the record date for the split is expected to be on or about July 27, 2012. Each shareowner of record on the close of business on the record date will receive one additional share of common stock for each share held. The new shares are expected to be distributed on or about Aug. 10, 2012.

Source: www.thecoca-colacompany.com/dynamic/press_center/2012/04/two-for-one-stock-split.html

---

for lower priced shares, but this is a commonly held belief which is acted upon by many publicly quoted companies.

Case Study 8.2 shows an extract from an announcement by Coca-Cola explaining its share split in April 2012.

Key messages

- Business risk remains high during a company's growth stage, so its financial risk should be low. This means an equity funding strategy, and minimal dividend payments, if any.
- Equity at this stage will be from investors who require a lower return than the venture capitalists who funded the launch stage. This might be through an IPO on a stock exchange, or via a private placement to a group of investors.
- Further investment should be made only if it is expected to generate a return higher than the relevant cost of capital which, for a company with no gearing, is the same as the cost of equity. However, there are some practical difficulties in calculating the cost of equity, either by CAPM or the dividend growth model.
- When further capital is issued, it is important to ensure that the interests of existing shareholders are not prejudiced. One way to do this is by the use of a rights issue, whereby new shares are offered first to the existing shareholders.
- Bonus issues and share splits change the number of shares in issue, but have no impact on the company's cash flows.

Suggested further reading

Any standard finance textbook will cover CAPM and the dividend growth model.

Jacobs, M. T. and Shivdasani, A. (2012), 'Do You Know Your Cost of Capital?', *Harvard Business Review*, July/Aug.

Discusses how companies miscalculate their costs of debt and equity, and their weighted average cost of capital by choosing the wrong parameters to feed into standard models.

Equity Underwriting and Associated Services (2011), Office of Fair Trading.

This research study, commissioned by the UK government, provides a lot of information about secondary public offerings, including rights issues, and the way in which underwriters work. It can be accessed via www.oft.gov.uk/shared_oft/market-studies/OFT1303.pdf

9   Mature companies

Learning objectives

After reading this chapter you should be able to:

1   Explain how the life cycle model relates to a company in the mature stage of its life.
2   Critique the financial strategy adopted by a mature company, making a decision as to which aspects of the life cycle model are relevant to its circumstances, and why.
3   Appreciate the theoretical impact on the share price of changing dividend pay-out ratios.
4   Understand how project finance works, and why projects are mainly debt financed.

Summary of the life cycle model in relation to mature companies

The end of the growth stage is often marked by some very aggressive price competition among rivals who have been left with considerable excess capacity as the anticipated continued sales growth in the industry fails to materialize. Once the industry has stabilized, the maturity stage of high but relatively stable sales at reasonable profit margins can begin. Clearly, the level of business risk has reduced again, as another development phase has now been successfully completed; the company should enter the maturity stage with a good relative market share as a result of its investment in marketing during the growth stage. The remaining critical business risks relate to the duration of this stable, maturity stage and whether the company can maintain its strong market share, on a financially attractive basis, throughout this period.

The strategic emphasis now switches to one of maintaining share and improving efficiency, which can make the transition between growth and maturity quite difficult to manage. However, the reduction in business risk enables the financial risk to be increased through the introduction of debt financing. This is now quite practical because the net cash flow should have turned significantly positive, enabling the debt to be serviced and repaid. The positive cash flow and ability to use debt funding for reinvestment needs are also important to shareholders as they allow the company to pay much higher dividends. Thus the dividend pay-out ratio is increased as a proportion of the now high earnings per share, increasing the absolute dividend payments significantly.

This increased dividend yield is required because the future growth prospects of the business are much lower than in the earlier stages of the life cycle. The lower growth prospects are reflected in a lower P/E ratio. Although shares are given a lower rating by the financial markets, this need not lead to a decline in share prices. Earnings per share should be high, and increasing (although not rapidly) due to efficiency gains, and perhaps volume gains. The resulting high eps offsets the reducing P/E multiples, and the net result should be a much more stable share price, as more of the investors' expected return is now provided through dividend yield rather than the capital gains which dominated the previous stages. These issues are illustrated in Working Insight 9.1.

When the reducing business risk and corresponding reduction in required return are added to the equation, it becomes clear that managing this transition requires some clear communication between the company and its investor base.

The rest of this chapter fleshes out this summary, and discusses various aspects of finance that might be relevant to the mature company, as well as examining project finance, the 'mature start-up'.

Managing the transition to maturity

For executives who have steered a company successfully through its growth phase, it can be difficult to accept that their company's main product will eventually mature and that it should be managed accordingly. Companies often spend large amounts of money searching

---

Working Insight 9.1

Financial strategy parameters

	Mature businesses
Business risk	Medium
Financial risk	Medium
Source of funding	Retained earnings plus debt
Dividend policy	High pay-out ratio
Future growth prospects	Medium to low
Price/earnings multiple	Medium
Current profitability, i.e. eps	High
Share price	Stable in real terms with low volatility

desperately for ways to prolong the earlier high rates of growth, even though the financial justifications for such expenditures become increasingly tenuous.

This inevitability of product maturity should, when it arrives, lead to a significant change in managerial focus. The earlier emphasis on growth, both in the overall market and in the share of that expanding market, should give way to a much greater concentration on profitably maintaining the level of sales which has now been achieved. This means a change in managerial style is desirable because the previous critical success factors are no longer as relevant in a period of much more stable sales volumes. Although many management teams can manage the transition from start-up to growth, relatively few are as successful at moving from the growth stage to the maturity phase of the life cycle. It may therefore become beneficial to make some changes at senior manager level, to facilitate the required changes in managerial style.

Of course, corporate maturity can be staved off for a long time. Although individual products will become mature, the company can extend its life cycle by having a portfolio of products within the business, and bringing in relevant new products so that the business can continue to grow. However, even if sales growth tails off, that might not be an indication of maturity. Having mentioned the problems caused by failing to acknowledge a product's move into the maturity stage, we should also point out that it can be very expensive to assume that a product is mature when in reality it is still growing. A particularly long recession can depress the sales growth of many products to such an extent that companies might regard them as mature, if not already declining. An upturn in the economy can restore the high-growth prospects of many such products, and if the wrong strategy has been implemented, the company could find that it has lost share in what is now once again a rapidly growing market.

Maximizing the long-term value of the business means that the changes required during the transition to maturity must be reflected in its financial strategy. In the initial stages of the life cycle shareholders expect most of their return to be generated from capital gains as the share price increases over time. These capital gains are produced by the company progressively overcoming many of the factors responsible for the very high business risks it faced as a start-up. It is also possible that during the growth stage the company may outperform the market's expectations, due either to the higher growth achieved by the product or to the greater market share gained by the particular company. However, once the maturity stage has been reached, these issues have largely been resolved so that the remaining business risks relate to the length of the maturity stage and the levels of profits and cash flows which can be generated during this relatively stable period. This means that the business risk associated with a mature business is reduced to medium, which implies that investors should be prepared to accept a lower return than in the earlier, higher-risk phases of the life cycle.

Such a lower return will only be accepted if the required change in shareholders' expectations is positively managed by the company.

Adding value through financial strategy

Yet again we must consider the components of the remaining business risk and relate them to the level and type of return which should now be offered to the shareholders.

As a company matures, its level of unique risk normally reduces because the cash flows become much more predictable and stable. The proportionate impact of the systematic risk component of the company therefore becomes greater. The beta factor which drives this level of risk trends towards a value of one, the beta of the markets as a whole.[1] This normalization process is due to the lower growth of the product, which tends to reduce the impact of external environmental changes for companies which had relatively high betas during their growth stages. Conversely, companies with very low betas in the high-growth phase (which are very rare) tend to become more responsive to changes affecting the overall market over time.

The demand for the product has now matured. This stable rate of consumption is more likely to be affected by general changes in the economy, as new users are no longer entering the market in large numbers and existing customers are not increasing their rate of usage.

If these factors can be applied to most mature companies, the base cost of equity capital for all such companies will be in a much smaller range than in the earlier stages of development. This smaller range will also be much closer to the expected return on the stock market as a whole. Thus it is important that the company convinces its shareholders that it does now have a lower-risk profile, and that they should accept this lower rate of return without reducing the share price to restore the actual rate of return to its previously higher levels. One obvious way to communicate this lower-risk profile is for the company to prove it by delivering less volatile financial results from year to year.

Another major way is to start to change the way in which shareholders expect to receive their return. In the earlier stages, their financial return was achieved by capital gains, but this is less possible once the company has matured. Profits will be less volatile but they cannot be expected to continue to grow dramatically; what future growth can be achieved will come mainly as a result of improvements in efficiency rather than large real increases in sales volumes or values. Indeed these improvements in profitability should become the emphasis of the reinvestment made by the business, as there will be few growth projects available to deliver the required returns. Instead of investing heavily in marketing for growth, marketing expenditure at maturity is concentrated on maintaining the existing market share; instead of spending on new fixed assets, reinvesting the current depreciation expense should enable the company to maintain its productive capacity.

This decline in the need to invest in rapid growth comes at a time of high profitability for the business, with the result that the company, for the first time, is a significant net cash producer. Also, these high profits and lack of the earlier tax deferral opportunities (through high levels of capital investment, for example) mean that the company is normally now a taxpayer. This increases the expected present value of any potential tax shield which could be created by the use of debt financing. Also the assets involved in the business are normally now at their maximum tangible value, producing strong, stable cash flows. This reduces the potential costs of any financial distress which might be created by the use of a level of debt financing which could not be serviced or repaid by the company. The positive cash flows being generated by the business on a relatively stable basis reduce the probability that these lower costs of financial distress would be incurred, because it is now much more likely that the company will be able to pay the interest on any borrowing obligations and to make the principal repayments as required.

Thus the inverse correlation between business risk and financial risk is borne out as the reducing business risk can be offset by increasing the financial risk through raising some debt funding. Such a change in the financial strategy from almost exclusively equity financing

---

1   It need not ever reach 1, as the market represents an average of all companies, and some companies and industries are inherently more susceptible to market movements than others.

to incorporating an increasing proportion of debt funding can add considerable value to the shareholders of a maturing company.

The key is for the company to find a useful way of utilizing this newly acquired access to additional sources of funding, which can further increase the value of the company. The management team also has to adjust its style to managing for cash, given the increased riskiness of the financing structure.

Although gearing-up the financial structure is a logical way to proceed in the financial life cycle, many management teams would prefer not to do so, as their job is made more comfortable by having a cushion of equity in a lower-risk business. However, the nature of the financial markets is that a company with an inefficient capital structure often becomes a takeover target, particularly for private equity, as discussed in Chapter 18.

Developing a dividend policy

The most useful application of this additional cash flow is to start to make higher dividend payments. An increasing dividend pay-out ratio serves several purposes including acting as a good signalling device to shareholders that future growth prospects are not as exciting as in the past. In earlier stages of development, future growth provided the dominant element of shareholders' return; now they must accept that it will be replaced by an increasing element of dividend yield, which is supported by an increasing dividend pay-out ratio out of the high, stable post-tax profits. The company can now support, with both profits and cash, a consistently high level of dividends. The reinvestment needs of the business can be met from the lower retention ratio on existing profits supplemented by raising a reasonable proportion of debt funding.

The P/E multiple will reduce as the market reassesses the potential for future growth. However, the increasing level of earnings and dividends should maintain the share price at the high levels achieved at the end of the growth stage, as long as the transition is properly managed. If shareholders are encouraged to keep believing in the growth fairy long after she's flown away, the share price will rise too high on expectations that cannot be realized. Generally, the reaction of stock markets when they realize this error is to overreact in the opposite direction, and the share price can often fall significantly when it becomes clear that the expected growth is not going to be delivered. It is by no means uncommon for a company to become a takeover target during a period of short-term rapid share price collapse caused by badly managing the expectations of the market.

In theory, shareholders should be indifferent as to whether the company pays dividends or reinvests the profits into the business. If the reinvestment is in positive net present value projects, the share price should rise to reflect the expected increased level of future cash flow arising therefrom. However, this assumes that a company can always reinvest its profits at a rate of return which is at least equal to the shareholders' expected return on their investment. During the early stages of the life cycle there are many attractive investment opportunities and a demand for funds to invest. With the arrival of the maturity stage the need for reinvestment reduces significantly just as the availability of finance increases substantially.

This means that the company runs a potential risk of retaining profits for which it has no profitable use, which can lead to a declining overall rate of return for the business. Alternatively, the company can start to invest these funds in other areas in the hope of developing new growth opportunities and new sustainable competitive advantages with which to exploit these growth opportunities. These diversification strategies have already been discussed; at this point it is sufficient to say that they have the potential to destroy shareholder value.

Working Insight 9.2

STAR plc – a growth company

Today's share price of 125p for Solar Technology And Resources plc (STAR) is supported by an expected 1p dividend to be paid out of expected earnings per share of 5p. It is known that shareholders expect future growth to be maintained at 15% p.a., and that the steady state cost of equity for an equivalent company to STAR is 10% p.a. The present dividend policy represents a 20% pay-out policy.

Using Gordon's dividend growth model:

$$K_e = (D_1 \div P) + g$$
$$= (1 \div 125) + 15\%$$
$$= 0.8\% + 15\%$$
$$= 15.8\%$$

Only 0.8% of shareholders' requirement for a 15.8% return is met by the dividend yield; therefore 15% must represent required capital growth.

We can demonstrate in two ways that STAR is seen by the markets as a growth company.

(a) Present Value of Growth Opportunities

At steady state, STAR's P/E ratio would be 1/0.1
  = 10 times

Share price at steady state is 10 × 5p
  = 50p

Current share price is 125p

Therefore, 75p of the current share price represents PVGO: 60% of the price.

(b) Steady State P/E

Current P/E is 125 ÷ 5 = 25 times

Steady state P/E is 10 times

Therefore current P/E is considerably greater than steady state P/E, demonstrating the market's growth expectations.

The way in which dividend policy can enhance shareholder value can best be illustrated by some simplified numerical examples. In Working Insight 9.2 the financial details for STAR plc are given, which indicate that it is currently positioned as a growth company with a relatively low dividend pay-out ratio. It is intended to use Gordon's dividend growth formula (despite its simplifying assumptions, the results in these examples are not misleading and the arithmetic is kept relatively straightforward) to analyse the likely impact on shareholder wealth of possible changes in this dividend policy.

In this example, shareholders expect growth to be maintained at 15 per cent per annum but this expectation is in the knowledge of the current dividend policy of the company. Thus, as shown in Working Insight 9.3, the shareholders are basing their growth expectation on the company achieving a return on reinvestment of 18.75 per cent p.a. in the future. It should be

---

Working Insight 9.3

Relationship of growth and return on reinvestment

The rate of internally funded sustainable organic growth is determined by the retention ratio and the return which is achieved on these reinvested funds; so that

g = retention ratio × return on reinvestment
  = (1 – pay-out ratio) × return on reinvestment (*ROR*)

For STAR this gives

$15\% = (1 - 0.2) \times ROR$

Therefore $ROR = (15\% \div 0.8) = 18.75\%$

---

remembered that, in the absence of any additional information, this expected return on reinvestment may be based on the return on equity being achieved by the company.

An important question is whether this rate of retention is adding to shareholder value, or reducing it. In STAR's case, the expected return on reinvestment (18.75 per cent) is greater than the total return demanded by the shareholder with the current strategy (15.8 per cent). It appears to be logical for the company to retain this level of its current profit provided that the directors believe it can achieve 18.75 per cent return on reinvestment.

However, it may be possible to improve this position by changing the dividend pay-out ratio. This can most easily be illustrated by considering the position if a nil pay-out ratio or a 100 per cent pay-out ratio were adopted. (These extremes each make one element in the formula equal to zero; they are therefore used for arithmetic clarity rather than to advocate that companies should adopt one or other extreme position.)

If the company were to switch to a nil pay-out policy, a rational investor would expect the future rate of growth to increase in order to compensate for forgoing the immediate dividend income.

Theoretically the company should be able to reinvest the additional retained profit at the same rate of return but, in the real world, companies do not have an infinite supply of equally attractive investment projects. Most capital investment budgeting processes select the most attractive projects first and so it is normal to find a law of diminishing returns applying when a company is given an increase in its capital expenditure levels, causing a minor reduction in the average rate of return on the reinvestment. (However, occasionally an increase in available expenditure actually results in an increase in the average rate of return because it enables the company to undertake a particularly attractive project which had previously been rejected due to lack of available funding.)[2] Provided that the rate of return of each project exceeds the cost of capital, value will be created despite the average return falling.

---

2 In theory, of course, this could not occur because the company should raise new funding in order to undertake all projects which generate an expected return in excess of the company's cost of capital.

Working Insight 9.4

STAR plc – 100 per cent retention ratio

g = retention ratio × return on reinvestment

If no dividends are paid, the retention ratio is 100 per cent

$$g = 100\% \times ROR$$
$$= 100\% \times 18.75\%$$
$$= 18.75\%$$

Therefore, using Gordon's dividend growth model:

$$K_e = 0 + 18.75\%$$
$$= 18.75\%$$

This represents an increase in expected return by shareholders, which was 15.8%. This would only be logical if they were to perceive an increased risk due to this change in financial strategy. Otherwise, the share price should increase to reduce the return to the normal level of expected returns. With a 100% retention ratio this cannot be reflected in this simplified formula.

For simplicity, an assumption has been made in these examples that the return on reinvestment is unchanged with the movements in dividend policy.

As can be seen in Working Insight 9.4, the 100 per cent retention ratio mathematically leads to an increase in the expected growth rate which more than offsets the lack of dividend, thus apparently increasing the shareholders' return. However, if there is no change in risk profile, the shareholders' required return should not increase, and so a share price rise is more likely, to keep the expected return at its previous level of 15.8 per cent.

Changes in required rates of return are caused by changes in perceptions of risk. So the question to ask is: does changing the dividend pay-out ratio affect shareholders' risk perceptions? Theory may at first appear to indicate that this should not be so because if shareholders are indifferent between dividends and capital growth they should not demand different levels of return if the mix provided by any company changes. However, a high retention rate is only logical for a growth-orientated company and the risk profile of such companies is higher than for similar but more mature businesses. Hence, it could be argued that an increase in the retention rate should indicate higher future growth expectations and the greater volatility associated with higher growth may increase the risk perception of investors.

Looked at another way, the shareholders might be more worried about a company which keeps the vast majority of its current profits when compared with one which pays a much higher proportion of these profits out as current dividends. With a high retention policy, shareholders are not only backing the continued success of the current business strategy but are also trusting that the company's managers can identify and successfully implement financially attractive new investment projects. Clearly this is less worrying (i.e. less risky) if the new investments are closely related to the existing successful areas of operation of the company.

In Chapter 13 we discuss again the issues surrounding companies' dividend policies, and the use of share buy-backs to supplement those dividend policies: buy-backs can be used by maturing companies to re-gear themselves, taking on a capital structure that more appropriately reflects the new stage in their life cycle. There, we will also discuss the apparent preference of investors for dividends rather than capital growth. This is sometimes known as the 'bird in hand' theory, after the British folk-saying 'A bird in the hand is worth two in the bush'.

The other extreme dividend policy for STAR is to pay out all of its current profits as dividends. As shown in Working Insight 9.5, this means that no future growth should be expected. Therefore all the return to shareholders comes through dividend yield, and earnings are likely to stay at their current level. This potentially places the company in a steady state position, as discussed in Chapter 2, and the expected steady state return for shareholders in STAR was already given in Working Insight 9.2 as being 10 per cent. If this is the new rate of return expected by shareholders (reflecting their reduced perception of risk due to the higher dividend pay-out policy as discussed above), this can only be achieved by a fall in the share price to 50p.

Such a dramatic potential fall should not be surprising for a high-growth company because, as noted in Working Insight 9.2, 60 per cent of the current share price represents the present value of the future growth opportunities. If the company were to change its dividend policy to a 100 per cent pay-out ratio, these future growth opportunities would disappear, as would their present value component of the current share price. Thus this reduced potential share price of 50p for STAR represents the present value of the current earnings stream,

---

Working Insight 9.5

Impact of a 100% dividend pay-out policy in a growth company

If all current profits are paid out as dividends, the future growth expectation must be zero, i.e.

g = retention ratio × return on reinvestment
  = (1 − pay-out ratio) × return on reinvestment
  = (1 − 1) × ROR
  = 0

For STAR plc the maximum sustainable dividend payment is 5p (i.e. the current eps). If the share price stays at 125p, the shareholder's return is reduced to

$Ke = 5 \div 125 + 0 = 4\%$

Shareholders previously wanted a return of 15.8 per cent. However, the company can now be regarded as having moved to a steady-state position (100 per cent pay-out policy) and, as per Working insight 9.2, investors should now expect a 10 per cent return. This can only be achieved by a reduction in share price, thus

$10\% = 5p \div P_1 + 0$

Therefore

$P_1 = 5 \div 0.1 = 50p$ (a reduction of 75p, or 60%)

where P_1 is the share price after announcing the change in dividend policy.

without taking into account the future growth opportunities. In practice the stock market makes this adjustment to the share prices of high-growth companies which, for whatever reason, are now not expected to produce the previously anticipated growth, irrespective of whether the company acknowledges the change by increasing its dividend pay-out ratio.

This illustration of the impact of changes in dividend policy for a high-growth company can be contrasted with the impacts on a declining business, as shown in Working Insight 9.6. The expected return on equity for DOG Inc. is now dominated by the dividend yield component, which is not surprising considering the 75 per cent pay-out ratio. However, the shareholders are assuming, in their expected growth rate of 2 per cent p.a., that the company's return on reinvestment is only 8 per cent p.a. This is considerably below their required rate of return of 11 per cent, thus giving the impression that the company is destroying shareholder value by retaining even 25 per cent of current profits. If this is so the share price should rise in response to a further increase in the dividend pay-out ratio. The potential impact of a move to a 100 per cent pay-out ratio is shown in Working Insight 9.7, which indicates a likely rise in share price as the destruction of shareholder value is reversed.

It would be logical to expect that an increase in the retention ratio of this company would lead to a significant decline in share price, and the effect of increasing the retention ratio to 50 per cent is shown in Working Insight 9.8. The low return on reinvestment means that the growth component is still very low, so that the dividend yield has to be high to compensate. This will only be achieved if the share price falls, as this automatically increases the dividend yield for any given dividend payment. The required reduction in share price signals the greater level of shareholder wealth which is being destroyed by the application of such an inappropriate financial strategy.

These illustrations indicate the importance of the dividend policy during the maturity stage, which is the bridge between high growth and decline for the business. The company should leave the growth stage with a low dividend pay-out ratio but should enter the decline stage with a 100 per cent pay-out ratio, or very nearly that level. The rate of transition is governed by the financially attractive reinvestment opportunities available to the company.

Working Insight 9.6

DOG Inc. – a declining business

Dear Old Geriatrics Inc. has a share price of 100p. The company is expected to pay a dividend of 9p per share out of earnings per share of 12p. Shareholders only expect annual growth of 2%.
Using Gordon's dividend growth model gives:

$$Ke = (D_1 \div P) + g$$
$$= (9p \div 100p) + 2\%$$
$$= 11\%$$

But
$$g = \text{retention ratio} \times \text{return on reinvestment}$$
$$2\% = 0.25 \times ROR$$

i.e.
$$\text{return on reinvestment} = 2\% \div 0.25 = 8\%$$

Working Insight 9.7

Switch to a 100% pay-out ratio in a declining business

If all current profits are paid out, $g = 0$ under Gordon's model. Thus, if the share price is unchanged

$$Ke = (D_1 \div P) + 0$$
$$Ke = (12p \div 100p) + 0 = 12\%$$

However, shareholders only required 11% rate of return when 25% of profits were being reinvested. If their risk perception has been reduced due to the higher pay-out ratio, the required rate of return should also reduce rather than increase. If we were to assume that the expected return stays the same, this would give:

$$P_1 = D_1 \div Ke = 12 \div 11\% = 109p$$

where P_1 is the share price after announcing the change in dividend policy.

(The logic of maintaining the previous cost of equity capital is that DOG Inc. has been categorized as a declining business, and therefore dividends will not be expected to be maintained at this same level forever; growth will actually be negative in the future.)

Working Insight 9.8

Increasing the retention ratio in a declining business

The expected return on reinvestment is assumed to be maintained at 8%. If the retention ratio is increased to 50 per cent, the expected dividend payment reduces to 6p. If we assume that shareholders' required return remains at 11%, this gives:

$$Ke = D_1 \div P_1 + \text{growth}$$
$$= D_1 \div P_1 + (\text{retention ratio x return on reinvestment})$$

i.e.

$$11\% = 6 \div P_1 + (0.5 \times 8\%)$$
$$= 6 \div P_1 + 4\%$$

where P_1 is the share price after the announcement of the change in dividend policy.

$$P_1 = 6 \div 7\%$$
$$= 85.7p$$

This represents a decline in the share price of about 14% due to retaining profits in a declining business to earn less than the cost of capital.

Project finance: the mature start-up

While discussing companies in the mature stage of the life cycle, it is appropriate to mention project finance – for example, the financing of infrastructure projects such as roads, bridges, or power plants. Technically, these are start-ups, in that an asset and stream of income are being created which did not exist before. Therefore, if the life cycle model were being followed blindly, with no regard to the principles behind it, one should expect equity financing. In fact, project finance is done, quite properly, through debt instruments.

Project finance is the long-term financing of capital-intensive projects that are self-contained in that the project cash flows are used to pay all the investors; there is no recourse to the rest of the business because they are set up in SPVs (special purpose vehicles) for this single purpose. There will be a small number of project sponsors who provide the equity, and a consortium of banks providing a significant amount of debt, in several different tranches which will be paid down at different times over the project life, customized to suit the particular project's cash flows. The debt is generally more expensive than it would be for a 'normal' company, reflecting the fact that there is no recourse to an underlying business with a separate stream of income. The debt is normally raised in loans rather than as bonds on a market, and strong covenants will be in place to protect the senior debt.

Project finance is governed by a series of contracts – often hundreds of contracts – between the various parties, who include, quite apart from the equity and the debt syndicates, construction companies, suppliers, and the purchasing organization.

Working Insight 9.9 sets out generically the key characteristics of project finance that set it apart from normal start-ups and make debt finance appropriate.

Working Insight 9.9

Project finance: a very different type of start-up

	Start-up	*Project finance*
Business risk	Very high, as the product, market and management team are all unknowns.	High during the construction stage, but low once the project is up and running. Risks are managed down, either through contracts or by specialist insurance. Extensive due diligence is carried out before the project is funded.
Cash flows	Negative in the launch stage, and continue to be negative in the growth stage due to working capital and capital expenditure.	Negative in the construction phase, but positive thereafter.
Future operations	Uncertain, as the market trajectory is not known.	A reasonable level of predictability. Projects often have a fixed life, and sometimes have a guaranteed minimum level of income.

Case Study 9.1

Project finance: the wind farm

A financing on which your author worked was building a wind farm on an empty site in Wales. A licence had been obtained under the UK government's Non Fossil Fuel Obligation, whereby the government was trying to reduce dependence on carbon-generating fuels. The licence gave the right, for a period of over twenty years, to sell into the National Grid all electricity generated by the wind farm at a price well in excess of the normal price for electricity, index-linked to inflation. So, the project involved raising the money, building the wind farm, and operating it for the full period of the licence.

Although logistically this was a complex task to coordinate and manage, in financing terms it was quite low risk. The manufacturer of the turbines was under contract to complete the build on time, or to pay liquidated damages, so the construction risk was mitigated. The manufacturer had also guaranteed a certain level of efficiency of the turbines, which meant that the likely level of electricity generation was known. The government had agreed to buy all that was produced, and the price was known, so there was little sales risk. And the contracts to maintain the turbines had been agreed several years in advance, so that too was a known cost. The project had been put together in such a way that the only risk that was being taken was whether or not the wind would blow in Wales!

The cash flow profile of the project was that it would be heavily cash-negative in the first year, during the construction phase, and then would be cash generative thereafter. Thus, only a small amount of the finance was in the form of equity. Most of the money was put in as debt of varying types, so that the debt could be repaid once the wind farm was up and running. A distribution policy was devised, included in the legal agreement between all of the parties, which provided for the majority of the cash flow to be paid out, with minimal retention as there was no prospect of growth in this business.

Case Study 9.1 gives an example of a relatively small project, to show how the risk profile differs from a normal business opportunity.

In the UK, the government has used the Private Finance Initiative to contract out to private sector businesses the building and running of public services such as hospitals, schools, etc. Such investment opportunities have many of the characteristics of project finance: there is an element of risk during the construction phase, but then the risk diminishes and a utility-type return should be available. Operators who understand this have increased their returns from these projects by charging the government a high rate for finance, reflecting the initial riskiness of the project, but then refinancing it themselves with much cheaper debt once the asset is up and running.

Key messages

- As companies approach maturity, the level of business risk reduces and so it is appropriate to take on more financial risk: debt should increase. Also, with fewer growth opportunities, the dividend pay-out should also increase.
- Investors' return in this stage comes more from dividends and less from expected capital growth.
- As a company increases its dividend pay-out, the theoretical cost of equity and expected share price can be recalculated.

- The nature of project finance means that start-up infrastructure projects are often, correctly, financed as mature businesses once the initial construction phase is complete.

Suggested further reading

Lartey, R. (2012), *The Essential Elements of and Issues in Project Finance*, available at http://ssrn.com/abstract=2027511
   Sets out the key characteristics of project finance, distinguishing it from corporate finance.

10 Declining businesses

A case for euthanasia?

Learning objectives

After reading this chapter you should be able to:

1   Explain how the life cycle model relates to a company in the decline stage of its life.
2   Evaluate a deep discount rights issue.
3   Calculate the theoretical financial impact on an over-geared company of raising new equity.

Summary: applying the overall model to declining companies

Unfortunately, the strong positive cash generation of the maturity stage cannot continue forever, and demand for the product will eventually start to die away. As demand fades, cash inflows fall. Once sales start to decline irreversibly, it is no longer sensible to maintain previous levels of spending on marketing activity. Reducing this spending means that net cash inflows can be maintained during the early stages of decline.

Despite this move to decline and the inevitable ultimate death of the product, the associated business risk should be regarded as still reducing from its level in the previous maturity stage. Yet another of the original unknowns, i.e. the length of the maturity stage, has now been resolved and the only major remaining risk is for how long will it make economic sense to allow the business to continue.

This low business risk should be complemented by a relatively high financial risk source of funding. This can be achieved by a combination of a high dividend pay-out policy and the utilization of debt finance. The reinvestment strategy in a dying business is likely to be low,

Working Insight 10.1

Financial strategy parameters

Declining businesses

Business risk	Low
Financial risk	High
Source of funding	Debt
Dividend policy	Total pay-out ratio
Future growth prospects	Negative
Price/earnings multiple	Low
Current profitability, i.e. eps	Low and declining
Share price	Declining and increasing in volatility

because the future growth prospects are now negative, and this implies a high dividend pay-out policy. Indeed dividends paid during this stage can exceed post-tax profits if there is inadequate financial justification to reinvest depreciation. (Reinvesting depreciation is a normal way of maintaining the scale of the existing business but this may not be logical during the decline stage.) Consequently dividends may equal the total of profits and depreciation, in which case it should be clear that part of the dividend payment really represents a repayment of capital.

This indicates how debt financing can be introduced into a declining business. Although assets may not be replaced as they are fully used up, some funds are inevitably tied up in the business during this period. If these funds are provided by equity investors, they will require a risk-adjusted return on this investment. However, the cost of debt is lower than the cost of equity, so a refinancing operation may enable some of these equity funds to be released by the company prior to its eventual liquidation. Lenders to the company will not want to take on an equity risk for a debt-based return, but they should be willing to lend against the ultimate realizable value of the assets which are locking up shareholders' equity. These borrowings can be paid to shareholders by way of dividend or share repurchase, and again clearly represent a repayment of capital.

The negative growth prospects translate into a low price/earnings multiple for the shares which, when allied with the declining trend in earnings per share, results in a declining share price. However, as long as the shareholders are aware that part of their high dividend payments are effectively repayments of capital, this declining value should not cause undue concern. These issues are illustrated in Working Insight 10.1.

The final financial strategy

The decline stage of the life cycle should not be regarded as a depressing end. It is a chance to review financial strategy and to make appropriate changes to the business as the company moves from maturity through to decline. For example, an analytical review of the cost structure of the business will be needed.

In the launch stage the very high business risk indicated that, as far as possible, costs should be kept variable and long-term financial commitments should be avoided. The high investment requirements of the growth stage usually lead to an increase in the fixed cost base, but the high business risk still means that the proportion of fixed costs should be carefully monitored. It is only when the greater stability of the maturity stage is reached that the business can accept the increased risk associated with a high level of fixed cost. The resulting efficiency gains are important to the continued improvement in operating performance.

When sales volumes start to decline, such a high level of fixed costs would quickly move the company into a loss-making position. Therefore it is important that the proportion of fixed costs is reduced, for example, by renewing contracts on a short-term or completely variable basis. This represents a reversal of the trend through the earlier stages of the life cycle, and is advocated in spite of the continuing reduction in the business risk profile. It reflects the need to use a much shorter-term timescale for financially evaluating all decisions during this stage.

The major risk associated with a declining business is that sudden relatively small changes in the external business environment can make the business uneconomic, so that immediate closure is forced. If major costs are still of a fixed nature or if new expenditures have been justified over a long future period of continued benefits, the financial impact of such a sudden forced closure can be extremely adverse. The company can effectively hedge itself from some of these adverse consequences by focusing on short-term financial impacts, for example, by adopting financial payback as a means of justifying expenditures rather than using discounted cash flow techniques.

A similar logic can be used in assessing the economic performance of the business during the decline stage. Return on Investment is the most common accounting technique used by companies for assessing business performance. This compares some measure of periodic profit with the investment required to achieve that profit. Depreciation is normally charged as an expense in calculating the profit; this assumes that the business intends to maintain its asset base by reinvesting the depreciation expense. Once the company moves into decline this may not be a valid assumption. Furthermore, the reducing scale of activity may enable the company to reduce the funds tied up in working capital. This means that the available cash generated from the business may exceed the operating cash flows.

If this increased cash balance is not required by the business, it should be paid out to shareholders: as illustrated in Chapter 9, the potential return on reinvestment in a declining business is often below the shareholders' required rate of return. This creates a high dividend pay-out ratio which will often exceed 100 per cent, highlighting that part of these dividends are really repayments of capital. As a result, shareholders should not be unduly concerned with a declining share price – as long as they are being compensated with a sufficiently high dividend yield.

This part of the financial strategy is dictated by the declining opportunities for financially attractive reinvestments in the business. However, the reducing business risk has led to the overall financial strategy model advocating that the debt funding ratio should be increased during this stage.

We know that debt is cheaper than equity because of the lower risk to the investor. Two other factors are relevant – the advantage of the tax shield, and the downside of the costs and likelihood of financial distress. Choosing to use debt means balancing out these offsetting factors. Thus in a mature business, it is possible to add value through borrowing because the positive impact of the tax shield normally outweighs the much smaller adverse consequences of potential financial distress. However, the declining business will eventually be less likely to pay corporation taxes due to its reducing profit streams, so that the value of the tax shield will ultimately fall.

On the other hand, the nature of corporation tax systems could change this. In most major economies, corporation taxes are affected by factors other than pure accounting profits. For

---

Working Insight 10.2

Adding value by borrowing in a declining company

The terminal value of a particular asset is £100,000 and the company is expected to continue operating for another five years. The shareholders' after-tax expected return on equity is 10% p.a. but the company can borrow at an after tax rate of 6% p.a.

The present value to the shareholders of the expected terminal value of the asset is

$$£100,000 \div (1.10)^5$$
$$\text{or } £62,092$$

However, if the company were to borrow funds against this terminal value at 6% it could obtain £74,726 now, which could be distributed to its shareholders.

In practice, the lender would want to maintain some buffer to allow for fluctuations in the actual terminal value or date of realization: but there is still an opportunity for significant shareholder value creation.

---

instance, many governments allow companies to claim accelerated depreciation allowances for tax purposes, which create differences between taxable profits and accounting profits. Other regimes have given allowances for additional capital invested in inventories. These fiscal adjustments are normally given as incentives for companies to invest, so they are geared to reduce tax liabilities while the company is growing. It is an inevitable consequence that these adjustments therefore tend to increase tax payments when a company is running down its investment base. Thus declining companies often face a higher effective rate of tax on their profits which can actually increase the value of a tax shield.

Declining companies do not need to use much funding for reinvestment since, as we have established, they are reducing the net value of their asset base. This debt-carrying capacity can therefore be used to produce cash which is paid out to shareholders sooner rather than later. This is achieved by borrowing against the terminal realizable value of the assets locked into the company. If this capital were not realized now, the shareholders would receive a final capital distribution when the company was eventually wound up. By borrowing against these assets now, it should be possible to increase the present value of the related distribution which can be paid to shareholders using the logic that the cost of debt is always lower than the cost of equity (particularly if a tax shield exists). This is mathematically illustrated in Working Insight 10.2.

The debt funding for a declining business is therefore focused on realizable values of assets and this dramatically reduces the costs associated with future financial distress. Indeed the structuring of the borrowings will be designed to make it easy for lenders to take possession of and realize the value of their security when the business no longer has an economically viable use for these assets. Consequently the use of a high level of debt funding in a declining business is not really contradictory to the theory, as long as the theory is sensibly applied.

Alternative business strategies to delay or avoid death

If the appropriate financial strategy is adopted by the company, the decline stage of the life cycle and the ultimate liquidation of the company are not necessarily injurious to shareholder wealth. However, these events are not normally looked at as neutral or non-threatening by the managers involved in the company. The final phase of the life cycle represents one of the most severe challenges to the concept of agency theory, because it may appear essential to the managers that ways must be found to avoid the final act of winding up the company, even though continuing may not be in the best interests of shareholders.[1]

There are many alternative strategies employed by businesses to try to delay or avoid their inevitable deaths, only some of which can be beneficial to the shareholders. One obvious approach is to diversify into other areas but, if the diversification is left until the core business has moved into its decline stage, it will be very difficult for the company to finance the diversification from a declining cash flow. (The potential lack of shareholder wealth creation from diversification has already been considered.)

Perhaps a more attractive course of action is to examine the main reasons why the company is now in decline. Referring back to the original Boston matrix, it is clear that a major difference between a cash cow and a dog is the lower market share held by the dog company. This may indicate a possible strategy for adding value to the business, particularly if it is expected that the decline stage may itself last a long while. If there are a large number of small companies in this market, they all face a slow, lingering, painful unproductive death. However, one of the companies could decide to change the dynamics of the industry by acquiring several of its small competitors. The cost of these acquisitions should not be too great, as the companies will be making poor current financial returns and be expecting things to get worse in the future. It is possible that a very small premium over the realizable asset value of each business may secure its purchase.

Once the company has achieved a much more dominant market share, it may be able to improve its overall financial return quite significantly. This could be done simply by rationalizing the total capacity of their group so as to remove capacity from the industry, if this is depressing selling prices. Alternatively the greater market share can be used to change the dynamics of the relative bargaining power with both customers and suppliers; thus increasing the share of the value chain gained by this company. In many cases, the end result is that the company discovers that the industry was not really in decline at all; the companies in the industry were in decline due to the disastrous industry dynamics which had been allowed to develop. Thus, as shown in Figure 10.1, the many small businesses are turned back into the single large cash cow.

If this type of rationalization strategy is successful, it is an example of the synergy benefits of acquisitions which are discussed later in the book.

Deep discount rights issues

Any attempt to rationalize a very mature or declining industry by a series of acquisitions requires finance to be raised. A logical alternative would be to raise at least some debt, since debt financing is attractive at this latter end of the life cycle. However, some equity funding may be considered appropriate and this could be raised via a rights issue to the existing shareholders. (It is most unlikely that the shareholders of the target companies would find anything other than a full cash offer for their existing shares to be at all attractive; they want to get out of the industry sooner rather than later.) In Chapter 8 the impact of doing a narrow

---

1   The wider stakeholder population, which includes employees and suppliers, would also prefer to see the company continue in business.

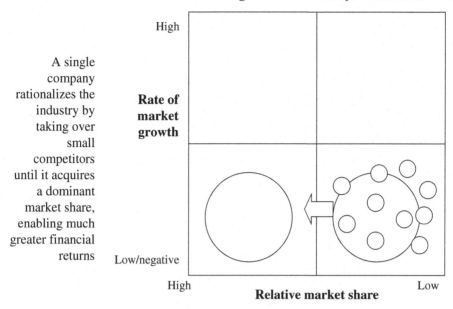

Figure 10.1 Declining industry transformation strategies (using Boston matrix).

discount rights issue was evaluated and here a similar illustration is used to highlight how a deep discount rights issue works.

The example given in Working Insight 10.3 shows a company trying to raise substantial funds which it intends to use to repay some of its excessive outstanding debt. The suggested means of raising new equity is to sell it at a big discount to the existing share price, i.e. a deep discount rights issue. The deep discount simply means that more shares have to be issued to achieve any given fundraising objectives. Thus in this example the company has to offer a two for one rights issue (i.e. issuing two new shares for each share held) at a price of 25p. Had the rights exercise price been set at 50p, a one for one rights issue would have been sufficient; at 100p, the £250 million could have been raised by selling only 250 million new shares. Remember that any extra shares over this minimum 250 million should therefore be regarded as bonus shares.

As discussed in Chapter 8, this means that the terms of the rights issue should not matter, as they cannot make any theoretical difference to the value of the company. However, companies and their advisers obviously believe pricing of rights issues is important, because otherwise they would not spend so much time and money deciding how best to attract investors to subscribe new money.

A large risk associated with a narrow discount rights issue is that the rights-inclusive share price could fall below the exercise price of the rights during the rights offer period. This risk could be hedged, but these underwriting costs were described in the earlier chapter as 'inefficiently high'. If the scale of the discount were increased, there might be a lower perceived risk of the rights having no value. In Working Insight 10.3, the current share price of £1 is predicted to fall to 50p because of the deep discount offered and the consequent number of new shares which have to be issued. However, the rights are being offered at an exercise price of 25p so that the market price would have to halve again before the rights had no value. The company may decide not to underwrite the issue or, if underwriting is taken up, the premium charged should be significantly reduced as the risk of the effective put option being exercised by the company is now lower.

Working Insight 10.3

Deep discount rights issues

Death Or Glory plc wants to raise some new equity funding in order to repay some of its existing debt financing. At present it has 500m issued shares trading at £1 each, giving the company a market capitalization of £500m. This market capitalization supports an existing debt level of £1 billion, giving a debt to market equity of 2:1 which is considered too high. If £250m of new equity could be raised, this debt to equity could be reduced to 1:1 as long as the new funding were used to repay or offset some of the outstanding debt.

The company's advisers have suggested a rights issue of two for one at 25p per share which would raise £250m, excluding costs. The impact of the proposed rights issue can be seen as

500m issued shares @ £1	⇒	£500m market capitalization
1,000m new shares @ 25p	⇒	£250m rights issue
1,500m total shares ⇒50p	⇒	£750m new capitalization

The rights value would be 25p per share (exercise price of 25p compared to market price at 50p), so that the gain of 25p × 2 rights = 50p compensates for the loss on each existing share of 100p – 50p = 50p, i.e. the two for one rights issue results in no gain and no loss if the share price responds properly.

(At least, it would be lower if investors behaved totally rationally but there is a great deal of psychology in pricing rights issues. If the market believes that successful growth companies raise new equity through narrow discount rights issues, it tends to accept that a company offering a narrow discount rights issue is successful and has good growth potential. Conversely, if deep discount rights issues are normally made by very mature or declining companies with negative growth prospects, the market might assume that any company making such an issue must have those attributes.)

A key issue is how investors will respond to such an offer. Investors owning 1,000 shares in DOG plc receive their notifications of their rights to buy another 2,000 shares in the company at the very reduced price of 25p per share. Even if they like the deep discount, taking up the offer requires them to invest another 50 per cent (£500) on top of the current value of their investment in DOG (£1,000). This is a high proportionate increase in investment in one company and for a rational investor it might unbalance their investment portfolio. Other investors may be feeling unhappy about their investment in the company, because, in this example, it is over-leveraged and has no positive growth prospects.

There is a strong possibility that many investors may not want to take up their rights. This possibility is increased when the alternative of selling the rights and obtaining cash is added in. Instead of investing an additional £500, the investor with 1,000 shares should be able to sell the associated 2,000 rights and receive £500 in cash. Of course if the market responds properly, there is no resulting change in value from either course of action but the perception of investors may be different.

If a lot of investors decide to sell their rights, the law of supply and demand means that the rights value will fall. The rights exercise price is fixed so that, if the rights value falls, the share price must also fall by a considerable amount. The decline in share prices closes the gap between it and the rights exercise price, thus making the rights offer look even less attractive than before. Deep discount rights offers have been known to fail when investors simply lost confidence in the company and its shares; not least because the company was offering lots of new shares at 25p when they are supposed to be worth £1. The danger is that investors start to believe that the £1 share price was wrong and that 25p is a better reflection of the true value of all the shares.

Deep discount rights issues are also used in company restructuring, as discussed in Chapter 17.

Adding value by reducing debt ratios

Death Or Glory plc is actually raising these new equity funds in order to increase shareholder value by reducing its debt-to-equity ratio. How this can work is illustrated in Working Insights 10.4 and 10.5, which indicate the way in which excessive risk perceptions lead to greater demands for returns, which can drive down investment values.

Normally an increase in the proportion of equity funding would lead to an increase in the weighted average cost of capital (WACC), because the cost of equity is greater than the cost of debt. However, if the existing funding mix contains substantial risk premiums which can be reduced or removed by a change in financial strategy, the overall WACC can actually reduce after the injection of new funding. This would obviously lead to an increase in equity value as discussed in Appendix 1 and highlighted in Working Insight 10.5.

Working Insight 10.4

Reducing risk perceptions and adding value

Death Or Glory plc currently has to pay a premium interest rate of 10% before tax (compared to the normal rate for similar companies of 8%) due to its high debt-to-equity ratio. Its shareholders' required return is also higher, due to increased perceptions of the risk of financial collapse: thus DOG's cost of equity capital is 16% compared to the 12% demanded from similar companies with normal leverage ratios.

Extracts from DOG's financial data are as follows:

	£m	
Operating profit	250	
Less: interest expense	100	(£1 bn @ 10%)
Profit before tax	150	
Taxation	50	
Profit after tax	100	
Number of shares	500m	
Earnings per share	20p	
P/E multiple	5 times	
Share price	100p	

Note: A P/E multiple of five is applied, as this is slightly below the inverse of the company's cost of equity capital (16%). This reflects the fact that (a) the company is declining rather than at steady state, and (b) there is a risk premium due to the over-gearing.

Working Insight 10.5

Post-rights issue position

If DOG raises £250m through a rights issue it will be able to reduce both its borrowing cost and its cost of equity. However, the relative proportion of equity in its financial structure will rise, as the new funds are used to repay some of the existing debt. Assuming nothing else changes, the post-rights P&L can be restated as follows.

	£m	
Operating profit	250.0	
Less: interest expense	60.0	(£750 m @ 8%)
Profit before tax	190.0	
Taxation	63.3	
Profit after tax	126.7	
Number of shares	1,500m	(1 bn new shares issued)
Earnings per share	8.45p	
P/E multiple	6.7 times	
Share price	56.6p	

The company's cost of equity has decreased to 12 % due to the lower perceived risk of financial collapse. However, as a declining company, the P/E will still be lower than the inverse of the cost of equity. In Working Insight 10.4 we reduced the 'steady state' P/E of 6.25 by 20% to arrive at 5; here we reduce the 'steady state' P/E of 8.3 by a similar proportion, to 6.7 times. In practice, the P/E may be slightly higher than this, reflecting a re-rating by the market.

If the stock market saw no value added from DOG's rights issue, the post-rights share price should fall from 100p to 50p as shown in Working Insight 10.3. However, the reductions in both borrowing costs and shareholders' expected returns mean that the share price should move to 56.6p rather than to 50p; thus producing increased value for the existing shareholders due to the reduction in risk premium demanded.

Key messages

- No further investment should be made in declining businesses, so the cash flows will be neutral or positive. The low business risk means that funding should be through debt. Dividend pay-out should be the maximum possible, constrained only by the availability of retained profits or cash generation.
- If the company has taken on too much debt, value can be created by reducing the level of gearing.
- Raising equity for an over-geared company can reduce its WACC, as the resulting lower risk reduces the costs of both debt and equity.

Suggested further reading

Equity Underwriting and Associated Services (2011), Office of Fair Trading.
   This research study, commissioned by the UK government, provides a lot of information about secondary public offerings, including deep discount rights issues. It can be accessed via www.oft.gov. uk/shared_oft/market-studies/OFT1303.pdf

Part 3

Financial instruments

11 Financial instruments
The building blocks

Learning objectives

After reading this chapter you should be able to:

1   Explain the fundamental characteristics of debt and equity.
2   Identify and contrast the different risk-reduction mechanisms used by investors and lenders.
3   Analyse a financial instrument to determine the yield, upside, and risk-reduction mechanisms it adopts.
4   Understand the basics of interest rate management tools.

Introduction

Investors need to make a return on their money. That return can come from a yield or a capital gain, or both. The amount of return they require depends on the level of risk that they perceive they are taking. Within this simple framework there is a vast panoply of financial instruments that can be created to serve the different needs of companies and their investors.

Throughout this book we have been talking about debt and equity. Now is the time to define our terms more carefully. What do we mean by 'debt', and how do we differentiate it from 'equity'? In this chapter we will answer those questions, and explain the building blocks used to create all financial instruments, showing how the distinctions between 'debt' and 'equity' become blurred as different instruments are designed. Chapter 12 will describe some of the more common financial instruments, and discuss how and why they are used.

Risk and return

It is worth noting that the risk–return continuum provides an overall regulation of what we can do with financial instruments.

For example, if we lend money to a blue-chip company (invest in its debt) the company is contracted to pay us a fixed level of interest at agreed intervals, and to return our money when the debt falls due for repayment. Should the company fail to do this we will have redress to the law, and perhaps have security[1] over its assets; lending to such a company is a relatively low-risk activity, and thus we should only expect a relatively low return.

Contrast this with the situation were we to invest in the ordinary shares of the same company. As shareholders we may or may not be paid a dividend, depending on the company's results and the directors' intentions. We may, if the company succeeds in the stock markets, be able to sell the shares for a huge capital gain at some point in the future; but there is no guarantee of this – the company might fail, and we could lose everything in a liquidation.

So, whereas we can reasonably anticipate the returns that we will obtain on the debt investment, there is huge volatility in the expected return from an investment in shares. That volatility of anticipated return is the risk we take, and it is for this that we need to be compensated. Whatever rate debt pays us, we will demand a much higher return from our shares, as illustrated in Figure 11.1.

As discussed in Chapter 1, it is also worth noting that individual investors perceive risk in different ways, and thus demand different levels of return for what is technically the same amount of risk. Your author has a very low-risk threshold for personal investment, preferring the certainty of a secure retirement to the possible glory of earning millions on speculative investment. This risk–required return profile looks like that shown in Figure 11.2.

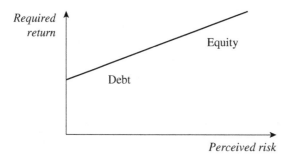

Figure 11.1 The relationship between risk and return.

---

1   The term 'security' has two separate meanings. 'Securities' is a generic term for financial instruments. The term is also used to refer to a mechanism which gives the investors some further means through which they can be repaid if the company defaults, for example, the ability to repossess assets.

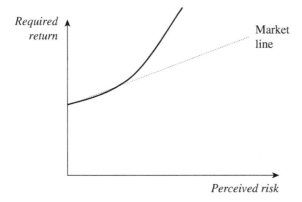

Figure 11.2 The risk-averse investor.

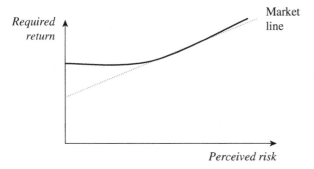

Figure 11.3 The speculative investor.

However, a venture capitalist may see the risk–return spectrum in an entirely different way. Such an investor is really not interested in low-risk investments, as their whole *raison d'être* is in making high gains on more speculative investments. Their risk profile looks more like that shown in Figure 11.3.

Knowing that the market includes investors with different appetites for risk, a company can design its financial instruments to suit a particular class of investor. In the next section, we discuss the parameters within which this can take place.

The building blocks of a financial instrument

The return investors require depends on their perception of the risk inherent in the investment. That return will comprise some combination of yield and the upside which comes normally from a capital gain. Thus, the three building blocks we can manipulate are:

- Risk
- Yield
- Upside.

Each of these is now considered in turn.

Risk

In order to reduce the return that the company has to pay, the risk to the investor has to be managed down. This can be done in several ways: giving the investor a way out; providing security to the investor; providing guarantees, often from a third party; and using restrictive clauses known as covenants.

1. *Giving the investor a way out:* If a company guarantees to redeem a financial instrument, the investor is taking less risk than if their ultimate repayment is to come from a sale of the security on the markets. Accordingly, one way to reduce investors' risk is assure them of a way out, by repayment or redemption, or conversion into another valuable asset. Furthermore, all other things being equal, a security that is due for repayment in two years should be safer for the lender than one which will be repaid in twenty years – just because so much more could happen to the business in the longer time period. Therefore, investors' risk is reduced still further if the investment life is relatively short.
2. *Providing security:* The company can provide security to the investor, often referred to as a 'charge' on the company's assets, such that if it fails to meet the terms of the agreement, the investor can protect their downside in some way. For example, a debt may be secured on a property owned by the company (the collateral); should the borrower fail to pay interest, or to repay the loan on the due date, the lender can seize the charged property and sell it off in order to recover the monies owed. This gives the investor another way out in case the company fails to meet its contracted obligations.

    Although the law varies in different jurisdictions, it is often the case that security comes in two flavours – fixed and floating. Broadly, the difference between them is that a fixed charge (lien) is one over specific assets such as buildings or fixed plant, and a floating charge (lien) is a charge over assets which change on a regular basis, such as inventories or receivables. The reason for the difference is that the holder of a fixed charge generally has to give permission before the owner can sell or transform the asset; this would be impractical for floating charge assets, which change their form in the ordinary course of business.

    In a liquidation, the holder of a fixed charge can use the proceeds of selling those specific assets in order to recover their due debts. Holders of floating charges can be repaid from the monies released by selling these assets, but they have a lower priority to the fixed charge holders and to various statutory creditors. However, any type of security puts the lender in a better position than the unsecured creditors.

    If a lender takes security, it is important to ensure that the security will be worth something if sold separately from the failed business. We spoke in Chapter 4 about strategic assets, ones that are rare, inimitable, and valuable. If these are too company-specific, then however valuable they are to the ongoing business, they will be inappropriate to use as security for the lender as they would have no resale value. Such assets, not being conducive to carrying debt, should be financed by equity.
3. *Providing a third party guarantee:* Investors need to ensure that their downside is limited. However, there is no law that says that the company itself has to provide this assurance. If the company is unable to provide the assurance, it is possible that a third party could do so. For example, a holding company or a major shareholder might agree to guarantee the loan as might, for a fee, a bank or insurance company.
4. *Covenants:* These are conditions in a loan contract which protect the lender by stating what the borrower may or may not do. Some of these, known as *maintenance covenants*, are tested at regular intervals, so that the lender can assure themselves that the indebted company will be able to meet its obligations. Others, called *incurrence covenants*, are

tested only at specific times: for example, when the borrower seeks further debt, an incurrence covenant might be in place to restrict the amount of new borrowing.

There are two types of covenant: positive and negative. Positive covenants are loan conditions which state what the borrower must do. For example, the borrowing company must deliver management accounts within a certain period after the month end; must deliver audited annual accounts within a given time-frame; must maintain agreed levels of accounting figures and ratios (such as the level of equity or the working capital ratios).

Negative covenants are clauses which prevent the borrower from undertaking certain actions. For example, negative covenants will prevent directors' remuneration being increased above a pre-agreed level, so that the business loan is not immediately transferred to the directors' benefit. In the same way, there will be covenants preventing large dividends being paid, or setting a maximum level of pay for non-directors. There will also be covenants in place preventing the company from taking further loans, unless the lender gives consent. Negative covenants will also prevent the company from spending large amounts on fixed assets that have not been previously agreed with the bank: this ensures that the monies borrowed are spent on the new factory rather than the CEO's Ferrari!

The main use of covenants is that a breach of the covenant terms can enable the lender to demand repayment of the loan, even though its term is not yet due. The ability to demand such repayment is valuable to lenders, allowing them to recover their money before things get worse. However, it should be noted that in some instances lenders will accept a breach of covenants, as they are aware that calling in the loan could result in the company going into liquidation without their being able to realize their money.

Working insight 11.1 gives some examples of maintenance covenants which relate to a company's financial reports, and Case Study 11.1 gives an example thereof, in respect of Eurotunnel.

There can be some flexibility for the borrowing company if the covenant agreement includes a provision for a *covenant switch*. This type of clause (which is not very common) enables the company to change the terms of the covenant, often on a one-off basis, to another covenant that it might find easier to meet. For example, Crest Nicholson, a UK housebuilder had a covenant on interest cover (EBIT ÷ interest) specifying that the ratio had to exceed 3:1.

Working Insight 11.1

Example of covenants relating to the company's finances

Interest cover	EBITDA must exceed a certain multiple of the company's interest payments
Debt/EBITDA	The ratio of net debt (or total debt, or senior debt as appropriate) cannot exceed a certain multiple of EBITDA
Gearing	The balance sheet ratio of debt to equity must be below a certain level
Cash-flow cover	Operating cash flows to exceed a target multiple of debt service cash flows

The 'debt' or 'interest' in the calculation could relate to total debt or senior debt or any other appropriate definition.

Case Study 11.1

Eurotunnel – an example of covenants

Eurotunnel SA, which operates the Channel tunnel between England and France, has a substantial amount of borrowing, with six different tranches of senior debt, each with different terms. Its debt covenants include a Debt Service Cover Ratio (DSCR), to be tested every six months.

DSCR is calculated as the ratio of the available cash flow for servicing of debt, to the debt service. The cash flow is defined as EBITDA less capital expenditure, tax, working capital movements, and various specified payments. Debt service comprises the finance charge plus all scheduled repayments. Extensive definitions underlie all of these terms.

The covenant was set such that the DSCR should be no less than 1.2 times for five years (until 2012), and then no less than 1.1 times thereafter. Breach of the covenant could lead to the mandatory repayment of the loans.

An additional covenant governs the payment of dividends, which is not permitted if the debt service covenant falls below 1.25 times. (Other covenants also restrict dividends, so that the lenders cannot be disadvantaged by funds leaving the business for shareholders.)

Source: Groupe Eurotunnel Registration Document 2011 and filings at www.secinfo.com

---

However, there was a covenant switch clause allowing the company a one-off chance for two years to change to a cash-based interest cover ratio of 1.75:1. This effectively gave the company a two-year grace period if its profits fell but its cash cover could be maintained.[2]

It is essential that all parties to the loan agreement understand the accounting conventions being used when calculating these covenanted ratios, and the implications of changes to accounting policies. This has always been a problem, as not all of the lawyers involved in drafting agreements will be very accounting literate; it has been known for covenants to be meaningless due to sloppy definitions.

The adoption of International Financial Reporting Standards (IFRS) in most jurisdictions led to great changes in the way assets and financial instruments were shown in the balance sheet, and the way in which interest and financial charges were shown in the income statement. Companies which appear highly solvent under one set of accounting conventions can seem remarkably vulnerable under a different one.

In addition to the various rights discussed above, which tend to be attached to debt instruments, some types of equity may also include risk-reduction rights. This is most common in venture capital deals, particularly with institutional investors. For example, the investor may have rights of veto over certain transactions, such as a sale of part of the business. Or they may have additional voting rights in all or some circumstances. (See also the discussion on anti-dilution and liquidation preference in Chapter 7.)

Yield

The yield of a security includes any payment made to the investors during the period for which the investment is outstanding, other than payments which reduce the capital balance.

---

2   Source: Crest Nicholson listing particulars, February 2013. The covenant switch also carried clauses preventing any dividends being paid during the period.

Thus, practical examples include interest on loans and dividends on shares. Share repurchases or loan redemptions would not be included in yield, as they are capital items.

The yield can be a regular payment, such as contracted quarterly interest, or can be on a more irregular basis, such as an occasional dividend. It can be for a set amount, again such as interest, or at the discretion of the paying company. The fact that a yield is at the discretion of the paying company does not necessarily make it an unpredictable amount – Chapter 13 points out that companies which pay dividends try to maintain a track record of level or increasing payments; this is an example of a discretionary payment which the investor has come to expect.

Interest rates on debt can be fixed rate or floating. Floating rate loans charge interest based on a premium over a reference rate such as LIBOR (London Interbank Offered Rate) or EURIBOR (Euro Interbank Offered Rate). For example, the contracted interest rate might be set at LIBOR plus 100 basis points (a basis point is 1/100 of a per cent). If LIBOR is 5 per cent, then the interest rate paid on the loan will be 6 per cent; if LIBOR rises to 5.5 per cent, the loan will be charged at 6.5 per cent.

Case Study 11.2 illustrates how Eurotunnel's different loans all carry different yields, including some that are effectively index-linked to inflation.

Floating rate interest can reduce risk for the lender, as it ensures that the lender will always receive 'market' rates on the loan. However, it leaves the borrowing company vulnerable to rises in market rates. For example, the credit crisis affecting country risk led to interest rates rising rapidly in several European countries during 2011/2012. Companies whose borrowing was linked to underlying rates were forced to pay much higher levels of interest, at a time when business was suffering a fall in demand. In order to minimize the borrower's risk in this, interest rate management tools such as caps and collars can be used, as discussed in the final part of this chapter.

Yield need not be as predictable as regular interest payments, or dividend payments on a particular trend. As discussed in Chapter 9, the author was involved in designing a capital instrument to finance the construction of a wind farm, in which the main financial objective

---

Case Study 11.2

Eurotunnel – examples of yields

Groupe Eurotunnel shows six different types of senior debt on its balance sheet, each with different terms and a different yield. Repayments on the loans are in instalments, ending between 2041 and 2050.

Tranche A_1, in £. Bears interest at a fixed rate of 3.49%. The nominal amount of loan is index-linked to inflation in UK.

Tranche A_2, in €. Bears interest at a fixed rate of 3.98%. The nominal amount of loan is index-linked to inflation in France.

Tranche B_1, in £. Bears interest at a fixed rate of 6.63%.

Tranche B_2, in €. Bears interest at a fixed rate of 6.18%.

Tranche C_1, in £. Bears interest at a variable rate, LIBOR + 1.39%.

Tranche C_2, in €. Bears interest at a variable rate, EURIBOR + 1.39%.

Source: Groupe Eurotunnel Registration Document 2011

was to return as much cash as possible to the investors, subject only to bank restrictions. The yield on this instrument was determined as the amount shown as free cash flow (strictly defined) in cash-flow forecasts for the wind farm for the following six months; once the banks' requirements were met, all of the free cash was paid out.

Upside

The investor obtains an upside from selling the security for an amount greater than was originally invested in it; the upside is the capital gain. The upside can come from various different sources:

1   ultimate sale of the financial instrument to another investor;
2   redemption of the instrument at a premium by the investee company, the premium being paid in cash or in the securities of the investee company;
3   redemption at a premium, with the premium denominated in the securities of another company or in another asset.

Each of these is considered below.

1   *Sale of the financial instrument to another investor:* This form of exit is most commonly seen by purchasers of shares listed on a stock exchange. The shares are liquid, in that there are many potential buyers and sellers, and the market sets a price. The holder of the investment can choose to sell at the market price, or can continue to hold the shares in the hope that the price will rise. The difference between the ultimate sales proceeds and the initial amount invested is the capital gain. (This will probably be subject to tax in the hands of the investor, but such taxation is country specific, may be investor specific, and is outside the scope of this book.) The company that issued the shares has no interest in this disposal, which is strictly between the buying and selling investors. There is also no guarantee that the disposal price will be greater than the price originally paid for the investment.

2   *Redemption by the investee company at a premium:* Many financial instruments have a defined life, and incorporate a contract to the effect that the company will redeem the instrument at the end of this period. If the agreement is that redemption will take place at par, i.e. with no uplift, then the investor's return comes solely through the yield. However, there is often a redemption premium which gives the investor a capital gain. The premium may be for a fixed amount, or dependent on other factors. An example of a fixed premium might be:

Company A issues £1,000,000 of a security which will be repurchased in five years' time for £1,200,000.

This gives the investor a capital gain of £200,000 in addition to any yield on the security.
    It is also common for securities which give a repayment premium to carry 'zero interest' as a coupon, with the investor's return being totally rolled up in the final payment.
    Another way of structuring this transaction would be to issue the security at a discount:

Company B issues for £1,000,000 a security with a face value of £1,200,000. In five years' time the security will be redeemed at face value.

This 'deep discounted bond' achieves the same effect as in Company A, but the tax treatment may differ.

Instead of a fixed premium, the ultimate amount of capital gain may be unknown when the investment is made. For example:

Company C issues a security for £1,000,000. In five years' time the £1,000,000 will be repaid and, in addition, the investor will receive shares representing 2 per cent of the equity of Company C.

Here, the value of the upside (known as an 'equity kicker') is dependent on the value of Company C's equity in five years' time. The investor is taking the risk that Company C will perform well, and the potential upside will indeed be valuable. The deal could also have been structured in a different way, as follows:

Company D issues a security for £1,000,000. In five years' time the investor has the option either of receiving £1,000,000 cash in redemption of the security, or of receiving 200,000 of Company D's shares.

In this example, the investor obviously expects that 200,000 of Company D's shares will be valued at more than £1,000,000 in five years' time – i.e. that the share price will exceed £5 per share. If the share price is higher than £5, the investor will obtain the capital gain by converting the security into shares in Company D. If Company D has not performed well, the investor will instead ask for the £1,000,000 in cash.

3   *Redemption by the investee company with a premium in securities of another company or in another asset:* Yet another way to obtain the capital uplift would be to enter into an agreement that gave the investor rights over another company's securities.

Company E issues a security for £1,000,000. In five years' time, the investor can either redeem the security for £1,000,000 cash, or can exchange it for 100,000 shares in Company F. As in the case of Company D, the investor is gambling on a share price rise, this time it is the price of Company F that is critical.

Normally, if the capital upside is structured to come from the shares of a third company, there will be a link between the issuing company and the third party. For example, Company F might be a spun-out subsidiary of Company E, or maybe Company E holds shares in Company F as part of a trade investment which it seeks, long term, to reduce. Similarly, there is no reason why the upside should not come from the proceeds of sale of another asset, for example, a business property. The key point is that the issuing company should be able to deliver to its investors the asset(s) providing the upside at the time they are required.

Another way to ensure the upside is a technique adopted by venture capital investors, known as *liquidation preference*, which combines risk reduction with protection of the potential upside. The terminology is slightly misleading: this is not necessarily to do with a distressed sale, but relates to the way in which any proceeds of disposal of the shares are distributed, which could be in a normal sale as well as a liquidation. If the investor has a liquidation preference, they are entitled to be paid out prior to the other investors – so, if there is insufficient money to pay everyone, they get preference. Furthermore, they often demand a preference multiple: a share with a 3 × liquidation preference would be paid out three times the face value of the shares before any other investor was paid. An example of liquidation preference is given in Chapter 7.

Defining 'debt' and 'equity'

Now that the basics have been explored, we are ready to look at the two fundamental financial instruments – debt and equity. How do these compare on our three headings?

Debt is a low-risk instrument from the lender's point of view (although, of course, it is high risk to the borrower). A contract is entered into which specifies how long the monies will be outstanding, and schedules their repayments; legally, the lender is a creditor of the company. The agreement also states what interest (the yield) is to be paid, and how. The lender's downside is often protected by taking security over specified assets of the borrower. Further downside protection may be obtained through the use of covenants – loan clauses which state clearly what the borrower may and may not do while the loan is in place. During the term of the loan repayments are made, to the agreed schedule, which fully repay the capital balance. There is no upside for the lender; the return comes only by way of yield.

Contrast that with equity, in the form of ordinary shares. This is permanent capital for the company. The investor puts money into the company with no guarantee of any return at all. The yield comes, if it comes at all, at the directors' discretion, dependent on the levels of cash and profit, and the company's future investment needs. If the company does well, there may be an upside, in that the shares can be sold at a profit. However, there is no guarantee that the company will do well, or that its value will be recognized by the market. This is a high-risk investment.

Table 11.1 summarizes the basic characteristics of debt and equity.

To give an example: in 1976 Apple Computers received its first order, and needed $15,000 for the working capital to make the circuit boards. If your author had at that time lent $15,000 to the fledgling Apple, she would have handed over the money, received interest for a few years, and then been repaid the $15,000. If instead she had invested $15,000 of private equity in Apple stock … she would not have needed to work so hard for the royalties on this book![3]

Manipulating the building blocks

We have established that the financial instrument must offer investors a return commensurate with the risk they perceive, and that such return will be derived from a yield and/or a capital gain. From these basic concepts, two important ideas can be developed:

The expected return on a financial instrument must be consistent with the investor's perceived risk.	Therefore, target the instruments at categories of investor who will understand the risks involved, and not charge a premium for their lack of understanding.
The return will come from yield and upside.	Therefore, an instrument with very high yield would be expected to provide little or no upside, and investors agreeing to receive no yield would anticipate the possibility of a high capital gain.

---

3   Although to be honest, she is very risk-averse and there is no chance she would ever have made that investment, even if asked.

Table 11.1 Characteristics of debt and equity

	Debt	Equity
Risk to the investor	Low, protected by security and covenants	High
Yield	Interest, normally contractually agreed	Dividends, at the discretion of the directors
Potential upside to the investor	None	Very high

We established in Chapter 5 that companies in the launch and growth stages of the life cycle should be financed mostly with equity; those in later stages can afford debt financing. The reasons behind this financial strategy relate to the business risk of the different stages, and to the companies' requirements for funding for growth. These arguments can be extended to consider the different types of financial instrument that a company may wish to use.

Figure 11.4 illustrates the yield–gain continuum of possibilities for providing return to investors. On the left-hand side of Figure 11.4, investors receive a return from yield only. This is appropriate when business risks are low. As business risk increases (and, generally, the need for funds for growth also increases) it becomes advisable to provide the return less by yield and more as capital growth. At the extreme right-hand side of Figure 11.4, high-risk companies use instruments with no yield at all.

Chapter 12 discusses various different types of financial instrument on the market, and shows how these principles are met in practice.

Interest rate management tools

Interest rate management tools are used to lower the financing risk for companies which have borrowed at a floating rate. Floating rate loans bear interest based on a reference rate plus a premium. If the reference rate falls, the company will pay less interest. However, unexpected increases in market interest rates could lead to the company having to pay a

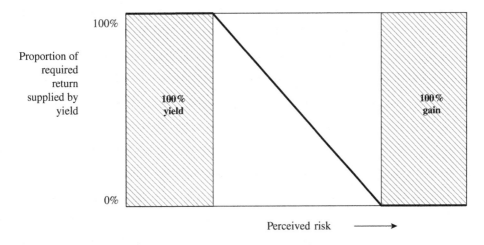

Figure 11.4 Companies' risk profiles and the yield and capital gain to investors.

much larger-than-anticipated charge:[4] the interest rate management tools can help protect against this.

Reference rates

The reference rate most commonly used globally is LIBOR (London Interbank Offered Rate – the rate at which banks will lend to each other in London, in various different currencies). (Equivalent rates exist based on other countries – for example, EURIBOR (EU), HIBOR (Hong Kong), SHIBOR (Shanghai), etc., but LIBOR is the most widely used internationally.) When we refer below to LIBOR, much of what we say applies to all reference rates.

There are several different types of LIBOR, representing money being lent for varying periods and in different currencies. The rates most commonly used as reference points for floating rate debt are three-month LIBOR and six-month LIBOR. A rate for each LIBOR is set every working day by a selection of reference banks, and it will vary depending on supply and demand and market conditions.[5]

As an example, CapCo might borrow say £1m for two years at a rate of three-month LIBOR plus 200 basis points (2 per cent). On the first day of the loan, three-month LIBOR might be 3 per cent; this means that CapCo will pay interest at 5 per cent (3% + 2%) for three months. At the end of the three months, the new rate for three-month LIBOR would be used to set the rate of interest due for the next three-month period. If six-month LIBOR had been used as the reference rate, CapCo's interest would have remained at that level for six months.

Caps, floors, and collars

CapCo may be comfortable borrowing when LIBOR is 3 per cent, and may be relaxed about LIBOR rising to, say, 6 per cent. However, at levels above that, there may be problems in meeting interest payments. In order to protect its position, the company can buy an interest rate *cap*. This is in effect an insurance policy that prevents the company having to pay interest at more than a given rate.

For example, Barland Bank has lent CapCo £1m for two years at three-month LIBOR plus 200 basis points. Three-month LIBOR is currently 3 per cent. The company wishes to ensure that even if LIBOR rises above 6 per cent, it will not have to pay any more than a total of 8 per cent on its loan (i.e. 6% + 2%). Accordingly, it can buy a LIBOR cap at 6 per cent. The impact of this is illustrated in Working Insight 11.2.

There are several points to note about buying the cap. First, the cap need not be acquired from Barland Bank, who provided the loan. In fact, Barland need not even know about the existence of the cap – CapCo has in fact bought it from EuroNordbank, and it is a separate financial transaction to the loan. This leads to the second point: technically, having a cap does not prevent the company having to pay high interest rates to its

---

4   If market interest rates rise, the company could face a 'double whammy'. Not only will the company's interest charge increase, but the economic factors behind the rate rise may lead to depressed sales, low profits and cash flow problems. Alas, the interest rate management tools only deal with the interest charge – the rest is still management's problem.

5   At the time of writing, the future of LIBOR is in doubt due to a major scandal in the way the rate was being set and manipulated. The Wheatley Review of LIBOR, published by HM Treasury September 2012, sets out details of the events and proposals for the future.

Working Insight 11.2

Illustration of an interest rate cap at 6%

LIBOR	Interest rate paid to Barland Bank (premium of 2%)	Interest rate received from EuroNordbank (selling the cap)	Net interest rate paid by CapCo
2%	4%	–	4%
3%	5%	–	5%
4%	6%	–	6%
5%	7%	–	7%
6%	8%	–	8%
7%	9%	(1%)	8%
8%	10%	(2%)	8%

lender – it just means that it can offset this extra interest by the receipts from the bank which sold it the cap. So, if LIBOR were to rise to 8 per cent, CapCo would have to pay Barland interest at 10 per cent, but would receive interest back from EuroNord amounting to 2 per cent, leaving it paying a net 8 per cent. And the third point to note is that although the loan is for £1m, the cap could be for less than that amount, or more, if CapCo wishes to speculate on interest rates.

Acquiring the cap will cost CapCo an up-front payment, the level of which depends on the rate capped, and the time for which it is needed. For example, if our company wanted to cap LIBOR at 4 per cent, it would be a great deal more expensive than capping at 6 per cent; similarly, a six-month cap would be cheaper to buy than a two-year cap.

Should CapCo wish to avoid paying for its cap, it could enter into a transaction to sell a *floor* to a bank. Just as buying a cap means that the company's interest rate will never move above a certain amount, selling a floor means that even if market rates fall, the company will not be able to take full advantage of it. So CapCo might sell EuroNord (or another bank) a LIBOR floor at 2 per cent. This would mean that should LIBOR fall to, say, 1.5 per cent, CapCo would be paying Barland interest on its loan at 3.5 per cent (1.5% + 2%) but would also be paying 0.5 per cent (2% – 1.5%) to EuroNord which owns the floor.

The purchase of a cap and a floor together is known as a *collar*. Terms can be set such that the amount that the company has to pay for purchasing the cap can be exactly offset by the amount the bank is paying it for the floor. This is known as a *zero cost collar*. Working Insight 11.3 illustrates the full impact of the collar on CapCo.

For the ease of display it has been assumed that the two parts of the collar are acquired from the same bank. In practice, a company could buy the cap from one financial institution and sell the floor to another.

Interest rate swaps

Another type of interest rate management tool is an interest rate swap. This is generally used as a mechanism for companies which have borrowed at a floating rate to convert their stream of interest payments into those of a fixed rate loan. (Swaps can also be done from fixed rate

Working Insight 11.3

Illustration of an interest rate collar, with a cap at 6% and a floor at 2%

LIBOR	Interest rate paid to Barland Bank (premium of 2%)	Interest rate paid/ (received) from EuroNordbank (selling the collar)	Net interest rate paid by CapCo
1%	3%	1%	4%
2%	4%	–	4%
3%	5%	–	5%
4%	6%	–	6%
5%	7%	–	7%
6%	8%	–	8%
7%	9%	(1%)	8%
8%	10%	(2%)	8%

Case Study 11.3

Groupe Eurotunnel swaps

Tranche C_1

The loan of £350m 'bears interest at a floating rate (LIBOR) plus a margin of 1.39% which is entirely hedged by a fixed/floating interest rate swap for which Eurotunnel pays a fixed rate of 5.2135% and receives a floating rate (LIBOR)'.

Tranche C_2

The loan of €953m 'bears interest at a floating rate (EURIBOR) plus a margin of 1.39% which is entirely hedged by a fixed/floating interest rate swap for which Eurotunnel pays a fixed rate of 4.853% and receives a floating rate (EURIBOR)'.

Source: Groupe Eurotunnel Registration Document 2011

into floating rate, but these are less common.) The company enters into an agreement with a bank (again, not necessarily the bank providing the loan), and this effectively fixes the reference rate for the loan, thus protecting it against future interest rate rises.[6] Although the loan agreement remains for a floating rate instrument, the actuality is a stream of fixed rate payments. Case Study 11.3 shows how Groupe Eurotunnel disclosed swaps on some of the loans shown in Case Study 11.2

Interest rate swaps are common for larger loans, for two reasons. First, market convention is that the loans tend to be made at floating rates, and so the borrowing companies require a

---

6 We say that it fixes the reference rate rather than the interest rate paid, as the rate paid might still be subject to changes if the company's credit-worthiness declines.

mechanism to protect against rate rises. And, second, because swapping from floating rate to fixed provides the same sort of protection against rising interest rates as does a cap, but at a cheaper price. As with caps, the amount and duration of a swap need not exactly mirror those of the loan itself.

The reason that swaps are cheaper than caps is that there is no 'optionality' in a swap. In the earlier example of caps, CapCo was protected against rises in LIBOR, but when LIBOR fell it would pay lower interest. With a swap this is not an option – the rate paid remains fixed regardless of the level of LIBOR. Some borrowers, seeing how much they are paying when rates fall, regard this as unfair, but they need to remember that the bank taking the swap has had to protect its own position in the financial markets, and so could only unwind the swap at a financial penalty based on current market rates.

One reason that borrowers take floating rate loans and swap into fixed is that many financial institutions prefer to deal this way. Another is that using a swap gives the borrower the flexibility to refinance the loan without trying to unwind any protection – the swap is portable to a new loan.

Key messages

- Financial instruments need to produce a return to match the investors' perceived risk. This return comes from a mixture of yield and capital gain. The capital gain can be market-generated or can be pre-agreed by the investee company, or a mixture of both. The yield can be fixed, or can be at a variable, floating rate.
- Risk can be mitigated by having covenants to protect the investors' position, or by taking security over assets of the company.
- Low-risk instruments tend to give all of their return as yield, for example, as interest payments. High-risk instruments give their return as gain. In the middle of the risk–return continuum, instruments can be structured giving a combination of the two.
- Interest rate management tools such as caps and collars or swaps can be used by the company to protect its position in the event of an increase in reference rates.

Suggested further reading

The Groupe Eurotunnel case studies in this chapter were all drawn from the company's 2011 Registration Document, available via www.eurotunnelgroup.com/uk/shareholders-and-investors/publications/registration-documents

Wheatley Review of LIBOR, published by HM Treasury September 2012 can be accessed via www.hm-treasury.gov.uk/wheatley_review.htm

Following the international scandal when it was disclosed that LIBOR rates had been manipulated, the UK government commissioned Martin Wheatley to undertake a review of the structure and governance of LIBOR and the corresponding criminal sanctions regime. This website accesses the discussion paper and the various responses received to it, as well as the proposed changes to regulation.

12 Types of financial instrument

Learning objectives

After reading this chapter you should be able to:

1   Distinguish different types of financial instrument, assess the broad categories
    into which they fall, and contrast their fundamental characteristics.
2   Discuss the continuum of financial instruments, and explain why the terms of
    a particular instrument will affect its position on the continuum.

3 Describe how credit rating agencies work.
4 Understand in broad terms the accounting treatment of financial instruments.

Introduction

As discussed in Chapter 11, financial instruments can be constructed from any commercially acceptable combination of risk protection, yield, and upside potential. Thus, companies can select potentially a wide variety of financial instruments to meet their exact needs, and those of their investors.

In this chapter we examine the factors affecting the choice of financial instrument, and discuss the characteristics of some of the commonly used financial instruments. We show that the distinction between 'debt' and 'equity' is blurred, and that there is in fact a continuum of financial instruments which have debt-like and equity-like characteristics. Option theory can be used to identify in any situation which instrument has preferential claims over others; this is perhaps the best way to define 'debt'.

What do companies need?

As set out in Chapter 4, the basic tenet of sound financial strategy is that the company should match its financing risk to its level of business risk. Companies with a high level of business risk should try to ensure that they do not add to the volatility of their results by taking on financial risk. Similarly, companies with a low business risk will find it worthwhile to use financial instruments that increase their risk profile but reduce their average cost of capital.

Chapter 11 looked at the risk of financial instruments from the point of view of the investor, and stated that debt was relatively low risk, and equity high risk. For the company, of course, the risk relationship is reversed. Borrowing is a high-risk activity for companies, as they have to find the resources to make interest payments and repay the principal. Equity is low-risk finance for a company as it is permanent, the shareholders having no contractual right to payments from the company.

In addition to the fundamental business risk–financial risk relationship, companies structuring long-term financial instruments should concern themselves with two other variables: cash and profits.

Companies which are cash constrained are best served by using financial instruments that do not demand any significant outflows of cash, at least in the short term. Growing companies, needing their resources to fund expansion, do not wish to pay out such resources to repay their lenders; they are better off with equity, or with an instrument that delays payouts. However, companies which are generating significant cash flows may be able to use debt, knowing that they have the means to repay it.

The profit impact of the financial instrument is a somewhat different matter. Although we have previously pointed out that shareholder value has only an indirect link to current profit, the effect on profits (and in particular eps) will also need to be considered by companies in their financing structure, as it might impact the market's perception of them. Profit reduction due to interest payments may lead companies away from the use of debt, or towards an instrument that dilutes profits in the longer term but not the short term.

Differentiating financial instruments using option theory

Shortly, we will introduce a model of the continuum of financial products, ranking each in order on the risk–return continuum. Before we do that, this section discusses option theory as a method of making these rankings. An option gives the holder the right to buy or sell a security, but not the obligation so to do. (Option theory is discussed more fully in Appendix 2.)

The right to buy something is known as a *call option*; the right to sell is a *put option*. These concepts can be helpful in trying to distinguish between different classes of debt and equity sources of funding, provided we have a clear understanding of the relative rights and responsibilities of each party providing finance to a company.

It is generally accepted that in a company with outstanding debt, the equity can be regarded as a call option on the assets of the business, at an exercise price equal to the value of the outstanding debt. This is because if the shareholders want to maintain control of the business, they must ensure that the debt obligations are met, otherwise the debt holders will exercise their rights as creditors of the company, and (by appointing a receiver or liquidator) take control of the assets. Thus the repayment of the debt is the amount to be paid to take control of the unencumbered assets of the company.

An alternate way of looking at this is that the shareholders could be seen as holding a put option on the company's assets to the debt holders. If the gross value of the company exceeds the value of debt, the shareholders will exercise their call option, repaying the debt and regaining control. Should the gross value of the company be less than the value of debt, shareholders can utilize their put option and effectively walk away from the business, letting the creditors take control of the assets. (Of course, this only works in situations where the shareholders have limited liability.)

How does this help us to clarify the graduations from debt to equity? It certainly helps to rank the order of priority of these different types of funding, because it focuses attention on which parties have options. However, you will see when we reach the next section that in practice there is a whole series of options held by each type of financial instrument over its neighbours.

The discussion on methods of risk protection in Chapter 11 suggested that the primary method of protecting the downside is that the instrument should have another way out. This is a good place to start in defining debt: debt has another way out. If the business fails to meet its contractual obligations, the lender can realize the security charged in its favour. Thus, we could say that the lender has a call option on some of the company's assets, which they can exercise if redemption is in doubt: the lender has the right, but not the obligation, to call in the receivers.

In ranking financial instruments, the types of option in existence – and who has the right to exercise them – are important in determining priority. In the example above, the share-holders always have the option not to repay the debt. Normally, the lenders' call option on the assets is only of value if there are sufficiently restrictive covenants surrounding the loan that the lenders can act to recover the monies before the value of their security has been damaged. If the lenders have minimal covenants in place, such that they can only act once the company has defaulted, then the option is worth a lot less than one which could be exercised at an earlier stage, as the assets might already have lost much of their value.

Lenders should also try to protect themselves against the subsequent creation of superior options to their own. They should have covenants in place to prevent the exercise of call options by lenders with a position that should be subordinated to their own. (For example, using terms that will be defined in the next section, one would not expect the lender of junior debt to be able to call in the receivers if the holders of senior debt did not so wish.)

Some lenders might choose deliberately to relax their protections, in order to make their loan products more attractive to potential borrowers. For example, in times when financial institutions have been anxious to lend, we have seen what are known as 'covenant-light' ('cov-lite') or 'covenant-loose' loans. Just as the name suggests, these loans have minimal or very few covenants covering leverage, interest cover, asset expenditure, etc. This is attractive to borrowers, as fewer covenants make it less likely that they will be breached and, more importantly, give them much more flexibility in the way in which they can run their businesses. Accordingly, borrowers are inclined to take these loans, often agreeing to a higher interest rate in order to compensate the lender for the increased risk.

However, cov-lite means that it is more difficult for lenders to be able to protect their position if things start to go wrong. This proved a problem during the credit crisis and recession that started in 2008. Although cov-lite loans became scarce in the few years following, by the time this book was being written cov-lite loans were again being offered by some lenders, seeking yield.

Tradable financial instruments

One further point to be noted about financial instruments is that they can be the subject of a private transaction, or can be traded on public markets. We are accustomed to this for equity, but it is also true of debt. For example, a company could borrow directly from its bank (a private transaction), or could raise bonds on the markets. From the lender's point of view, publicly traded debt has the advantage that it gives another way out – the lender can sell the debt before it falls due, releasing the capital for other uses.

In the same manner as private debt, debt securities can be fixed or floating, and for short-, medium-, or long-term periods. (Short term is defined as fewer than twelve months, but is often much less.)

For debt to be traded on a market, both the issuing company and the particular instrument must follow disclosure rules, in the same way as do companies listing their equity. However, debt can be issued which is tradable among market professionals but not to the public at large, and the disclosures for this are much lighter.

The advantages of raising tradable debt rather than borrowing privately through a bank include the fact that it diversifies the company's funding sources, raises its profile, and can be cheaper with fewer covenants. However, tradable loans provide less flexibility in the event of a potential default, as there are so many parties to the negotiation (and, in the case of bearer bonds, the identities of those holding the paper will not immediately be known). Also, issuers have to consider the potentially high level of cost to arrange the issue, and the costs of disclosure.

If the debt is publicly tradable, it is important to realize that the lender may be able to make a capital gain (or a capital loss) on selling it. The value of traded debt fluctuates depending on its coupon (interest rate based on the nominal amount of the principal) and market rates. Thus, with the low interest rates prevailing at the time of writing, a debt instrument issued several years ago with a coupon of 10 per cent will probably trade at greater than £100 per £100 nominal value. Of course, by the time the debt falls due, provided no default is anticipated, the instrument should be trading at exactly £100 per £100, as that is what the investor will be getting.

> **Case Study 12.1**
>
> ### Repurchasing debt – Société Générale
>
> In June 2012 Société Générale announced that it had bought back €1.7 billion of its own 'Lower Tier 2 Hybrid notes',[1] going on to report, 'With this transaction, the Group achieves a profit before tax of approximately EUR 300 million'. What this meant was that it had paid about €300m less than the book value of the debt. The repurchase also had the effect of improving the bank's regulatory Tier 1 ratio.
>
> *Source:* www.investor.socgen.com

The value of debt also varies with the creditworthiness of the borrower, in a usual risk–return relationship. Case Study 12.3 towards the end of this chapter illustrates this in an accounting context for Barclays Bank.

The fact that a debt is publicly traded may make little difference to the borrowing company, which still has to service the interest and repayments. However, it does give the directors the flexibility of being able to repurchase the debt in the market, and cancel it. There are potentially two reasons for a company to want to buy back its debt. First, if the debt carries an interest rate higher than current market rates, a company might choose to buy it back to refinance it at a lower interest rate, which will have less impact on profits in the future. And, second, if the debt is trading at below par, the company might choose to buy it back in order to book a profit. For example, during summer 2012 several European banks bought back their own debt, as illustrated by Société Générale in Case Study 12.1.

The continuum of modern financial instruments

Financial instruments can be created with any combination of risk protection, yield, and potential gain. It is useful to be able to set them out on a continuum, showing which are the riskier (for the investor) and how the potential returns might change. If this is done, companies have a framework from which they can begin to determine how they should finance themselves.

The continuum set out in Figure 12.1 runs from secured debt as the safest instrument (for the investor) up to ordinary share capital as the riskiest. Other securities are shown at points on the risk–return continuum between these two extremes. Not all of the securities discussed in this chapter are included. The oval in Figure 12.1 is there to highlight the fact that the positioning of the securities on the risk–return line is inevitably somewhat arbitrary. The actual risk–return position of any security will depend on the specific terms of the contract under which it is written. Thus, although it is possible to state that high-yield bonds (junk bonds) are riskier than senior debt and will provide a greater potential return, it is not possible to say whether high-yield bonds are riskier than mezzanine, or vice versa. The chart should be read with a certain degree of flexibility, and an appreciation that the terms of each individual transaction are vital to an understanding of who has what options over which assets, and so which instrument is taking the greater risk.

---

1 Of banks' capital, Tier 1 is the core (safest) capital followed by Upper Tier 2, then Lower Tier 2.

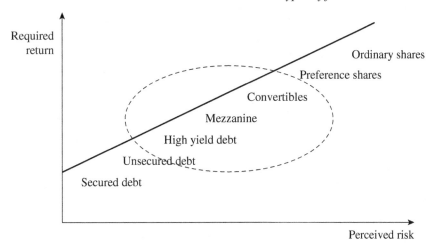

Figure 12.1 Illustrative continuum of financial instruments.

The principles behind Figure 12.1 can also be used in a functional definition of gearing. In evaluating accounting ratios we calculate gearing based on net financial debt, which includes all types of financial (negotiated) borrowing. However, for practical purposes, if I am a lender, then the only debt that concerns me is anything that ranks ahead of my debt in terms of priority: anything to the left of my security will count as 'debt', but anything to the right has fewer rights and so can be treated as 'equity'. Doing the calculations that way can provide useful insights.

Set out below are brief descriptions of some common securities and how they are used.

Secured debt

Downside protection: charge over assets; covenants
Yield: interest
Upside potential: none

Secured debt is a loan made to the company on the strength of good security, with a registered charge being taken over certain assets (or all of the assets) of the company. Strong covenants would be in place to ensure that the company could not misuse the monies advanced, and to ensure that the lender would have advance warning of any decline in the company's position. The loan agreement would set out details of the amount of the loan, and the repayment terms (see Working Insight 12.1). As the loan is relatively low risk, it should carry a relatively low rate of interest. Accordingly, companies that can afford to borrow (mature businesses with good cash flow and strong asset backing) would make use of this type of instrument.

A company may borrow different tranches of secured debt carrying different conditions. Debt with the strongest claims on the company would be known as *senior debt*. From this, we can determine that securities known as *junior debt* will have much weaker claims on the

Working Insight 12.1

Loan repayment terms

In setting the repayment terms for a loan, it is important to pay note to the company's need for the funds and its ability to make repayments. Repayment schedules can be tailored to meet any combination of needs of the company and the lender. Some of the most common types of repayment are as follows.

Regular repayments: these might be monthly, quarterly, semi-annually, or annually. The loan is repaid in equal instalments over its life.

Bullet repayment: the whole loan is repaid in one 'bullet' at the end of its life.

Balloon repayment: repayments in early years are relatively small. In later years of the loan the repayments might grow, but the main quantum of the loan is repaid at the end.

Capital holiday: if the company will be unable to make loan repayments in early years, it might be sensible to allow for a repayments holiday for, say, the first two years of the loan. Repayments after that might be by regular instalments, or by way of a balloon.

company, and should charge a higher rate of interest to compensate for their greater risk. Where a company has several different tranches of debt (for example Groupe Eurotunnel as shown in Chapter 11), there will be an inter-loan agreement to establish their relative rights.

Leasing

Downside protection: ownership of assets; covenants
Yield: interest
Upside potential: none

Leasing is a form of secured debt, with the lending being made against a specific asset. Normally, the lease contract is entered into at the same time as the asset is acquired. The lessor retains legal ownership of the asset, and can reclaim it if lease payments are not met. The accounting treatment is to show the leased asset as a fixed asset[2] of the company, and the lease liability under current and long-term liabilities.[3] There can be great tax benefits in leasing assets, as the lessor company may be able to use the tax allowances relating to the assets, and so pass on a reduced finance charge.

2   Fixed assets are technically known as 'non-current' assets, and long-term liabilities as 'non-current' liabilities. Strictly speaking, we should use these terms, but it is ugly language, and we prefer the terms used by most business people.

3   The type of lease described is a 'finance lease'. Leases which relate to the short-term rental of an asset may be classified as 'operating leases'. Assets held under operating leases do not, at the time of writing, have to be capitalized on the balance sheet. However, it appears likely that this accounting treatment will be changed. It should of course be remembered that unless there is an effect on the tax paid, a change in accounting treatment has no impact on shareholder value, merely on the reported profits.

Hire purchase is a similar type of contract. The main difference between hire purchase and a finance lease is that under hire purchase the assets technically belong to the borrowing company, whereas leased assets belong to the lessor.

Companies can also raise lease finance on assets that they already own. Such transactions, known as 'sale and leaseback', often (but not always) relate to property. A company will sell its property to a finance company in order to obtain a lump sum payment, and then will lease back the premises so that it can continue using them. The amount of the lump sum payment will depend partly on the value of the premises, but also on the credit status of the borrowing company and the agreed ongoing rent: a profitable company that is prepared to pay a high rent will be able to obtain a larger lump sum than one which wants to minimize future rental payments. Later in the book, Case Study 17.1 illustrates a company that used sale and lease-back as one part of its strategy to reduce its overall level of debt.

Securitization

Downside protection: charge over assets; may be guarantees
Yield: interest
Upside potential: none

Securitization is an example of a broader category of instruments, known as *structured finance*. This is a blanket term to cover a range of types of debt tailored to an individual company's needs and often secured on future cash flows rather than on assets. Generally, structured finance can give companies financial flexibility at a relatively low interest rate.

Structured finance has spawned a profusion of varieties and acronyms. We have the CMO (collateralized mortgage obligation), CDO (collateralized debt obligation), CLO (collateralized loan obligation) and many others. The key word here is 'collateralized', meaning that an income stream has been turned into collateral for a loan. For the sake of simplicity, in this chapter we consider only generic securitization.

Securitization is used by companies that have a strong and predictable income stream on which to 'securitize' a loan. Effectively, the company creates a security by selling the future income stream in exchange for a lump sum payment. Although the company itself may not be very creditworthy, its income stream is, and so the lending is based on this.

Securitization has been around since the 1970s, when the US Government National Mortgage Association, a government organization responsible for purchasing mortgages from mortgage originators, issued its 'Ginnie Maes' as the first mortgage-backed securities. Although each individual mortgage carries a chance of non-repayment, by putting together a package of mortgages carrying the same level of credit risk, the portfolio carries a lower default risk, and so is more valuable to the purchaser.

Securitization has three significant advantages to the company.

- It can diversify sources of funds for businesses which otherwise would not be able to obtain debt from these markets.
- It can lead to a lower cost of funds. If the company itself has a poor credit rating, the asset-backed debt may have a much higher one.
- Because the lenders have the securitized assets they do not need covenants from the company, which gives management more freedom in running the business.

When it first became popular, securitized debt could often be treated as an off-balance sheet transaction, reducing the company's balance sheet gearing. However, under current financial reporting rules, the treatment will depend on the specific terms of the agreements.

Many different types of assets produce an income stream that can be securitized. Examples of securitization include: mortgages; commercial and other loans; credit card receivables; road tolls; car loans; trade receivables; and licence payments. The length of the securitization period will depend in part on the characteristics of the assets being securitized. Possibly one of the most unusual securitizations, a pioneer of its time, was the 'Bowie Bond', securitized in 1997 on ten years of future royalties of the past albums of the singer David Bowie.

The cash flows of a simple securitization are illustrated in Figure 12.2.

The company transfers the assets to be securitized into a special purpose vehicle (which may be a company or a trust, depending, *inter alia*, on the tax regime). It is important that there is a clean break between the originator and the SPV, so that investors are not subject to the company's risk. Investors make a loan to the SPV based on the income stream which will accrue to it: in Figure 12.2 this is the interest and principal repayments over the lives of the loans. The originating company receives a lump sum from the asset sale, plus a regular fee for ongoing management of the asset portfolio on behalf of the SPV. Over the lifetime of the arrangement, the investors receive the cash flows from the asset pool.

If the security of the asset stream is not considered to be good enough, the company (or a third party such as a bank or monoline insurance company) may enhance the credit status of the SPV. This credit enhancement works by ring-fencing the risks, and putting them to the appropriate party. The key determinants of the credit rating are:

- Assets type, and likelihood of risk of default.
- Cash flow – so that bondholders can get their regular cash for interest. When cash flows are less than 100 per cent certain, the credit enhancement can take the form of an escrow account to cover temporary shortfalls.

The assets securitized will be divided into several tranches, each with a different degree of risk attached, and so carrying different credit ratings and interest rates. One of the factors underlying the subprime mortgage problems of 2007 was the difficulty in

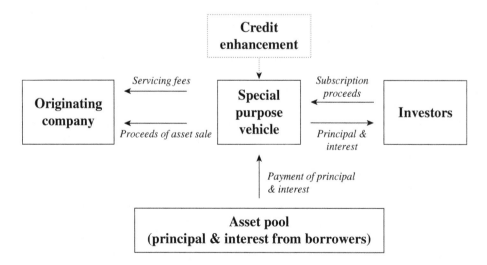

Figure 12.2 Securitization flows.

assigning a credit rating to some of these instruments, and the over-optimism of the financial markets – and particularly the credit rating agencies – as to their combined creditworthiness.

At this point it is worth taking a few moments to discuss the credit rating agencies. These are private institutions which publish their opinions on the creditworthiness of corporate debt. (They also consider sovereign debt, but that is outside the scope of this book.) We are all familiar with the term 'Triple A rating' – AAA is the highest rating awarded by one of the two largest rating agencies, Standard & Poor's. It implies that the debt being graded is very high quality, and extremely unlikely to default. Debt instruments judged less creditworthy are graded as AA, then A, then BBB etc, with plus or minus symbols used as modifiers to differentiate more finely. The other giant rating agency, Moody's, has a similar ratings, starting at Aaa. The third agency of significance, Fitch, uses AAA. A different referencing system is used for short-term debt.

Understandably, a debt instrument rated as, say, AA will carry a lower rate of interest than one rated lower, as A, perhaps. This reflects the perceived risk–required return relationship.

The rating agencies base their judgements on information supplied by the companies themselves, and from other sources. Their business model includes receiving fees from the companies that they rate, which generally need the ratings in order to be able to sell the debt. There is a certain conflict of interest inherent in this arrangement, which after the credit crisis was found to have influenced some of the opinions issued in favour of granting higher ratings in order to attract more corporate business.[4]

Other forms of asset-based finance

Downside protection: charge over assets
Yield: interest
Upside potential: none

Asset-based finance is a generic term for a range of different forms of finance. In addition to leasing, discussed earlier, lenders can take security over a company's inventories, or over its receivables. This topic is explored further in Chapter 20 on working capital.

Unsecured debt

Downside protection: may be covenants
Yield: interest
Upside potential: none

Unsecured loans bear interest at a higher rate than secured debt, to compensate the lender for the greater risk.

---

4 A useful source of information on this, and on securitizations, is the widely read thesis written by Anna Katherine Barnett-Hart for her undergraduate degree at Harvard, 'The story of the CDO market meltdown: an empirical analysis'. This is downloadable from www.hks.harvard.edu/m-rcbg/students/dunlop/2009-CDOmeltdown.pdf

---

High-yield debt

Downside protection: may be a charge over assets; may be covenants
Yield: interest
Upside potential: none

High-yield debt used to be known as 'junk bonds'. This is sub-investment grade debt, issued with a rating of below BBB– (Standard Poor's rating) or Baa (Moody's rating).

Junk bonds were a very popular source of company finance in the 1980s. However, in the recessions of the early 1990s there were a lot of defaults, and the instrument became less attractive. Perhaps this was the cause of the change of name from 'junk' to 'high-yield'! The bonds came back into fashion in the 1990s, as investors sought instruments that gave a high yield. However, the yields are very susceptible to changes in economic and market conditions, which affect the likelihood of default: the relationship between perceived risk and required return plays out very clearly in the changes in the market price of these instruments.

Payment in kind (PIK)

Downside protection: may be a charge over assets; may be covenants
Yield: interest is rolled up, so no yield payments until the end of the lifetime
Upside potential: none, although rolled-up interest is paid out when the bond is repaid

---

Many high-risk bonds, although nominally giving a high yield to investors, in fact gave no cash return at all. Interest on these instruments is paid in kind (PIK), by issuing further bonds to cover the interest. Thus an investor buying £1m of such bonds could after a few years end up being owed £2m. Such a policy works only if the company can ultimately afford to repay the capital due, which mounts up very quickly at high rates of interest, compounded. Because the interest is not being paid out, they are inherently more risky than equivalent bonds which give a regular yield, and so should carry a greater interest rate.

PIK bonds have become increasingly popular in recent years, used particularly in private equity transactions.

A variant of the PIK bond is the PIK-toggle. Here, a bond pays interest but the issuer can at any time choose to make the interest payment as a payment in kind rather than in cash. The issuer can also at any time choose to toggle back to paying cash interest. PIK-toggle is obviously a useful option for the issuer to have, but makes the loan much riskier for the lender, who will demand a higher interest rate.

Mezzanine debt

Downside protection: may be a charge over assets; covenants
Yield: interest
Upside potential: equity kicker on redemption

We once heard mezzanine described by a banker as 'what we issue when we can't afford to lend any more, but the company can still afford to borrow'. By this, he meant that the borrowing company had exhausted all the 'good' security, and its financial gearing ratios were higher than a risk-averse lender would live with comfortably, but it was accepted that the company's cash flow and growth prospects merited further borrowing.

Mezzanine can carry covenants, although these might not be very useful, as they would not take precedence over senior covenants.[5] Accordingly, mezzanine debt is higher risk than senior, and thus attracts a higher return. As it would normally be infeasible for the loan to carry a rate of interest high enough to compensate for the lender's risk, in addition to the interest a mezzanine loan will often carry *warrants* (see below). Thus the return on mezzanine will be a mixture of interest yield and potential capital gain, as illustrated in Figure 12.3

An example of a mezzanine loan is as follows. MezzCo wishes to borrow £10m for seven years, and has exhausted all of its 'normal' debt capacity. A specialist mezzanine provider

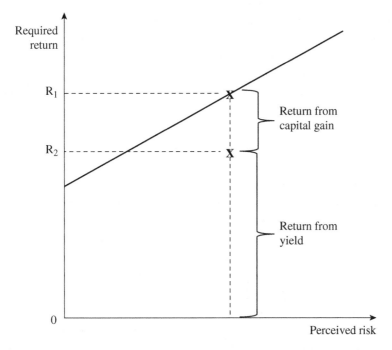

Figure 12.3 Return on mezzanine.

Given the riskiness of the instrument, the required return would be R_1. However, the company cannot afford the profit and cash-flow impact of a yield of R_1. Instead, it pays a yield of R_2 and offers an equity kicker which it is anticipated will fill the gap with a capital gain.

5 Your author once managed an investment in a mezzanine loan to a company which had been in breach of the mezzanine covenants for two years. However, the senior loan covenants had not been breached, and so the mezzanine lenders were powerless to enforce their position. We merely noted in the files, on a monthly basis, that the covenants were in breach.

(which might be a finance house that writes only mezzanine, or could be the mezzanine arm of a bank) will lend the money. The deal is structured such that the loan bears interest at, say, LIBOR plus 3 per cent over the life of the loan. At the end of the seven years the full loan will be repaid, and the lender will also have warrants giving the right to buy say 2 per cent of the company's share capital, at a very low price. This gives the lender a running yield, and enhances the return with the possibility of a capital gain on redemption.

Mezzanine is a private transaction rather than one which is traded on the financial markets.

Convertible debt

Downside protection: may be a charge over assets; may be covenants
Yield: interest
Upside potential: opportunity to convert into equity

This is debt which is convertible into equity (generally ordinary shares). The advantage of this to the lender is that there is a chance to participate in the share capital of the company, and so to make a capital gain. Because of this, the interest rate on convertibles is lower than that on non-convertible debt. The general principle is the same as that illustrated in Figure 12.3.

To give an example of convertible debt, consider ConCo. ConCo is currently trading at a share price of £1 per share. The directors wish to raise £100m capital, and have considered their alternatives: issue new equity, raise debt, or issue a convertible. They are reluctant to issue new equity, as they can foresee the share price rising considerably in the near term, and feel that issuing equity now, at only £1, would be an unnecessary dilution for their existing shareholders. Furthermore, they realize that issuing £100m of equity now would substantially change the voting structure of the company's shares, and they would like to maintain their controlling position for as long as possible.

ConCo has also considered issuing straight debt. The problem with this is that the company's existing lenders would not permit further senior debt to be issued, as this would damage their own position. Anyway, ConCo is already paying out large sums in quarterly interest charges, and taking on further debt would only exacerbate that cash outflow from the company.

Accordingly, ConCo determines that it will issue convertible debt. The terms of the debt are as follows:

> Outstanding for 10 years.
> Carries interest at LIBOR plus 1 per cent.
> Carries conversion rights into ordinary shares at £2 per share.

This means that the holders of the debt will earn a running yield of LIBOR plus 1 per cent (not a large amount, considering the risk they must be taking) over the ten years of the loan. At the end of the ten years, they have a call option – the choice either to be repaid their £10m, or to convert it into shares in ConCo at £2: 50 million shares. Obviously, the lenders hope that shares in ConCo will be trading at considerably more than £2 in ten years' time. If the shares are trading at, say, £3, the lenders will undertake the conversion, and can immediately sell their 50 million shares for £150m, making a capital gain of £50m. The capital

Working Insight 12.2

ConCo: returns from convertibles

ConCo has borrowed £100m on a 10-year convertible carrying interest at LIBOR plus 1%. LIBOR is currently 5%. The conversion price is £2, which compares to today's share price of £1. The cash flows to the investor are:

£m	Year 0	Years 1–9	Year 10
Initial investment	(100)		
Yield		6	6
Redemption/sale of shares			≥100

If the shares are trading at less than £2 in Year 10, the investor will demand repayment of the £100m, otherwise, they will convert. The overall return obtainable depends on the growth in the share price over the period, as shown below.

Annual growth in share price	Share price in Year 10 (£)	Value of 50 m shares (£m)	Overall compound return on investment
8%	2.16	107.9	6.6%
9%	2.37	118.4	7.3%
10%	2.59	129.7	8.0%
11%	2.84	142.0	8.8%
12%	3.11	155.3	9.5%
13%	3.39	169.7	10.3%
14%	3.71	185.4	11.1%
15%	4.05	202.3	11.9%

Thus, if the investor requires a return of, say, 10%, they should only invest in this convertible if they believe that the share price will increase by more than 13% compound over the 10 years. (A check for reasonableness of this could be done by looking to the PVGO and the growth inherent in the current share price, as discussed in Chapter 2.)

The calculations underlying this Working Insight are given in a spreadsheet on the book's website.

gain boosts the return, making it more commensurate with the risk being taken. Working Insight 12.2 sets out an example of the returns, and the level of growth the investor might require.

From the issuing company's point of view, convertibles have many advantages, as follows.

- Issuing convertibles rather than equity avoids issuing shares at the current price. This defers any dilution of eps, and also retains voting rights in their existing proportions for a while longer.
- Issuing convertibles rather than equity means that the eventual issue of equity (the conversion) will take place at a higher share price in the future, benefiting existing shareholders as it will dilute them less.

- Issuing convertibles instead of debt means that the ongoing servicing of the instrument (interest payments) is lower, thus conserving the company's cash resources and improving its reported profitability.
- Convertibles represent self-liquidating debt, in that – if all goes according to plan – the debt will never need to be repaid but will be converted into equity instead, thus preserving resources in the company.

Convertible and exchangeable bonds often have additional levels of sophistication in their structure. For example, the holder might have a put option which allows for redemption at a fixed price at a predetermined date, giving them a chance to exit an underperforming investment. If the investment is *over*-performing, i.e. the share price has soared way beyond the conversion price during the life of the bond, then often the issuing company has a call option (a 'soft call') allowing them to redeem the bonds, thus forcing the holders to convert.

Convertibles seem at first sight to give the best of both worlds – they free the company from having to sell equity cheaply, and they give the lender some downside protection so that even if the share price does not rise, the investment can still be repaid. There is of course a catch – in finance there is no free lunch. If ConCo's shares are still trading at £1 in ten years' time, then the convertibles will not be converted. In this case, the lender will have effectively lent the money to the company at LIBOR plus 1 per cent – a return that in no way reflects the risk taken. Furthermore, if the shares are only trading at £1 in ten years' time, it implies that the company is not trading to expectations; indeed, it could be facing problems. Having to repay £100m unexpectedly (because it was assumed that the holders would convert rather than ask for repayment) might be difficult.

If things do go according to plan, the convertibles will be converted and the company will never have to find the £100m for the pay-out. This expectation that they would be self-liquidating led to companies treating convertibles as equity in their balance sheets when the instruments first became common, in the 1980s. The view taken was that as the capital would never need to be repaid, it was equity rather than debt. However, the accounting standards bodies took a different view, arguing, very reasonably, that there is a potential liability unless and until the conversion option is selected. Accordingly, until recently the instruments were shown on companies' balance sheets as debt, and the ultimate dilution should they be converted was noted.

This accounting treatment was changed with the general adoption of International Financial Reporting Standards (IFRS). The required treatment is now that the convertible be treated as two separate instruments, debt and equity, classified in accordance with the substance of the contract. There is a liability, included in the financial statements at its present value (based on the interest rate that would be charged if it were 'normal' debt). This liability is deducted from the face value of the entire instrument, which results in the value of the equity component. This treatment has made the use of convertibles less attractive for some companies.

Case Study 17.2, which relates to company restructuring, sets out the example of Knight Capital, which was rescued by an injection of $400m in the form of 2% cumulative perpetual convertible preferred stock, with extremely dilutive terms.

Appendix 2 explains how convertibles are valued.

Exchangeable bonds

Downside protection: may be charge over assets, may be covenants
Yield: interest
Upside potential: opportunity to convert into the equity of another company

Case Study 12.2

Temasek – exchangeable bonds

The Singapore sovereign wealth fund, Temasek, issued exchangeable bonds for S$800m in 2011. The bonds were exchangeable into shares in Standard Chartered, the bank, of which Temasek held 18% of the capital, worth about S$6bn. The bonds were unusual in that they had a zero coupon, i.e. no yield. However, Temasek is AAA-rated, so the downside risk was considered low. The price for the exchange was set at 27% premium above the stock price on the date of issue of the bonds; this might be seen as aggressive for a three-year return, but apparently the markets expected such growth.

Source: Financial Times

Exchangeables are very similar to convertibles, in that the lender has the right to repayment or to convert into another asset. The difference is that the assets into which conversion is offered are not the securities of the company issuing the bonds, but the assets of a related company. This can have several advantages for the issuing company, including limiting the dilution of its own shareholders, and enabling it to offload investments that it no longer wishes to hold. Case Study 12.2 illustrates this.

Subordinated debt

Downside protection: probably none
Yield: interest
Upside potential: none

As its name implies, this debt is subordinated to the claims of other creditors. Because it is riskier, it should carry a higher interest rate.[6]

One particular example of subordinated debt is hybrid bonds. These have very long maturities: for example, the subordinated hybrid issued by Henkel, the German multinational. Case Study 12.3 sets out the terms of this bond, as an example of such an instrument.

Preference shares

Downside protection: minimal
Yield: fixed dividend
Upside potential: none

Preference shares are a type of quasi-equity – they do not give a right of ownership of the company and do not normally give a capital gain. (Also, they are not the same as

6 However, subordinated debt is sometimes lent by the owners of the business, or the previous owners in order to facilitate a buyout, in which case the coupon might not fully reflect the commercial risk.

Case Study 12.3

Henkel: the 99-year bond

- Raised €1.3 billion.
- Issued in 2005, and maturing in 2104 (99-year term). However, the investors' risk is mitigated by the fact that the bond is redeemable after 10 years.
- Interest is at 5.375% for the first 10 years, and then at 3-month EURIBOR plus a premium of 2.85%.
- The bond is subordinated, and Henkel has the option to defer interest payments under certain specified circumstances, relating to a fall in its cash flows.

As would be expected given the risk, these interest rates represented a premium over the prices being paid for more normal medium-term bonds at the time.

The ratings agencies treat the hybrid debt as 50% equity when they are evaluating the company's position, which gives it an advantage over traditional debt as regards its gearing calculations.

Source: www.henkel.com

'preferred' shares as discussed in Chapter 7 on venture capital investments.) Their main feature is that they carry a fixed dividend, which takes precedence over the dividend paid on ordinary shares. The dividend is often cumulative: if it is unpaid in any year, the arrears are carried over to be paid in future years. Although the shares do not normally carry votes, it is often the case that they will carry a vote if, and for as long as, their dividend is in arrears.

The 'preference' in the title also refers to the fact that in a winding-up these shares get paid out before the ordinary shares. (This gives a marginal reduction in risk compared to the ordinary shares, but is nothing to get excited about.)

Preference shares may be redeemable at the direction of the company, in which case the redemption is normally at par: as stated above, there is no right to a capital gain. However, preference shareholders may be able to make a capital gain if the shares are traded on the market, and market interest rates have changed significantly since the shares were issued. For example, a £1 12 per cent preference share carries an annual dividend of 12p. If market rates reduce to 6 per cent, the value of the share in the market could rise to £2.

Instead of being repayable or redeemable, or in addition to those possibilities, some preference shares may carry a right to conversion into equity, similar to convertible debt.

Ordinary shares

Downside protection: none
Yield: dividends
Upside potential: unlimited

The holders of the ordinary shares are the ultimate owners of the company. They are entitled to the profits after the other sources of finance have received their interest or dividends. This is the true risk capital of the company. In the event of a liquidation, the ordinary shareholders are the last to be paid out.

Warrants

Downside protection: none
Yield: none
Upside potential: opportunity to acquire the company's equity

Warrants are financial instruments issued by a company in its own shares. Ownership of a warrant gives the holder the right to acquire shares in the company on or after a certain date, at a certain price (which, it is hoped, will be less than the then market price). In this, they are similar to call options.

Warrants resemble options, but differ in that they are issued by the company itself, generally related to other fundraising, whereas options are instruments used by investors for speculation or hedging.

Options

Downside protection: none
Yield: none
Upside potential: opportunity to acquire the company's equity (call option) or to sell it (put option)

As explained in Appendix 2, an option gives the holder the right to do something, but not the obligation to do it. The buyer of options may do so to hedge against a risk, or to speculate. The seller of options is taking a significant risk, as the price of the underlying assets may move out of line with expectations. The difference between options and warrants is that whereas warrants are issued by the company in question, any third party can write options over any company's securities.

Microfinance: a non-traditional form of lending

It is worthwhile considering briefly a non-traditional form of lending, to see how it fits the model. *Microfinance*, or *microcredit*, involves providing loans to low-income individuals, families, and groups, often in the developing world through specialist microfinance institutions. In terms of the three variables we consider in evaluating financial instruments, microfinance has no upside for the lender. There is frequently no conventional downside protection, as there are few assets over which to take security. However, the downside is often protected by making a loan to a group rather than to individuals, as it has been established that this carries less likelihood of default. The loans do carry interest, at a rate sufficient to make a return for the lender.

Accounting for financial instruments

The treatment of financial instruments under International Financial Reporting Standards (IFRS) is complex, and well beyond the remit of this text. Nevertheless, it is important that

---

Case Study 12.4

Debt on a bank's balance sheet – misleading?

On 14 November 2011 the *Financial Times* carried a letter from Chris Lucas, Group Finance Director of Barclays Bank. Mr Lucas pointed out that accounting standards which demanded that debt be 'marked to market' were creating large unrealized profits for the banks at a time when their situation was worsening.

Marking to market means that the balance sheet shows debt at the amount at which it is, or could be, traded in the markets, rather than at the amount actually owed by the company. As a company's credit rating decreases, investors' required return will increase, thus the market value of its debt falls. The fall in value of a liability shows as a gain in the financial statements.

An accompanying article in the newspaper* stated that three major UK banks had between them booked almost £10bn of such gains in the three months to September 2011, and five large US banks had 'revealed gains equivalent to more than four-fifths of their combined $16bn in net profits for the third quarter'.

*'Barclays calls for clarity on fair value debt', *Financial Times*, 14 November 2011

---

we set out some basics of the subject, as they have direct relevance to the financial strategies that companies choose to adopt.

To grossly oversimplify, the historical situation was that financial instruments which carried a right to repayment were treated as debt, and everything else was considered as equity. Once issued, financial instruments tended to be left on the balance sheet at their original values. Nowadays, those same instruments are split into their component parts, each of which is shown at 'fair value' under debt or equity as applicable. The disclosure in the financial statements will reflect the characteristics of each instrument. So, as discussed earlier, a convertible is no longer included in the balance sheet as a liability at its face value, but is included as a liability (the net present value of the future committed cash flows) and an embedded option (the right to convert in the future). Furthermore, as circumstances change, for example, the share price rises, or market interest rates vary, the rules on 'marking to market' make it possible that the balance sheet value and the charge against profits will also change.

This has consequences to both balance sheet and income statement. Instruments such as preference shares, which traditionally were included with equity, might now be treated as debt.[7] This affects the company's interest charge, its interest cover and its gearing ratio. The former will reduce profits and the latter two may be the subject of debt covenants, which will need to be redefined. Some companies have reportedly changed their financial structures just to avoid the complications and profit impact of this reclassification of financial instruments, despite the fact that the underlying economics of the situation remain unchanged.

Case Study 12.4 sets out one of the issues faced by those analysing the financing side of the balance sheet.

---

7   We say 'might' rather than 'will', because the treatment required will depend on the exact terms of the preference share: for example, preference shares redeemable at the option of the company are accounted for differently to those redeemable at the holder's option.

8   Barclays calls for clarity on fair value debt', *Financial Times*, 14 November 2011

In order to understand a company's true financial situation, in terms of who owes how much to whom, one really needs to understand the relative rights of the different types of investor and lender.

Key messages

In the beginning there were 'debt' and 'equity'. However, the capital markets have long since diversified their financial instruments, and the continuum shown in Figure 12.1 illustrates that there are many choices in financing a company. When selecting or evaluating a source of finance there are several important things to remember.

- Keep it simple. If it is possible to structure the deal using 'plain vanilla' debt or equity, this is probably the best thing to do. Generally, fancy financial structures mostly benefit the investment banks who sell them (or the academics who write about them).
- The financial instrument chosen should have a risk profile to complement the company's business risk profile. Companies with low business risk can afford to take on high-risk debt instruments, to lower their average cost of capital. High-risk companies are best to stick to equity instruments.
- Cash requirements and profitability will also affect the choice of instrument.
- The accounting treatment of financial instruments may not be a good indicator of the true situation. Use option theory to help classify the instrument.
- The continuum of financial instruments indicates that there is no single definition of 'gearing'. The gearing of a company is the relationship between its debt and its equity; the continuum shows that there are few absolutes, but a lot of grey areas. When calculating gearing, always do it from the point of view of a particular security: other securities to the left of it in the continuum count as 'debt' as far as it is concerned, as they have better rights against the company's assets. Securities to the right on the continuum line have fewer rights, and can be treated as equity.

Suggested further reading

There is an excellent series of videos on YouTube presented by Paddy Hirsch, a senior editor of Marketplace. Clearly, and with humour, they explain financial instruments, securitizations, etc. They can be accessed also from the Marketplace website, via www.marketplace.org/topics/business/whiteboard

Gilligan, J. and Wright, M. (2010), *Private Equity Demystified – An Explanatory Guide* (2nd edn, ICAEW Corporate Finance Faculty), London.
This comprehensive document, free to download, is prepared by a leading academic and practitioner. Relevant to this chapter is a section entitled 'What are collateralised debt obligations, collateralised loan obligations and structured investment vehicles?'.

13 Dividends and buy-backs

Learning objectives

After reading this chapter you should be able to:

1 Set out the main arguments in favour of and against companies paying dividends.
2 Identify different types of dividend policy.
3 Explain why companies might prefer to undertake periodic share purchases rather than pay dividends.
4 Understand why different types of investor might have a preference for either dividends or buyouts.

Introduction

In Part 2 of this book we examined the various dividend strategies appropriate for companies at different stages in the life cycle. In this chapter we bring together those thoughts on dividend strategy, and supplement them with consideration of alternatives to dividends, such as share repurchases or buy-backs. We also examine some of the theories behind dividend payment.

Summary of the overall model as related to dividends

The payment of dividends is constrained by two main factors: ability to afford the cash out-flow from the company, and existence of distributable profits. In terms of the financial model

Working Insight 13.1

Dividend strategy and the life cycle model

	Cash availability	*Profit availability*	*Dividend policy*
Launch	No spare cash available. All cash is needed for investment in developing the business.	None. Probably making losses.	Nil dividend pay-out.
Growth	Cash is needed for development and investment in growing market share.	May be profitable.	Nil dividend pay-out is preferable. However, new shareholders might prefer a nominal pay-out.
Maturity	The company is now cash positive and has fewer opportunities to invest in profitable growth.	Profitable.	A medium to high dividend pay-out is preferred.
Decline	The company is cash positive, with no reinvestment potential.	May be profitable; has retained profits.	Full pay-out of available cash as dividend, even in excess of current profits.

developed in Chapter 5, this translates into dividend strategy as shown in Working Insight 13.1.

The bones of this model are broadly accepted by the market, and so one finds a clientele effect in investors – those who seek dividends are likely to be attracted to mature or declining companies, whereas shareholders preferring their return in capital gains look to earlier-stage investments. However, this does not hold true completely, and we have known earlier-stage companies start to pay dividends in order to attract interest from a wider range of potential investors.

Some thoughts on why companies pay dividends

Appendix 1 shows how Modigliani and Miller took the view that, in the perfect world in which their theories were developed, dividends are an irrelevance. Paying dividends reduces the overall size of the company, thus decreasing the value per share in direct proportion to the dividends received. Shareholders could choose to sell shares in order to realize funds, and do not need the declaration of a dividend to facilitate this.

However, Modigliani and Miller based their work on a world of perfect information, in which both taxes and transaction costs were ignored. In the real world, dividends are not irrelevant. Before we look at the ways in which they are paid, let us consider just some of the reasons suggested for why they are paid in the way they are: taxation, agency issues, and signalling.

One argument is that companies' dividend policies are influenced considerably by the tax systems – both corporate and personal – under which they operate. This seems plausible, in that shareholders might prefer to receive capital gains, taxed at a low rate, rather than dividends which are taxed highly. Furthermore, investors can choose when to trigger a capital gain by selling shares; they do not have a choice about paying tax on dividends so this too is an argument in favour of dividend policies being influenced by tax issues. However, research provides only

Working Insight 13.2

What does a dividend change signal?

Interpretation	Increase the dividend level	Decrease the dividend level
Good news	The company is prospering, and we can afford to pay out more of our profits without damaging our prospects.	The company has changed its strategy and the directors see these very profitable investment opportunities, which will provide more shareholder value than will mere payment of dividends.
Bad news	The directors have run out of ideas for profitable growth. *The model suggested in this book indicates that increasing the dividend level could be seen as a signal of advancing one stage in the life cycle.*	Profits and cash flow are falling, and the company is facing trouble in the foreseeable future. *The model suggested in this book indicates that decreasing the dividend level could be seen as a signal of moving back one stage in the life cycle.*

moderate support for this as a stand-alone theory, and if it were truly the case, companies in regimes which tax dividends more highly than gains would never pay dividends: this is not so.

(However, it is notable that Microsoft, extremely profitable and having over $40 billion of surplus cash, only announced its first dividend in 2003, once US tax laws were revised to exempt shareholders from income tax on dividends received from tax-paying corporations.)

A case is also made for dividends as a manifestation of agency theory. If a company has surplus cash, the management effectively has three choices as to how to deal with this: they can invest it in positive net present value projects (in which case, the cash is not really surplus); they can waste it on negative net present value projects; or they can distribute it back to the shareholders. Companies that sit on mountains of cash tend to make the investing community quite nervous, as there is always the danger that it will be misused. Therefore, giving it to the shareholders as a dividend is seen as a positive sign of good corporate governance. If surplus cash is repaid, then when the executives need additional funding in order to invest in new projects there is an automatic vetting mechanism, in that either lenders or shareholders will have to be convinced of the power of their investment proposal. Research findings suggest that companies in jurisdictions with weaker governance signal their good intentions by paying out higher dividends, which facilitates future fundraising.[1]

Perhaps the strongest argument about how companies pay dividends, and one that relates directly to the theories propounded in this book, is that dividends are seen as a signalling mechanism to the market. Here, changes in dividend levels are far more important than the actual dividends themselves. It is undoubtedly true that changes in dividends carry a signalling effect – any cursory reading of the financial press for a few weeks will demonstrate this. However, as Working Insight 13.2 illustrates, reading those signals may be somewhat complex.

---

1   Lemmon, M. L., Gan, J., and Wang, Z. (2011), 'Can Firms Build Capital-Market Reputation to Substitute for Poor Investor Protection? Evidence from Dividend Policies', http://ssrn.com/abstract=1787603

Working Insight 13.3

Smoothing dividends over a period

The directors of DivCo plc believe the company to be in its mature stage, and ideally would like to pay out 50% (no more) of annual profits as dividends to shareholders. However, the company's business model includes taking on large contracts, the profits of which can fall either side of a year end, significantly affecting year-on-year profitability. The dividend paid in Year 0 was £35m. The following tables demonstrate (a) a 50% pay-out ratio and (b) a smoothed dividend policy.

	Year 1	*Year 2*	*Year 3*	*Year 4*	*Year 5*
Profit after tax £ m	100	120	110	150	130
(a) Dividends using a 50% pay-out ratio	50	60	55	75	65
(b) Smoothed dividend policy	40	46	53	61	70

A company's situation and reputation will affect how the dividend signals are interpreted. For example, when Apple, a very fast-growing company with $100bn of surplus cash, announced in 2012 that it would pay its first dividend for seventeen years, the CEO emphasized that this would not affect their growth prospects, and the market believed him.

Generally, boards are reluctant to change their dividend policy without good cause. However, although some companies maintain a reasonably constant dividend pay-out ratio, many do not. Companies rarely change dividends exactly in line with changes in profits: if they did, one bad year could lead to a fall in dividends, with disastrous results for market sentiment. Particularly for companies in cyclical industries, a dividend pay-out policy that reflected a constant pay-out percentage would lead, over the cycle, to a level of dividend that varied considerably. This is not what shareholders have come to expect. For such businesses, it may be more appropriate to vary the dividend cover but maintain (or smoothly increase) the level of dividend. This would just be a different way of managing shareholders' expectations. Working Insight 13.3 demonstrates how this might work in a company suffering changed profitability.

The smoothed dividend policy illustrated in Working Insight 13.3 reflects merely increasing annual dividends by 15 per cent each year, a figure which management believes will be well covered by forecast profits for the next few years. In Year 5 this leads to a dividend pay-out which reduces dividend cover below two times. This continued increase in dividend payments would (they hope) be seen by the financial markets as a signal of their continued confidence in the company's prospects, and their belief that the fall in profits in Year 5 was a 'blip' in a growing trend.[2]

A real-life example of a company operating smoothing is shown in Case Study 13.1.

---

2   The smoothed dividend policy in Working Insight 13.3 was determined on a totally arbitrary basis by the authors. In Appendix 1 we discuss the research of Lintner in 1956, who concluded that companies actually apply an adjustment factor to their target pay-out ratio each year, to allow for such smoothing. Lintner's work was ground-breaking in its time, and a useful development of theory. However, practical experience with finance directors and boards suggests that the dividend decision is often made on pretty unscientific grounds – the main criterion being 'a bit more than last year'.

Case Study 13.1

Antofagasta – dividend policy in a cyclical industry

Antofagasta is a London-listed Chilean mining company. The graph is taken from the company's 2011 financial report. The ordinary dividend grows progressively over the cycle. Total pay-out has varied considerably, but the pay-out percentage has remained constant apart from the special pay-out in 2010 which reflected the successful completion of two projects. The 35 per cent pay-out is set at a level which can be managed over the economic cycle.

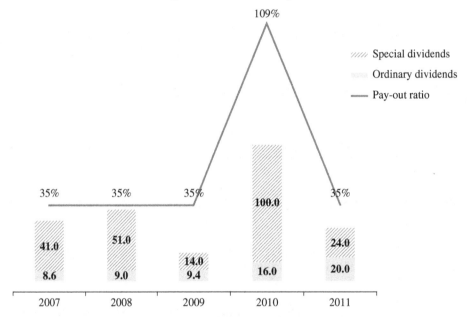

Antofagasta dividends per share (cents) and pay-out ratio (%)
Source: www.antofagasta.co.uk/pdf/presentations/Aplc2011FYpresentation20120313.pdf

The practice of smoothing dividends is widely followed in Europe and the USA. However, it is not universal. In some jurisdictions, companies have to set a mandatory pay-out level in their internal regulations. For example, in Brazil there is a compulsory dividend of at least 25 per cent of adjusted profits, although companies can and do choose to set higher levels. This annual minimum dividend (which can, subject to certain safeguards, be suspended if the company's circumstances so demand) can then be 'topped up' with an additional dividend to reflect performance in the year, and the projected cash demands on the business. In a similar manner, in early 2013 the Shanghai Stock Exchange stated that it would demand that companies pay out at least 30 per cent of profits as dividend.

In recent years, institutional investors have pressed for companies to increase their dividend pay-outs. There are three possible reasons for this. The first is a search for yield, in a market of very low interest rates. Second is the agency explanation suggested above, to keep control over executives' spending. And, third, investors have encouraged companies to increase their gearing, creating value through financial engineering. Of course, we must point out that value creation from gearing only takes place if the company is suitable for high leverage; if not, then it will make the investment more risky without necessarily increasing value proportionately. Although such financial engineering often provides benefits for private equity companies (see Chapter 18), such companies have close management contact with their investments, and are able to act quickly if things appear to be going wrong. For a publicly listed company shareholders do not have this insight, so might be taking on the gearing risk without having access to appropriate mitigation strategies.

Stock dividends

There is another way of paying dividends, in which the company declares a dividend but does not actually pay out any cash. This is normally known as a stock dividend or scrip dividend, and many companies give their shareholders the option to take their dividends either in cash or in the form of new shares.

In some jurisdictions there can be an advantage in stock dividends for some shareholders, as the stock dividend might not immediately be charged to tax.

When shareholders are offered stock dividends, it is always possible for those investors who want to receive cash to sell these new shares in the markets to realize the cash equivalent of their dividend. This is the same argument as used in theory to justify indifference of shareholders to the dividend policy of the company, and hits the same problem of transaction costs.

One perceived advantage of the stock dividend is that it enables shareholders to increase their holdings without incurring dealing costs. This, of course, is only valid if some of the shareholders sell their shares, or elect to receive a cash dividend; otherwise, all that happens is each shareholder's absolute holding increases, but their percentage holdings remain the same. Theoretically a straightforward stock dividend is the same as a bonus share issue; the company is simply capitalizing part of its distributable profits in order to issue new free shares. If the shareholder can choose between a cash dividend and being given more shares, the alternative stock dividend can be seen as a rights issue, with the exercise price being the total dividend divided by the number of shares offered.

A company declaring a stock dividend is effectively retaining the cash in the business for reinvestment. The critical question for shareholders therefore is whether the expected return on that increased reinvestment is financially attractive, so that it increases the total value of the company. From this perspective it can be seen that the declaration of a stock dividend is completely irrelevant – no cash is leaving the company. If stock dividends do not affect the company's reinvestment strategy, they are not part of the real dividend policy of the company.

Share repurchases (buy-backs)

Paying dividends is a logical way of distributing cash to investors if that cash is no longer required by the company. However, another way of achieving the same aim is for the company to repurchase some of its own shares using its excess cash to finance the purchase. The repurchased shares are held in the balance sheet as 'treasury stock', and can later be reissued, at an appropriate market price.

This is an area where the legal and tax positions vary by country. Some countries allow share repurchase, others still do not permit it, or impose severe tax penalties if it is undertaken. Some regimes are broadly neutral between buy-backs and dividends, whereas others give buy-backs a tax advantage over dividend payment.

Working Insight 13.4

Repurchase of shares: impact if taken up pro-rata by existing shareholders

Cash Rich Holdings plc has £100m in surplus cash on its balance sheet. It currently has 500m shares trading at a market price of £2 each. Rather than declaring a higher dividend, it announces that it intends to purchase 10% of its existing shares in the market at £2 per share. If all shareholders accept the offer pro-rata to their current shareholdings, nothing will change after the event.

For the holders of 10m shares before the deal, they would sell 1m shares and receive £2m in cash. After the repurchase, they own 9m shares but this represents the same 2% of the company which they owned before the deal, i.e.

$$\frac{9 \text{ million}}{450 \text{ million}} = \frac{10 \text{ million}}{500 \text{ million}}$$

When looked at in terms of the real impact, a share repurchase scheme should be regarded as a one-off discretionary dividend offer to shareholders. Thus, as shown arithmetically in Working Insight 13.4, if all shareholders accept the repurchase offer pro-rata to their shareholdings, they will own the same proportion of the company after the repurchase but will have received a cash payment from the company. This sounds remarkably like a dividend! If any particular shareholders do not want to receive cash at this time, they do not need to sell any of their shares. Their proportionate shareholdings will increase to compensate for the non-receipt of the cash payment: whether the compensation is inadequate or excessive depends on the reaction of the share price to the news of the repurchase.

The market reaction to the repurchase should be conditioned by the appropriate dividend policy for the company and whether this repurchase can be logically explained in this context. For example, if a mature company disposes of one of its business units it might have no need of the large cash balance it receives as a result. It could pay this cash out as a dividend but this level of dividend would be unsustainable in the future. Confusion among shareholders could be avoided by clear communication of the extra payment as a special one-off dividend, stating the source of the cash inflow.

Alternatively the company could use the cash to repurchase some of its own shares in the market, thus indirectly paying a one-off dividend to those of its shareholders who choose to sell shares at this time. There is an accounting impact of repurchasing shares which can make it appear more attractive to some companies than the straightforward higher dividend payment. This is, that share repurchase can be used to increase earnings per share, whereas they will actually be reduced by the higher dividend payment.[3] As illustrated in Working Insight 13.5 this increase is achieved for companies with relatively low P/E multiples, which tend to be mature, cash positive businesses where high dividend pay-out ratios are appropriate.

In a perfectly efficient market, the share price should not be affected merely by changes in earnings per share unless these changes reflect real alterations in future cash flow.

---

3   The higher dividend payment will reduce the company's cash resources; if nothing else, profits will be reduced because the company is not earning interest on its deposits.

Working Insight 13.5

Impact of share repurchases on earnings per share

Extracts of the latest profit and loss account of Mega Cash Holdings plc are

	£ millions
Operating profit	130
Interest income	20
Profit before tax	150
Taxation	50
Profit after tax	100
Dividends paid	50
Retained profits	50

The company has 500 million issued shares, so that the earnings per share are 20p (profit after tax of £100 million divided by 500m shares). The current share price is £2, representing a P/E multiple of 10. The interest income of £20m is generated by the investment of a cash mountain totalling £400m at a pre-tax interest rate of 5%.

The company wishes to assess the impact on eps of using the cash mountain either to pay a one-off extra dividend or to repurchase 200m shares (no change in share price is assumed as a result of the share repurchase and operating income and effective tax rates are kept the same). We assume that the normal dividend pay-out is maintained at 50% of profit after tax.

	Impact of dividend	*Impact of share buy-back*
Operating profit	130	130
Taxation	43	43
Profit after tax	87	87
Dividends	443	43
Retained profit	(356)	44
Earnings per share	17.4p	29p
No. of shares	500m	300m

The use of the cash mountain removes the interest income from the profit and loss account thus reducing eps in the dividend payment case.

The distribution of cash now, whether in the form of dividends or share repurchase, should have the same impact on the company's future cash generation capability; this assumes that there are no differences in the tax treatment of the two cash distributions. Consequently the total value of the company should be the same, which leads to a difference in share price since after the share repurchase there are fewer issued shares remaining. This difference in share price means that the P/E multiple applied to the company should still be the same in both cases, as is shown in Working Insight 13.6.

It is quite possible to generalize the conditions under which share repurchases will increase earnings per share, as is explained in Working Insight 13.7 but, as mentioned above, this should theoretically have no impact on the share price.

Working Insight 13.6

Impact of share repurchases on share price and price/earnings multiple

It is assumed that the original market capitalization (£1 billion) of Mega Cash Holdings plc valued the cash mountain at its face value of £400m. This implies that the after-tax trading profits of the company of £87m are capitalized at a P/E multiple of 6.9; so that

Profit after Tax (excl. interest income)	£87m
multiplied at implied P/E of	*6.9*
gives market value of	£600m
plus face value of cash	£400m
Market capitalization of company	£1,000m

After the cash distribution, this market capitalization should therefore fall to £600m (ignoring the tax impacts).

	Dividend distribution	*Share repurchase*
Market capitalization	£600m	£600m
Issued shares	500m	300m
Resulting share price	£1.20*	£2.00
eps (from Working Insight 13.5)	17.4p	29p
P/E multiple	6.9	6.9

*The share price falls after the dividend payment, because this cash payment represents 80p per share (ignoring the tax impact).

The 'rule' on the eps impact of buy-backs set out in Working Insight 13.7 is illustrated in Working Insight 13.8

Case Study 13.2 shows how Siemens implemented a share repurchase in order to re-gear its balance sheet and take advantage of low interest rates.

Over the last decade, stock repurchases have become more popular with companies. One reason for this is that previously they were illegal or tax inefficient in many countries: now these restrictions have been lifted. But many other reasons have been given for the explosion in companies buying back their own shares rather than paying dividends. Working Insight 13.9 sets out many of these, some of which have more face validity than others.

It is worth highlighting the first of the reasons suggested in Working Insight 13.9, that a share repurchase can increase eps. For many executives in listed companies around the world, eps is one of the key performance measures on which their pay is determined. An increase in eps can be personally rewarding for those determining the financial strategy.[4]

---

4 It is interesting to note that executive contracts often contain provisions stating that the eps calculation will be re-based if there is a bonus issue of shares, but rarely that such a recalculation will take place for a share repurchase. This is probably just an oversight.

Working Insight 13.7

Assessing the impact of share repurchase on eps

Let N = number of shares in issue
   n = number to be repurchased
   p = price of shares to be bought
   K_d = bank interest rate on money borrowed (or not earned) for repurchase
   t = tax rate (corporate)
   PAT = profits after tax before the share repurchase
Then,

$$eps = PAT \div N$$

and after the buy-back

$$\text{new } eps = [PAT - npK_d(1 - t)] \div (N - n)$$

If eps is to be enhanced by the transaction, $eps <$ new eps

i.e. $PAT \div N < [PAT - npK_d(1 - t)] \div (N - n)$ ⠀⠀⠀⠀⠀⠀⠀⠀(1)

Equation 1 can be simplified down to:

$$PAT > NpK_d(1 - t)$$
$$PAT \div N > pK_d(1 - t)$$

i.e. $eps > pK_d(1 - t)$ ⠀⠀⠀⠀⠀⠀⠀⠀(2)

i.e. share price paid for the repurchase, $p > eps \div K_d(1 - t)$ ⠀⠀⠀⠀⠀⠀⠀⠀(3)

If the share price paid is greater than this, eps will be diluted; if the price paid is less than calculated by (3), eps will be enhanced. (*And let us just say again, this impact on eps does not itself create or destroy shareholder value.*)
Restating equation 3 we can see that at equilibrium (i.e. where new and old eps are the same)

$$eps = \text{share price paid} \times \text{after-tax cost of debt}$$

This shows that eps is reduced by interest on the amount borrowed for the repurchase. So if interest rates are high, or the price paid is high, eps may not be boosted.
But – if the directors believe that profit is going to rise in the future, it will be worth the eps effect as eps will rise even more for the fewer shares that are left.
This is the same as:

$$P \div eps < 1 \div K_d(1 - t)$$ ⠀⠀⠀⠀⠀⠀⠀⠀(4)

Eps will be enhanced if the P/E multiple of the repurchase is less than the inverse of the post-tax opportunity cost of funding used to repurchase the shares.

As stated, one of the reasons often declared for undertaking share buy-backs rather than declaring dividends is that buy-backs are more flexible than dividends and do not give rise to a shareholder expectation of future activity. However, shareholders are generally intelligent, capable of understanding that special one-off dividends will not be repeated every year, as suggested in Case Study 13.3.

Working Insight 13.8

Impact of share repurchase on earnings per share

In Working Insight 13.5 we showed the impact of a buy-back on Mega Cash Holdings. Mega was receiving interest on its cash mountain of 5% before tax, 3.33% after tax. Its shares were trading on a P/E of 10 times.

Using equation (4) derived in Working Insight 13.7, the share repurchase will increase eps provided that the P/E multiple of the buy-back is less than the inverse of the post-tax opportunity cost of funding used to repurchase the shares, i.e.

$$P/E < 1 \div K_d(1 - t)$$

For Mega, the buy-back was done at the then-current market value, i.e. at a P/E of 10 times. Provided that the post-tax cost of funds was below 10%, the buy-back will enhance eps. As shown in Working Insight 13.5, the buy-back did indeed have this effect.

In the unlikely event that the company had used its surplus £400m to buy back 66.7m shares at £6, a P/E of 30 times (the inverse of the 3.33% debt cost), there would have been no impact on eps, as shown below.

	Before £m	*After £m*
Operating profit	130	130
Interest income	20	0
Profit before tax	150	130
Tax	50	43
Profit after tax	100	87
Number of shares	500m	433.3m
Earnings per share	20p	20p

Case Study 13.2

Repurchasing shares to take advantage of low rates

In August 2012 Siemens, the German industrial company, announced a €3bn share repurchase. Its stated intention was to borrow long-term debt (at a time when interest rates were historically low), and use the funds to buy back shares. The following month, the company issued the following press release.

> Siemens has issued some €2.7 billion in bonds at the lowest interest rates ever obtained on the European bond market. The bonds, which were issued on August 30 at today's value, will primarily be used to finance the company's share buy-back program, which was launched at the beginning of August. Siemens intends to repurchase up to €3 billion in company shares by the end of 2012. As of last Friday, the company had spent some €1.1 billion for this purpose. 'Our plan to swap expensive equity for historically cheap debt capital is being executed in grand style. The fixed interest rates we've obtained will ensure

that we'll continue to profit from today's extremely favorable conditions over the long term', said Siemens CFO Joe Kaeser.

The bonds are being issued in four tranches. Two-year bonds with a volume of €400 million carry an interest coupon of 0.375 percent, while 7.5-year bonds with a volume of €1 billion offer investors an interest rate of 1.5 percent. Thirteen-year bonds with a volume of GPB350 million carry an interest coupon of 2.75 percent. And investors will receive 3.75 percent interest per annum on 30-year bonds with a volume of GBP650 million. These are the lowest interest rates that a company has ever obtained for euro- and sterling-denominated bonds with these maturities. Nearly two-thirds of the euro-denominated bonds went to German and French investors. British investors purchased more than 80 percent of the sterling-denominated bonds. All four tranches were rated A+ by Standard & Poor's and Aa3 by Moody's.

Source: www.siemens.com

An example of the great flexibility a company can create when returning cash to shareholders was shown by Emap, a UK media group, which effectively gave them a choice between a dividend and a share repurchase, as set out in Case Study 13.4

Do buy-backs add value?

Given that share buy-backs have become common, what is the market impact of a company's announcement that it is about to undertake such a transaction? Well, as with dividends the signalling effect may vary. Generally, markets are in favour of buy-backs, as they eliminate

---

Working Insight 13.9

Reasons for companies to repurchase their own shares

Reasons which apply only to share repurchases

- To increase earnings per share (as demonstrated in Working Insight 13.7).
- To strengthen management incentives by reducing the number of outstanding shares so that management ends up with a higher percentage of the company. (Note: this obviously can lead to agency conflicts.)
- Buy-backs are considered to be more flexible than dividends, as they are seen as one-offs and do not reflect a trend. (But see case study below.)
- To buy out 'weaker' shareholders who may otherwise sell to a hostile bidder. (Again, note the potential agency conflict.)
- To give shareholders a choice of how to take their return.
- To offset eps dilution from the exercise of share options.

Reasons which would apply equally to dividend payments

- To improve management's business focus by limiting their opportunities to invest in non-core or value-reducing projects.
- To reduce the cost of capital.

Case Study 13.3

Heritage Oil – a one-off dividend

In August 2010 Heritage Oil, an oil exploration company, paid a one-off dividend of 100p per share in order to distribute the proceeds from disposal of some of its assets. The company's explanation of the dividend made it clear that the dividend reflected the asset disposal. Its financial statements stated, 'The company has not declared or paid any other dividends since incorporation and does not have any current intentions to pay further dividends in the foreseeable future.'

An interesting adjunct to this is the impact of the dividend on the company's convertible bonds. Once such a special dividend is paid out, the company's share price will fall, which is prejudicial to holders of such convertibles. The company stated that it would not amend the terms of the convertible instrument to reflect this, but instead would pay out the dividend to all of the convertible bondholders as if they had already converted into Ordinary shares.

Source: www.heritageoilplc.com/special_dividend.cfm

the 'slack' for directors, and often the company's share price rises disproportionately. However, as with dividend increases, if the market believes that the directors are proposing a buy-back because they have run out of investment ideas, the negative impact could damage sentiment about the company's future.

It is also worth noting another reason why investors might like buy-backs that leverage a company. For most stock markets, the average holding period of equities has fallen, and investors now stay with a stock for months rather than years. This being so, they could be swayed by their short-term gain from a buy-back rather than the longer-term benefit of growth through investment.

Case Study 13.4

Emap – returning money to shareholders

In 2006 Emap received approximately £380 million from the sale of one of its divisions. Part of its long-term plan was to return such proceeds to shareholders. Emap structured the return as a share buy-back.

The company capitalized reserves to create a new class of shares, the B shares. As part of a capital reorganization, shareholders were given one new B share for every existing ordinary share they held. Shareholders then had three choices.

(1) Receive a one-off dividend of 110p per B share (taxable as income), after which the B shares would become effectively worthless. Or
(2) Have Emap redeem their B share for 110p, which would be treated for tax purposes as a capital gain. Or
(3) Hold the B shares until the start of the next tax year (about 6 months later) for redemption at 110p. This too would be a capital gain, but might be preferable for tax planning.

Source: emap.com

Case Study 13.5

Berkshire Hathaway – buying back cheap shares

In September 2011 Berkshire Hathaway, the investment vehicle for Warren Buffett, announced that for the first time it was to undertake a share repurchase scheme. The board of directors was authorized to buy back shares at prices no greater than a 10% premium on the then-current book value of the shares. Set out below is an extract from the company's regulatory announcement.

> In the opinion of our Board and management, the underlying businesses of Berkshire are worth considerably more than this amount, though any such estimate is necessarily imprecise. If we are correct in our opinion, repurchases will enhance the per-share intrinsic value of Berkshire shares, benefiting shareholders who retain their interest.
>
> Berkshire plans to use cash on hand to fund repurchases, and repurchases will not be made if they would reduce Berkshire's consolidated cash equivalent holdings below $20 billion. Financial strength and redundant liquidity will always be of paramount importance at Berkshire.
>
> *Source:* www.businesswire.com/news/home/20110926005712/en/Berkshire-Hathaway-
> Authorizes-Repurchase-Program

It is interesting that many companies appear to announce share buy-back programmes without actually undertaking them. This way they get the flexibility of financial choice, and benefit of the positive market sentiment without all the messiness of losing control of the company's funds! However, this does mean that the market often treats more seriously a formal purchase plan than just a vaguely expressed intent to buy back shares on the market.

Of course, in the final analysis share buy-backs only add value for the shareholders if they can be achieved at a buying price below the fundamental value of the company. Buying back shares which are overpriced by the market – however it affects the eps or market sentiment – is not a value-enhancing strategy. This is illustrated clearly in Case Study 13.5 which sets out the conditions under which Berkshire Hathaway will buy back its shares.

The mechanics of a buy-back

The practicalities of repurchasing shares are more complex than those for declaring a dividend (which means of course that significant fees may be paid to investment banks and advisers, in turn implying that the company has to be very certain that this is a route it wishes to follow). The regulations will differ in each country.

The buy-back decision, because of its 'one-off' nature, is more complicated than the dividend decision. As we have stated, with dividends the question to ask is generally 'how much more than last year should we pay?'. With buy-backs three key issues to be addressed are:

1   How much can the company afford to repurchase? Issues to consider are whether or not there is surplus cash in the business; the impact on the company's debt-to-equity ratio of a buy-back; and whether available reserves will permit the desired level of buy-back.
2   Is it the intention to give all shareholders an equal chance of selling their shares to the company? This will have an impact on the method by which the buy-back is undertaken, as discussed below.

3   Are the shares currently under or overvalued? Buying back shares at an undervalue could be seen as a useful financial strategy. Buying back shares in an overvalued market is merely a transfer of value to the shareholders who exit.

Methods of repurchase of shares

Provided that a company has met with local legal requirements such as having sufficient reserves and obtaining shareholder approval for the transaction, there are two main ways in which it can repurchase its shares: buying them on the stock market, or a tender offer. The former is the most common method: buying shares on the market is relatively quick and straightforward, and the company can choose when to make the purchase.[5] For repurchases of relatively small amount of shares – say, 2–3 per cent of the outstanding capital – this is an effective way to proceed.

If the company wishes to buy back a higher volume of its shares, or if it wishes to make an offer to all of its shareholders, not just those who are active in the stock market, then a tender offer is better. In a tender offer the directors state a price range at which they will repurchase the shares, and advertise this widely to shareholders. The ultimate price paid reflects the shareholders' willingness to tender their shares.

Conclusion

Companies can in some circumstances create value for shareholders by returning money to them. They may choose to return cash to shareholders in two main ways – by paying dividends or by entering into share buy-back arrangements. Although in many instances the position for the shareholders is the same – they receive a cash payment – the signalling effect by the company can be very different, as can the impact on its financial results. Accordingly, the decision as to how to give the shareholders their return is one that is closely linked to the company's position and future strategy.

Key messages

- Dividends and share buy-backs both involve giving cash to the shareholders.
- Dividends paid by issuing more shares, rather than being paid in cash, may have advantages in some circumstances.
- The level of dividend pay-out should increase over the company's life cycle, with payments increasing as the company matures and has more cash and profits available.
- Many companies are reluctant to reduce dividends year on year, even over the economic cycle. However, in some jurisdictions, dividend policies based on a minimum pay-out ratio are the norm.

---

5   Logically, companies would only buy back their shares on the market if they believed that the shares were undervalued. That would mean that shareholders who wished to stay with the company would benefit, and those who thought the current price fair would be able to exit. However, as most listed company directors seem permanently to regard the market as underpricing their shares (even at the height of a boom) this analysis may be overly academic.

- Various theoretical arguments are advanced to explain dividend policy. These include tax reasons; protecting surplus cash from poor management decisions; and as a signalling mechanism to the market.
- Buy-backs may be undertaken for these reasons, and also to increase earnings per share or change the relative holdings of shareholders. Buy-backs are also commonly used to re-gear a company, reducing the overall cost of capital.
- A share buy-back can be a useful way to return cash to shareholders while not raising expectations of future dividends. It may also carry tax advantages.
- The signal given by increasing dividends or organizing a buy-back can suggest that the company expects to have growing profits and cash flow, and so can spare the extra money. Or it can suggest that the company has run out of suitable investment ideas. The context of the pay-out decision is important to the markets.
- The impact on eps of a share repurchase can be positive or negative. Usually, the positive impact of reducing the number of shares more than compensates for the negative impacts of reducing interest income.

Suggested further reading

Dhanani, A. and Roberts, R. (2009), *Corporate Share Repurchases: The Perceptions and Practices of UK Financial Managers and Corporate Investors*, Edinburgh: Institute of Chartered Accountants of Scotland.
This survey research, supplemented with interviews, captures the views of investors and company managers as to how and why share repurchases are undertaken, and how they are perceived.
Jiang, B. and Koller, T. (2011), 'Paying Back Your Shareholders', *McKinsey Quarterly*, available at http://www.mckinsey.com/insights/corporate-finance/paying_back_your_shareholders.
Discusses factors affecting the decision between dividends and buy-backs.

Part 4

Transactions and operating issues

14 Valuations and forecasting

Learning objectives

After reading this chapter you should be able to:

1 Apply the three main methods of valuing a company – assets, multiples, and discounted cash flow.
2 Appreciate the advantages and disadvantages of each method of valuation, and the need for sensitivity analysis.
3 Explain why a suite of forecasts needs to comprise an integrated income statement, cash flow, and balance sheet.
4 Question the assumptions underlying any forecast by understanding some common behavioural biases.

Introduction

In this part of the book we deal with financial strategy in terms of the transactions a company might undertake – listing its shares on a stock exchange, making an acquisition, receiving private equity, or restructuring. These transactions have a common thread – each of them involves the preparation of a forecast or a valuation in order to enable it to proceed. In undertaking an acquisition we obviously need to know how much the target business is worth to us; raising funds requires a cash-flow forecast to determine how much is needed, and for how long. In this chapter we consider some methods of company valuation, before going on to discuss how the underlying forecasts might be put together and the biases we need to address in so doing.

Valuing companies

Outline of valuation approaches

The first thing to realize about company valuation is that there is no right answer. Yes, it involves spreadsheets and formulas, but valuation is an art, not a science. It is driven by the valuer's opinion of how the business will perform in the future, the perceived risk, and the investors' required return. Given the potential range of these inputs, there is no real reason why any two valuers should come up with the exactly the same numbers for a company.

When we speak about the value of a business, we are referring to the value, for a company, of its *equity*, the ordinary shareholders' funds. This is what is left after all the other stakeholders' claims have been deduced from the value of the assets. However, in calculating the value of the equity, we often start with the *enterprise value*, the value of the organization regardless of the means of finance. Given that the acquirer can impose their own financing structure on the business, valuing the underlying enterprise independent of the sources of finance makes good sense.

There are three broad approaches to company valuation: balance sheet or asset-based methods; discounted cash flows (DCF); and multiples of profits. Of these three, DCF is probably the most useful, and profit multiples probably the most widely used.

Assets basis of valuation

We could just look at a balance sheet for the 'total equity' figure and use that as the company's value. We could, but we don't. Balance sheets are not a good representation of company worth. Working Insight 14.1 gives some examples of why this is so.

Sometimes, for valuation purposes, balance sheets are amended to reflect key assets at a market value rather than historic cost. This is better than using an unchanged balance sheet for the valuation, but still does not address all the problems. However, in some industries, asset-based valuations are commonly used, for example, property companies or investment companies, where up-to-date asset valuations are included in the financial statements.

It might be the case that the business owns assets that are 'separable', i.e. they could be sold off without affecting its ongoing business. As an example, the business could be run, mostly over the telephone and internet, from a Manhattan penthouse owned by the company. Clearly, a valuation of the whole company would have to include the value of that property, as it is a separable company asset.

The most appropriate time to use balance sheet values is if the company is being acquired to be broken up, because the realizable value of its constituents is greater than the going concern value.

Working Insight 14.1

Reasons why the balance sheet is not a good indicator of value

Balance sheets are backward-looking	The balance sheet reflects what has been spent on a business, not what it could generate in the future.
	Many assets are shown on the balance sheet at historic cost, and the amount that they cost when they were bought may not be representative of what they are worth now.
Accounting policies are not designed to reflect value	Accountants have never really got to grips with recording goodwill or other intangibles on the balance sheet. So the basic approach we adopt is to ignore them. If a company has bought its intangibles (e.g. acquired goodwill on an acquisition), then the purchased intangibles can be shown on the balance sheet, but never at more than they cost. If the intangibles were generated internally, they cannot be show on the balance sheet. (For example, Coca-Cola is one of the most valuable brands in the world, but because the brand was developed internally rather than acquired, it is not ascribed any value on the balance sheet.)
	Debt shown on a balance sheet can in some circumstances be stated at its market value rather than the actual liability. This has the peculiar effect of understating the liabilities of a failing business: because their debt is risky, the market is applying a discount to it.
	Accounting policies vary between businesses and, despite attempts to create universal standards, between countries. This means that the equity could vary under different rules.

Discounted cash-flow approach

Buying a company should be evaluated on the same principles as making any other investment – the sum paid in Year 0 should be less than the discounted value of the future cash flows, thus generating a positive net present value for the purchaser. In order to value a company using this method the expected cash flows must be determined, as must a suitable discount rate.

The most common DCF approach is to discount free cash flow at a weighted average cost of capital. The steps in such a valuation can be explained using the seven drivers of value, as set out in Working Insight 14.2.

This approach to DCF valuation, determining enterprise value by discounting the free cash flow at the WACC, is probably the most widely used and useful discounting approach. However, it is also possible to calculate the equity value directly, by discounting cash flows to equity at a cost of equity. Other DCF methods are also valid. The reading list at the end of this chapter gives sources for those wishing to explore this in more depth. A very simple spread-sheet is available on the book's website to demonstrate how the drivers contribute to value.

Although DCF analysis contains a lot of assumptions, a great advantage of it is that it can easily support a sensitivity analysis, with the underlying figures being changed to reflect different potential scenarios. This will indicate which of the value drivers is/are the most important for the business. A good understanding of the value of the business can be built up in this way, which can be used to direct due diligence in an acquisition, or to inform a post-acquisition operating plan.

Working Insight 14.2

Valuing a company using DCF

1 Determine a suitable time period for the valuation	Companies have an indefinite life, so common practice is to forecast out for an initial period, and then take a 'terminal value' from that point onwards. The initial period should in theory be taken as the period of competitive advantage, but in the absence of a clear indication of when that might be, a forecast of 6–10 years is often used.
2 Calculate the Free Cash Flow (FCF) from operations for that period	FCF is the cash flow generated by operations ignoring any cash flows related to financing (such as dividends, interest, loan repayments, etc.).
	Calculate FCF for each year as follows: Sales Less Costs and Expenses = EBITDA Adjust for: Tax on EBITDA Capital expenditure Movements in working capital = Free Cash Flow
3 Estimate Terminal Value (TV) at the end of the initial period	TV is the value of the business at the end of the initial period – effectively, the value of all cash flows beyond that period. Normally calculated as a perpetuity or a growing perpetuity of the final year FCF. (See spreadsheet on the book's website for examples.)
4 Calculate an appropriate discount rate	Generally the weighted average cost of capital, based on an appropriate financing structure for the target company.
5 Determine the Value of operations	Discount the FCF and the TV at the WACC.
6 Add in the value of non-operating assets, to arrive at the Enterprise value	Companies often hold assets which are easily separable, and could be sold off without affecting the value of operations. For example, in 2012 Apple had cash and marketable securities in excess of $100bn. It is difficult to imagine that the company needed all of that to conduct its operations, so a valuation of the company would value the *business* and then add on the $100bn as a non-operating asset. If the non-operating assets comprise a significant investment in another business, this too will have to be valued. At this stage, the value you have calculated is the *Enterprise Value*.
7 Deduct net debt to arrive at Equity Value	The final stage of the valuation, to arrive at the value of equity, is to deduct net debt from the enterprise value.

Valuation on multiples

Although valuation using DCF is the most rigorous, being based on a considered view of the likely cash-flow generation of the target business, valuation on multiples is the most commonly adopted approach. The logic behind a valuation on multiples is to compare the target business with a listed company (or preferably several companies) in a similar area of activity. As the businesses are in the same line of operations, the thinking is that the ratio of company value to profits should be broadly similar.

So, broadly, for the comparator companies, assuming that market capitalization reflects value, we say that:

$$\text{Value}_{\text{comparators}} = (\text{Average profit after tax})_{\text{comparators}} \times (\text{Average P/E ratio})_{\text{comparators}}$$

Therefore, for our target company in the same business we can assume that

$$\text{Value}_{\text{target}} = (\text{Profit after tax})_{\text{target}} \times (\text{Average P/E ratio})_{\text{comparators}}$$

If the target company operates in more than one distinct business sector, then the valuation should be conducted on a *sum of the parts* (SoTP) basis. Profits related to each division should be multiplied separately by the relevant multiple for the comparator companies in that industry, and then the divisional values totalled. If divisional profits sum to more than the overall corporate profit (which will happen if corporate overheads have not been allocated to divisions), then a deduction to the value should be made by capitalizing the corporate cost base at an average multiple.

The steps to complete a simple valuation on P/E multiples are set out in Working Insight 14.3.

If the target company has non-operating assets (as discussed earlier), then the business valuation should be adjusted accordingly. A simple way to do this is to add the value of the non-operating assets to the value determined on multiples. However, if the non-operating assets have generated income in the year, then that income needs to be excluded from the income included in the P/E calculations, otherwise we are double-counting. Similarly, the market capitalizations of the comparator companies should be checked to see if they are distorted by non-operating matters.

Although this valuation method is quite easy (particularly as the P/E multiples of most companies can be found in the financial media) it does not take much financial knowledge to spot its flaws. There might not be any listed companies that are truly comparable. Furthermore, the value of listed companies reflects market sentiment rather than just their own position, and so at any time could be artificially high or low. These issues are flaws that relate to any valuation on multiples. More specific to a P/E multiple valuation is that by being based on profits after tax, the P/E multiples reflect the capital structures of each of the comparators, which might be very different to the target company's capital structure. This particular issue can be addressed by using EBIT or EBITDA multiples in the valuation. (EBITDA has the advantage of not being so distorted by accounting policies. EBITA might also be used.)

A valuation on EBIT[DA] multiples works on the same principle as a P/E valuation, but the underlying equation relates to enterprise value rather than equity value. So we calculate an EV/EBIT[DA] multiple for each comparator and apply the (adjusted) average to the target company's EBIT[DA]. The steps in this are shown in Working Insight 14.4.

A very simple spreadsheet is available on the book's website to demonstrate multiples-based valuation.

Working Insight 14.3

Steps in a valuation based on P/E multiples

1 Determine a sustainable profit after tax for the target business	A sustainable profit after tax is one that is not affected by one-off items that might have distorted the current year, such as redundancy costs, windfall profits or expenditure that would not be continued by an acquirer.
	Start by determining a sustainable operating profit (EBIT) and then apply to this the interest and tax related to an appropriate financing structure, to get the profit after tax.
2 Determine a suitable multiple	Find companies that are similar to the target company in terms of size, sector, etc. Average their P/E ratios (making sure that you understand why outliers are different from the pack and deal with them appropriately).
	It may be appropriate to adjust the average P/E multiple at this point. For example, if using the technique to value a private company, valuers often reduce the quoted comparator figure by 25–50% to allow for the fact that private companies tend to be smaller with fewer growth prospects and more risk. On the other hand, if the target has better prospects than its sector, the multiple could be increased.
3 Apply the multiple to the target profit after tax	Multiplying the calculated P/E by the target's profit after tax gives an equity value for the target company.

A fundamental problem with all valuations on multiples is that they rely on the underlying market being 'correct'. However, if stock market prices are unrepresentative, any value based on these will be similarly misleading.[1] During the dot.com boom, technology and media companies were overvalued, and basic engineering companies often undervalued; any valuation based on comparisons with these would have produced misleading results.

The use of market multiples for valuations can be further misleading due to the way in which shares are traded, with prices reflecting market expectations rather than underlying value, as discussed in Chapter 2.

One other use of multiples is worth noting in valuing a business. In some industries, custom and practice suggest that businesses will change hands on a multiple of turnover, or a multiple of a physical quantity such as the number of units sold in a year. It is worthwhile being aware of these rules of thumb, but essential to understand the underlying logic before using them.

It is always worthwhile reverse-engineering your valuation on multiples, to see what it implies for levels of profit and growth if it were the outcome of a DCF model. Similarly, it

---

1 This was demonstrated convincingly in Cooper, M. J., Dimitrov, O., and Rau, P. R. (2001), 'A Rose.com by Any Other Name', *Journal of Finance*, 56(2): 293–324. They documented a large and seemingly permanent value increase for companies which changed their names during the height of the boom to dot.com and other internet-related terms, whether or not the companies made changes to their underlying businesses.

Working Insight 14.4

Calculating value based on EBIT[DA] multiples

1 Determine the market capitalization of each of the companies in your chosen peer group.
2 Determine the value of net debt in each of the companies in the peer group. (Often, the book value of debt is used as a proxy for its market value.)
3 Add these together to get the Enterprise Value (EV).
4 Determine the sustainable EBIT[DA] of each of the peer companies.
5 Calculate the EV/EBIT[DA] ratio for each of the peer companies.
6 Determine an average or median – again, exclude outliers once you understand why they are outliers.
7 This multiple, adjusted if appropriate, can be applied to the EBIT[DA] of your target company.
8 Multiplying the target's sustainable EBIT[DA] by the multiple gives the target's Enterprise Value.
9 Deduct the target's debt (at market value where appropriate) to get its Equity Value.

---

is useful to take a DCF valuation and check whether the multiples it implies appear realistic in the current market.

Valuing a loss-making business

One issue which seems to give some concern is how to value a loss-making business. The solution to this rather depends on two things – why the business is making a loss, and why you want to value it. Once these questions have been answered, the normal valuation methods are available.

For example, let us say that a normally profitable business made a loss last year, but this is very clearly a one-off loss, due to specific circumstances that are unlikely to be repeated. That being the case, the loss should not impact on the calculation of sustainable profits (for a valuation on multiples) or on the future cash flows (for a valuation on fundamentals). You might choose to apply more risk factors to the valuation, knowing that losses are a possibility, but this very much depends on the circumstances.

For a business that has been loss-making for several years, the problem is a bit trickier until you understand why it is making a loss, and what you intend to do about it. If you are buying the business in order to obtain a specific asset or assets, then the losses are not that relevant – the value of the business will relate to the value of that asset(s), net of any costs that will be incurred in closing the rest of the business or selling it on. However, if you are buying the enterprise as a going concern, you need to think about what you are going to do to change the nature of its operations, how long that will take, how much the restructuring will cost, and what level of profitability is expected after the turnaround.

Once the future profit forecast is established, then the enterprise can be valued either on multiples or on fundamentals. Using multiples, the simplest way is to project forward to a point at which there are profits, apply a suitable multiple (based on today's markets, but adjusted for risk) and then discount the resultant sum to a present value at a suitable cost of capital. Using discounted cash flow to generate a valuation on fundamentals is probably more useful, as this will set out clearly the cash flows in the loss-making period and the future profitable period. In scheduling these, the buyer has to take a good look at what they are acquiring and the plans for turnaround.

Preparing forecasts

Valuation using discounted cash flow requires a forecast of future profits and cash flows. Most business activity involves some sort of financial forecasting. We need forecasts to help determine how much money to raise, whether we can afford to pay a dividend, whether to introduce a new product, what price to pay for an acquisition – for pretty much everything, really. In this section we consider the main issues to consider when preparing financial forecasts. This is not a technical primer, and does not address topics such as how to use spreadsheets: we focus on obtaining and understanding the numbers rather than manipulating them.

The process of forecast preparation can be broken down as follows:

1   Determine the reason for the forecast and the required timescale.
2   Obtain the supporting data.
3   Prepare the forecast.
4   Analyse what it is telling you.
5   Do a sensitivity analysis.

And then repeat stages 2 to 5, as appropriate.

Each of these stages is outlined below. We then look briefly at the fascinating area of behavioural finance, to highlight the biases we all have in considering numbers.

Why do we need this forecast?

There are two main types of financial forecast. Monthly or weekly (or occasionally daily) forecasts are used to determine what the cash position will be, in order to ensure that funding will be sufficient for the organization's needs. The preparation of these should be a regular activity, part of the management information process, and the timetables and information sources should be well understood within the business. This contrasts with forecasts used to support decisions, generally involving annual cash flows over a period, which require some sort of discounted cash-flow analysis in order to support an investment decision.

The key questions to ask before commencing forecasting are: who needs this information, and why? And, having established this, we should be able to address the next two questions: how accurate does it need to be, and to what timescale?

It is vital to understand these terms of reference. In particular, a clear appreciation of the aim of the forecast will help with the next stage, data collection, as it will enable us to differentiate relevant and irrelevant data.

Obtaining the data

> Supposing is good, but finding out is better.
> *(Mark Twain)*

A forecast is only as good as the data that go into it. Those data can come from sources internal to the organization, or from external sources, or from both; they can be verified, or unchecked; they can be taken from people with a vested interest in the outcome of the work, or from parties with an interest but no axe to grind, or from those who really don't care and don't have the time to help you, anyway.

We won't insult your intelligence by categorizing the above on a continuum of 'good' and 'bad' data sources. But we do suggest that, in any report or business plan prepared around the forecasts, you make explicit what sources you used.

The supporting data should be non-financial as well as financial. Indeed, it is always best to start with the non-financial information, and only look at the numbers once you have understood the strategic picture. A forecast prepared in splendid ignorance of industry trends and the business environment is unlikely to stand up to scrutiny.

Preparing the numbers

Include a balance sheet

In 1494 Fra Luca Pacioli wrote his *Summa de Arithmetica*, which included a description of double-entry bookkeeping. He recommended that all transactions be recorded in a systematic way, with a debit and a credit entry, and that the clerk should always ensure that the debits and credits balanced. That was sound advice back in the fifteenth century, and is still good today.

Many financial forecasts are prepared in order to obtain an understanding of cash flows – for example, to support a fundraising exercise or valuation. In most cases, the cash flows come out of a forecast income statement, and the underlying data relate to sales and costs, which translate into debtor receipts and creditor payments. However, a common problem is that people try to short-cut the process by just preparing the cash-flow forecast, or just preparing an income statement and cash flow, but not taking the time to put together a forecast balance sheet.

The advantage of drawing up a forecast balance sheet – quite apart from giving you the ability to analyse same and obtain useful insights – is that it forces the preparer to consider transactions more carefully, for example, to match sales and debtor receipts, and to take account of inventory movements. Ensuring that the closing line on the cash-flow forecast agrees to the 'bank' line on the balance sheet gives a logic check. Without preparing an interlinked income statement, cash flow, and balance sheet, you have no way of knowing if your forecast is arithmetically sound.[2]

An example of why it is good practice to prepare a balance sheet was seen in a proposal reviewed by your author, approached for venture capital funding. The plan indicated that the operation became cash positive after eighteen months. No balance sheet was offered, but when one was prepared from the data supplied, it showed that cash was only highly positive because inventories of raw materials were highly negative!

Include narrative

Most people are more fluent with words than numbers, and would prefer to take in information verbally rather than undertake a detailed analysis of someone else's spreadsheet. In preparing a forecast or business plan it is vital to include a narrative explaining the assumptions, and highlighting those that are key. A written analysis of the business proposition and the forecast outcomes, together with a discussion of the risks and the possible alternatives is also useful in most circumstances.

---

2 However, the fact that your forecasts balance does not mean that they are accurate or reasonable. Arithmetic consistency is a necessary condition for good forecasts, but not sufficient.

Analysing the outcomes

Having prepared the forecast, the next stage is to sense-check it. What is it telling you, and how does that tie in with your strategic analysis?

For example, in a DCF analysis, projects should only be accepted if they generate a positive net present value (NPV). But consider what a positive NPV actually means – it tells you that this project is planned to earn a return over and above the standard cost of capital; it is going to make super-profits. The ability to make super-profits is generally predicated on having a competitive advantage. Thus, whenever you are faced with an investment appraisal that looks good, you should make sure you understand just what competitive advantage is being exploited, and ensure that it really does exist.

Don't be fooled by small numbers. If your business plan depends on taking 'only 2 per cent of the market', you need to understand who is already servicing that 2 per cent and how they are going to react to your entry into the market.

Don't use the spreadsheet as a substitute for thinking, projecting forward trends over a long period. It is dangerous to extrapolate growth at the same rate year after year. Consider what the total market is for a product, and how soon it will be saturated; think about whether it is feasible for your gross profit percentage to continue to rise annually once the initial savings have been made; critically examine your assumption that inventory days will continue to fall.

The same thinking underlies projects that look bad, but that you know should be profitable. If your strategic and market analysis says that it is a good opportunity, but the NPV comes out negative, then consider what you might have missed out.

For example, a small restaurant chain analysing whether it would be worthwhile opening another branch in the same geographical area would correctly take account of the fact that some diners coming to that new branch would have switched allegiance from another of its outlets, and would not represent an overall increase in sales for the group. However, another way to look at this is to argue that if this chain does not buy the premises for a restaurant, another restaurateur could open up there. As there is a limit to the number of meals people can eat, chances are that the chain's other restaurants in the area would lose business anyway. If the loss of sales is inevitable whatever is done, it is not relevant to this decision. This analysis with a declining base case is illustrated in Figure 14.1

Finally, always be aware of the limiting factor in your forecasts. For most businesses the limiting factor is the level of sales – all other assumptions hang from that. But in some businesses it might be the availability of skilled labour, or the size of the factory. (Your author once prepared a very complex spreadsheet to support the valuation of a distribution business. The underlying assumptions came from three separate directors. It was only when the numbers were presented back to them that the logistics director pointed out that the volumes being predicted by the marketing director were physically impossible to achieve from premises of the size they occupied. This led to some tension in the meeting, and to a major change in the company's strategic plans.)

Sensitivity analysis

Prediction is very hard – especially about the future.[3] Almost the only thing you know for certain about the forecasts you have prepared is that they will be wrong. What is important

---

3   This aphorism has been variously attributed to Mark Twain, Niels Bohr, and Yogi Berra. And probably to many others.

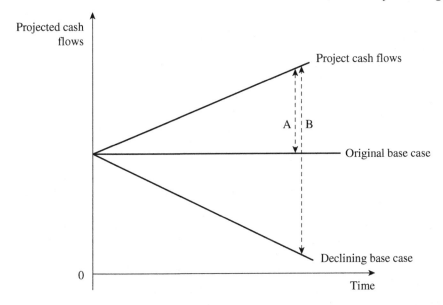

Figure 14.1 The declining base case in DCF analysis.

The original analysis shows the project cash flows as generating value 'A' above the base case of doing nothing. However, strategic analysis shows that the 'doing nothing' option will not leave profits where they are, but will result in a steady decline. Accordingly, the value of the new project is not 'A', but 'B'.

is to understand how wrong they are likely to be, and whether or not it matters. This is where sensitivity analysis comes in.

Sensitivity analysis involves changing one or more of the forecast variables, to see how that impacts upon the outcome. Working Insight 14.5 sets out some of the several ways in which it can be approached.

Of the various ways to approach sensitivity analysis, the one that is the most widely followed is intellectually the least satisfactory.

Many people do sensitivity analysis by changing the variables (e.g. sales, or material costs) by 10 per cent, either individually or in parallel, and seeing what happens. The reason that this is intellectually sloppy is that there is no logic behind the choice of 10 per cent other than the fact that it is easy. For a start-up project, making a forecast of sales volume

---

Working Insight 14.5

Some methods of sensitivity analysis

1 Change each input variable individually to determine the impact on the forecast.
2 Reverse-engineer the forecast to determine the tolerance on each input – how much would it have to change before the project was unsatisfactory.
3 Prepare the forecast under several different scenarios.
4 Monte Carlo analysis, using the computer to generate forecasts using different ranges of inputs, based on their underlying probabilities.

that is within 10 per cent of the final outcome would be an impressive achievement; for an existing company, being 10 per cent out on a forecast of production costs might be unusual.

Accordingly, a more satisfactory approach is to change each of the underlying variables – individually or in parallel – by an amount that reflects the level of uncertainty in your estimates. That might involve flexing the sales volumes by 40 per cent but the labour costs by only 5 per cent. This more accurately mirrors the uncertainty you face.

Another way to do sensitivity analysis is to turn it on its head. Instead of asking 'how wrong am I likely to be?', ask 'at what point does an error make the project unviable?'. So, if a forecast is showing a positive net present value, how much would sales have to fall for the NPV to be zero? How much would costs have to rise? Calculate each of these, and then go back to the original source of the estimate and ask their views on the numbers obtained.

For example, if a fall in sales of 23 per cent would strip all of the value out of a project, explore with the sales and marketing departments how their forecasts were determined. It might be that their estimates are deliberately on the low side, so an additional 23 per cent decline is unlikely. It might be that some targeted market research could give a better feel for what is happening. Whatever the result, at least you are facing the decision with a better understanding of the risk.

Also, don't forget that changes in variables can interact with each other. An increase in interest rates will increase finance charges, but may also reduce sales; a fall in demand will reduce sales, but may also cause increases in material prices, as economies of scale are lost. And don't forget to test what happens if sales *increase* rather than decrease – quite often, this is what leads to a cash crunch.

Working Insight 14.6 illustrates some ways in which variables might be flexed to determine sensitivities.

Another sensitivity to run might be on exchange rates. For example, Carlsberg is a Danish brewer with about 40 per cent of its sales in Russia. Any sensitivity analysis for that business should include an evaluation of how it would be affected by movements in the kroner–rouble exchange rate.

A more complex way to do sensitivity analysis is to prepare multiple scenarios. An advantage of looking at different scenarios – both good and bad – is that it can give a better feel for the riskiness of a project, and forces the preparer to consider different eventualities, and thus prepare for them.

Finally, Monte Carlo analysis can be used to evaluate sensitivities. Here, we accept that our forecast figures are not single numbers, but ranges. For example, we put 'Sales = 100' into a forecast but what we mean is 'Sales is likely to be somewhere between 60 and 140, with 100 being our best guess'. In a Monte Carlo analysis each major input into the forecasts is assessed, with probabilities being assigned to the numbers in the range. These are then fed into a computer model, and a random number generator simulates the project some thousand times with the inputs being represented in accordance with their probabilities. The resultant output shows just how often the project would be value-creating, and how often it would fail. Having this range of outcomes gives considerably more information to management than would the point forecasts that are normally used.

One outcome of the sensitivity analysis is a better understanding of the critical success factors for the business – which of the value drivers really matter. Another benefit is a better understanding of risk: a range of potential outcomes, can be more meaningful as a decision support than merely increasing the project discount rate to allow for risk. And, as a practical

Working Insight 14.6

Changing variables in the forecast

Driver of value	Some examples of changes to explore
Sales volumes	Decrease or increase by $x\%$; slow (or accelerate) the sales growth plan by one year, or two years; change the rate of growth of the market as a whole, or the market penetration rate.
Profit margin	Change input costs individually; assume selling prices fall over time; assume that production costs or expenses change in a different pattern to that anticipated; look at the effect of a movement in the ratio of fixed and variable costs.
Tax rate	Flex the tax rate.
Working capital	Change the assumptions for inventory days, and debtor or creditor terms.
Capital expenditure	Examine the impact of price changes in the future, and of delaying or bringing forward capacity changes. Consider the impact of leasing rather than buying.
Timescale of competitive advantage	Run the forecast for one year more, or one year fewer, to see the impact. Change the terminal value assumptions in a DCF analysis.
Cost of capital	Flex the cost of capital. Change the timing of interest payments and loan repayments where appropriate in a forecast to evaluate funding requirements.

point, preparing and understanding detailed sensitivity analyses that show upsides and downsides can inform the way the project is undertaken.

One final point on forecasting. When preparing a cash-flow forecast to support borrowing requirements, consider just how much funding to request. If your base forecast shows a borrowing requirement of £1m, then asking just for £1m shows poor judgement – work out what the worst case looks like and make sure that you have capacity to borrow at least up to this level. (You needn't borrow that amount – that would be inefficient use of capital – but it is useful to have the headroom for further borrowing if it is needed.)

Behavioural finance

When you have to make a 'blue skies' forecast, with no prior knowledge of the subject, where do you start?

One of our favourite pieces of research was undertaken by Amos Tversky and Daniel Kahneman. They showed that we all use a limited number of heuristic principles to help us cope with complex number-related decisions. Working Insight 14.7 summarizes what they had to say about 'anchoring and adjustment'; the process whereby we fix on a number and then just make small alterations up or down from it.

Anchoring and adjustment is one example of behavioural finance, a fascinating area of study that examines how we behave towards numbers. It has much significance for the

---

Working Insight 14.7

An example of anchoring

Tversky and Kahneman reported an experiment whereby participants spun a wheel of fortune, containing the numbers 0 to 100. They were then asked to indicate whether the percentage of African countries in the United Nations was higher or lower than the number obtained from the wheel, followed by their estimate of the percentage.

The wheel of fortune was rigged, so that it produced either 65 or 10.

Although the rational readers of this book will appreciate that there is no possible connection between a wheel of fortune and the African constituents of the UN, the experiment showed that the participants 'anchored' their predictions on the wheel of fortune. So, for example, those whose wheel showed 65 indicated that African countries made up some 45% of the UN; those who saw the wheel land on the number 10 took the view that, on average, it was 25%.

Source: Tversky, A. and Kahneman, D. (1974), 'Judgment under Uncertainty: Heuristics and Biases', *Science*, 185(4157)

---

practice of corporate finance. On a small scale it illustrates why we approach sensitivity analysis by moving only 10 per cent away from our original estimates. A more fundamental issue is how we can use anchoring to set expectations on a deal price, with the aim of getting the other party to adapt our initial offer rather than re-examine from first principles. And it is interesting how often analysts' valuations of companies turn out within reasonable proximity of the current market price, which acts as an anchor to their underlying assumptions for the business.

Other behaviours of which you should be aware are the tendency of forecasters to be over-optimistic, and overconfident in their abilities (both as forecasters and as entrepreneurs); and the very human desire to seek out data that support our initial views and ignore data that might prove us wrong. Commercial examples of these tendencies can be found in pretty much every business plan ever prepared, and in every acquisition that generated so much momentum that it never even occurred to the participants that it was a bad deal. People also tend to evaluate probabilities based on their resemblance to other situations rather than looking at the raw data, and to avoid ambiguity, even at the risk of being 'certainly wrong'.

One further bias is useful to understand. The way in which a decision is framed will influence our view of the risks. People seem to have more of a desire to avoid losses than to make gains. This has significant implications for the behaviour of managers faced with a choice of whether to wind up a poor project, or to throw good money after bad in the hope of recovery. It also means that executives will find it easier to forego a discount than to accept a surcharge, even though the financial outcome could be the same. Working Insight 14.8 illustrates this.

Understanding the issues in behavioural finance is valuable to the corporate financier. Knowing how you think can improve your success in forecasting. Knowing how others think can improve your business acumen. If this brief insight into the subject has whetted your appetite, some other resources are shown at the end of this chapter.

Working Insight 14.8

The impact of framing on decisions

150 people were asked to indicate their preferences in the following pair of choices. The numbers in brackets show how the participants voted.

Choose between:
A A sure gain of $240 (84%)
B 25% chance to gain $1,000 and 75% chance to gain nothing (16%)

Choose between:
C A sure loss of $750 (13%)
D 75% chance to lose $1,000 and 25% chance to lose nothing (87%)

For decisions A–B the majority choice is risk-averse, even though the expected outcome is slightly lower than taking the gamble; for decisions C–D the majority choice is risk-seeking. Such risk-seeking behaviour is seen every time a company decides to 'throw good money after bad' rather than close down a loss-making project. It was seen in the extreme in the way Nick Leeson, the 'rogue trader' brought down Barings Bank rather than admit to the deficit in his trading book.[4]

Source: Tversky, A. and Kahneman, D. (1986), 'Rational Choice and the Framing of Decisions', *Journal of Business*, 59(4): 251–78

Key messages

- Valuation is an art, not a science. There is no one value that can be attributed to a company – it depends on who is going to own it, and what they plan to do with it.
- There are several different methods that can be used to value a company. Valuation on fundamentals (discounted cash flow) is probably the most useful; valuation on multiples probably the most widely used. It makes sense to conduct a valuation using several different methods.
- Financial forecasts need to be prepared properly, and incorporate an income statement, cash flow, and balance sheet.
- Sensitivity analysis is vital, to understand the key drivers of a forecast and appreciate the margin for error.
- Forecasts depend on assumptions, and human beings are hard-wired to be irrational in their assumptions. Behavioural finance highlights some of the issues we need to consider.

Suggested further reading

On valuation

Aswath Damodaran, Professor of Finance at the Stern School of Business, New York University, is one of the leading authors on valuation. He has several books available, addressing different aspects

---

4 The Barings collapse in 1995 is widely reported on the internet, and in books and a film.

and at different levels of complexity, but all of them very readable. He also blogs on the subject, publishes his book chapters through SSRN, and makes available on the web his MBA classes. All of his information can be accessed through his website http://pages.stern.nyu.edu/~adamodar

Holthausen, R. W. and Zmilewski, M. E. (2012), 'Valuation with Market Multiples: How to Avoid Pitfalls When Identifying and Using Comparable Companies', *Journal of Applied Corporate Finance*, 24(3): 26–38.

Discusses problems with valuation on multiples, and shows how variations in value drivers affect multiples.

On the cost of capital

Jacobs, M. T. and Shivdasani, A. (2012). 'Do You Know Your Cost of Capital?', *Harvard Business Review*, July/Aug.

This article reports a survey of practices followed by companies in calculating their cost of capital. There is a wide variety of approaches, and the outcomes differ considerably.

On forecasting

Davies, R., Goedhart, M. and Koller, T. (2012), 'Avoiding a Risk Premium That Unnecessarily Kills Your Project', *McKinsey Online Journal*, available at http://www.mckinsey.com/insights/corporate_finance/avoiding_a_risk_premium_that_unnecessarily_kills_your_project.

Argues that increasing the discount rate to allow for risk can penalize potentially good projects.

On behavioural finance

Kahneman, D. (2012). *Thinking, Fast and Slow* (London: Penguin).

An excellent, very readable book from a Nobel Prize-winning researcher in psychology. Kahneman's aim is to 'improve the ability to identify and understand errors of judgment and choice, in others and eventually in ourselves'.

www.behaviouralfinance.net

This website collects together definitions and academic articles on many aspects of behavioural finance.

15 Floating a company

Learning objectives

After reading this chapter you should be able to:

1 Explain why a company might want to float its shares, and differentiate cash-in and cash-out floats.
2 Analyse the different stages of an IPO in relation to a marketing model of 'seven Ps'.
3 Understand the process for a listed company to issue further equity.
4 Set out the reasons why a company might delist its shares, and the potential conflicts of interest this entails.

Introduction

In Chapter 8 we discussed how flotation on a recognized stock market may be an appropriate strategy for growth companies seeking to raise capital and provide an exit for their venture capital investors. This chapter addresses in more detail the reasons why a company might float (or list, or undertake an IPO – these terms are all synonymous), and the mechanisms by which it can do so.

The first point to note is that the IPO process is not really a 'finance' issue. Although the decision as to whether listing is appropriate is one that should be driven by financiers (based ultimately on the corporate strategy), the actual process of listing is a marketing issue. In Figure 1.2 in this book we stated that investment is a two-stage process: investors invest in the company; the company invests in projects. Arranging the sale of the company's products to its target market is widely accepted as an issue for marketers, who advise on the most appropriate positioning and methods of sale. Similarly, arranging the sale of the company's shares to its target market of investors is also a marketing issue. Accordingly, part of this chapter borrows a model from our marketing colleagues in order to analyse the listing process.

The chapter also considers how companies undertake a secondary offering once they are already listed, and goes on to look at the issues that arise when the directors decide to delist the shares.

Why go public?

An IPO is expensive and time-consuming. Before entering into the process, the owners of the business need to understand clearly their objectives, to see if the IPO is the best solution for them. Only then can questions of how to float be addressed.

The two fundamental reasons why a company might seek a listing can be categorized as 'cash-in' and 'cash-out'. A cash-in float is one which is done for the purpose of raising funds for the company's continued expansion. Cash-in floats are for growth companies, which issue new shares to obtain the funds they need. Contrast this with a cash-out float, where the main purpose of the listing is to obtain an exit for some of the existing shareholders, rather than to raise new money. In such a float, few new shares are issued; instead the existing shareholders sell all or part of their holdings to the new shareholders. Such a flotation would be appropriate for a more mature company. Figure 15.1 illustrates the characteristics of the two types of float.

As stated earlier, a flotation is a marketing exercise, and it is important that the marketing message is clear, so that 'customers' (the potential investors) are not confused. A cash-in float signals to the market that the company is seeking growth; this is likely to be confirmed in the explanation in its prospectus of its proposed dividend policy. A cash-out float is more appropriate for mature companies, which are likely to pay higher dividends and will attract a different type of investor.

It is possible to mix the two. Over the past decade there has been a notable increase in the number of companies combining the motives. This can be successful when the story is clear, for example, when it is obvious that a founder or venture capital investor wishes to exit or realize part of their investment, but there is still a growth story for the incoming shareholders.

An example of a cash-in and cash-out float was UK fashion retailer, SuperGroup (owner of the Superdry brand), set out in Case Study 15.1

A mixed message sends the wrong signals to the market. Your author was asked a few years ago to advise on financial strategy for a growing, profitable software company. The owner/director, who was a key employee of the company and had overseen all of its development to date, wanted to float the company, realize his investment and then 'go off to the Bahamas to play golf'.

Sadly, he had to be advised that the market was unlikely to accept this as a value proposition – for key personnel to bail out of what was obviously positioned competitively as a growth company was going to invoke a certain level of cognitive dissonance among prospective shareholders; to put it bluntly, who would buy the shares if he had so little faith that he was selling out?

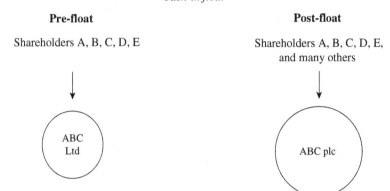

Cash-in float

Pre-float

Shareholders A, B, C, D, E

ABC Ltd

Post-float

Shareholders A, B, C, D, E, and many others

ABC plc

In the cash-in float, the company increases in value, due to the new funding attracted from new (and possibly existing) shareholders.

Cash-out float

Pre-float

Shareholders A, B, C, D, E

ABC Ltd

Post-float

Shareholders A, D, and many others

ABC plc

In the cash-out float the company has not raised any new funds, but the shareholders have changed.

Note: For convenience, the pre-listing company is referred to as 'Ltd' (limited) and the post-listing company is referred to as 'plc' (public limited company). It should be noted that under UK company law it is possible for a company to be a plc without being listed on a stock exchange.

Figure 15.1 Two categories of float.

Although a cash-out float is intended to realize the investment, this may not happen completely in the short term. Sometimes there will be a 'lock-in' (also known as a lock-up) period of between three months and two years following the float, during which a significant shareholder has agreed not to sell its shares. (This helps provide a more orderly market, but does mean that for a shareholder who really needs an exit, a trade sale might be a more appropriate route than a flotation.) Lock-in arrangements were common in the very highly priced floats of internet companies in 2011 and 2012. For example, when Facebook floated in May 2012 there were various lock-up periods for insiders of the company, with some being able to sell shares after three months, and others in up to eighteen months.

We have discussed two main purposes for a listing – cash-in and cash-out. Working Insight 15.1 sets out those and other potential objectives for the owners and the company.

Case Study 15.1

SuperGroup

SuperGroup undertook its IPO in March 2010. The company issued 25 million new shares at a price of £5 per share, raising gross proceeds of £125 million (about £120 million after costs). The number of shares in existence after the listing was about 79 million, meaning that the new shares comprised some 31% of the enlarged share capital. Such an IPO would normally be viewed as cash-in, because the shares for the IPO were newly created rather than being sold by their existing owners. However, the prospectus showed that only £15m was going towards the growth of the business, and the remaining £105m was being used to pay down loan notes.

Paying down debt is a valid use of the proceeds of a cash-in float, as it frees up financial resources for future growth. However, in this case the loan notes had been created during a pre-float reorganization of the business from its previous status as a limited liability partnership. They were owed to the management and owners of the business, and paying them off was in effect a cash-out use of the funds raised on listing. This was made clear in the prospectus, which stated, 'Approximately £100 million of the net proceeds of the Institutional Offer will be used to enable the Loan Note holders to realise part of their investment in the Group'.

However, the prospectus also showed that management were retaining a substantial investment in the company (for example, the CEO's shareholding of 48% pre-listing would be 33% after the IPO). This, together with the strong growth trend in sales and profits, meant that the market treated it as a growth story.

Source: SuperGroup prospectus

A listing might also be undertaken just because market prices are so high the owners can see an opportunity to make a great deal of money selling part of their stake. Many believe that this logic was behind some of the flotations of large private equity companies in 2007, which followed a buyout boom.

One issue to consider as part of the listing decision is the level of the 'free float' of shares. Just because a company is listed does not mean that all of its shares are available for purchase

---

Working Insight 15.1

Reasons for floating a company

- Cash-in, to raise funds for the growth of the business.
- Cash-out, to provide an exit or partial exit for investors.
- Desire to have shares which can act as a currency in acquisitions (as discussed in Chapter 16).
- Listed shares will provide a better incentive for management (e.g. through share options) than unlisted shares with no clear valuation or exit route.
- Wish for future financial flexibility (a listed company tends to have more financing options than an unlisted one).
- Diversification for shareholders who wish to spread their investment holdings.
- Diversification of the shareholder base away from, say, just one small family.
- Desire for prestige, for either the company or the directors. (It goes without saying that the former reason is more appropriate than the latter.)

by the public: a significant proportion might remain in the hands of insiders. For example, if a founding family chooses to float the company to raise funds, but retains ownership of 40 per cent of the company with no intention to sell, the free float is only 60 per cent of the shares. If the free float is perceived as being too small, then the market might be less willing to buy the shares, and listing on certain exchanges might not be appropriate. However, in recent years we have seen some companies adopting a 'small float' strategy, deliberately choosing to float only about 10 per cent of their shares, with the dual advantage of maintaining control with the original owners, and creating artificial scarcity in order to stoke demand and push up prices.[1]

The IPO process

In this section we examine the IPO process using the seven Ps of marketing: the product, place, price, positioning, promotion, people, and process.

Product

The product that is being sold is the company's shares. Given that the main reason for holding shares is to obtain their flow of dividends and ultimate capital gain, the attractiveness of the shares is a reflection of the attractiveness of the company and its business proposition.

The company is more likely to have a successful float if it can show a growing profit trend: an indication of future prospects. Directors with a strong personal track record of business success are another factor in its favour. Likewise, it can be useful to have a 'cornerstone investor', a known investor (normally an institution) which has already invested in the company, thus adding credibility and legitimacy. Also, investors will be more comfortable with buying shares if they know that the business of the company is not in any way mingled with the separate interests of the directors. (For many private companies, directors'/shareholders' and company's interests are seen as one and the same thing, which means that a certain amount of pre-float grooming needs to take place, for example, to make the accounting policies consistent with good practice, tidy up the balance sheet to write off those debts that are never going to be recovered and remove the family villa in Spain!) And it goes without saying (and indeed is generally a stock exchange requirement) that the company's accounting systems will be in order, and its internal controls will be sufficient.

Each particular stock market has its own regulations, which companies have to meet in order to obtain an initial listing, and to comply with on a continuous basis in order to maintain it. For example, in the USA the governing body is the Securities & Exchange Commission (SEC); in the United Kingdom it is the UK Listing Authority (UKLA). As the rules differ between markets, and change frequently, little purpose is served by setting out the current versions in this book. However, Working Insight 15.2 sets out some of the considerations that a company may need to address.

Another factor which will make a company's shares more attractive is a good corporate governance structure, so that investors' rights are protected. However, this can be against the preferences of management, and is discussed in the next section in the context of some high-profile listings which chose to disregard this characteristic.

---

1   For example, LinkedIn has a free float of less than 10 per cent, and the scarcity of the shares was said to have been a factor in the price increase at IPO.

Working Insight 15.2

Possible regulatory requirements for a listing

- Accounts with unqualified audit reports have been published for a certain number of years prior to the float.
- The company has a substantial business, with a trading record. (This requirement is often waived in markets wanting to attract high-potential start-ups in attractive sectors.)
- The directors are suitable people to be running a publicly quoted company.
- The company is not controlled by any shareholder with a conflicting interest.
- At least *x* per cent of the company's shares will be in public hands after the float.
- A minimum post-float market capitalization level is to be expected.

Place

Once the decision has been made to float, the next questions is: where? Companies will target potential investment markets in much the same manner that they target markets for their products. There are two key issues to consider: what type of investor is likely to buy our shares; and which stock market is best suited to our needs?

As regards the type of investor, the issue has been highlighted many times already in this book. Investors who seek dividend income are unlikely to be attracted to growth companies which retain most of their earnings. Similarly, those looking for a capital gain are not going to be persuaded by the prospectus for a mature company.

As to the choice of stock market on which to float, this is a more complex decision. There is a wealth of exchanges from which to choose. In the USA there is NYSE (the New York Stock Exchange) or NASDAQ (National Association of Securities Dealers Automated Quotations) or several other exchanges. The Hong Kong and Singapore markets attract a lot of Asian and international business, and the Shenzen and Shanghai exchanges are also significant players. In Europe there are the various bourses of the individual countries, or pan-European platforms. The UK currently has its main market, the London Stock Exchange (LSE), and its offshoot AIM, the Alternative Investment Market. And of course other countries each have their own markets, whose operations and investors may be more or less sophisticated. Figure 15.2 sets out the funds raised through IPOs in various international markets in 2011.

		US$bn
1	Hong Kong	36.1
2	New York	31.4
3	Shenzhen	26.2
4	London	19.2
5	Shanghai	16.3
6	NASDAQ	10.7
7	Singapore	7.6
8	Spain	5.3
9	Brazil	4.4
10	Korea	3.6

Figure 15.2 IPO fundraising in major stock exchanges in 2011.
Source: Dealogic data from www.hkex.com.hk/eng/newsconsul/newsltr/2012/Documents/2012-01-02-E.pdf

		US$bn
1	NYSE Euronext (US)	11,796
2	NASDAQ OMX (US)	3,845
3	Tokyo Stock Exchange Group	3,325
4	London Stock Exchange Group	3,266
5	NYSE Euronext (Europe)	2,447
6	Shanghai Stock Exchange	2,357
7	Hong Kong Exchanges	2,258
8	TMX Group (Toronto)	1,912
9	BM&FBOVESPA (Brazil)	1,229
10	Australian Securities Exchange	1,198

Figure 15.3 Market capitalizations of major stock exchanges at end of 2011.
Source: www.world-exchanges.org/files/file/stats%20and%20charts/2011%20WFE%20Market%20
Highlights.pdf

Although Hong Kong leads in the value of IPOs (and has done so for a couple of years), the table looks very different when considered from the point of view of market capitalization, as Figure 15.3 shows.

The stock exchanges are all in competition with each other to attract listings. Working Insight 15.3 sets out some of the factors a company should consider in making its decision.

The choice of market and country depends partly on the prestige and liquidity of the particular market and partly on what the company does. Rational investors know that the market capitalization of a company should represent the discounted value of its future cash flows. However, technology companies have tended to be more highly valued on NASDAQ than on NYSE or LSE, while natural resources companies have often favoured a London listing. Investors may tend to prefer dealing in certain markets, and they perceive less risk in industries with which they are familiar: hence a rational explanation is that investors accustomed to these sectors assign them a lower-risk level and thus a higher value. (In this respect it is interesting that LinkedIn, which described itself as 'the world's largest professional network on the Internet' chose to float its shares on NYSE rather than NASDAQ, sending a message that it sees itself as a professional services company rather than an internet company.)

Investors are also comfortable with companies whose names they know, which is why most companies list in their home market. It might be foolish for a company with no trading

Working Insight 15.3

Factors to consider in choosing a market on which to list

- Geographical location.
- Liquidity of trading.
- Size of the market, and of the companies on the market.
- Regulatory, reporting, and governance requirements.
- Specialization of the exchange in your sector, and relative valuation of companies in your sector on this market.
- Diversification of the investor base.
- Costs, both of the IPO and ongoing.

presence in the USA to list its shares there; it would be unlikely to receive much press coverage or analyst attention, and so could flounder in the backwaters of the market. However, companies which have a large trading presence in another country often choose to have a secondary listing on one of that country's markets; increasing their name-awareness in their product market by obtaining exposure in the capital markets. (Chapter 19 on international finance discusses secondary listings further, including the use of Global Depository Receipts (GDRs).)

Another matter to consider in the choice of stock exchange is its corporate governance regulations. Governance in a stock exchange is a clear illustration of the risk–return trade-off. In Chapter 6 we discussed governance, and the need to protect the investor (particularly the minority investor) whilst still ensuring ease of doing business. For stock exchanges, the more regulations they have, and the more disclosure they require, the happier the investor might be – but the more frustrating it can be for the listed companies themselves. Exchanges have to find a balance between regulation and laissez-faire. This is a matter for competitive strategy between exchanges. It is notable that a strengthening of governance regulation in exchanges in China and Brazil is reported to have increased the numbers of companies wishing to list there, as the markets have become more attractive to domestic and global investors.[2] Even established markets such as London have introduced 'premium listing', to differentiate those companies complying with basic EU governance standards and those adopting more stringent standards.

For international companies, the choice of exchange is wide. For example, the Italian luxury goods company Prada chose Hong Kong for its float in 2011. The advantage of floating in Asia was to capitalize on its well-known brand (over 30 per cent of Prada's sales were in Asia), to raise that brand-awareness further, and to gain investors with an appetite for luxury companies in a fast-growing market.

Sometimes, companies deliberately choose to list on an exchange with lower governance or disclosure requirements. Examples from the sporting arena are shown in Case Study 15.2.

Finally we come to size. Size matters. For example, although the listing regulations for the LSE state that companies with a market capitalization as low as £700,000 can list on this market, such a company would be foolish to try. A glance at the financial press shows that the LSE's largest companies are capitalized at well over £100 billion; at the time of writing, about 15 per cent of the companies listed on the LSE represented over 85 per cent of the market capitalization.[3] Among these giants, how much attention are analysts and investors likely to pay to a minnow? (This issue is picked up again at the end of this chapter, when we look at reasons why companies delist from a market.) Thus, although it might be painful to the directors' egos, it is probably more useful to be a medium-sized company on a small exchange than to be a tiny company on a large one.

Price

An obviously important consideration in the flotation process is the price at which the shares are listed. It would be nice to be able to tell you that the company's advisers consider in detail its projected cash flows out into the future, and discount them at a cost of capital to

---

2   See, for example, Chavez, G. A. and Silva, A. C. (2009), 'Brazil's Experiment with Corporate Governance', *Journal of Applied Corporate Finance*, 21(1): 34–44.

3   The LSE's monthly Main Market Factsheet can be downloaded from www.londonstockexchange.com/

Case Study 15.2

Companies choosing a market on governance or disclosure requirements

Williams Grand Prix Holdings

Williams, the Formula 1 team, floated on the Frankfurt 'Entry Standard' stock exchange in March 2011. Williams is a UK-based company. It is believed that it chose to list in Frankfurt because the rules on disclosing revenue segmentation (such as details of sponsorship and television rights) were less restrictive there than London, and that was seen as a commercial advantage.

Manchester United

The UK football club, Manchester United, is owned by the Glazer family. During 2011 and 2012 there were rumours that they would list the company. Locations under discussion included Hong Kong and Singapore, before they finally settled on New York. The reason that London was never on the cards as the exchange for this UK company was that the Glazer family wanted to have a two-tier share structure in which they retained all the votes, and also wished to minimize business disclosures. This would not be possible in the UK governance environment, but was acceptable on NYSE where the company also took advantage of the JOBS Act which treated Manchester United (an organization founded in the nineteenth century) as a new company entitled to follow reduced governance regulations.

---

arrive at a valuation. Nice, but alas untrue.[4] Although valuation on fundamentals does undoubtedly take place, much of the art of pricing IPOs depends on finding suitable comparators and using their price/earnings multiples as a benchmark. Market multiples have far more significance in the process than academic purists would care to admit. Similarly, the absolute value of the shares plays its part: Professor Keith Ward, author of earlier editions of this book, worked on one flotation before which the company did a one-for-one share split in order to double the number of shares, halving the potential share price so that it would not seem expensive when compared to its nearest comparator!

On the subject of pricing, what does 'good' look like in a float? When Company X's shares are listed at 100p and climb to 200p in the first few hours, is that good? When Company Y's shares float at 100p and fall to 50p by the end of the first day, is that good? The answer to both of those questions is 'no'.

If the share price soars in the first few hours or days of trading, the implication is that the advisers have got it wrong. The shareholders who bought into Company X on the listing have made a 100 per cent profit; they are happy. But the company could have issued half as many shares and raised the same amount of cash, so it has unfairly diluted its existing shareholders by issuing shares at an undervalue. Or it could have raised twice as much money by issuing the same number of shares. As for Company Y, its new shareholders no doubt feel bitter about being 'conned out of their money' by an overpriced issue. The company has

---

4 Untrue in the author's experience. However, a study of the Belgian market reported in the *Journal of Business Finance & Accounting* suggests that DCF is used, albeit only marginally, more than multiples. Deloof, M., De Maeseneire, W., and Inghelbrecht, K. (2009). 'How Do Investment Banks Value Initial Public Offerings (IPOs)?', *Journal of Business Finance & Accounting*, 36(1–2): 130–60.

Case Study 15.3

IPO pricing is tricky

Connecting with LinkedIn

LinkedIn, the professional social networking site, floated its shares in May 2011 at a price of $45. The closing price at the end of the first day was $94, giving a market capitalization close to $10bn.

A Reuters article reporting the IPO included a comment from an anonymous (and ecstatic) employee, 'We recognise that there's potentially a bubble right now'.

Not really liking Facebook

The Facebook IPO in May 2012 had been eagerly anticipated and much hyped. The expectation was that there would be great demand for the shares, and the 'pop' on day 1 would reflect the glories of the dot.com years, with the initial investors making instant profits as they sold on.

The IPO price was set at $38, representing a market capitalization of about $100bn, which was considered by commentators to be high. Although positioned as a growth company, many insiders, both executives and institutions, took the opportunity to cash out a proportion of their holdings. This was not seen as a problem, as they still had a significant number of shares.

The share price never rose. It closed flat on its first day of trading, and then started to decline. Reasons given for the lack of 'pop' included a technical glitch on NASDAQ which delayed trading, and also stories of briefings that the analysts had cut their estimates to a selected number of clients. At the time of writing, this latter point is the subject of litigation from shareholders.

Source: www.reuters.com

obtained the funds it sought, and has created value for any exiting shareholders, but at the expense of its future goodwill in the investment community. Next time it tries to raise capital, investors will remember this debacle and be suspicious.

In a 'good' float the shares are priced at about 10 to 15 per cent less than where the advisers expect the closing price to be at the end of day one. Such a discount – which is easier to describe than to manage – enables the new investors to feel mildly content with their investment, whilst providing reasonable value to existing shareholders. Case Study 15.3 illustrates both extremes of pricing.

So, a good IPO leaves something on the table. This phenomenon of IPO underpricing has been well explored by academics. Various reasons have been suggested for it, such as the fact that it compensates the investor for information asymmetry, the fact that the directors and advisers know more than the investor.[5]

The pricing decision is assisted by the bookrunners gauging investor interest at different price levels (see Process, below). Also, IPOs often have a type of price stabilization known as an over-allotment option, or greenshoe. With this, the bookrunner has the right to buy extra shares from the company and sell them on in the market. At the IPO the bookrunner sells more shares than they actually hold, knowing that they can exercise the greenshoe if

---

5 For more information, see Ljungqvist, A., 'IPO Underpricing', in *Handbook in Corporate Finance: Empirical Corporate Finance*, ed. B. Espen Eckbo. A draft chapter (2004) is available at SSRN: http://ssrn.com/abstract=609422

needed, obtaining those extra shares from the company. However, if the share price had fallen after the IPO the bookrunner would not exercise the greenshoe to buy the shares from the company, but instead would buy them (at the lower price) in the market. One advantage of this over-allotment option (apart from making profits for the bookrunners) is its impact in stabilizing market prices immediately after the IPO.

Positioning

In discussing price, we noted the importance of market multiples. Because of this, the positioning of a company is critical. The aim is for the market to identify it with peers which have high multiples; in this way, any price set on relative values will be high. Positioning a company in the right geographical market is important, as is the market size, and sector into which the company is placed. For example, a utility that can be reclassified as a service company could in most circumstances expect a substantial uplift in its share price, as the comparator service businesses are perceived as having more growth than other utilities, and this effect rubs off on our target utility.

Promotion

During the IPO process, the role of investor relations is important – it is part of the marketing effort in selling the company to the markets. But post-float, investor relations (IR) is equally necessary. Companies need to ensure that their investors understand their businesses and strategies, and that they are followed by sufficient analysts to ensure a good flow of information to decision-makers in the markets.

A company will generally use specialist financial public relations consultants to assist in its investor relations on the float. Such specialists should understand the investor markets, and also the detail of the regulatory requirements, as it is important that information reaches the markets in an appropriate manner.

Investor relations post-IPO reflect the whole of communications with the investor and analyst communities and the media, including published documents, the Annual General Meeting, presentations, the website, etc. It is generally led by the company's finance director, who, together with the CEO, will spend a significant proportion of his/her time post-float in discussions with and delivering presentations to analysts and investors. In larger listed companies, there will be a dedicated investor relations individual or team. The aim of IR is to establish a liquid market for the shares, trading at a fair price, with supportive shareholders and a following of analysts who understand the company. It is not just an activity for the flotation process; IR is a vital activity throughout a company's listed lifetime.

It is worth spending a moment to discuss analysts, the individuals who follow a sector and the companies within it, and make pronouncements on the 'true' value of the organizations. They come in two flavours – buy-side and sell-side. The ones that we, the public, hear of are the sell-side analysts. Sell-side analysts work for investment banks or stockbrokers. They publish their research, with the aim of encouraging their institutional investor clients to buy (or sell) the target company's shares through them, thus generating commission on the transactions. Having a following of many sell-side analysts can amplify the company's IR message, as its activities will be reported to many potential investors. However, because their recommendations are public, and because some of the companies on which they report may also be clients, there can be an incentive to downplay any negative opinions, as they or their employer might not wish to offend an important (potential) client. Such behaviour was rampant during the dot.com boom, but is said to be less so now. Buy-side analysts have no such restrictions. They work exclusively for their employer, making recommendations internally which influence whether their own fund managers buy or sell the shares. Their research is not disclosed outside their own firms.

People

As we will see when we come to Process, an IPO is a complex task, involving many different parties. Working Insight 15.4 sets out brief details of these protagonists and their roles in the drama.

In addition, the company needs to consider another aspect of People – those on its board. In many jurisdictions the rules of the stock exchange demand one or more independent directors. Thought should be given to who is on the board, and what they can bring in terms of industry and business knowledge, and prestige and comfort from a governance point of view.

Process

Having selected the market and groomed the company for its float, the final consideration is the method of flotation. There are several possibilities: for example, a public offer, a placing, and an introduction. In all cases, in all markets, detailed registration documents will have to be completed and approved by the market regulator (e.g. the SEC or UKLA).

In a public offer (which is the most expensive way to float a company and therefore generally only used for large issues, or those where a lot of retail interest is expected) the sponsor will offer shares widely to both private and institutional investors, generally at a fixed price. The prospectus will be advertised widely in national media, adding to the complexity and costs of the issue.

Placings are a cheaper means of listing, and are the most popular choice among companies and their advisers. The shares are offered to a selected number of institutional investors, with whom normally the sponsor has (or would like) a business relationship. This can result in a relatively narrow investor base for the company, but that in itself may not be a disadvantage – the cost of communicating with a wide retail investor base is considerable. A placing has the advantage that pricing the issue can be fine-tuned: because the bookrunners are in constant contact with relatively few institutional investors. They can run a book-building process based on a 'pathfinder' prospectus (a prospectus with pricing details omitted). From this, pricing expectations can be judged and monitored more clearly, gauging the level of interest at different price points before the final decision is made and the shares issued. This price discovery mechanism also means that there is less risk of the shares being left with the underwriters.

Finally, a company can also come to the market by way of an introduction. This takes place when a company's shares are already widely held (either on another exchange or, for example, by employees), and it has no need to raise further capital. The introduction is a means of enabling the shares to be traded on an exchange, to the benefit of the existing shareholders who may otherwise have difficulty selling them. It may later be followed by a share issue.

Having set out the alternatives, we will focus on the most common method of floating, the placing, and explore further what is required. The listing process will differ by stock market: what follows is a broad description.

Working Insight 15.4

Who's who in an IPO

Sponsor

Often an investment bank or corporate finance adviser. They project-manage the issue, liaise with the various parties, and advise on all aspects. They effectively (but not necessarily legally) share responsibility with the directors for the contents of the listing particulars.

Broker/bookrunner

Will advise on the ultimate offer price and market the issue to the investment community. Prepares the directors for the roadshow. May arrange the underwriting. Smaller issues might just have one bookrunner, often the sponsor, but larger floats will have two or three, with many more for very large issues. The bookrunners are responsible for running the order book showing how demand for the shares is building during the process.

Underwriters

The main underwriter (who may be the sponsor or another bookrunner) guarantees (for a fee of between about 2% and 7% depending on the issue, and the stock exchange chosen) that the company will be able to sell its shares, as they will take them should the issue not be popular in the market. This risk is laid off to sub-underwriters (who receive a large part of that fee).[6]

Reporting accountants

Prepare the accountants' report on prior years' results. Review the company's cash-flow forecasts. Carry out due diligence on behalf of the sponsor.

Lawyers

Lawyers to the sponsor and separate lawyers to the company. Review all legal documentation and ensure compliance with relevant regulations.

Financial public relations firm

Promote the company within the investment community prior to and post-float.

Registrars

Responsible for sending out the share certificates and managing the share register.

Receiving bankers

To whom the payment for shares is sent.

Security printers

Print the extensive documentation required for a listing, to tight deadlines.

---

6 Effectively, the underwriter sells the company a put option on the shares, and the sub-underwriters sell a put option to the underwriter. Underwriting is discussed in Chapter 8, with respect to rights issues.

Working Insight 15.5

Illustrative contents of listing particulars

- Details of the shares to be issued, and full details of the share capital of the company, including the rights of different types of share.
- Information about the business of the company, its performance, risk factors affecting it, and the markets in which it trades.
- Information about the directors and key personnel, and on governance policies and procedures.
- Confirmation that the company will have sufficient funds in the foreseeable future.
- Information about any unusual contracts entered into by the company of which shareholders should be aware.
- Details of any ongoing or potential litigation.
- An indication of the company's dividend policy after flotation.
- Accountants' report on previous years' financial results, and other relevant financial information.
- Anything else that might be of interest or relevance to the potential shareholders.

The first thing to note is that listing is not cheap. There are many documents, and many advisers, and costs mount rapidly.[7] The company will need to prepare a prospectus (otherwise known as listing particulars), sample contents of which are illustrated in Working Insight 15.5. It will need to produce (although not for publication) cash-flow forecasts to be verified by reporting accountants, confirming its ability to survive on the funds to be raised. Those accountants will also produce a due diligence report, again not for publication, addressed to the company and its sponsors, confirming the company's financial and trading position and reviewing in detail its governance and internal control systems. A report on its prior years' audited results will also be prepared, to be included in the listing particulars. And then there are investor presentations, press releases, and a wealth of legal documents.

A further issue to consider about the flotation process is the time it takes. Were you to look at the promotional documentation issued by many of the leading stock exchanges, they set out an illustrative timetable for IPO that starts with appointing advisers and ends some five or six months later on 'impact day' when the shares are quoted on the market. In practice, the listing process can take a lot longer than that. Indeed, if advisers think it desirable for the company to engage in pre-float grooming, tidying up its balance sheet and capital structure and ensuring a steady trend in profit growth, the process can take several years.

Is it worth it?

The first section of this chapter set out the advantages of listing for a company. Having looked at the complex decisions and processes involved, the question has to be asked: why would you want to float; is it worth it? Certainly, for growing companies seeking access to a

---

7 For example, Oxera suggest that legal, accounting, and advisory fees for a listing on LSE can take between 3 per cent and 6 per cent of the proceeds. See *The Cost of Capital: An International Comparison*, LSE/Oxera, June 2006. However, for a smaller company, the costs can take a considerably higher percentage of the funds raised.

new and extensive source of funding, flotation is a good way to proceed, provided economic conditions support an active market. But a note of caution should also be exercised. In this section we set out some of the reasons *not* to seek a public listing.

1   An IPO involves a lot of time and cost, as discussed earlier. More significantly, during the period when the company is preparing for listing its senior management will be unable to focus on the business itself. Their time will be taken up in endless meetings, and in making the rounds of the investing institutions to pitch to their prospective investors. Unless this is carefully planned, the company's business can suffer during this period.
2   As the CEO or chairman of a listed company, less of your time is spent on running the business, even post-float, as a considerable proportion of your time will be involved in dealing with investors and analysts. The larger the company, the more investor attention it attracts and the greater this time commitment.
3   For both the company and its directors, flotation involves a heightened public awareness of what they are doing. Directors of listed companies become public figures; sometimes, even their private lives are reported upon by the press. For the company, results and strategies are analysed in close detail, often critically, by commentators who may have only a scant understanding of the industry dynamics.
4   Corporate governance requirements on listed companies are considerable, and independently minded executives may feel that they interfere with the smooth running of the business.
5   Many directors take the position that investors have a short-term view. This is why they focus on manipulating earnings per share in quarterly or half-yearly results; they claim that the market would not understand the long-term implications of a strategy that decreased short-term profitability.[8]
6   Once listed, the company may become vulnerable to a hostile takeover. (Takeovers, hostile and otherwise, are discussed in Chapter 16.)
7   Once listed, the company becomes far more susceptible to market conditions, and may see its market capitalization fall through no fault of its own.
8   There have been periods when markets are effectively closed to IPOs, with a lack of investors due to economic conditions.

Given this list, the directors and shareholders have to decide whether they really want a listing, or whether their objectives could be achieved in another way. The shareholders also have to make another decision: given that they choose to obtain a listing, are the current directors the people they want to present to the investment community, or is a change in management appropriate at this stage? (In family-dominated companies this can be a particularly problematic issue.)

Seasoned Equity Offerings

Although most of this chapter has been about Initial Public Offerings, companies that are already listed can go back to the market to raise further equity. This is known as a Seasoned (or Secondary) Equity Offering (SEO).

---

8   Although there is certainly some truth to this, the market is not totally short term, and investors do need to see drivers for future growth, as share prices cannot be sustained just on the next few years' dividend payments.

Case Study 15.4

Peugeot launches €1bn rights issue

In March 2012 the *Financial Times* reported that Peugeot had launched a €1bn rights issue in order to fund its alliance with General Motors. The then-current share price was just over €14. For every 31 shares owned, shareholders were being given the chance to buy 16 new shares at €8.27 per share, quite a substantial discount, reflecting volatile market conditions.

In the USA and many other jurisdictions, SEOs are marketed like IPOs. However, the UK and some other jurisdictions give existing shareholders a pre-emption right, meaning that new shares have to be offered to existing shareholders before they can be offered to the general public. Here, the new shares are subject to a *rights issue* whereby existing shareholders are given the right to buy x new shares for every y shares they own. If the shareholder chooses not to take up their rights, these are sold in the market and the shareholder receives the net proceeds. Case Study 15.4 illustrates.

Rights issues are generally made at a discount to the current market price, to ensure that the issue is a success. Although theoretically the issue could be made at any price without impacting the shareholders' wealth,[9] in practice a deep discount may be seen as a sign of weakness in the company, indicating that its advisers believe the share price might fall.

Delisting

We have considered in detail how and why a company might list its shares. However, in recent years many directors of listed companies have chosen to delist their shares, taking their companies private. Occasionally this is involuntary, the company having fallen foul of the rules of its exchange, for example, companies on NYSE whose share price falls below $1 for a period, or companies falling below a minimum income threshold. More often, the privatization is voluntary, and the logic behind this action will now be considered.

A key reason for companies being taken private is that the directors believe, sometimes correctly, that the market is undervaluing them. This is often true of smaller companies in out-of-favour sectors. It was mentioned earlier that most of the attention of analysts and investors is concentrated on the larger companies – for example, the FTSE 100 and the FTSE 250, which together comprise the 350 largest companies (by market capitalization) in the LSE. The Main Market of the LSE contains over 1,000 listed companies: therefore a lot of these are relatively neglected.

There is little liquidity in smaller company shares, for two reasons. First, because few analysts (if any) provide research on them, they are not widely known. This means that they do not register on the radar as potential investments, and also that they are perceived as risky simply because less information is available. Second, as a practical issue, many large financial institutions will have a minimum dealing size, and would be unable to buy or sell a stake in a small company without significantly moving the share price. (Indeed, there might not be

---

9 Chapter 8 gives further explanation and mathematical illustrations. Using these Peugeot numbers, the theoretical post-rights price would be €12.05.

Case Study 15.5

Benetton delisting

In March 2012 the Benetton clothing group delisted from the Italian Stock Exchange. The Benetton family, which controlled about 73% of the company's equity, acquired the remaining quarter of the shares in a public tender. One reason behind this delisting was a significant fall in the company's market capitalization (the *Financial Times* reported that it was about €800m, having been about €2bn a decade earlier). Another reason put forward by commentators was the need to restructure and refresh the business, which could be done more easily under private ownership, out of the market spotlight.

Source: Financial Times

---

enough shares on the market for them to buy it at all.) And, of course, such extreme movements in the share price, quite apart from acting to nullify any potential profit on the transaction, will lead to additional volatility in the share price, and thus establishing it further as a risky stock.

In such circumstances, directors (sometimes prompted by interest from a prospective private equity buyer desirous to undertake a public-to-private transaction – see Chapter 18) often decide that it would be in their and the company's best interests if it were taken private. If the company was originally floated as a cash-out float, then the financing for this should be easy to arrange, as mature companies tend to have strong cash flows against which the company could raise debt.

Similarly, for a company that floated to raise cash and which has since become mature, there is now an ability to raise debt funding and the added incentive that the original reason for the float – to raise cash for growth – is superseded, so there is no further advantage to a listing. Even if the directors still believe the company to be in its growth stage, if its shares are rated poorly there is no further opportunity to raise additional capital at a sensible price (i.e. one which does not greatly dilute existing shareholders), and so the reasons for being listed have disappeared. Case Study 15.5 sets out the Benetton delisting as an example.

Another reason why a poorly rated company may wish to go private is a fear of takeover, particularly if it is apparently a well-performing company in an out-of-favour sector. Although hostile takeovers (discussed in the following chapter) are generally hostile to the directors rather than the shareholders, for many smaller companies these parties overlap significantly, and the individuals concerned may decide that it is in their own best interests to privatize.

The agency issue between directors and shareholders raises another concern. Directors are meant to act in the best interests of the shareholders over whose interests they are stewards. However, if the executive directors of a company make a bid to take it private, their interests diverge from those of the non-director shareholders. Because of this, in many jurisdictions there is a requirement (or at least an expectation) that the non-executives play an active role in such privatizations, taking independent advice in order to inform the shareholders whether the bid is reasonable at an acceptable price. However, this is no guarantee that shareholders will obtain value from the transaction. In February 2013 the announcement that US computer company Dell was being taken private by its management in a $24.4bn deal was followed within days by shareholders filing an action which stated that directors were violating

---

Case Study 15.6

CCX: going private to preserve the group

In January 2013 Brazilian billionaire Eike Batista announced that he would delist CCX, a coal company spun out of his business interests in 2012. The price to be offered for the shares would be R\$4.31, which was about double their trading price. The offer was that shareholders in CCX would instead receive shares in other listed companies that were part of his empire.

The reason given for this was that CCX was facing deteriorating market conditions and needed a new strategic plan, which would be done more easily off-market. Furthermore, negative news on one of his companies might have affected the share prices in the rest of his group.

In Chapter 6 we gave some examples of poor practice in companies controlled by block-holders. It is worth remembering that they can also act in the interests of minorities.

Source: Financial Times

---

their legal duties to shareholders by allowing the company's founder and a private-equity fund to 'obtain Dell on the cheap'.[10]

Even if the company's shares are not underperforming, the directors may decide that privatization is a preferable option. This is often because they feel that the market is too short-termist, and is restricting the company's long-term growth opportunities. Or they might feel that the public scrutiny of their own performance is unacceptable, and wish to regain the independence of action that they had as executives in a privately held business.

A more unusual reason for delisting is shown in Case Study 15.6, which also shows an unusual mechanism, exchanging the target's shares for shares in another company.

Of course, delisting a company is carried out more easily when the directors still own a substantial shareholding. This means that (a) the vote in favour of delisting is more certain to be passed (although those directors would in many jurisdictions be unable to vote their shares), and (b) less cash needs to be found to finance the deal, as fewer shares are in public hands needing to be bought out. But it does sometimes happen that a management buy-in team makes an offer to take private a listed company, often against the wishes of the existing management. This might happen in circumstances where the market is undervaluing a good company. The bidding management can see the possibility of running the company privately for a few years, then refloating it at a more propitious time.

Key messages

- An Initial Public Offering (IPO) is a useful means for a growing company to raise money (a cash-in float) or a more mature one to provide an exit for some of its shareholders (a cash-out float). Companies that are already listed raise money through a Seasoned Equity Offering.
- A cash-out IPO might not provide a full exit for shareholders, as they might be obliged (for legal or market reasons) to retain some of their shares for a further period.

---

10 Text taken from: 'Dell directors sued over \$24.44 billion management buyout', by Jef Feeley www.bloomberg.com/news (accessed 7 February 2013).

- The decision as to whether to float is a financial one, but the flotation (IPO) itself is a marketing exercise, with the product in question being the company and its shares.
- The choice of which stock market to use is dependent on various factors including the company's home and trading region(s), its size, and its industry. Some companies chose to have a secondary listing on another market, to access a wider pool of investors.
- Different stock markets have different regulatory requirements. Stronger regulation might give more confidence to investors (meaning lower perceived risk and therefore a lower cost of capital and more potential players in the market). In order to list its shares, a company will have to meet its market's requirements, which often include matters such as its trading record, structure, and reporting systems.
- The listing process can be time-consuming. It will almost certainly be expensive, with many advisers and much documentation. The method by which the shares are listed will also have an impact on the cost.
- Price-setting for a listing is an art rather than a science. A successful float will result in the company's share price at the end of the first day being slightly higher than the listing price.
- Many boards choose to delist their shares, taking the company private. This may be because there is no longer a need to raise money, or because they are disappointed at the price the market is attributing to their business. Sometimes, an outside team bids for the company, buying it with private equity backing. The process of privatization is fraught with the potential for conflicts of interest.

Suggested further reading

A Guide to Listing on the London Stock Exchange (2010), London Stock Exchange (and others). www. londonstockexchange.com/home/guide-to-listing.pdf

This 112-page book comprises chapters written by lawyers, investment bankers and other professionals, and covers in detail every aspect of the listing process, including listing depository receipts. Although focused on London, much of the information is relevant to other exchanges.

Strategies for Going Public: The Changing Landscape for IPOs (2012), via www.deloitte.com

This report by Deloitte; American Stock Transfer & Trust Company; and Skadden, Arps, Slate, Meagher & Flom LLP & Affiliates comprises 86 pages plus detailed appendices. It focuses on how to effectively prepare for an IPO in the USA, including the IPO process, technical terms, and language that are commonly encountered, and the regulatory requirements that organizations will need to take into account as they seek to go public.

Investor Relations – A Practical Guide (2010), London Stock Exchange. www.londonstockexchange. com/home/ir-apracticalguide.pdf

A 70-page booklet produced by the London Stock Exchange in conjunction with Investor Relations professionals.

The Kay Review of UK Equity Markets and Long-Term Decision Making: Final Report (2012), Professor John Kay for Department of Business, Innovation & Skills. www.bis.gov.uk/kayreview

The Kay Review was commissioned by the UK government, and published in July 2012. Its focus is corporate governance and the encouragement of a longer-term view of markets. It provides some interesting information about how the markets work, with useful graphs and tables.

Equity Underwriting and Associated Services (2011), Office of Fair Trading. www.oft.gov.uk/shared_ oft/market-studies/OFT1303.pdf

This market study looks in detail at secondary issues by FTSE 350 companies, describing the way they raise the capital and the role of the various parties.

16 Acquisitions and selling a business

Learning objectives

After reading this chapter you should be able to:

1 Understand how and why companies make acquisitions.
2 Critically evaluate the synergies claimed for an acquisition, and how they affect the valuation of the target business.
3 Explain the different ways in which an acquisition can be financed, and understand how to select the most appropriate funding strategy.
4 Appreciate the governance and finance issues surrounding hostile bids.
5 Identify situations where an earn-out might be of use, and explain the advantages and disadvantages of this deal structure.
6 Outline some key areas of consideration in the sale of a business.

Introduction

We established in Part 1 of this book that companies need to grow in order to generate capital gains for their shareholders and to justify the growth value already priced into their shares. There are two main ways to obtain this growth: organically, and by acquisition. Organic growth is often less risky, but it can be difficult for larger companies: doubling in size is simpler for a company with £10 million turnover than for one turning over £1 billion. Accordingly, many companies look to acquisitions as a means to obtain the appropriate growth within the required time-frame.

We tend in finance to refer to 'mergers and acquisitions' (M&A). In an acquisition, one company (often, but not always, the larger) purchases the other. A merger is more of a meeting of equals; two companies of approximately the same size come together to form one new venture. In past decades it was sometimes useful, for financial reporting purposes, for companies to present a deal as a merger when in fact it was really an acquisition. However, changes to accounting standards have made this less relevant. In this chapter the term 'acquisition' is used to cover both types of transaction.

The chapter focuses on the financial aspects of acquisitions, and skates swiftly over the surface of many strategic and operating matters, while mostly ignoring regulatory concerns. By the nature of this book that has to be the case, as we have insufficient space to cover the subject in the depth it deserves. Some information about international M&A is included in Chapter 19, and guidance to further reading sources is included at the end of this chapter.

Why make an acquisition?

Academic research shows that most acquisitions fail, in that they do not meet the original expectations of the acquiring party.[1] Although such research can be vulnerable to misinterpretation (it is difficult to evaluate the aims and outcomes of transactions assessed from a distance) its results are widely disseminated in the popular and business press, and so must be known by many CEOs and finance directors. Nevertheless, acquisition activity is widespread, and not all of it can be driven by a desire to provide large fees to investment banks. So, why make an acquisition?

In our opinion, reasons for acquisition activity fall into two camps – good reasons and bad reasons. The overriding 'good' reason is the creation of shareholder value; we have, after all, established this as a key corporate financial objective. More specifically, the good reasons can be analysed as follows:

1   To complement the business strategy by filling gaps in product range, market segments, geographic territories, technological know-how, etc.
2   To support value-creating growth that cannot be achieved organically.

And possibly:

3   To prevent a competitor from making the acquisition.

We will come back to reasons one and two shortly. However, at this point we have to admit that we do have some doubts about this third reason, as often it is ego-driven. On balance, we have included it under 'goods' rather than 'bads' on the basis that allowing a competitor to

---

1   Schoenberg, R. (2006), 'Measuring the Performance of Corporate Acquisitions: An Empirical Comparison of Alternative Metrics', *British Journal of Management,* 17(4): 361–74.

Case Study 16.1

An acquisition to thwart a competitor

Your author was involved in advising a medium-sized private company on an acquisition. The managing director, an experienced businessman, was seeking advice on the valuation of the potential target. He had valued it at £10m, but the vendors would not sell for less than £12m. He wanted to buy the company, but did not want to overpay.

On questioning, it turned out that if his company did not buy the other business, their chief competitor would. And if that company were to make the acquisition, it would set back our client's growth plans by several years. Thus the added value of making the acquisition was significantly higher – getting it for £12m was a bargain.

expand could in some circumstances lead to an erosion of one's own competitive position, thus destroying value in the future – see Case Study 16.1. Therefore, making an acquisition to prevent this – provided that the overall effect is value-enhancing – is a legitimate strategy.

The bad reasons for acquisitions, of which there are, alas, many examples, are:

4   To show better financial results (e.g. to increase eps, whether or not this increases shareholder value); and
5   Managerial utility (a polite way of saying 'it's much more fun to buy companies than it is to run them successfully, so that's what we're going to do').

On the basis that we seek to inculcate good habits in our readers, we intend to ignore the 'bad' acquisition reasons from now on, and to focus on the good ones. And these can all be summarized in a term often used in describing corporate finance transactions: 'synergy'.

Almost every acquisition we have ever seen or been involved in has been praised (by the protagonists) for the synergy created. In fact, the term is used so often that it is probably illegal to do a deal without mentioning it! But in the context of acquisitions, what exactly does it mean?

The common shorthand used to explain synergy is '2 + 2 = 5', i.e. if we put these two parts together, the subsequent whole is worth considerably more than its components. However, this is the sort of woolly terminology that can be used to justify any deal, so let's see what we can do to strengthen our understanding of the concept.

In terms of competitive strategy, synergy can be described as the creation of a sustainable competitive advantage, or the removal of a previous competitive disadvantage. Achieving significant economies of scale or gaining greater control over channels of distribution or sources of supply may enable the enlarged business to improve its financial return. In these cases the financial justification for the acquisition should be that it would be much more expensive and/or more risky to try to achieve the same improvement in financial return by organic development of the business.

Another way of considering the value of synergies is to look at the accounting goodwill created in a deal. Goodwill in the financial statements represents the excess of the purchase price over the identifiable value of the assets (both tangible and intangible) purchased. There is a 'winner's curse' – almost always, the winning bidder in an acquisition has offered the highest amount. This being so, they should question what they were getting for that goodwill, i.e. why the target was actually worth more to them than to others. What synergies does this acquirer have that were not available to competitors? Unless these can clearly be identified, it is possible that the acquirer overpaid.

Working Insight 16.1

Examples of synergies relating to the value drivers

Value driver	*Examples of some possible synergies*
Increase sales growth	Use Target distribution network for Bidder products, or vice versa. Complementary products can increase volumes for both.
Increase operating profit margin	Cost efficiencies (e.g. economies of scale or scope, or better procurement practices). Increase selling prices, e.g. due to economies of scope.
Reduce cash tax rate	More tax-efficient location of operations.
Reduce incremental investment in capital expenditure	Combine operations and sell off surplus assets.
Reduce investment in working capital	Combine operations and reduce inventories.
Increase time period of competitive advantage	Strengthened branding or R&D from the business combination.
Reduce cost of capital	Should only occur if one of the companies is not already financed in the most efficient manner.

Developed from this, the checklist in Working Insight 16.2 can be used to identify and quantify synergies, and to ensure that they are managed operationally.

An even tighter definition of synergy can be obtained by referring back to Rappaport's seven drivers of value, discussed in Chapter 1. Working Insight 16.1 suggests some possible areas for synergy relating to these.

The checklist set out in Working Insight 16.2 provides a way to quantify the potential synergies from an acquisition. It takes away the 'wishful thinking' element of the deal, and sets out clear post-integration targets. If more deals were subject to this kind of analytical rigour, fewer deals might be done, but they would be more value-enhancing.

The website accompanying this book includes a simple example of a synergy spreadsheet, which quantifies the value of each separate synergy. Completing such an analysis helps focus the acquirer's mind – and their due diligence process – on what is important.

Case Study 16.2 sets out some examples of stated synergies in acquisitions.

Discussion of deal synergies leads us conveniently to the next section: how should the deal be valued?

How much to pay?

It is often said that acquirers overpay for deals. Certainly, an analysis of where value lies in an acquisition will lead the researcher to conclude that in general the vendor shareholders obtain a better deal than the acquiring shareholders. But the 'overpay' proposition tends to be made on the basis of prices paid for acquisitions of listed companies – these are often at a premium of 30 per cent or more over the target's pre-bid share price.

To assume that an acquirer is overpaying merely because the bid price is greater than the pre-existing share price is a fallacy. There are two reasons for this.

Working Insight 16.2

Synergy checklist

Strategic
1. Which of the value drivers will be affected by this transaction?
2. In which direction?
3. Why?

Financial
4. By how much will it change?
5. When will this happen?

Operational
6. What critical success factors need to be in place to ensure this happens?
7. What needs to be measured?
8. Who is responsible for making it happen?

First, it is a misconception to assume that the market capitalization of a company (the current share price multiplied by the number of outstanding shares) represents the value of that company. It doesn't. The current share price for any company represents the price at which most shareholders were not persuaded to sell their shares. Only a tiny fraction of any company's capital changes hands on any day, and the quoted price is merely the price of the latest transaction. If this were an overvalue, it presumably would persuade most rational investors to sell out. Even if the quoted share price exactly equalled the 'fair' price, it is reasonable to assume that more shareholders would sell (assuming that shareholders' expectations of future performance are distributed normally around the mean of 'fair' price). Thus the market

Case Study 16.2

Examples of reported potential acquisition synergies

LVMH buys Bulgari
In March 2011 LVMH, the French luxury-goods group, announced its agreed acquisition of high-end jeweller Bulgari. In its report of the transaction, Reuters stated: 'Bulgari will benefit from world No. 1 LVMH's global retail network, improve margins through cost-sharing and help the owner of Louis Vuitton handbags close the gap with bigger watch and jewelry companies.' It went on to report that the high price would be justified by the savings that could be made.

Avis and Zipcar
January 2013 saw the announcement that car hire company Avis Group would acquire the car-sharing company Zipcar. The suggestion was that as well as complementary markets (car-sharing is replacing car rental in some countries), there would be a synergy in fleet optimization, as Avis needed the most vehicles for its peak mid-week business, and Zipcar for its busiest times at the weekend.

Sources: Reuters, Financial Times, Dan Primack (*Fortune*)

capitalization could be perceived as an undervalue, and shareholders need to be offered a premium to persuade them to sell.

Second, shareholders understand markets. A bidder for the whole of a company's share capital is creating a situation in which demand exceeds supply; the share price obviously goes up to reflect this. And the shareholders realize that acquiring 100 per cent of the company puts the acquirer in a far more powerful and valuable position than an investor acquiring a small stake: accordingly they make the bidding company pay for this value.

The issue for the bidder is to ensure that the amount paid for the business does not exceed the value it will generate. Here is where the analysis of synergies from Working Insight 16.2 can be used. Figure 16.1 illustrates how value is added in a deal.

The value diagram in Figure 16.1 starts on the left-hand side of the page with the value of the company to the vendor. This may be the market capitalization, but a bidder would be better to undertake an analysis of value under the target company's existing strategy and management. From this point the bidder can add in the value created by each of the identified synergies; the seven broad drivers included in Working Insight 16.1 may be broken down at this stage, to identify, for example, how much value will come from better procurement practices, how much will come from elimination of duplicate expenses, or how much will be generated from manufacturing efficiencies. Account also needs to be taken of the 'negative synergies', for example, customers whose business will be lost due to the new ownership of the business.

For illustration, Figure 16.1 includes only three types of synergy. Adding those to the base value leads us to the target's potential value to the acquirer. However, this is not the amount that should be paid for the target business. Investment banks and lawyers do not come cheap, and substantial deal costs may be incurred before the transaction is complete, thus reducing the deal's potential value. More significantly, reorganization costs such as redundancies and relocations need to be considered. As well as causing a huge personal cost to those involved, they involve significant financial costs, often over several periods. The sum that remains is an indication to the bidder of the maximum amount that they should be prepared to pay for the target company.

This is where things often go wrong. The bidding team, with this maximum fixed in their minds, are often prepared to pay up to this amount. To use the terminology of behavioural

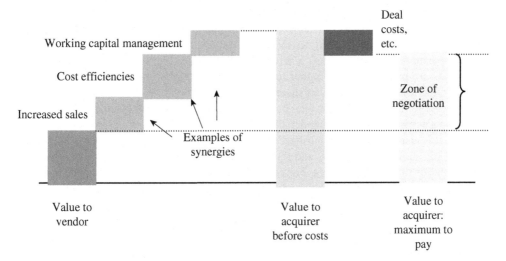

Figure 16.1 Adding value in an acquisition.

finance set out in Chapter 14, they tend to 'anchor' on this sum. This has the effect of giving to the vendor shareholders the benefit of all of the synergies that the company intends to generate – before it has even started. In other words, paying the maximum value for the target company represents a transaction at a net present value of zero: a fun exercise for management, but hardly a value-enhancing strategy. In a good deal, the price paid will probably be greater than the vendor's value, but should be significantly less than the bidder's maximum.

If the value to the vendor is higher than that to the potential bidder, then (unless vendor or bidder is particularly stupid) the deal will not proceed. Similarly in a competitive bidding situation, it is logical (but again not always true) that the bidder who can create the most value is the one who will win the deal. However, emotion often takes control at this point, and directors are tempted to increase their offers in a competitive situation, perhaps believing that if there is competition, the target business really must be good! This being the case, it is useful to re-evaluate the synergies using a different template.

Synergies have already been considered in terms of the impact on the seven value drivers. But it is useful to look at them in terms of their specificity to the bidding company.[2] There are three different possibilities:

1   Synergies that any bidder could realize. (E.g., arising through better management.)
2   Synergies that any bidder within the industry could realize. (E.g. arising through consolidation of manufacturing, or distribution chains.)
3   Synergies unique to this bidder. (E.g., involving the application of a particular brand or R&D capability.)

Working Insight 16.3 illustrates this.

It can be difficult to add value in an acquisition. Acquisitions raise shareholders' expectations. After all, as shareholders in Bidder we can go out and buy shares in Target. So, if Bidder itself chooses to buy Target, it must be expecting to add some value that we as individual investors could not create. Furthermore, an acquisition premium will almost certainly have been paid – so Bidder has paid more for Target than we would have ourselves. And, finally, we must remember that the share price of both companies undoubtedly has a PVGO element, with future growth already priced into the shares. Thus if the acquisition is to create value, the combined organization has to outperform the growth already included in its share price. Working Insight 16.4 illustrates this.

In this section we have, perhaps, made M&A sound very logical and rational. Although some deals are priced like that, rather too many are driven by emotion and non-financial matters, rather than by principles of shareholder value.

An owner selling a business that has been built up over decades will have a different point of view to a corporate restructuring department anxious to offload a troublesome subsidiary, or one that is just too small to contribute to corporate strategy. This will influence the price they ask, the strategy they adopt, and the emotion they bring to the deal. All of which are useful data for the potential buyer. For example, a colleague of the author's once paid just $1m in a transaction for which the vendor had sought $10m. This was done by obtaining a

2   These ideas were suggested in Baldi, F. and Trigeorgis, L. (2009), 'Assessing the Value of Growth Option Synergies from Business Combinations and Testing for Goodwill Impairment: A Real Options Perspective', *Journal of Applied Corporate Finance*, 21(4): 115–24.

Working Insight 16.3

Specificity of synergies

BigChem wishes to acquire SmallChem. A stand-alone value of SmallChem is £20m, and BigChem has calculated the value of synergies as follows:

	£m
Increasing sales volumes	2
Improving operating margin	3
Better working capital management	1
Total synergies	6
Stand-alone value of SmallChem	20
Value of SmallChem to BigChem	26

However, as a cautious bidder, BigChem has also sliced the potential synergies in another way:

	£m
Available to any other bidder	1
Available to other bidders in the industry	4
Specific to BigChem, due to application of patented technology	1

It has also looked at the potential competition, and is aware that GiantChem (a competitor) also has a specific synergy due to leveraging the strength of its distribution chain. This could amount to as much as £2m. This means that while BigChem can potentially pay up to £26m for the target, SmallChem is worth £27m to GiantChem, and if the latter were to enter the bidding, then BigChem would be likely to lose.

deep understanding of the vendor's position, and realizing that he wanted to retire before the end of the tax year, and time was not on his side.

Due diligence

Acquisitions are generally expensive, and often risky. Before any transaction is completed, the buyer needs to ensure that proper due diligence is undertaken. Due diligence is an investigation of the affairs (financial, commercial, and other) of the target company. Conducting good due diligence carries several advantages:

Working Insight 16.4

The need to add value in acquisitions

Target has eps of 10p, a share price of 200p and pays a dividend of 2p per share. Its cost of equity is 10%, which means that, with a dividend yield of 1%, investors are expecting growth in the share price of 9% per annum. Such expectations imply a share price of 308p in five years' time.

Bidder buys Target for 250p per share. Assuming, for simplicity, the same growth expectations, annual growth of 9% means that a share price of 385p is required by Year 5. This implies eps growth (assuming no change in the P/E ratio) of 14% per annum. Unless Bidder can increase Target's growth rate by an additional 5% per year (or grow its own profits as a result of the acquisition), it is destroying value for its shareholders.

Working Insight 16.5

Some common areas for due diligence

Financial performance	Review of historical financial statements. Review of management accounting information. Review of forecasts.
Information systems	Adequacy of the internal controls of the business and assessment of its management information systems.
Commercial aspects	Include a review of competitive positioning, dependence on large customers/suppliers, trends in sales volumes and prices, state of the forward order book.
Technical operations	Production technologies in use; information technology systems and their compatibility with Bidder's.
People	Understanding who's who and where knowledge lies; unionization and legal issues; terms of employment and how they might integrate with the Bidder's; organizational culture and likely conflicts with the Bidder.
Intellectual property	What is used, what is owned, what is patented or trademarked, which legal entity actually holds the licences.
Environmental and corporate responsibility	Contingent liabilities, for example, related to previous use of sites, or asbestos in buildings; a wide range of corporate responsibility issues;[3] reputational issues related to being associated with that business.
Legal and governance issues	Details of major contracts; compliance with regulation; company's compliance systems surrounding, for example, Foreign Corrupt Practices Act (USA) or Bribery Act (UK). Also an understanding of the main risk management mechanisms in the organization and its attitude towards corporate governance.
Pension liabilities	Status of pension fund(s) verified separately with clear understanding of legal position; review of the power of pension fund trustees in relation to the acquisition or the future running of the organization.
Taxation	Full review of tax situation including tax impacts of the acquisition.

We must point out that the above is indicative and does not cover the full range of issues on a due diligence checklist.

- It ensures that you know what you are buying, and are aware of any potential pitfalls.
- It can help in determining valuations, ensuring that you don't overpay.
- It can be focused on the potential synergies, to evaluate whether they are achievable.
- It can assist the buyer in developing a post-acquisition integration plan.

Working Insight 16.5 lists some common areas into which due diligence may be conducted. In practice, acquiring companies and their professional advisers will have comprehensive checklists of matters to be checked.

---

3 Corporate responsibility issues will vary depending on the type of business and its location. A good source to use as an initial checklist is the Global Reporting Initiative, www.globalreporting.org, whose guidelines set out matters to be considered in producing a corporate responsibility report.

The detailed due diligence carried out pre-acquisition should be used to check the realism of the initial valuation assumptions. Due diligence is always worthwhile, but in scoping the level of work a balance has to be struck between the significance of the deal, the likelihood of its going ahead, and the cost and timescale of the due diligence exercise.[4] Key issues to address must be the main value drivers for the business, and sensitivity analysis should be done to establish how critical these are, with due diligence used to confirm that the minimum required level should be reasonably achievable. If the deal value is predicated on synergies, attention should specifically be paid to issues surrounding those synergies.

In addition, the detail of the accounting policies needs to be understood, as the acquirer needs to know what the asset values and underlying cash flows are, and also what the target's profits will be under the acquirer's accounting policies. In these days of 'fair value' in accounting, when mark-to-market and mark-to-model valuation techniques are common in financial statements, this has become increasingly important.

Due diligence might be conducted on the target company's premises or, more commonly these days in a large transaction, through the use of a data room, as explored later in this chapter.

Financing the deal

Deals can be financed by an exchange of shares, or through some form of cash, or a combination of these. In an exchange of shares, the shareholders of the target company exchange their shares in Target for shares in Bidder. A cash deal involves Bidder paying cash (from its existing resources, or financed through raising debt or by issuing new shares on the market) to the Target shareholders. Thus a share exchange adds the Target shareholders to the shareholder base of Bidder; a cash bid means that Target shareholders do not participate in the future of the combined company.

Deal finance can be considered in two separate ways: we can look at value-enhancing strategies, and we can consider eps-enhancing strategies. Naturally, we believe strongly in the former, but a jaundiced view of the markets indicates that many companies put enhancement of eps above shareholder value, so this is where we will start.

Financing acquisitions using eps-enhancing strategies

If the acquisition finance is to be structured so as to enhance eps, there are two 'rules' to note:

1   If the Bidder P/E is higher than the Target P/E, using equity to finance the deal will increase eps; if Bidder P/E is lower than Target P/E, then using equity will dilute eps.
2   If the company's post-tax interest rate is lower than the inverse of the Target P/E ratio, then using debt will enhance eps; if the interest rate exceeds the inverse of Target P/E, then using debt will dilute eps.

These two 'rules' will now be explained using Working Insights 16.6–16.9.

Working Insight 16.6 illustrates the fallacy of basing deal assessment on whether or not it is immediately eps-enhancing. The Bidder–Target combination is 'bad' because it dilutes eps; the

---

4   See Chapter 17 for an indication of how to conduct the acquisition of a business out of liquidation, where there is little time available for due diligence.

Working Insight 16.6

Funding with equity: relationship between bidder and target P/E and eps dilution

Bidder is acquiring Target. Each company has 1,000 shares in issue, and is trading at £10 per share. For convenience, assume that each company could be bought for its market capitalization (£10,000) by issuing shares at the existing share price. (These assumptions can be relaxed without invalidating the principles shown, but they make the case easier to explain.)

	Bidder	Target
Profit after tax	£1,000	£500
Earnings per share	£1	£0.5
Share price	£10	£10
P/E ratio	10	20

1. Bidder to buy Target at £10,000, issuing 1,000 new shares.

Revised share capital of Bidder (number of shares)	2,000
Combined after-tax profits	£1,500
Revised eps	£0.75

If Bidder, a low P/E company, buys Target, a higher P/E company for shares, the eps is diluted from £1 to 75p. Financial markets may see this as 'bad'.

2. However, what if instead Target were to buy Bidder, issuing 1,000 new shares so to do?

Revised share capital of Target (number of shares)	2,000
Combined after-tax profits	£1,500
Revised eps	£0.75

Thus the combination of Target/Bidder is eps-accretive, it has increased eps from 50p to 75p – obviously a good deal!

In practice of course, judgement as to whether it is a good or bad deal should lie only with an assessment of whether shareholder value is increased, not the impact on eps.

Target–Bidder combination is eps-accretive and therefore 'good'. In either case the same assets have been combined – it's just a matter of arithmetic, as explained in Working Insight 16.7.

The other 'rule' to enhance eps relates to debt financing. Working Insight 16.8 sets out how this works.

Again, this is purely arithmetic; the detail is set out in Working Insight 16.9.

Another use of the maths illustrated in the last few Working Insights is to calculate, for a potentially dilutive transaction, just how much needs to be earned in first-year synergies in order to make the deal earnings-neutral. Working Insight 16.10 illustrates this.

Case Study 16.3 shows how, despite what we say about eps dilution being unimportant, the market thinks otherwise.

Working Insight 16.7

'Bootstrapping' to enhance eps

The following is a mathematical proof of why the purchase of a low P/E company by a high P/E company will lead to an increase in eps for the acquirer.

Bidder		Target	
Earnings	E_b	Earnings	E_t
Share price	P_b	Share price	P_t
Market value	MV_b	Market value (value of the bid)	MV_t
P/E	PE_b	P/E	PE_t

Therefore number of Bidder shares in issue = $MV_b \div P_b$
Number of Bidder shares needed to acquire Target = $MV_t \div P_b$

After the acquisition, the new company will have the combined earnings of Target and Bidder (assuming no synergies). Therefore, the new eps after acquisition will be:

$$eps_{new} = (E_b + E_t) \div \text{total new shares}$$
$$eps_{new} = (E_b + E_t) \div (MV_b/P_b + MV_t/P_b)$$
$$eps_{new} = (E_b + E_t)P_b \div (MV_b + MV_t)$$
$$eps_{new} = (E_b + E_t)P_b \div ((PE_b \times E_b) + (PE_t \times E_t)) \tag{1}$$

We want the eps of Bidder after the deal to be higher than it was before the deal, i.e. $eps_{new} > eps_{old}$

eps_{new} was calculated in equation (1)
eps_{old} is simply $P_b \div PE_b$

Therefore we want:

$$(E_b + E_t)P_b \div ((PE_b \times E_b) + (PE_t \times E_t)) > P_b \div PE_b$$

Multiplying this out, it becomes

$$PE_b \times (E_b + E_t) > ((PE_b \times E_b) + (PE_t \times E_t))$$

Which simplifies to

$$(PE_b \times E_t) > (PE_t \times E_t)$$

i.e., $PE_b > PE_t$

So, if the acquisition is to enhance Bidder's eps, the P/E of Bidder must be higher than that of Target.
    This automatic increase in eps due to the nature of the acquisition finance is known as 'bootstrapping'. However, readers should be aware that the term bootstrapping is widely used in finance, and has several different meanings.

Working Insight 16.8

Using debt finance to enhance eps

Target has post-tax earnings of £500 and is being acquired for £10,000. Bidder can borrow at 6.25% and pays tax at the rate of 20% which reduces its cost of debt to an after-tax 5%.

> Bidder is buying profits after tax of £500. The cost of financing the acquisition by debt is £10,000 @ 5%, i.e. £500. Thus, in the first year the extra interest cost exactly cancels out the acquired profits.

The after-tax debt cost, 5%, is the inverse of Target's P/E ratio of 20. If Bidder could borrow at less than 5%, the deal would be eps-enhancing in Year 1. If its borrowing cost exceeded 5%, eps would fall.

Working Insight 16.9

Using debt finance to enhance eps

The following is a mathematical proof of why financing the purchase of a company by borrowing at a rate less than the inverse of its P/E ratio will lead to an increase in eps for the acquirer.

Bidder		*Target*	
Earnings	E_b	Earnings	E_t
Share price	P_b	Share price	P_t
Market value	MV_b	Market value (value of the bid)	MV_t
P/E	PE_b	P/E	PE_t
After-tax cost of borrowing	Kd		

Bidder will borrow the sum of MV_t in order to finance the deal.
The after-tax interest charge on MV_t will be $(MV_t \times Kd)$

After the acquisition, the new company will have the combined earnings of Target and Bidder (assuming no synergies), less the net interest. i.e. $E_b + E_t - MV_tKd$

No new shares will be issued, so the new eps after acquisition will be:

$$eps_{new} = [E_b + E_t - MV_tKd] \div (MV_b \div P_b)$$

Whereas eps previously was:

$$eps_{old} = E_b \div (MV_b \div P_b)$$

We seek enhancement of eps, so ideally $eps_{new} > eps_{old}$
Which means that:

$$(E_b + E_t - MV_tKd) \div (MV_b \div P_b) > E_b \div (MV_b \div P_b)$$

This simplifies to:

$$E_t > MV_t Kd$$

Which is a very long-winded way of saying that the profits we are acquiring should exceed the interest charge we are paying.

The price being paid for Target (MV_t) can be expressed as $PE_t \times E_t$
Therefore:

$$E_t > PE_t E_t \times Kd$$

Which simplifies to:

$$1/PE_t > Kd$$

Or, as stated in rule 2 (p. 269), if the after-tax cost of debt is less than the inverse of the target P/E ratio, the deal will be eps-accretive.

Financing acquisitions using value-enhancing strategies

As stated earlier, acquisitions can be undertaken by offering the target shareholders shares in the bidding company (an acquisition for shares) or offering them cash, either from its balance sheet or newly raised. The choice of financing methods will depend at least partly on the business risk of bidder and target companies. The bidding company should not upset its long-term financial strategy without good cause.

Working Insight 16.10

What synergies are needed to make the deal earnings-neutral?

Working Insight 16.6 showed that if Bidder were to acquire Target for shares, its eps would be diluted from £1 to £0.75. If eps is to remain at £1, additional post-tax profits need to be generated from the synergies of the deal, in Year 1.

With 2,000 shares in issue, eps of £1 means after-tax profits of £2,000. This is an increase of £500 over the combined profits of the two entities.

An increase of £500 in post-tax profits and a tax rate of 20% mean an increase of £625 in pre-tax profits. This is the required synergy level in Year 1.

Alternatively, this calculation could be done by taking Bidder's P/E as the highest P/E payable without dilution, and determining what profits this represents.

Bidder P/E is 10 and the price paid for Target is £10,000 which implies profits of £1,000. Target currently makes profit of £500, so the synergy needed in Year 1 is £500, post-tax, which is £625 pre-tax.

The arithmetic is easy. However, in practice, achieving a 25% uplift in combined profits in Year 1 might present some difficulties to management.

Even if the board sees past the short-term lure of being earnings-neutral in Year 1, it is always useful to carry out this calculation. The level of required synergies needs to be mapped against the anticipated changes in value drivers, to establish the credibility of the targets.

Case Study 16.3

Eps dilution does matter in practice

Hewitt and Aon: eps-accretive

In 2010 it was announced that Hewitt Associates would merge with a subsidiary of Aon Corporation, to create an even larger global HR consultancy. The press release announcing the transaction emphasized the impact on eps, as follows, 'Aon expects the transaction to be accretive on a GAAP EPS basis in 2012 and on an Adjusted EPS basis in 2011. Aon expects the transaction to be significantly accretive to cash earnings in 2011.'

Disney and Lucasfilm: diluting eps

The October 2012 announcement that Disney would acquire Lucasfilm, the makers of *Star Wars*, was greeted positively in terms of its potential strategic and financial impact, but resulted in a share price fall for Disney. This appears to have been due in part to the fact that the deal would be eps-dilutive in 2013 and 2014, with the result that analysts marked down their forecasts. One analyst was reported as saying that investors would be 'disappointed with the dilutive deployment of capital' despite it being a good deal.

Sources: www.aon.com and www.cnbc.com

It is important to note that although an acquisition for shares involves issuing new equity, an acquisition for cash need not be financed by raising debt. The bidding company could issue shares in the market and use the proceeds of the sale to pay cash for the target company. Figure 16.2 illustrates the alternatives.

If the target company shareholders receive cash (however raised) for their shares, that is the end of their involvement with the company. However, in deals which pay the target shareholders in shares, they have an ongoing relationship with the company. Thus in share-based deals the vendor shareholders have various matters to consider:

Are both companies fairly valued?	If the target is overvalued, then the acquirer has made a poor deal.
	If the acquirer is overvalued, then the target's shareholders will receive proportionately too few of its shares in exchange for their company.
What are the prospects for the combined company?	Target's shareholders are accepting shares in the combined entity and need to understand the risks and rewards of the ongoing business.

One of the best pieces of advice given by your author was to a friend who had been offered a large sum (payable in shares) by a quoted dot.com wishing to buy his fledgling internet company. The advice was 'don't see it as selling your company – what you're doing is using your business as a currency to buy a small stake in a larger concern over which you have no control; do you feel comfortable about that?'. A year later his company was thriving . . . the quoted dot.com had gone into liquidation.

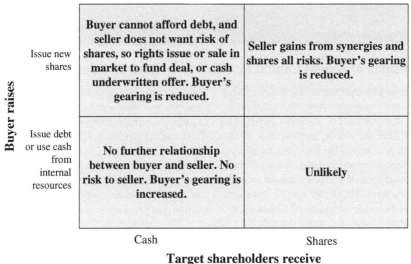

	Cash	**Shares**
Issue new shares	Buyer cannot afford debt, and seller does not want risk of shares, so rights issue or sale in market to fund deal, or cash underwritten offer. Buyer's gearing is reduced.	Seller gains from synergies and shares all risks. Buyer's gearing is reduced.
Issue debt or use cash from internal resources	No further relationship between buyer and seller. No risk to seller. Buyer's gearing is increased.	Unlikely

Figure 16.2 Financing acquisitions.

If a transaction is done for shares, the parties have to determine how the price is stated: as a fixed number of shares, or a fixed value. There will inevitably be a delay between announcing a deal and completing it. A deal which offers the vendor a fixed number of the bidder's shares leaves the vendor exposed to the risk that the bidder's share price will fall in the interim. On the other hand, a deal at a fixed value of shares protects the vendor, but leaves the bidder's shareholders vulnerable to dilution should the share price fall.

Of course, a transaction need not be all shares or all debt, but can be a combination, or the consideration could also be a different type of financial instrument. Case Study 16.4 illustrates a mixed financing.

Regulatory issues

If my small private company wishes to take over your small private company, chances are that nobody else will be interested; certainly, there will be little if any regulatory involvement. But if either of the companies is listed, then the transaction will be subject to the rules of the stock exchange(s) concerned, which may, for example, have set rules to ensure a level playing field, such that an acquirer cannot buy the target by stealth without the other shareholders being aware of the transaction, or to make sure that all shareholders are treated equally in the deal.

If the companies are significant in size, or in their strategic importance, then national or transnational regulators will become involved. These might be concerned with protecting markets from becoming monopolies, or with ensuring that strategic companies do not fall into what might be considered unfriendly ownership. Examples of areas for regulation are shown in Working Insight 16.11.

Rules differ by stock exchange and in different parts of the world. Any prospective buyer should be aware of the potential regulations and the costs involved in compliance.

Case Study 16.4

Acquisition of Knight Capital by GETCO for cash and shares

In Chapter 17 we set out a Case Study of Knight Capital, a financial services company engaged in market making and electronic execution, brought down by a computer fault and rescued by a group of investors. The investors included GETCO LLC, a private equity owned rival. Three months after the rescue, in November 2012, GETCO made a bid for Knight, and the reverse takeover was agreed the following month.

Knight shareholders had a choice of how they would take their consideration. For each share they could receive $3.75 in cash, or one share of common stock in the new (listed) holding company for GETCO and Knight. Investors in the shares would also receive warrants to be exercised at price thresholds of $4 and $4.50 in four and five years respectively.

The deal value was approximately $1.4 billion, a 51% premium to the company's pre-bid share price. The cash alternative was available up to a cap of $720m – if Knight shareholders in aggregate elected to receive more than that sum, then the cash alternative would be distributed pro rata, with shares for the balance. However, major shareholders had agreed to limit their cash consideration to 50% of their investment, in order to make the cash available to other shareholders.

An assumption is that the cash alternative was necessary because investors might have been reluctant to accept equity in GETCO which, being private equity owned, did not have a public record.

Sources: Financial Times and www.prnewswire.com

Working Insight 16.11

Some examples of areas for takeover regulation[5]

Takeover regulations could include provisions on:

Equal treatment
All the shareholders of a class should be treated the same, regardless of who they are and how many shares they own.

Mandatory bids
Once the bidder has a majority of a certain level, they are obliged to make an offer to the minority, on equivalent terms.

Transparency of ownership and control
Any build-up of ownership above a certain low threshold should be made clear to the market.

---

5 These and many more such regulations are discussed in Goergen, M., Martynova, M., and Renneboog, L. (2005), *Corporate Governance Convergence: Evidence from Takeover Regulation Reforms in Europe.* www.cepr.org/meets/wkcn/5/5528/papers/Goergen.pdf

Hostile bids and defence strategies

An offer made to acquire a listed company which is rejected by the target company's directors is known as a hostile bid. It is important to realize that the bid is hostile to the *directors* – the company's shareholders may actually welcome the bid.

Why would the target's directors reject the bid? There are two main reasons:

1   Because they believe that the bid undervalues the company; i.e. they consider that they can create more value for shareholders by continuing to run the company themselves.
2   Because they wish to retain their jobs.

It goes without saying that we see the first reason as totally valid and the second as probably against shareholders' interests, and representing an agency conflict. However, an examination of directors' actions in bid situations suggests that reason 2 often applies in practice.

Directors fending off a hostile bid need a defence strategy (which generally comes courtesy of a host of highly paid advisers). The best defence strategy is to ensure that the company is correctly valued by the markets at all times. Given that quoted company acquisitions generally demand a significant price premium, if the company is fully valued, the potential acquirer is either creating synergies or is overpaying. In either of these situations, a bid is likely to generate value for the target shareholders.

As well as continually communicating with the markets to ensure an appropriate valuation, directors of listed companies should maintain a contingency plan of what they would do should an unexpected offer be made. This will help them to react more swiftly and efficiently to the offer. Such reaction will include the preparation of a comprehensive defence document to explain to shareholders why they should not accept the offer, and a concerted effort to woo key shareholders such as major financial institutions.

Within the UK, there are various strategies that can be adopted by the directors of the target company in order to fend off the bid. We list these in Working Insight 16.12, but with a health warning: although they might enable the company to remain independent, they may also destroy value for the shareholders. (This is yet another example of an agency conflict between owners and managers.)

In other countries, a wider range of defence strategies may be available. For example, 'poison pills' are allowed in the United States and in various European countries. Some examples of these defence strategies are shown in Working Insight 16.13.

Again, we would point out that poison pills and the like may benefit the directors of the target company, but rarely add value for its existing shareholders unless they lead to an increased offer which is then accepted. It is very difficult to justify many of the tactics that directors use to defend against hostile bids. Poison pills impede the efficient working of the capital markets and deprive shareholders of a tool by which they can discipline an inefficient management.

Earn-outs

Another way of structuring an acquisition is through an earn-out, in which the eventual price paid for the business depends in part on its performance in the early years following the transfer of ownership.

Working Insight 16.12

Defence strategies available to UK companies

- Make an acquisition, thus making your company larger, and more difficult for the predator to digest.
- Use of the 'Pac-man' defence: make a bid for the predator company itself.
- Dispose of some key assets which would be particularly attractive to the predator.
- Find a 'white knight' – another company which will acquire you, and will be more acceptable to the directors.
- Have the bid referred to the competition authorities, which may or may not prevent it, but will almost certainly delay it considerably.
- Enter into a joint venture of part of your business with another company, which would be difficult for a predator to unravel.
- Arrange cross-shareholdings with industry associates, or with partners up and down the supply chain.

Earn-outs are often used in the acquisition of private companies, for example, in situations where the acquiring company wishes to retain the services and commitment of the director/ shareholders of the target, perhaps because they are crucial to operations. In a business which is very dependent on personal relationships, the bidding company may wish to retain the directors' commitment for long enough to ensure that the goodwill and contact base are secure.

The earn-out deal might be that the vendor shareholders receive £X immediately on completion of the deal, and a further £Y if profits of a certain level are achieved within one, two or possibly three years of the deal being done. This gives the key director/shareholders an incentive to perform well during the earn-out period, as shown in Case Study 16.5, which demonstrates a rather unusual form of the transaction.

Working Insight 16.13

Some examples of other defence strategies

- Issue new shares at a discount to friendly shareholders, thus continually diluting the acquirer's shareholding. (This is known as a 'poison pill', although that term has been used more widely to discuss other types of defence strategy.)
- Set up a 'staggered board' such that only a certain number of directors can be made to retire each year. Although this might not prevent the takeover, it means that some of the outgoing directors could retain their jobs for several years. Another version of this is the classified board, whereby different classes of director serve for different term lengths. Either mechanism means that an acquirer needs to win proxy battles for more than one year to take control of the board.
- Set up provisions in the company's internal regulations such that a super-majority (say, 80%) is required to agree a takeover rather than the customary 50%. Alternatively, used dual-class shares, with one class having more rights, effectively able to block a takeover.

Case Study 16.5

MITIE: growth through earn-outs

A UK company that has grown through earn-outs is strategic outsourcing and support services group MITIE (which stands for Management Incentive Through Investment Equity).

MITIE's website explains its model as follows:

> The 'MITIE Model' is for entrepreneurial management teams who have an idea for growing a business as a part of MITIE. It's structured so that the management team takes an equity stake of up to 49% in a business which they grow over a five to ten-year period, and is eventually acquired by MITIE in full.

MITIE has acquired over 100 start-up businesses in that way, and claims a 95% success rate. (It does not give a definition of 'success'.)

MITIE business managers interviewed by the author see this combination of private equity and earn-out as being highly effective as an incentive mechanism to grow their businesses.

Source: www.mitie.com and discussions with MITIE business managers

It should be obvious that earn-outs will be most effective in situations in which the vendor shareholders are also the key management of the company, generally in private companies. If the management are not shareholders, an earn-out will not benefit them, and management contracts might be a better way to achieve their commitment. If the shareholders are not managers, they may be very reluctant to agree an earn-out, leaving their ultimate consideration in the hands of managers over whom they no longer have any sanction.

However, there are circumstances where a listed company can be sold with an earn-out, in this case known as *contingent value rights* (CVTs). CVTs are generally of shorter duration than a standard earn-out, and are designed to relate to the settlement of a specific uncertainty which is affecting the valuation of the target company. So, for example, if one event, such as the settlement of outstanding litigation, or the licensing of a particular pharmaceutical drug, is stalling the transaction, the deal can proceed based on the assumption that it will not be settled in the company's favour, but with CVTs in place such that the vendor shareholders receive a further payment if the eventual outcome is beneficial.

Returning to unlisted companies, earn-outs may also be used as a means to resolve differences of opinion as to a company's potential, and thus its value. It often happens that the target company is small, but with great prospects. Naturally, the vendors wish to receive consideration for the potential that they are selling to the bidder. However, the bidder, quite reasonably, could argue that it will not pay for unrealized potential that cannot yet be proved. An earn-out may be used to resolve this situation, with the initial price reflecting the target's current performance, and further payments being made if certain milestones are achieved.

Structuring a deal as an earn-out has both advantages and disadvantages to the acquirer, as set out in Working Insight 16.14.

For the seller, an earn-out also has advantages and disadvantages. They have the potential to get more money, but it is not a clean break. Working Insight 16.15 shows the earn-out from the seller's point of view.

Working Insight 16.14

Features of an earn-out to the acquirer

Advantages

- Only pay for what is achieved.
- Defers payment, thus retaining cash resources (for a cash deal) or delaying dilution of eps and control (for a deal financed by issuing equity).
- Maintains the interest of key management during the transition period.

Disadvantages

- Difficult to achieve synergies in combining the businesses, as the continuing management will demand a free hand to run 'their' business.
- The earn-out management have an incentive to run the business for the short term, focusing on a particular year's profit targets. Longer-term investments in fixed assets, marketing, training or research may be neglected.
- In a share-based deal, if the bidder's share price falls in the intervening period, it could end up issuing far more shares for the final consideration than was intended.

The important thing in any earn-out (apart, obviously, from the price) is the need to define the terms very clearly, in terms of how the business should be run during the earn-out period, and what counts as 'profit'. Working Insight 16.16 suggests some matters to consider.

One final point is worth mentioning about earn-outs. Before undertaking such a transaction (as buyer or seller), consideration should be given to the accounting and tax treatments

Working Insight 16.15

Features of an earn-out to the vendor

Advantages

- Has the potential to result in a higher sales value.
- Deferring payment can sometimes have tax advantages.
- Keeps an involvement in the business (and a salary over the earn-out period), which may be desired.

Disadvantages

- Unless covenants are in place to prevent the new owners from making radical changes, the nature of the business might be changed adversely, meaning that the profit potential can never be reached.
- Receipt of the final consideration is delayed.
- Receipt of the final consideration is dependent on the acquirer having the financial resources to meet its commitments. (If that consideration is in equity rather than cash, it is also dependent on the share price of the acquirer.)
- Ongoing involvement in the business might not suit a seller who wishes to sever ties and move on.

Working Insight 16.16

Matters to consider in an earn-out

Ernie has agreed in principle to sell his milk delivery business to BigCow, but they are haggling over the price. Ernie's profits and cash flows have risen by 15% every year over the past five years, and he believes that this rate of growth will continue; BigCow are more pessimistic about the market, and do not wish to overpay for a business that they think is approaching maturity. An earn-out is mooted, whereby BigCow will pay Ernie a sum now that reflects current profitability. He will run the business for them, as their subsidiary, for a suitable period, and if it makes the profits he anticipates, they will pay him a substantial earn-out; if the business does not make the required profits he will not receive any further payment.

Some of the matters to be dealt with in the agreement include:

How is profit to be determined?	At what level in the income statement? (E.g. EBITDA, EBIT, net earnings.) What accounting policies will be used, and what happens if regulation on accounting policies changes?
Who will be responsible for management decisions?	If Ernie is fully responsible for managing the business, it is within his ability to drive success (well, short-term success, at least), but BigCow will not be able to make synergies. If BigCow has control over the business it is unfair to expect Ernie to be able to make the earnings he anticipated, perhaps with a new business model being imposed.
How long is the earn-out period?	
Is there to be a cap on the level of the earn-out?	
Is the earn-out to be made in cash or in BigCow shares?	
What happens if BigCow wishes to sell the business during the earn-out period?	
What happens if BigCow goes into liquidation?	
What happens if Ernie is unable or unwilling to work for the agreed period?	
	These and many other issues need to be resolved before the deal is signed.

that will be applied. Accounting rules often mean that the contingent element of the consideration has to be shown in the acquirer's financial statements at the date of the initial transaction rather than the date (if ever) that it gets paid. Tax treatments need to be considered to ensure that the vendor does not end up with a tax liability on monies not yet received.

Selling a business

Having considered acquisitions, it is worth turning briefly to examine matters from the point of view of a vendor selling a business.

Every owner of a private company should consider their eventual exit strategy. Do you intend to build the company up quickly and then sell out in five years' time? Is your goal capital growth in the short or long term, or are you seeking a good lifestyle out of the business until normal retirement age? Even if you intend to 'work until you drop', who will inherit the business from you, and what state will it be in? Will they want to inherit the role of managing it, or will its sale be their priority?

There are two main reasons for a private company owner having the eventual exit strategy in mind. The first one is that owners who seek a lifestyle from the business will run their operations in different ways to those going for aggressive growth and an eventual sale. In particular, owners planning to sell out in a few years should be scanning the environment for potential acquirers, and perhaps grooming their companies for that eventual sale, in a similar manner to pre-float grooming discussed in Chapter 15. The second reason for owners to consider their eventual exit strategy is so that they can react more quickly to any out-of-the-blue offer for the business.

Large corporates too need to consider their ownership strategy. They should continually scan their portfolio of subsidiaries to determine whether they are still aligned with corporate strategy, or whether any of them would be worth more to another owner.

For larger businesses the exit could be in the form of a trade sale or a public flotation of the shares. It has become more common, particularly for businesses backed by private equity, to pursue both of these alternatives simultaneously; preparing for a float while actively marketing the business to trade or other private equity buyers. Although this takes considerable effort, it can have the advantage of increasing the price, and providing a more certain exit.

Larger businesses face a further problem if they are choosing to divest themselves of a division or part of the business rather than the whole. Care needs to be taken to establish what stays and what goes. Some parts of the business will be clearly separable, but others will be shared, in terms of expenses or indeed revenue streams. If the infrastructure of the business to be divested has been provided by the central group, then provisions may need to be made to make it self-sufficient, depending on the resources available from the purchaser. Likewise, the sale of that business could leave the remaining group with an uneconomic level of overhead, as its infrastructure cannot be downscaled quickly.

When and how to sell

If an offer comes in out of the blue, the shareholders (or corporate HQ if it is part of a group) need to consider how to react to it. But if there is a plan for sale, consideration has to be given to when and how.

The answer to the 'when' question is 'sooner than you think'. Corporate finance professionals generally advise planning to sell while the business is actively growing, rather than holding on until the maturity stage, as there is more potential to be priced into the deal.

The answer to 'how' rather depends on the size of the company. For smaller businesses, the directors (or more likely their advisers, to maintain confidentiality in the early stages) can

---

Working Insight 16.17

Selling a business – some of the key stages

1   Choose advisers, undertake pre-sale grooming, possibly set up vendor due diligence.
2   Information memorandum to be prepared.
3   Identify potential purchasers and make contact.
4   Initial meetings are likely to be off-site; after receiving indicative valuations, preferred bidders can have site visits.
5   Negotiations around price, deal structure, and conditions will lead to Heads of Agreement with preferred bidder.
6   Due diligence is done. (May use a data room.)
7   Legals completed – contracts, warranties, etc.

Source: Based on *Selling a Business* (2009), Corporate Finance Faculty of the ICAEW.

---

sound out potential acquirers to determine their level of interest. Often the business owner will have an idea who might be interested in buying; if not, a shortlist can be drawn up based on a search of companies of the relevant size in an appropriate industry. Larger businesses might opt for a similar controlled sale process, or, increasingly, might sell the business through an auction. There is no one correct method of sale: it depends on context.[6]

Working Insight 16.17 outlines some key stages in a generic sales process.

It is also worth considering one more question here: what to sell? Generally the vendor is trying to sell a company, but the bidder does not actually want that company – they want the business that is inside the corporate shell. This difference matters. If the bidder acquires the company, then legally they take on everything to do with that corporate entity: its undeclared liabilities, its past frauds, its dead inventory – everything. Far better for them to be able to buy just the assets they choose, and leave the rest with the vendor. This can be done in a transaction whereby the bidder buys specific assets from the company: for example, the name and intangibles, certain fixed assets, certain inventory, and the receivables. Everything else can be left behind for the vendor to deal with.

This is good for the buyer, but leaves the vendor with a problem. When the corporate shell sold those assets it would have made a capital gain, on which it needed to pay tax. The vendor, having paid off the liabilities, now has a cash-rich company and needs to get the money out for herself. However, taking the funds as dividend will trigger a personal tax liability, as will taking it as wages, or winding up the business. In a transaction where the bidder acquires the assets, the vendor ends up with double taxation – the company pays it, and the person pays tax on what is left. If the sale is of the company itself, then there is only one charge to tax.

Given that the bidder would often prefer a deal to buy the assets, and the vendor would prefer selling the company, there can often be room for negotiation on price to complete the deal.[7]

---

6   Boone, A. L. and Mulherin, J. H. (2009), 'Is There One Best Way to Sell a Company? Auctions versus Negotiations and Controlled Sales', *Journal of Applied Corporate Finance*, 23(1): 28–37.
7   It should go without saying – but we will say it anyway – full legal and tax advice should be taken in structuring your sale; please do not rely on a book written by academics, even if they were once practitioners!

Due diligence and confidentiality of data

Any acquirer is going to want to do due diligence – as discussed earlier in this chapter it is an essential part of the value-determination process and protects buyers against unexpected shocks after the deal is completed. But from the point of view of the vendor, due diligence is difficult. If the vendor is trying to keep quiet about the business being sold (which, to be honest, is rarely succesful no matter what a vendor does), then having teams of strangers crawling over everything is not really conducive to secrecy. And even if there is no secrecy about the potential sale, in a situation where there are several potential bidders in the early stages (which is what you want to happen), then the disruption from several separate due diligence teams is considerable. Nonetheless, due diligence is needed.

There are two solutions to this – vendor due diligence and/or a data room.

Vendor due diligence is due diligence commissioned by and conducted on behalf of the vendor of the business before the bidders are invited to consider the company. Although in the later stages of a bid the potential acqurers will need to conduct further due diligence of their own, managing the early stages in this way has several advantages. First, by seeing the results of a due diligence exercise before the information memorandum has been finalized, the vendor can be aware of potential flaws in the business, and can put measures in place to correct them. And, second, there is just one due diligence team involved, rather than several, which is easier for the business. Of course, the only way this can work is if the bidders know that the vendor due diligence is done thoroughly, and that they can rely on it legally. This is a well-understood and accepted process.

The second way to manage the due diligence process is to have a data room. It is very common in larger transactions for a virtual data room (VDR) to be set up, with all of the company's documentation held electronically on it, and bidders given password access to enable them to carry out their due diligence remotely.[8] For the vendor, this has many advantages in addition to the fact that there will be fewer visitors to the premises. By carefully managing passwords, bidders can be given increasing access to different levels of data; as the bids progress, the longlist is reduced to a shortlist and then to preferred bidders. Also, depending on the way the VDR is established, the vendor can track which areas most interest the different bidders, which can be a guide to how they are thinking.[9]

It would be remiss to discuss due diligence, allowing acquirers (sometimes competitors) to see the company's private data, without considering how the company can protect its confidentiality. It is customary to demand that potential bidders sign confidentiality letters (also known as NDAs, non-disclosure agreements) at all stages of the process, confirming that if they do not proceed with the acquisition they will hand back or destroy any data they have, without making copies, and will not use the knowledge they have gained from the process.

Confidentiality letters should always be used. However, it is almost impossible to ensure that all copies of all documents are returned or destroyed. And it is definitely impossible to order someone to forget what they have learned about the company. Thus, enforcing the terms of NDAs is tricky, and their authority is perhaps a moral one rather than legally enforceable.

---

8   A good source of information is Merrill Datasite, a provider of online VDRs. www.datasite.com

9   Bidders might not see this as an advantage. Another issue for bidders to consider is that although VDRs are very useful, and can speed up the process and enable, for example, term-searching through documents, their existence tends to focus attention on the target's paperwork, whereas some of the best due diligence findings come from just walking around the business and seeing what is going on.

If the vendor company has some data that are truly comercially secret – perhaps a formula or the terms of a contract – then it is probably more useful to hold back their disclosure until the transaction's completion meeting (bearing in mind that it could be a deal-breaker if not as expected).

Key messages

- Acquisitions, properly planned and executed, can increase shareholder value. In order for this to happen, the protagonists must be clear about how and why this will occur.
- Synergies can be evaluated using the value drivers model, and due diligence should be focused on the critical areas where value can be gained or destroyed.
- An acquisition raises performance expectations, as the bidder will generally pay more than market price for the target company, i.e. PVGO will increase. Synergies need to be quantified to support this.
- Acquisitions can be financed by cash, or through the issue of shares. If the target's shareholders take equity in the bidder, they retain an interest in the ongoing business and must be satisfied that it will perform under the new ownership, and that the bidder is fairly valued. If the deal is for cash, the target's shareholders have a clean exit.
- Although the choice of deal finance can be used to manipulate earnings per share movements, it should be based on the company's overall financial strategy.
- Public companies can be subject to takeovers hostile to the management. Various defence strategies are available to protect against such unwanted interest. Not all of these strategies will create value for the shareholders.
- An earn-out can keep key management with the company, and enhance the value the vendor receives. However, such deals can also cause operating problems for the future.
- Business owners should always be aware of the sale possibilities for their companies.

Suggested further reading

Huyett, B. and Koller, T. (2011), 'How CFOs Can Keep Strategic Decisions on Track', *McKinsey on Finance*, 38, winter: 10–15.
Looks at some of the behavioural biases that lead to errors in M&A and in deal pricing.
Fubini, D., Park, M. and Thomas, K. (2013), 'Profitably Parting Ways: Getting More Value from Divestitures', *McKinsey Online Journal*, available at http://www.mckinsey.com/insights/corporate_finance/profitably_parting_ways_getting_more_value_from_divestitures.
Discusses the strategic and operational issues that large groups face when divesting divisions, and suggests ways to improve the process.

17 Restructuring a company

Learning objectives

After reading this chapter you should be able to:

1 Diagnose when a company is in trouble, and identify ways in which its cash flow can be improved to stave off a cash crisis.
2 Identify potential sources of finance for a troubled company, and evaluate how appropriate they are.
3 Understand some of the regulatory mechanisms underlying company rescue or liquidation.
4 Explain what spin-offs and carve-outs are, and how they differ.

Introduction

Change is not comfortable; company reorganizations involve change. The implication of this is that company reorganizations are not undertaken lightly, but are done when something is wrong – either with the company, or with the market's perception of it. This chapter considers reorganizations that are done in this context, from refinancings to demergers, and the issues that are faced.

If there is something wrong with the company itself, then the reorganization needs to address the internal issues. If the problem lies with market perceptions, then the focus is on revising how the company is viewed. Although there will be many overlaps in these types of reorganization, it is convenient to discuss them under these headings.

Reorganizations addressing internal issues

Put very simply, companies can face problems due to having the wrong business configuration or the wrong financial strategy. Many, many books have been written about business strategy and change management, and we would do the subject no service by adding our necessarily brief comments to that discussion. Hence, we focus on reorganizations that address situations where a company has the wrong financial strategy.

A company's financial strategy may be wrong because it has too little debt, for example, a mature company which has remained equity financed. To correct this, the company could rebalance its debt-to-equity ratio, perhaps by paying out a special dividend or undertaking a share repurchase as discussed in Chapter 13. Alternatively, the company could put the money to good use by investing in a value-enhancing investment opportunity. Although the special dividend and buy-back may technically be seen as company reorganizations, they hardly present problems, unlike the reorganizations that need to take place because a company has over-borrowed.

A company may have taken on too much gearing for several reasons. It could have been a deliberate, if misguided, financial strategy which has not worked out as expected. Or it could be because the financial strategy suited the company's then business conditions, but changes in circumstances led to a fall in operating profits, and a resulting debt problem. Although the reason for the decline will influence how the company chooses to reorganize, there are several generic reorganization strategies:

1   Raise cash by improving operational efficiency.
2   Raise cash by selling assets: either outright sale of surplus assets; disposal of parts of the business; or a sale-and-leaseback transaction.
3   Raise cash by issuing new equity or another financial instrument.
4   Come to an arrangement with creditors to restructure existing debt.

In some jurisdictions, once it is decided that the company is savable under 'intensive care', the process of reorganization will be in the hands of the current management of the company: this is the case in the USA, where companies go into Chapter 11, giving management time to sort out the problem. Regulations in other parts of the world take the power away from the management – for example, the UK has a receivership process which puts a bank-appointed receiver in charge of sorting out the business. However, the generic strategies are valid for all jurisdictions.

Improve operational efficiency

This first approach, improving operational efficiency, should be the simplest for management to implement, as it is mostly under their control. Indeed, it is something that they should be doing as a matter of course, whether or not there is a cash crisis. The focus should be on improving profit margins (including letting go of products or customers that are unprofitable at a contribution level), consolidating fixed assets, and managing down inventories and receivables.

Sell assets

A good way to raise cash is to sell assets, ideally surplus assets. If the company clearly has assets which are not necessary for its operations, then realizing the value in them makes sense. However, if there are no obviously surplus assets, hard decisions have to be made, and the business might need to be reconfigured to facilitate disposal of some business units. Issues that may arise here include (a) determining which assets to sell; (b) finding a buyer; and (c) being prepared to take the accounting consequences.

In determining which assets to sell, sometimes what is needed is a fresh perspective on the business. Companies develop their own internal myths about which assets must be owned in order to run their business properly, or which business units are core to their offering. Sometimes a division which has been part of the corporate fabric for many years needs to be sold off to protect the viability of the others. Or, on a more modest scale, attitudes to asset ownership may need to be amended, and leasing considered as an alternative.

Of course, even if a company realizes that it has assets which could be sold, disposing of them at a good price might not be a realistic proposition. Knowing that a company is in financial difficulties, prospective buyers may bid low, or may decide not to bid at all, hoping to benefit from a distressed sale. Or, if the company's problems have resulted from poor economic conditions or an industry-wide collapse, there may be a glut of such assets on the market, or indeed no market for them. This is seen, for example, in shipping, where profits, and therefore asset prices, are closely linked to the business cycle. The resultant volatility in the price of vessels means that they are not always good collateral for a lender, and that one firm's financial distress can lead to asset prices falling throughout the industry.[1]

Rather than disposing of assets completely, a company can enter into a sale and leaseback, selling the asset to an investor and then leasing it back over a long period at an agreed rent. In this way the company receives the proceeds of disposal but maintains the use of the asset, albeit at the cost of an ongoing rental charge.

It is rare that a company could turn itself around just using one strategy. If the crisis is severe, or is likely to become severe, several different restructuring strategies will need to be managed in tandem to achieve the greatest effect. Case Study 17.1 illustrates the various strategies followed by French shipping company CMA CGA.

We mentioned earlier that a company has to be prepared for the accounting consequences of its disposals. This comment arises from an experience the author had when undertaking a pre-receivership investigation into a building company, on behalf of their bankers. The company was in a very bad situation – a fact not realized by the directors, who were not in the habit of using cash-flow forecasts as part of their management information. However, it did own an apartment in London, bought many years earlier when times were good in the housing market. It was suggested – strongly – that the directors sell the apartment as soon as possible in order to raise cash for the company. However, they refused on the grounds that the property had cost £400,000 at the height of the property boom; it would now fetch only about £250,000 and they did not want to sell at a loss. It was difficult to make them understand that they had already made the loss, and the only issue now was whether or not they realized it in the financial statements.

---

1   This example is taken from Albertijn, S., Bessler, W., and Drobetz, W. (2011), 'Financing Shipping Companies and Shipping Operations: A Risk-Management Perspective' *Journal of Applied Corporate Finance*, 23(4): 70–82.

Case Study 17.1

Keeping CMA CGA afloat

CMA CGA, a family-owned business, controls the world's third-largest container shipping fleet. In autumn 2012 it announced a series of measures taken to refinance itself in the face of an uncomfortable level of debt. These included:

- Raising new finance through a $250m convertible bond which would take 10% of the company's equity on conversion. The bond was sold to a sovereign wealth fund and an existing private investor.
- Asset disposals, including a 49% stake in one of its businesses.
- Sale and leaseback of about one-quarter of its fleet.
- Agreement with 72 banks to restructure loans of $4.6bn, including deferral of repayments and modification of covenants.
- Aggressive cost-cutting activities.

Source: Financial Times

The scenario of directors, and particularly non-executive directors, not realizing just how bad the company's financial situation is, is unfortunately not a rare one. Working Insight 17.1 sets out some factors for boards to consider.

Raise new finance

The company might be able to pull itself out of the financial mess by raising finance from existing or new investors. If raising equity from existing shareholders, a deep discount rights issue may be appropriate. (Deep discount rights issues were discussed in Chapter 10.) Whether the injection of funds is from current or new investors, it is likely to be highly dilutive to the existing shareholders, as illustrated in Case Study 17.2.

Often, when new finance is raised, an *equity cure* provision from the loan agreement is invoked to ensure that there is no technical breach of covenants. It allows the shareholders to remedy a covenant breach by injecting equity into the business. This might, for example,

Working Insight 17.1

Some warning signs that action may need to be taken

- The company is trading close to the limit on its bank facilities.
- Monthly management accounts continually show negative variances on sales and profits.
- There are no monthly management accounts, or they arrive late, with inadequate explanation.
- Several key people leave the company in a short period of time.
- Loss of several customers.
- Poor relationships with suppliers.

Case Study 17.2

Dilutive injection to save Knight Capital

In August 2012 Knight Capital, a financial services firm engaged in market making, electronic execution services and trading, was brought to its knees after a rogue algorithm led to trading losses of some $440m, nearly four times its net income.

Before the announcement of the 'software glitch' Knight had been a $1bn company, with shares trading at over $10 each. Markets reacted to the news with a price drop to about $4.

The company was saved by an injection of $400m from a consortium of investors including private equity houses and other trading companies. The funds came in the form of 2% cumulative perpetual convertible preferred stock carrying a 1x liquidation preference. Conversion into common stock would be at $1.50 per share, which would leave the new investors owning about 73% of the company. The security's terms allowed for conversion if the company's share price remained above $3 for any 60-day period.

The new investors also had the right to appoint three representatives to Knight's board.

When the terms of the injection were announced the company's share price fell further, to just over $3.

Postscript
In December 2012 it was announced that Knight Capital would merge with GETCO, a rival company that had been a major investor in the restructuring. (See Case Study 16.4.)

Sources: Financial Times, Knight Capital Form 8-K (6 August 2012), and www.cnbc.com

---

allow the new equity to be treated as additional EBITDA in testing the covenant immediately after the cash injection.[2]

Renegotiate existing debt

The third type of financial reconstruction relates to restructuring existing debt. If a company can convince its lenders that they will ultimately receive more by waiving interest payments or extending the term of a loan, then debt terms can be eased to aid the company's short-term survival. Such renegotiations normally only work in situations in which the creditor banks are owed a significant amount: it is said, 'if you owe the bank £5 million and can't pay, you have a problem; if you owe the bank £5 billion and can't pay, the bank has a problem!'.

One form of debt renegotiation is the debt-for-equity swap, in which existing loans are released in exchange for the creditors taking an equity stake in the company. The argument behind this is that if the creditors insist on their debt being serviced and repaid, the company will be forced into liquidation and they will lose their money anyway. However, if the debt is converted to equity, the creditors – now shareholders – will participate in the ultimate upside if this causes the company to recover. Negotiations in debt-for-equity swaps revolve around the proportion of equity which is issued to the creditors; obviously, this new equity

---

2 Obviously, adding a balance sheet amount to an income statement amount is not normally done – this is a technical way around a particular problem for a one-off calculation.

Case Study 17.3

Swapping debt into equity

Getting Eurotunnel out of a hole

An example of debt renegotiation occurred with Eurotunnel, the Anglo-French company which built and operates the Channel Tunnel. In summer 2007, the company's debt mountain of about €9 billion was halved, with the lenders swapping it into a majority of the equity in the restructured company, leaving the previous shareholders with only 13% ownership. The various claims of the shareholders and several tranches of debt took many months to negotiate. However, in the end the reconstruction had to be done – it had been anticipated that had the swap not taken place, the company might have had to be placed into liquidation.

Constructing a deal for Mouchel

On a much smaller scale than Eurotunnel, Mouchel, a UK civil engineering and professional services group, entered into a debt-for-equity swap with its bankers in August 2012. The banks bought all of the company's shares in exchange for writing off £87m.[3] The existing shareholders' investment was not wiped out completely – the agreement stated that they would receive a final dividend of 1p per share (the share price was just over 2p). The lenders took 80% of the equity, with management holding the remaining 20%.

Source: Financial Times

will significantly dilute the existing shareholders. Case Study 17.3 gives two examples of debt-for-equity swaps, of very different sizes.

There are likely to be many difficulties involved in debt renegotiation. As suggested, a fundamental problem is the different interests of the various stakeholders involved. If a company has over-borrowed there is rarely just one creditor; many banks might be owed money, with several different layers of debt, all with varying legal rights. This increases in complexity for an international or global business, where legal issues will vary by jurisdiction and assessing priorities on claims can be a minefield. Other stakeholders such as employees, suppliers, the government, and regulators might also have issues to resolve and have power in the situation. Each major stakeholder will probably appoint their own professional advisers to protect their particular interests. This adds to the number of people around the negotiating table, and can itself cause delays in completing a reorganization.

What if the restructuring doesn't work?

If the techniques suggested above cannot be implemented in time, or do not work, the company is heading towards liquidation. At this point the alternatives include agreement with creditors, some form of legal protection for the business, or, ultimately, bankruptcy. The regulations surrounding these various alternatives differ greatly between jurisdictions, and so the following paragraphs just give a flavour of what is available, without going into the legal detail.

---

3   It is worth noting that during 2012 UK banks were facing considerable criticism from government and media for their apparent unwillingness to lend to business. Furthermore, two of Mouchel's three banks had been bailed out by the UK government in the financial crash. That might have influenced their decision to save this company, with its 8,000 employees.

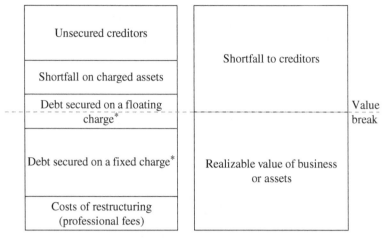

CLAIMS ON THE COMPANY   ASSETS ARE INSUFFICIENT
TO MEET ALL CLAIMS

* The debts secured on fixed or floating charges only take precedence to the value of
their security: beyond that they are unsecured.

Figure 17.1 Determining the shortfall for creditors.[4]

A first step is to prepare a balance sheet for the business at break-up values, to determine
the shortfall. Figure 17.1 illustrates this.

The realizable value of the business or assets will be calculated on a break-up basis. This
means, for example, that cash will be counted at 100 per cent of its value, but other assets
will reflect a discount related to the need to sell them quickly, or the chances of selling them
at all. This will depend on the industry and the type of asset. Land and buildings might be
marketable, specialist plant less so. One would expect the likely recovery from receivables to
be discounted significantly, and the expected sums that would come in from selling inventory
to be very low.

The dotted line in Figure 17.1 shows the *value break*, with a shortfall to the floating charge
creditors and no funds available to pay the unsecured creditors. The actions to be taken will
depend on the severity of the financial position and the likelihood of eventual recovery.

The stakeholders in a distressed company always have options. For example, shareholders
can choose to invest more, or can accept dilution or the loss of their investment; lenders can
put in more money on better terms, or swap to equity, or write off their investment; trade
creditors can agree to support a valuable customer, or can negotiate terms, or just write off
their debt. Stakeholders without a direct balance sheet claim also need to be considered. For
example, employees might face the hard choice of accepting redundancies or pay cuts (or in
some countries taking more direct action). How stakeholders choose to act will depend on the
relative power of each stakeholder, and their level of interest in the survival of the company.

The next step is to explore the legal alternatives open to the company. This will depend
on the legal jurisdiction. For example, the USA is considered to have a debtor-friendly

---

4 Figure based on Bryan, D., Tilley, A., Cork, S., and Moffitt, K. (2011), *Best Practice Guideline to Turnarounds*,
published by the Corporate Finance Faculty of the ICAEW, London.

regime: in a Chapter 11 reorganization the failing company can remain under the control of incumbent management, under the supervision of the courts. The management have an exclusive right to propose a reorganization plan and seek creditor agreement. While in Chapter 11 the company is protected from its existing creditors, whose claims are frozen until its situation is worked through. This contrasts with the UK, which has a more creditor-friendly regime, with the focus being on maximizing value for existing creditors, and where the management frequently are replaced.

The UK does have forms of consensual restructuring such as a Company Voluntary Arrangement (CVA) or a Scheme of Arrangement (SoA). These do not represent formal insolvency, but there will be an agreement between the company and its creditors (and in an SoA, its shareholders). The process is managed by an authorized insolvency practitioner. If a consensual restructuring is not possible, then an administrator might be appointed, an insolvency practitioner whose role is to manage the company's affairs with the aim of achieving the best result for creditors, preferably by effecting a rescue of the business. (Where certain assets are subject to charges, then a receiver might be appointed, whose role is to realize those assets to pay back the relevant creditors.)[5]

A further relevant aspect of UK insolvency law is the existence of the *pre-pack administration*. The pre-pack was designed to enable insolvent companies to be sold quickly, in order to protect the ongoing business, which would lose customers and employees if the process were to drag on. In a pre-pack, the sale of the business is agreed before the company formally enters administration, and takes place very quickly after that legal process is completed. The great advantage, as stated, is that the viability of a business can be protected. However, a disadvantage of pre-packs is that often the buyer of the business is a new company formed by the previous directors, which acquires the business free of debt in a process devoid of competition. The creation of such a 'phoenix' company can sometimes be perceived as unfair or an abuse of process.

Buying a distressed business

Before we continue, it is worthwhile taking a different perspective for a few paragraphs, and considering the potential acquirer of the distressed business or its major assets. There are bargains to be had in making such acquisitions, but the risks are high.

There will be very little time available to undertake due diligence, but it is essential to do as much as possible, and to clarify the legal position regarding any obligations with might come with the business.[6] The position of legal charges also needs to be clarified, and this will differ before and after legal insolvency proceedings commence. It is also important to verify the legal situation regarding contracts with suppliers, customers, and others, as often there will be clauses in agreements that terminate the contract on change of ownership.

In conducting such an acquisition, the potential acquirer will have to pay cash, and to have that money available immediately, as time is of the essence for the vendor. It is useful to take professional advice from an adviser who has experience in these situations.

It is also worthwhile to remember the very relevant words of Warren Buffett: 'When a management with a reputation for brilliance tackles a business with a reputation for poor

---

5 Information on insolvency practice in the UK can be found at Companies House, www.companieshouse.gov.uk
6 In the UK, for example, the terms and conditions of employees might be protected under the Transfer of Undertakings (Protection of Employment) Regulations (TUPE), which would limit the potential for restructuring.

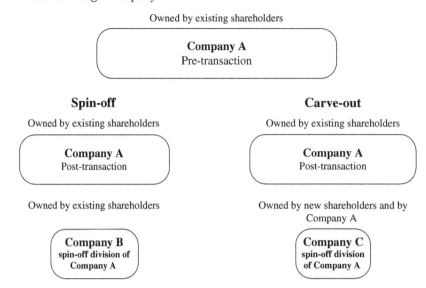

Figure 17.2 Spin-offs and carve-outs.

fundamental economics, it is the reputation of the business that remains intact.'[7] A business that has failed is always more difficult to turn around than has been anticipated.

Reorganizations to address market perceptions

Sometimes the problem is not internal to the company, but relates to the fact that it is trading at a market value considerably below a fair value for its shares (in quadrants C or D in the value matrix in Figure 1.6). In such cases, if they wish to forestall an opportunistic takeover bid for the company, the company's directors have several different options:

1   Demerger, to demonstrate the value in the group.
2   Blitz on investor relations to change market perceptions.
3   Take the company private.

The issue of taking a company private was discussed in Chapter 15 and will not be revisited here. Similarly, we will spend no time discussing how a company can improve perceptions with a concentrated focus on investor relations, explaining its true value to shareholders and analysts. In this section we focus on reorganizations as a way to address the issue of markets undervaluing the company: specifically the process of demerging or spinning-off units.

An explanation of some terminology is appropriate here. A demerger is where one listed company becomes two or more listed companies. This can be done as a spin-off or a carve-out. Figure 17.2 sets out how these differ.

In a spin-off, Company A divests itself of a division by putting that business into a subsidiary (Company B), and distributing the shares of B to its own shareholders, often by way of a dividend. The ownership of B will, at the time of the transaction, exactly mirror the ownership of A, and no money will change hands. It can be done with relatively low advisory fees, and can be structured to be a tax-free transaction for the shareholders.

7   www.iwarrenbuffettquotes.com/warren-buffett-quotes-on-business

This differs from an equity carve-out, in which a stake in Company C is sold to the public as an Initial Public Offering. (An equity carve-out is sometimes known as a partial IPO.) Company A maintains an investment in the subsidiary, and receives proceeds from the sale of shares to the market. The level of advisory fees and the regulatory interest reflect the fact that shares are being sold to new investors.

We should point out that the difference between the various transactions and straight sales of subsidiaries is generally one of size. A transaction would not be considered as a reconstruction unless the business disposed of formed a substantial percentage of the overall group value.

Why do companies undertake demergers?

Sometimes, demergers are undertaken in order to focus management on one side of the business, and put a separate management team in place to deliver value in a radically different type of business that has just happened to be part of the group. This is a matter of corporate strategy rather than corporate *financial* strategy. However, here we are discussing demergers (in their various forms) undertaken in order to improve the value attributed to the business by the financial markets.

Often, a group includes two or more very different classes of business. This can make it difficult for analysts and shareholders to understand, and such a lack of understanding leads to underpricing in the markets. Splitting the group into separate companies, each in a defined business sector, clarifies the situation and enables investors to select where to invest their funds. A company might also choose to carve-out a division to take advantage of that particular sector being very highly rated: it is a chance to receive proceeds from selling part of the asset at an opportune time. This is particularly relevant to businesses in need of cash.

Research and market sentiment indicate that the post-demerger market value of the separate companies is normally greater than that of the whole group before demerger (an example of the sum of the parts being greater than the whole). Some reasons put forward to explain this are shown in Working Insight 17.2, while Case Study 17.4 gives an example of a spin-off.

After the demerger, each separate company can make its own investment and financing decisions and approach the capital markets in a way that is appropriate to its own asset structure, revenue sources, and business objectives.

Working Insight 17.2

Why demergers are seen to add value

- Separation into clearly defined business segments leads to market transparency and greater understanding.
- Raise money by taking advantage of the market pricing one particular sector very highly.
- The different businesses can follow financial strategies more appropriate to their activities.
- Improvements in corporate governance and efficiencies arise in companies which were subsidiaries but are now separately accountable to the markets.
- Incentive structures can be put in place that link management performance directly to the unit's share price.
- Removal of the 'conglomerate discount'.

Case Study 17.4

Pieces of Mosaic

In 2011 Cargill, a privately owned agricultural company headquartered in the USA, agreed to spin off its stake in Mosaic, a fertilizer producer of which it owned 64%. The other 36% of Mosaic was already listed, but as the free float was less than 50% it was not realizing its market potential.

The reason for the deal, which was valued at over $24bn, was to satisfy the need of certain shareholders for funds. As with many family-owned companies, after several generations the ownership had become widely distributed among family members, and 17% of Cargill was owned by charitable trusts, which needed to diversify their investment to meet their objectives.

The reported deal structure was complex. About 40% of the company's investment in Mosaic was being exchanged for debt from third parties, thus reducing Cargill's gearing. The rest of the shares were effectively the currency in a share repurchase, being exchanged for shares in Cargill itself. The end result was a smaller, less indebted company in which some shareholders had reduced their investment and some had chosen to exit completely. All shareholders also owned some shares in the listed company, Mosaic, whose value should be enhanced by having a higher free float. (However, an extended multi-part lock-up agreement was put in place, presumably to establish an orderly market in Mosaic shares.)

Source: http://dealbook.nytimes.com/2011/01/18/cargill-to-spin-
off-its-mosaic-unit-in-complex-deal

Key messages

- Financial reorganizations can result from the need to correct external perceptions of the company, or can be because the company needs to revise its financial strategy, generally to correct an over-geared position.
- Rebalancing the debt-to-equity mix can be done by retrenching or selling surplus assets; by raising new funds; or by renegotiating existing borrowings, sometimes swapping them into equity.
- A reorganization often involves combining several different restructuring strategies. The strategies adopted will reflect the reason for the reconstruction.
- The process of restructuring is complicated for global companies by the differing legal rights of creditors in different jurisdictions.
- A demerger can change the market's perception of the company, clarifying the value in each of its parts. This can be done as a spin-off (giving the division to existing shareholders, often by way of a dividend) or a carve-out (in which the group retains ownership of part of the carved out division, but capital is raised for the group from new shareholders).

Suggested further reading

Carter, R. B. and Van Auken, H. (2005), 'Bootstrap Financing and Owners' Perceptions of Their Business Constraints and Opportunities', *Entrepreneurship & Regional Development: An International Journal*, 17(2): 221–39.
This article discusses a survey into 'bootstrap' methods (i.e. finance not from external sources) used by small US companies. It lists twenty-eight different techniques used, split between delaying payments, minimizing receivables, or other investment, sharing resources with other businesses, and private owner methods of finance.

18 Private equity

Learning objectives

After reading this chapter you should be able to:

1   Explain how private equity firms are structured, and how they make their money.
2   Understand the different types of leveraged deal, and how value is created for investors.
3   Create or use a financial model for structuring a private equity transaction.

Introduction

The transactions discussed in previous chapters – flotations, acquisitions, and restructuring – can all have a private equity element. Private equity (PE) has become an established part of the corporate landscape, with PE companies being significant players in many aspects of business life. In this chapter we look at the structure of the PE industry and then focus on PE transactions which contain a high degree of leverage.

In discussing 'the private equity industry' we are conscious that it is not necessarily one industry. There is a variety of private equity companies. A few firms, which garner most of the publicity, undertake extremely large, often international deals. But there are many PE investors operating mostly in their domestic markets undertaking large transactions, and more still that will be doing smaller deals. Hedge funds also participate in this market, and have different operating structures and imperatives. Furthermore, PE companies in different parts of the world face different challenges and act in different ways. By not differentiating these players we are doing them a disservice. Nevertheless, for the sake of brevity, that is what we will do. We occasionally, where appropriate, relate our comments also to fundraising from venture capital companies, which finance the smaller, higher-risk transactions.

The private equity industry

We need to start with a definition, and that is not a simple thing to do. In its broadest sense, private equity is finance provided in return for an equity stake not listed on public markets. Within that, there are various types of investment: a business angel putting money behind a start-up business is effectively issuing private equity, as is a large fund investing several billion dollars in a buyout. Figure 18.1 illustrates the universe of equity investment.

The Venn diagram in Figure 18.1 shows that private equity is non-public equity, and 'venture capital' is a subset of private equity. In some markets, the terms are used inter-changeably. However others, for example, the USA, use 'venture capital' to mean investment in early-stage businesses, and reserve 'private equity' for the larger buy-in and buyout markets. This book dealt with raising early stage venture capital in Chapter 7 on start-up busi-

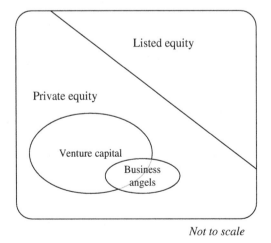

Not to scale

Figure 18.1 The universe of equity investment.

nesses. Accordingly, in the majority of this chapter we will discuss private equity as referring to the larger, leveraged transactions.

Many companies, large and small, regard themselves as private equity players. We now set out some characteristics of the companies, and of the markets in which they operate.

Private equity companies

Private equity[1] companies raise funds and invest them in businesses with the aim of increasing the value of those funds many times over. The return for their investors is dependent on this investment performance. The PE companies themselves make money from investment, and also from the fees they charge their investors.

The PE companies can obtain their funds in several different ways. Some have raised money on stock exchanges, some are 'captives', investing the money of their parent companies (e.g. they might be subsidiaries of large insurance groups), and some raise independent funds. PE funds (raised as stand-alones, or by captives or by listed PE companies) are the most traditional method of raising money to invest as private equity. Sources of funding might include banks, pension funds, insurance companies, large corporates, governments, and wealthy individuals. A PE company will raise a series of such funds, which will each have a limited life, for example, ten years. This means that investments tend to be made in the first half of the fund's life, and realized in the second half; the average lifespan of an individual investment is considerably shorter than ten years, and the time limit can influence investment behaviour, particularly regarding the need for exits as the fund's end date (the ten years, generally plus a two-year grace period) approaches. Furthermore, a PE company's funds will overlap, with each new fund being raised before the end of existing funds' lives. Thus, their mid-life performance is important as a marketing tool to attract new funds.

Funds are often structured as limited partnerships, as this is a sensible tax-effective structure that prevents double taxation.[2] Figure 18.2 sets out a very simple example of such a structure.

Investments are made by the PE fund, under the management of the Investment Manager provided by the PE company. The PE company also provides the general partner (all limited partnerships need at least one general partner with unlimited liability, but by making the general partner a separate company the PE company is restricting its own liability). The majority of the funding is provided by the limited partners (the banks, pension funds, etc.), who receive their reward by way of capital gains and yield, after deduction of the PE company's entitlements.

The PE company will take a management fee, as a percentage of the monies raised (often 1–2 per cent), and will also get a 'carried interest'. This carried interest gives the PE company a share of all investment returns above a certain level. A common agreement is that the PE company gets 20 per cent of any profits the fund makes in excess of 8 per cent (compound) per year.[3]

---

1 This section relates also to venture capital companies.
2 Partnerships are 'tax transparent' which means that the partnership itself is not taxed, but the partners are. If there were a corporate structure, income and gains from the investments would first be taxed by the company, then taxed again when withdrawn by the owners.
3 The PE company receives its fees on the monies raised, not monies invested, and continues to receive them every year until the fund is closed (sometimes at the same annual percentage rate, but sometimes at a lower rate in the later years of the fund). This causes an agency conflict with the limited partners, in that the PE company's incentive is to raise the largest fund it can, generating the highest fee level. Research suggests that PE companies get higher returns from fees than they do from carry. At the time of writing there is some discussion as to whether the '2/20' system (2 per cent fees, 20 per cent carry) is overgenerous.

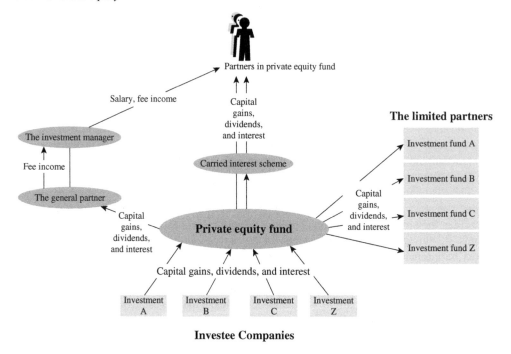

Figure 18.2 Structure of a typical private equity fund.
Source: Gilligan, J. and Wright, M. (2010), *Private Equity Demystified*, London: Corporate Finance Faculty of the ICAEW. Reproduced with permission

The surrounding infrastructure

For a PE industry to thrive, a suitable commercial infrastructure needs to be in place. As well as the PE firms, other sources of finance such as banks must be willing to participate. To support the transactions there needs to be a suitable professional class, including accountants and lawyers who understand this type of deal. Vendors of businesses have to accept private equity as an alternative when they are selling, and management teams must appreciate the potential if buyout deals are to be done. Also, a strong stock market or an active market for trade sales is an advantage, to facilitate exits. Without the combination of all of these, private equity becomes very challenging.

Another vital ingredient is the legal and regulatory background. Governance structures should ensure the safeguarding of rights, for example, as regards the proper execution of contracts, or the protection of intellectual property. Without this, investors, particularly those from another part of the world, are likely to be uncomfortable about committing their money: the balance of perceived risk and potential return might be just too unfavourable.

Private equity deals

In this chapter we are considering private equity investment into large companies. Most of these transactions are leveraged, to take advantage of the fact such businesses can support gearing, and debt is cheaper than equity. Working Insight 18.1 sets out some common types of deal.

Working Insight 18.1

Common types of private equity transaction

Leveraged buyout (LBO)	Generic term that covers any of the transactions below.
Management buyout (MBO)	In this transaction, the company's current operating management acquire the business, or purchase a significant shareholding in it.
Management buy-in (MBI)	A buy-in is similar to a buyout, except that the management team comes from outside the company. Sometimes they have worked together previously in another company, but often the management team is put together by the private equity investor.
Management buy-in/buyout (BIMBO)	A BIMBO is a transaction in which some members of the management team acquiring the company come from its existing management, and some of them are outsiders. Quite often the new CEO will be an outsider, but will retain some of the company's existing management team, who will also become equity investors.
Institutional buyout (IBO)	In an IBO, a private equity firm buys the company, following which the incumbent and/or incoming management will be given the chance to buy a stake in the business. The deal is driven by the institution(s) rather than the management. Such deals may be quicker to do, because the equity provider is negotiating directly with the vendor, rather than also with the management.
Leveraged build-up (LBU)	Here, a private equity firm acts as principal to buy a company with the intention of developing it into a larger group by making further acquisitions in a specific business area. This is also known as 'buy and build'.
Public-to-private (P-to-P)	The term refers to buying a listed company and taking it off the stock market. This transaction could be any of the above.

For the sake of convenience, we generally describe deals in this chapter as LBOs or buyouts, but our comments will mostly apply to all of the above types of PE deal.[4]

These deals all follow the same commercial logic – the PE investor seeks a return that is more than commensurate with the risk taken on the investment. The deal process is set out in Figure 18.3.

An argument in favour of private equity is that it has the potential to add value at each stage of this process.

1. *Find investment.* The PE company is actively seeking investments to make, and has a network of contacts to assist. Sometimes, potential deals are found before the rest of the market is aware of them. Often, PE companies choose to focus on a particular industry, which gives them an advantage in knowing where and how to look.

---

4 Although buyouts are less common than buy-ins, particularly in larger transactions, we refer to the former, as they provide a useful focus on the position of the management team.

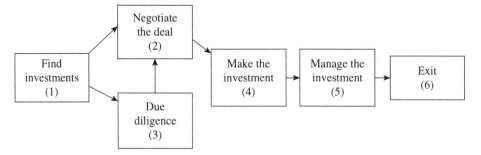

Figure 18.3 The private equity deal process.

2. *Negotiate the deal.* Many people in business may buy or sell a company once; private equity investors do it all the time, and so are more experienced at negotiation. Also, because their agenda differs from that of someone buying a business to run it, they might have less of an emotional commitment to the deal, and so walk away if the terms do not suit them. (Although this is not always the case – individuals working in this field are just as prone to behavioural biases as the rest of us.) They also have the advantage of having a substantial pool of money behind them, which encourages vendors to treat them seriously.

However, the days when PE investors could make a profit by buying cheap are long past. Vendors have moved away from selling to incumbent management teams, and many transactions are put to an auction, in which the PE company is just one participant (as perhaps is the incumbent management). PE companies might have the experience not to overpay, but they rarely manage to underpay.

3. *Due diligence.* The negotiation would be conducted in parallel with the due diligence. It is worth noting that PE companies take due diligence very, very seriously and commit far more time and resource to it than do commercial buyers. They will investigate both the business and the management team, using their internal resources and a host of outside advisers. In particular they will focus on how the business could be changed once under their ownership, which will be relevant to stage 5.

Because the financiers see themselves as investing in the management as much as in the business, a lot of attention will be paid to taking up references on the members of the management team. Such references may be from people suggested by the management team, but will also include trade and other sources, to obtain a good cross-section of views. The results of the due diligence could fall into three categories:

*   due diligence shows that the management team is capable of undertaking the transaction and successfully running the business – the transaction can proceed;
*   due diligence shows that the management team has a serious flaw(s) – the PE investors will probably withdraw; or
*   due diligence shows that most of the management team is satisfactory, but there is one (or more) weak member. In such instances, the PE company may demand that a manager be replaced. This can put severe personal pressure on a team of people who have been working together for years, but it may be the only way to get the deal done.

(The management team should also do due diligence on the providers of capital. How good are they as investors? Are they supportive of their investments? Do they take board positions in their investee companies, or do they manage in a more hands-off way? Do you like these people, and are you prepared to be tied to them for many years? It is a mistake to go into business with people whom you dislike or do not trust – even if they do seem to be the only source of finance.)

Because they have investigated their targets more thoroughly, PE investors are better equipped to determine the appropriate price, and also much better prepared to know how to drive value once the business has been bought.

4. *Make the investment.* Deal structuring is an important part of the creation of value for the PE investor, and is discussed separately in this chapter. PE companies are more aggressive in leveraging their investments than are other owners, and this, provided it is not done to excess, is one way in which they have in the past created value for shareholders. However, times have changed, and debt is not as easily available as it was a few years ago. Attitudes towards aggressive gearing have hardened, and so although the transactions will contain a lot of debt, it is no longer the main driver of returns.

5. *Manage the investment.* The main way in which value is created is by improving the quality of profits and cash flows in the acquired company. Most companies, once released from the control of a distant holding company, will be shaken up to re-evaluate costs and working capital management, as well as looking more carefully at their product–market decisions.

The PE investor should be able to bring experience and resource to help with the business improvements. A PE company with industry experience and contacts can add a lot to a business. More significantly, given the illiquidity of their investment (they cannot just sell if it goes bad) they need to make it work. Accordingly, they probably have a much greater interest than another investor, or than a remote parent company. This combination of knowledge, power and interest leads to a close relationship with the business and its management, which reduces the agency costs considerably. Add to this good corporate governance processes, a simple chain of command, and a short timescale in which decisions can be made, and there are distinct ownership advantages to private equity.

6. *Exit.* The PE company makes most of its return on the eventual sale of the business, and so the exit is crucial. This may be in the form of a trade sale, an IPO, or even a secondary buyout, selling on to another PE institution.[5] The exit will probably be planned at the time the investment is made, although changes in circumstances will obviously affect those plans. A trade sale is often a more attractive exit, as it enables the PE company to sell out completely; often in a listing they are obliged to hold a shareholding for a further period. However, the PE company might decide to 'twin-track' – running a sale process in parallel with a listing application, to obtain the most suitable exit.

Overall, PE investors are looking for good companies, with considerable growth potential, and good management teams to run them. Because the deal will carry a significant level of debt,

---

5 In mature markets there is a trend away from IPOs and towards secondary buyouts, reflecting the current difficulties in floating a company.

the company generally needs to be cash-generative, and ideally this cash-generating power will be protected by some unique factors giving a competitive advantage that is not easily imitable by competitors. They will aim to make money at all stages: buying as cheaply as they can; growing the business both in top line sales and in restructuring to reduce costs; and selling well.

Doing the deal

Before we look at deal structuring in depth, it is worth considering how buyouts arise, and the concerns of the various parties.

The impetus for a transaction

Management buyouts may be undertaken for a variety of different reasons, reflecting both the holding company's and the management's priorities.

The holding company's reasons might include:

- disposal of a non-core business, to regain focus
- release of funds to support the rest of the group
- passing on a family-owned business from which the owners wish to retire.

The management's reasons could be:

- to run the business autonomously without head office interference
- fear that the division will be closed down or outsourced unless they buy it
- a preference to run their own business than to be sold to a trade buyer.

Buyouts are sometimes driven by an ambitious management team which sees the potential for high growth of the business once it is outside the control of a bureaucratic parent. In other cases, the parent company might suggest the buyout, either as a means of releasing capital tied up in a division, to use elsewhere in the business, or because the division has become non-core, and the group would be more focused without it. In some instances, a buyout is undertaken because the management of the division see it as a preferable option to being outsourced or sold on to a trade buyer. For the larger, public-to-private transactions, the driving force might be that management and the PE companies see the potential to make a great deal of money.

Secondary buyouts, where the initial PE investor exits by selling to a second PE investor, are often driven by the first investor's need to close down a fund that is nearing the end of its life. The new PE investor might have ideas on how to shake up a business that has started to throw off cash after its first buyout.

The reason driving the transaction will be an important influence on the attitudes of potential financiers and other stakeholders.

Fiduciary duties of incumbent management in a buyout

In the early stages of a management buyout, specifically, the process will differ depending on whether the deal is being driven by the management or the owners of the company.

In some ways, the situation is simplest if the owners have expressed a wish that the management team should consider a buyout. Here, the management team are free to pursue the idea as they see fit, and to contact outside parties for financial advice and possible funding, knowing that in principle the transaction will be acceptable to the shareholders.

However, if the impetus for the buyout comes from the management team, then an interesting fiduciary position arises with regard to the owners of the company. Management are paid to act in the best interests of the owners, and have a duty so to do. Undertaking a buyout might be in the owners' interests, but it might not: indeed, they could object strongly to the proposal. Management thus have two choices: they either investigate the feasibility of a buyout before they approach the owners, or they do so afterwards.

Why should management choose to investigate the feasibility of a buyout before broaching the subject with the owners? If the team were to announce to the owners that they were considering a buyout, and then fail to obtain the finance, their position in the organization could be weakened. If they can sound out finances in advance, and if the deal is feasible, they can approach the owners secure in the knowledge that their aims are achievable, and in a potentially stronger negotiating position. If finance will not be forthcoming, they can quietly drop the idea.

The other alternative is for management to respect their fiduciary duties, and approach the owners before determining whether a deal can be done. This has the advantage of being totally above board. However, should the deal be unfundable, management will face a potentially job-threatening embarrassment.

The legal situation will be slightly different in each case. Management teams will probably want to test the lie of the land before approaching the company's owners, but they must be aware of a potential breach of their duties if they release confidential information (for example, management accounts) to outside parties without the owners' approval. Legal advice may need to be taken.

The paragraphs above make the assumption that the proposed buyout is of a division of a company. The situation differs slightly in a public-to-private deal, where the management, backed by private equity, wish to acquire the whole company and take it off the market. Here, it is important that the 'external' shareholders are not disadvantaged, and the board of directors needs to act to protect their interests. Case Study 18.1 sets out some of these issues as regards the acquisition of J Crew.

Advisers

In order to complete any funding deal, the management team will need to make contact with providers of equity and debt finance. They will also need to employ professional advisers: at the very least they will need a lawyer. It is also recommended that they use a financial adviser, an accountant, or other professional involved in raising finance.

There are two good reasons for using a financial adviser. First, even if the management team is very experienced in this area, they will have enough to do without project-managing the minutiae of the deal – it is useful to have an experienced agent on whom they can rely. The second reason for employing an adviser is more basic: PE and venture capital companies receive many hundreds of approaches every year from businesses needing finance, and they have to have a filtering system to sort out potentially good proposals from time-wasters. One of the most basic filters is only to consider proposals that come from professional advisers who are respected in the industry – that way the institution can assume that the adviser has vetted the plans, and that only reasonable proposals are reaching them.

This latter point often seems totally unreasonable to managers and entrepreneurs, who do not think the world should work this way, and believe that their plan deserves consideration on its merits. Quite possibly it does, but we live in the real world. Your author knows of a company whose business plan was rejected out of hand by a local venture capital company; the

Case Study 18.1

J Crew: public-to-private conflicts of interest

The announcement late in 2010 that private equity company TPG Capital was seeking, with a partner, to acquire listed US clothing company J Crew caused some consternation due to apparent deficiencies in the governance around the deal. TPG had previously been a major shareholder in J Crew, and they still held a seat on the J Crew board. Furthermore, as part of a turnaround strategy in 2003 they had appointed Mickey Drexler as chairman and CEO. They were now seeking to take the company private, with Mr Drexler leading the buyout and other members of the executive team involved.

Shareholders argued that the transaction evidenced several conflicts of interest. Apparently, Mr Drexler and his colleagues were in discussion with TPG for several weeks prior to informing the board of the transaction. Furthermore, Mr Drexler had previously received several other offers for the company about which he had chosen not to inform the board at all. Other conflicts included confidential information shared with TPG, and the discouragement of alternative bids which could have increased the value to J Crew shareholders.

Once the board was made aware of the offer an independent committee (excluding Mr Drexler, other members of the executive team who were involved in the deal, and the TPG board member) was set up to evaluate it. However, this committee, coming to the deal when it had gone so far already, faced difficulties.

The $3bn transaction went ahead, at the agreed price, in March 2011. In September 2011 a shareholder lawsuit relating to the conflict of interest was settled for $16m.

Source: Various media reports including http://blogs.wsj.com/deals and
http://dealbook.nytimes.com

entrepreneur went to a local financial adviser, who re-badged the proposal in his company's binder without changing a word of it; the business plan was read, and the investment was made. Sometimes you just have to accept that life is not fair – and play by the rules the market sets.

Selecting financiers

Different PE companies and venture capitalists have different investment criteria. For example, some will only invest in deals above £5m, or £50m, others might specialize in (or avoid) certain industries. The first point to note in selecting potential financiers is only to approach those who might be interested in your deal: to do otherwise is a waste of your time and theirs.

Once a PE company is on board for the deal, they will help to make introductions to other sources of finance, including bank and mezzanine lenders, and other PE companies with whom they might want to syndicate the deal. An advantage of syndicated ('club') deals is that they share the risk and also enable larger targets to be acquired than one PE company could afford on its own.[6]

Sometimes, bank finance can be arranged as part of the purchase, using 'stapled financing'. Here, the lead bank advising the vendor will guarantee to offer debt finance to the successful

---

6 A detailed review of syndication can be read in Jääskeläinen, M. (2012), 'Venture Capital Syndication: Synthesis and Future Directions', *International Journal of Management Reviews*, 14(4): 444–63.

bidder, up to a certain amount (and subject to the bidder meeting its specifications). In order to do this, the bank conducts due diligence before the bidding process, to establish the level that it will offer. Although this is often not taken up (the offered terms are used as a negotiating point with other lenders), it can speed up the transaction. It can also increase the offer price, as the level of debt offered will help anchor the parties' expectations of the eventual deal price.

If your investment proposal is very attractive to the investor community, for example you are looking to buy a large, profitable, cash-generative company that has just refurbished all of its assets, then you may be in the fortunate position of having PE companies vie for your favours. In such cases your advisers would run a 'beauty parade', in which selected firms would be invited to present to the management team to demonstrate why they should be the ones selected as lead investor.

However, for many run-of-the-mill propositions, the situation is reversed, and the management team has to convince an investor that they are worth backing. In such cases, it is important to deal only with a few potential investors at a time.

Some management teams try to send their business plan out to all of the potential investors, in the hope that someone will express an interest in their deal. This is a poor strategy. First, if there is a flaw in the business plan, it will have been exposed to the whole market, without the team having a chance to correct it. Sending the plan to just three or four firms would have given the management and their advisers a chance to understand why it was being rejected, and adjust it accordingly. The second reason that mail-shotting the market is a bad idea is that it makes you seem like a loser – if everyone could have your plan, no one will want it.

Deal structures

Structuring a private equity transaction involves balancing the needs of the various parties while meeting the funding requirements and capacity of the company. Three sets of issues need to be resolved:

- What funding is needed?
- What can the business afford? and
- What do the parties want?

What funding is needed?

The funding to be raised will primarily comprise the purchase consideration for the business, to be paid to the outgoing shareholders. This will have been determined based on a calculation of the value of the business being acquired. As with all corporate acquisitions, that price will be a matter for negotiation between the parties.

Funding will also be needed to develop the business. Private equity does not normally invest in businesses unless they anticipate growth – and that growth will almost certainly require additional funding. Financial forecasts should demonstrate how much of that funding can be released from internal sources (for example, by better management of working capital) and how much will need to be funded externally.

Finally, the massed ranks of professional advisers would be most upset were we to forget the final funding need – that of paying the deal costs. Accountants, lawyers, and other professionals will need to be paid, as will arrangement fees to financiers. Furthermore, there may be taxes due to the transaction (such as UK stamp duty). As a (very) rough guide, you might expect deal costs to add 5 per cent to a transaction.

Working Insight 18.2

Sustainable level of debt

ELBO Ltd had EBITDA of £10m last year but is confidently predicting increases in sales and margins, resulting in forecast EBITDA of £14.4m next year. The directors and the providers of finance have agreed that senior interest cover of 4x is adequate for safety. Interest rates on senior debt are 7%.

ELBO has operating profits of £14.4m.
Therefore, with interest cover of 4x, it can afford to pay an interest charge of £3.6m.
With interest rates of 7%, this represents a capital sum borrowed of £51.4m.

What can the business afford?

Here, the main consideration is the cash impact of providing a return on finance. We have established previously that debt is cheaper than equity, and when we discuss funding structures later you will see that these deals are financed substantially with debt. However, debt finance involves regular interest payments and a repayment schedule: the post-buyout company needs to be able to meet these requirements.

One way to evaluate a company's debt capacity is to select a suitable level of interest cover (EBITDA divided by interest charges), and work back to evaluate the level of debt this represents. Working Insight 18.2 illustrates such calculations.

Instead of this simple interest cover calculation the variables used for the numerator could be EBITDA less maintenance capital expenditure, or a variant involving EBITA or EBIT. The denominator, instead of the interest charge in the income statement, could be cash interest, or cash interest plus cash debt servicing, for example. Another alternative would be to calculate how much cash the business can afford to pay out in debt service in the early years, and base the loan on that. The book's online spreadsheet gives a very simple example.

The desired level of interest cover will reflect the company's business risk and industry, together with matters that reduce the lenders' risk, such as the assets available for security. Thought should also be given to how the business will change under the new ownership. Here again, the drivers of value can be used, evaluating which levers will increase profits and which will reduce cash tied up in assets.

There is of course more to a company's debt capacity than just considering the interest cover. Lenders will be interested in the level of security for their debt, and also, particularly, the ability to make repayments of principal. In this connection, companies which have easily separable assets – for example, property that can be sold and leased back, with the proceeds being used to pay down debt – are very attractive propositions for PE deals.

Although the traditional accounting ratios for measuring a company's indebtedness are gearing (debt/equity, or debt/capital employed) and interest cover, a commonly used ratio in corporate finance is Debt/EBIT or Debt/EBITDA. Working Insight 18.3 shows how Debt/EBIT relates to interest cover.

We should also point out that although in this chapter we will just refer to 'debt', in practice there may be several different financial instruments used, each with different rights and priorities, interest rates, and repayment terms. A tranche of senior debt, with low interest

---

Working Insight 18.3

Relating the Debt/EBIT ratio to interest cover

Let the level of borrowing be D, and the interest rate i. The Debt/EBIT ratio is represented by G.

$$G = D/EBIT, \text{ therefore } EBIT = D/G$$
$$\text{Interest} = Di$$
$$\text{Interest cover} = EBIT/Di = (D/G) \div Di$$
$$\text{Which simplifies to } 1/Gi \tag{1}$$

Equation (1) shows that the interest cover is the inverse of the Debt/EBIT multiple multiplied by the interest rate. So, a higher interest rate or Debt/EBIT will give a lower interest cover and thus a greater financial risk. This is intuitively obvious, but the maths is often ignored.

For example, in a transaction with a Debt/EBIT multiple of 4 times, where interest rates are 10%, the interest cover will be $1/(4 \times .1) = 2.5$ times. This would not be appropriate for an organization with high business risk and a need to conserve cash.

Often, rather than using the ratio of Debt/EBIT, the calculation is instead done as Debt/EBITDA. The logic behind this is that EBITDA better represents the underlying cash flow of the organization. However, we should remember that most companies require some investment in fixed assets, and reinvesting the depreciation is probably the minimum level of such investment. Thus, treating EBITDA as cash flow can misleadingly flatter the company's financial position. Because of this, ratios using EBITDA less maintenance capital expenditure may be a better indicator.

---

cover covenants and strong security, may be supported by senior subordinated debt, junior debt, and mezzanine, each with progressively weaker covenants and security, and carrying a greater return for the lender. Generally, and not surprisingly, larger deals have more complex debt structures. In such structures it is common to have the most senior debt being repaid in instalments, with more junior debt having, perhaps, a bullet repayment once the senior is cleared, or on the sale of the company.

What do the parties want?

The main parties to a private equity transaction are the management team, the providers of institutional equity, and the providers of debt funding. However, other stakeholders also have an interest in the deal and how it is structured. Figure 18.4 sets this out.

Each of the parties has a different set of requirements of the deal.

The *vendor*'s needs depend on the reason for the sale. Often, it is financially driven and they need money to fund the rest of their business. But the sale could be for strategic reasons, or because a family owner has no heirs, or something else entirely. Often, it is important for the vendor to make sure that they are not seen to sell at an undervalue, and this is sometimes resolved by their taking a stake in the Newco.

Management generally undertake the transaction in order to become their own bosses and to get rich through an ultimate exit. For an MBO, there may also be an element of doing the deal in order to preserve their jobs – if they don't buy the company it could be sold on, or closed down. Thus management's key requirement is a large share of the equity (for a feeling

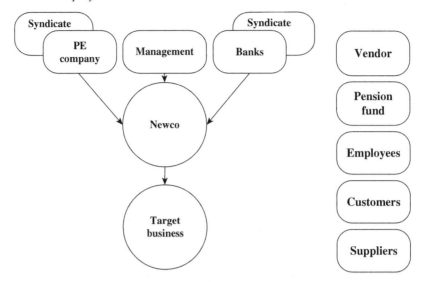

Figure 18.4 Parties to the transaction.

The standard structure for such a transaction is that a Newco is set up: a brand new company into which the investment is made, which then buys the target business. Sometimes there are two Newcos, one owning the other, with debt going to the lower one, and shareholder debt to the upper, passed down through inter-company loans.

of control, and for capital gain), and preferably a relatively low cash investment, as they are likely to have other financial commitments.

The *PE companies* are taking a risk in making this illiquid investment, and are doing so in order to make a good return. They need a suitable cash-to-cash return over the investment lifetime, often calculated as the IRR (internal rate of return). For example, they might require an IRR exceeding 30 per cent per annum over the life of the investment, and have to believe that the deal will give them this. If the PE company plans to syndicate the deal, bringing in other PE companies to take part of the investment, then the transaction terms have to be attractive to all of them. And it is worth bearing in mind that a smaller IRR on a large sum might be more attractive than a large return on a small initial investment.[7]

The *lenders* have a different view again. Lending debt should be a low-risk activity – which means that they have to be able to protect their downside. Hence the lenders will require strong covenants, and security where available. They will be less interested in the deal's potential upside (in which they do not share) than they will in protecting their position should the downside occur.[8]

---

7 The book's online spreadsheet shows the relationship between cash-to-cash return and IRR and time.
8 During the private equity boom of the mid-2000s, so-called 'cov-lite' loans became common. As the name implies, so keen were the banks to participate in these deals that these loans carried very few covenants. An argument made for this was that the absence of strict covenants gave the PE investors time to sort out the company if things started to go wrong. Earlier in this book we defined debt as a low-risk instrument which has another way out. By lending with few covenants, banks were taking more risk than the return appeared to justify.

In addition the other stakeholders – customers, suppliers, employees and their pension funds – have an interest in the future viability of the business, and will be particularly concerned with its financial stability and future methods of trading.

Relationships between the main parties (excluding other stakeholders) are complex, and constantly changing during the acquisition process. For example:

- in negotiating the purchase price of the business, the vendor is pitched against the combined might of the management team, the equity investors, and the banks;
- in negotiating the banking terms, the PE firm and management team are up against the banks;
- in negotiating the equity split, the PE investors are now on the opposite side to the management team;
- individual members of the management team may each be defending their own corner when it comes to negotiating equity terms and employment contracts.

The various rights and obligations of the parties will be spelled out in, for example, the sale and purchase agreement; the new company's internal constitution; shareholders' agreements; the loan agreements; and employment contracts for the directors and key staff.

Structuring the deal

With these constraints in mind, deal structuring can be simplified to a series of steps, as follows.

1 Determine how much finance is needed. This should be the total finance: sufficient to cover the deal price, working capital requirements, future cash requirements, and deal fees.
2 Ascertain how much of that finance can be taken as debt. Debt is a cheaper form of finance than equity, and the gearing of the deal will affect the equity returns, as demonstrated later. The level of debt will depend on the asset backing of the business, and the amount and quality of its cash-flow generation. Several different tranches of debt could be used, each with a different risk/return combination.
3 Determine how much funding the management will be able to put in. Investors will generally expect this to be 'hurt money' – at least one year's salary, often more if the individual is independently wealthy, or effecting their second buyout.
4 Knowing the total funding needed, the level of debt, and management's contribution, the balancing figure normally has to be supplied by the PE institutions. This will be split between ordinary shares and either preference shares or a subordinated loan. Factors to consider here are the percentage of equity that management will have in the business, and the prospective IRR on the institutional investment, payment terms, the dividend on ordinary shares, etc.

Working Insight 18.4 sets out the deal parameters from which we will build a possible financing structure.

The total financing for ELBO's deal is £85 million. As stated earlier, the first part of the finance to be evaluated is the new company's debt potential. Working Insight 18.5 illustrates this calculation.

Of the £85 million needed for the buyout to go ahead, debt will provide no more than £42.5 million. We will assume debt of £42 million, leaving equity sources to provide a further £43 million. We were told than management will put in £500,000, thus the finance from PE is £42.5 million. The next issue to consider is the form this finance will take.

Working Insight 18.4

Financing structure for an LBO: initial parameters

The management team of ELBO is putting together a management buyout from Parent, their holding company. They have approached a PE company, PE-Co, which has agreed to lead the deal. PE-Co has discussed the deal with BestBank, which is leading the debt.

Deal statistics are as follows.

- The parties have agreed a purchase price of £80m to be paid to Parent.
- A further £5m is needed to fund deal costs, etc.
- ELBO is confidently expected to make operating profit of £14.4m in the first year of operating after the deal. This is higher than the company is doing now, but the management will be able to operate more efficiently (and with more enthusiasm) once they are freed of the dead hand of group bureaucracy.
- BestBank has stated that it will lend at 7%, and has demanded a covenant that interest cover will not fall below 4x for the first year. They have also set a gearing covenant, that senior debt will never exceed 50% of total funding.[9]
- The management team between them are investing £500,000.

Determining the equity split

In determining how the institutional investment is made, there are several possibilities. The most obvious solution is for management and the institutions to invest on the same terms. Working Insight 18.6 illustrates this for ELBO.

ELBO has £43m of equity finance, of which management is putting in £500,000. If shareholdings are split in these proportions, management will obtain 500/43,000 of the equity – just over 1%. It is unlikely that they will see 1%, split between the members of the team, as sufficient incentive to invest their life savings and work flat out for several years.

Therefore a method has to be devised to give management proportionately more of the equity than their money alone would deserve.

This could be done by differential pricing, by which the different classes of investor pay different prices to invest. Working Insight 18.7 sets out a possible solution on this basis.

The position set out in Working Insight 18.7 seems to meet the needs of the situation, in that the company has the funding it requires, and management have an acceptable percentage of the equity. However, as is often the case with simple solutions, there is a catch. What if a trade buyer comes along the next day, offering to buy the company (including the debt) for £90m? Once the £42m debt is paid off, that would leave £48m for the equity – a profit of £5m in a day! However, £48m for the equity works out at £9.60 per share. Management will be delighted – they bought in at £1 per share, and can make a huge capital gain – their £500,000 has turned into £4.8 million. However, the institutions bought in at £9.44 per share, and would not be prepared to sell out at £9.60 – given the effort that they will have put into the transaction, a gain of £700,000 will not compensate them. So immediately we have a conflict of interest, and a very frustrated management team.

Differential pricing can easily lead to such conflicts of interest, which is one reason why it is best avoided. To overcome the problem of giving management sufficient of the equity to make it interesting, the deal can be instead structured using another instrument such as

Working Insight 18.5

Debt capacity in an MBO

The bank funding is first limited by the interest cover covenant, as set out in Working Insight 18.2.

Forecast operating profit	£14.4m
Interest cover (min)	4 x
Therefore, maximum interest charge	£3.6m
At 7%, this equates to borrowing of	£51.4m

However, the gearing covenant will supersede this, as debt cannot exceed 50% of total funding (£85m).

This equates to a borrowing of	£42.5m

Working Insight 18.6

Institutional investment on management terms

	£'000
Investment by management	500 (1%)
Investment by institutions	42,500 (99%)

Working Insight 18.7

Structuring the MBO using differential pricing

Assume that the management team buy their ordinary shares at £1 each, but the institutions pay £9.44 per share.

	Investment	No. of shares
	£'000	
Management @ £1	500	500,000
Institutions @ £9.44*	42,500	4,500,000
	43,000	5,000,000

Management now owns 10% of the company's equity, which they would probably see as a worthwhile investment for their trouble.

*Institutions put in £42.5m but can only receive 4.5m shares, hence the price of £9.44 per share.

Working Insight 18.8

Institutional gearing in an MBO structure

Assume that the institutional investment of £42.5m is invested as £4.5m in ordinary shares, on the same terms as management, and £38m as subordinated debt.

	Investment	No. of shares
	£'000	
Equity		
Management @ £1	500	500,000
Institutions @ £1	4,500	4,500,000
	5,000	5,000,000
Subordinated loan		
Institutions	38,000	
	43,000	

preference shares or subordinated debt to 'gear up' their stake. The way that this institutional gearing works is that the PE investors put in their funding in two separate instruments – ordinary shares and a subordinated loan. This is illustrated for ELBO in Working Insight 18.8.

In Working Insight 18.8, the institutions invest £4.5 million in ordinary shares at £1 each, and £38 million in a subordinated loan.[9] Management will own 10 per cent of the company. Any future buyer of the company would have to pay off the subordinated loan first (at par), with the balance of sales proceeds being split in proportion to the numbers of ordinary shares. This would lead to a situation in which the institutions and management are on the same side. Working Insight 18.9 completes the example with the full deal structure and exit calculations.

Based on Working Insight 18.9, who has obtained what out of the deal?

Management invested £500,000 and obtained £9million – an absolute gain of £8,500,000. This is an IRR of 162 per cent – an excellent deal!

The institutions put in £42.5 million (£4.5 equity and £38 million subordinated loan) and obtained £119 million – an absolute gain of £76.5 million, which represents an IRR of 41 per cent. This IRR would be increased by the annual interest on their subordinated loan. The institutional percentage return is nowhere near as good as management's, but it's quite respectable in terms of their original requirements from the deal.

The decision as to how much of the institutional capital goes in as ordinary shares and how much as subordinated loan is crucial in the deal structuring, as the institutional gearing is what gives the management its excellent return. As with everything, the level of institutional gearing

9   This need not be a subordinated loan; other instruments could be used – the key requirement is that the instrument is subordinated to other debt, and that it carries no capital gain. The choice of instrument will reflect, *inter alia*, tax regulation: 'thin capitalization' rules in many jurisdictions mean that interest will not be tax-deductible if the debt is considered to be excessive or not to be at arm's length, or relate to a foreign-controlled company. Preference shares might be used instead of a loan, which look better in the financial statements: otherwise the appearance of yet another debt instrument on the balance sheet will influence the gearing calculations made by outsiders.

Working Insight 18.9

Rewards on exit

Assume that the initial deal is as set out in Working Insight 18.8. Three years later, an offer is made to buy the company at an enterprise value (i.e. including the debt) of £150m. This reflects the considerable improvements that management has made to the company's trading position. £20m of the senior debt has been repaid since the deal was originally done.

	Year 0	Year 3
	Initial deal	*Exit*
	£'000	*£'000*
Finance required	85,000	
Sales proceeds		150,000
Less debt	42,000	22,000
Management and institutions	43,000	128,000
Less subordinated loan	38,000	38,000
Equity funding/return	5,000	90,000
Equity investment/return		
Management (10%)	500	9,000
Institutions (90%)	4,500	81,000

is a matter for negotiation: the more the institutions want to do the deal, the more generous their offer to management.

One figure which is used to determine how generous, or otherwise, the institutions are being is known as the *envy ratio*. This is most easily explained by example, as shown in Working Insight 18.10. The higher the envy ratio, the better the deal for management.

Because there are so many variables, it is possible to structure a deal in several different ways.

The website associated with this book gives a very basic Excel model with the structure of this deal. This enables you to change the terms yourself, to see what would happen if gearing were raised or lowered, or the management terms were more or less generous. (The

Working Insight 18.10

Illustration of envy ratio

For the ELBO buyout the institutions put in a total of £42.5m for ordinary shares and subordinated loan, and ended up with 90% of the equity. Management put in £0.5m and ended up with 10% of the equity. This values the company as follows:

From the institutions' point of view	42.5/90% =	47.2m	(A)
From management's point of view	0.5m/10% =	5.0m	(B)
Envy ratio (A/B)		9.4 times	

model also illustrates that the rolled-up interest on the subordinated debt can only be paid out of the sales proceeds of the business. As it stands, making the full pay-out in Year 5 cannot be done out of trading cash flows – the cash balance turns negative.)

Tweaking the terms

Sometimes it can be difficult to meet the conflicting needs of management, the institutions, and the lenders. For example, if the lenders will only lend a small proportion of the deal funding, then equity must be found to make up the balance. If management are putting in relatively little, the institutions have to make up the balance, and it can be difficult to give management a high percentage of the equity while still obtaining a high IRR for the institutions. There are two possible ways around this – paying a yield to the institutions, and using a ratchet.

YIELD

If the management seek a higher percentage of the equity but the institutional IRR is not good enough, one solution can be for the PE investors to take a yield during the investment period. An ongoing return on the subordinated loan or preference shares will improve the institutions' IRR without, we hope, restricting the company's ability to grow. Working Insight 18.11 illustrates this for the ELBO deal.

A yield can also be used as a tactic to ensure that the institutions do actually get their exit. In a company which is known to be cash generative, the dividend terms might be set such that the institutions' preferred ordinary shares (or sometimes all of the ordinary shares) receive an extra dividend that starts at, say, 10 per cent of distributable profits but rises annually by 5 per cent or more. The payment of such a high dividend can be used to focus management's mind on the possibility of an exit – to realize their potential capital gain before the

---

Working Insight 18.11

Institutional return with a yield

Revising the terms of the ELBO buyout, the subordinated loan now carries interest at 8%. The PE cash flows (ignoring tax) are as follows:

Figures in £'000	Year 0	Year 1	Year 2	Year 3
Investment:				
Subordinated loan	(38,000)			
Ordinary shares	(4,500)			
Loan interest		3,040	3,040	3,040
Capital returns				
Loan repayment				38,000
Sale of shares				81,000
Total cash flow per year	(42,500)	3,040	3,040	122,040

IRR = 46%

institutions have taken it all out by way of dividend. Even if there isn't an exit, the institutions still get their high IRR, through the yield.

RATCHETS

There are times when management and the institutions cannot agree about the future prospects of the business. Management want a high percentage of equity, believing that the company will do incredibly well. However, the institutions might argue that there is no guarantee that the company's performance will improve, and so they need a high equity stake to ensure their return. A ratchet can be the answer.

A ratchet is a device that enables the proportion of equity held by management to be altered depending on what profits the company achieves (or depending on any other variable specified). A *positive ratchet* starts management at a low equity percentage with the incentive that should they perform well their percentage will be increased. A *negative ratchet* starts them at a high equity percentage, but they will have to forfeit some shares if the company does not meet its targets.

Ratchets are effected by converting shares into different classes of share. For example, if management own ordinary shares and the investors own A shares, then the conversion terms of A shares into ordinary can be tweaked to give management a higher or lower percentage of the company. An alternative way to provide a positive ratchet would be for some of the A shares to convert into another type of financial instrument which carries little value.

Warning: ratchets solve the immediate problem of resolving the conflict between the parties at the commencement of the deal. In many cases they lead to even greater problems in the future when the ratchet is (or is not) triggered. They can also drive short-termist behaviour that is not in the best interests of creating long-term shareholder value.

Improving returns with more leverage

In the example above we have shown a simple deal, with an initial deal structure, improvements to the company, and a sale a couple of years later having paid down some of the debt. However, the PE company has had to wait until the ultimate exit before it makes its gain. The global financial crash has severely restricted the amount of debt available in the system, but pre-crash, a common way to bring forward that gain, and to improve it considerably, was to undertake a *leveraged recapitalization*. Although these are, for obvious reasons, less common than they were, it is worth spending a moment to consider how they work.

In a leveraged recapitalization the cash flow that the company has generated during its PE ownership is used to pay a large dividend to the owners, and more debt is taken on to refinance the company. This often happens very quickly, with cash being generated by selling off unwanted assets. The early dividend payment will greatly improve the PE company's IRR; indeed, it can mean that the whole investment is repaid after a relatively short period, and the PE company still retains a substantial percentage of a profitable business. Case Study 18.2 illustrates an extreme example of this.

Because an early leveraged recapitalization can have such an extreme effect on increasing the IRR of a deal, many PE investors prefer to evaluate transactions on the cash-to-cash return, the multiple of cash in to cash out. They see this as a more meaningful measure of how well they have done. Working Insight 18.12 illustrates.

Case Study 18.2

Leveraged recapitalization: Hertz Corp

Hertz, the car rental company, was a buyout from Ford in December 2005. The total deal size of about $15bn represented $4.4bn paid to Ford for the equity, $0.4bn of fees and expenses, and just over $10bn of the company's debt. The PE firms put in some $2.3bn, with the balance of the purchase price being financed by various tranches of debt.

Some six months after the deal was done, the company borrowed $1bn, which was then paid to the investors as a dividend, meaning that they had recouped nearly half of their investment. The resultant high gearing was reduced in an initial public offering that took place in November 2006 – within a year of the original buyout. This left the PE companies as major shareholders, but having considerably reduced their investment.

This transaction appears to represent gains made purely from financial engineering, rather than from any significant improvement in the underlying business.

Source: Compiled from Hertz annual report 2006 and various press sources

---

The other reason that investors like cash-to-cash as a measure of return is that it is a realized measure, taking account of the whole cycle of the investment, whereas IRR can be calculated for a portfolio including unrealized investments, and thus affected by the assumptions underlying valuations.

Comparing a PE transaction to an acquisition

This chapter discusses the acquisition of a target company by a PE investor. It is worth spending a few moments to consider how this differs from the acquisition of a target company by a corporate, as discussed in Chapter 16. There are a lot of commonalities, but some critical differences, as set out in Working Insight 18.13

Working Insight 18.12

Measuring returns

A private equity company does two deals in the same year, both for £100m. In the first deal they exit in Year 1 for £150m, the second deal provides an exit for £337.5m in Year 3.

  Both transactions create an IRR for the PE company of 50%.
  Deal 1 has a cash-to-cash return of 1.5 times.
  Deal 2 has a cash-to-cash return of 3.375 times, and is significantly more profitable.

The spreadsheet on the book's website gives an example.

Working Insight 18.13

Contrasting PE transactions and corporate acquisitions

	PE acquirer	*Corporate acquirer*
Use of a Newco	Newco must be created in order to set up shareholding structures in a suitable manner.	The existing company can be taken as a subsidiary of the acquirer.
Impact of debt	Debt relating to the acquisition is held in the Newco and does not gear up the PE fund.	Debt relating to the acquisition is not ring-fenced and affects the acquirer's capital structure.
Conditional payments	Ratchets can be used to increase/decrease management's shareholdings, depending on performance.	Earn-outs can be used to give the sellers further proceeds, depending on performance.
Changes to target business operations	Part of the acquisition plan agreed with management will be operational restructuring to improve profitability and reduce cash outflows.	The price paid probably includes an assumption that synergies can be created.
Management incentives	Linked completely to the eventual exit from the investment.	Will depend on the corporate objectives.
Purpose and timescale of acquisition	The acquisition is made with an ultimate profitable disposal in mind. Timescale is usually 4–6 years but will vary.	Probably made for strategic reasons with no expectation of selling on.
Funding the acquisition	A relatively high level of debt.	To meet the corporate financial structure.

Ethical issues in private equity

The private equity industry has long been regarded with suspicion by some elements of society.[10] There are undoubtedly ethical considerations involved in private equity financings, and we set out a brief overview of these in the following paragraphs.

Excessive use of debt. One of the means by which the PE companies make their return is by gearing up the investee companies. This means that the majority of the returns fall to the equity providers. However, very high gearing is often associated with company failure. If the investee company is too highly geared, the PE investors (who are diversified) are forcing the employees (who only have one job) to take inappropriate risks with no additional payoff. This applies in the initial structuring of the deals, and in particular to leveraged recapitalizations.

Societal impact of restructuring. Another complaint about private equity ownership is that PE-backed companies restructure – a euphemistic term for making a lot of the workforce redundant. It is argued that this improves operating returns, but at a wider cost.

---

10 Indeed, at times it seemed like much of the US presidential campaign debate of 2012 revolved around the private equity background of one of the candidates.

As authors, and as one-time market participants, we have mixed views about the two arguments set out above.

It is undoubtedly true that some PE-backed companies are over-geared. However, we have spent much of this book pointing out that debt is cheaper than equity, but that debt should be used appropriately to the company's needs, its business risk, and the stage in its lifecycle. If debt is used appropriately, then it provides advantages to all, without making the business significantly riskier. Likewise a leveraged recapitalization, provided that it does not damage the interests of other stakeholders is not particularly evil. It is only when gearing is excessive, and done with disregard to the valid interests of other parties (including in particular the workforce and the company's pension scheme), that it becomes a problem.

The point raised regarding the impact on the workforce of restructuring is one that is contested by participants in the PE industry, and we have no wish to get drawn into that debate. We would point out that a company that is run inefficiently is unlikely to survive in the longer term, and so value can be created, for many parties other than the PE investors, by trimming unnecessary costs. However, making cuts just for short-term profit improvements is unlikely to generate value overall and so is not recommended.

It is also worth pointing out that there is considerable research into the private equity industry. There are papers which conclude that private equity creates value for the economy, and papers that conclude that it doesn't. Similarly, some researchers show that investors in private equity funds do well, others demonstrate that their return is relatively poor. Summaries of the research can be found in the comprehensive guide by Wright and Gilligan, referenced at the end of this chapter.

Impact on the capital markets. A final argument made against the PE companies is the detrimental impact that public-to-private transactions are having on the capital markets. When management takes a company private and then refloats it a few years later at a higher value, it can leave a sour taste in the mouths of the institutional investors who had little alternative but to sell cheap, and are now being asked to buy back the same shares at a higher price. This has led to debates about management's conflict of interest, and the leakage of price-sensitive information to a variety of parties. At the time of writing, various formal and informal processes are under way to address this; for example, we are seeing some transactions where the existing shareholders retain a stake in the PE-backed business (known as 'stub equity'), and so have some participation in the ultimate gains, should there be any.

Key messages

- Private equity (PE) is the investment of equity outside a public stock market, in larger transactions. It has played an increasing part in corporate transactions over past decades.
- PE companies commonly raise funds for investment from groups of institutional investors and wealthy individuals. They might also use their own money or, if they are captives, their parent company's. The funds are generally structured as limited partnerships.
- In addition to their investment returns, the PE companies receive fees on the funds raised, and carried interest on returns above a hurdle rate.
- In order for PE to play a part in the economy the supporting infrastructure must contain the other players, such as experienced bankers, financiers and professionals. In addition, the legal and regulatory systems must be strong enough to reduce the perceived risk of investors.
- PE transactions include management buyouts and buy-ins, plus various other forms of deal where the ownership of a company changes hands. Often they involve a listed company becoming privately owned.

- PE transactions are usually highly geared. Investors make their returns from this gearing, and also from taking a close interest in managing the businesses, and a reduction in agency costs.
- In addition to the gearing of the transaction with several classes of debt, the PE investment itself will be geared up in order to increase management's relative stake in the business. This is often done by using preference shares or a subordinated loan as part of the financing structure.
- Advantages claimed for PE investors include a reduction of agency costs due to the closeness of the investor to the management and operations of the company. They have the opportunity to add value at every stage of the investment: finding a suitable transaction, evaluating it through due diligence, negotiating and financing the deal, running the business, and the eventual exit.

Suggested further reading

Gilligan, J. and Wright, M. (2010), *Private Equity Demystified – An Explanatory Guide* (2nd edn, London: ICAEW Corporate Finance Faculty).

This comprehensive document, free to download, is prepared by a leading academic and practitioner and covers both practical operations and academic research. There is also a 2012 update available to supplement the guide.

Bishop, M. (2012), *The Future of Private Equity: Beyond the Mega Buy-Out* (Basingstoke: Palgrave Macmillan).

Comprises a fascinating series of interviews with the great, the good, and the wise of the private equity world, covering investors from developed and developing economies.

Heel, J. and Kehoe, C. (2005), 'Why Some Private Equity Firms Do Better Than Others', *McKinsey Quarterly*, 24–6.

Discusses the active ownership of PE firms' investments that leads to increased value.

www3.imperial.ac.uk/business-school/research/innovationandentrepreneurship/cmbor. The Centre for Management Buy-Out Research monitors and analyses management buyouts, with and without private equity investment. It produces some excellent research.

It is also worth checking out the websites of various national private equity and venture capital bodies such as www.bvca.co.uk (UK), www.evca.com/html/home (Europe), www.cvca.com.hk (China), www.indiavca.org (India), http://lavca.org (Latin America), www.avcal.com.au (Australia), and www.pegcc.org (USA).

19 International corporate finance

Learning objectives

After reading this chapter you should be able to:

1 Appreciate how international corporate finance differs from the domestic variety.
2 Explain the three sources of currency risk – translation, transaction, and economic – and understand how they can be mitigated.
3 Understand the theory underlying exchange rate movements.
4 Evaluate different methods of financing an international acquisition, and appreciate their advantages and disadvantages.

Introduction

As someone once said, the world is becoming more global every day. Certainly, business is increasingly conducted on a global scale, and companies need to understand the implications for their business and financial strategies. In international corporate finance we face all of the complexities of the domestic variety, together with additional issues relating to dealing with foreign cultures, satisfying different stakeholders, and managing foreign exchange risk.

We have already explained that a detailed exposition of business strategy is outside the scope of this book; our remit is to explain financial strategy. Accordingly, in this chapter we will not venture into the 'whys' of investment overseas, but will instead focus on its financial aspects. We will assume that someone else has done the detailed analysis that concludes, for example, that:

- we have exhausted the growth potential of our local market, and international expansion is a more rational strategy than diversification; or
- it is more cost-effective to have operations in [name your country/region] than it is to continue to produce here and export to them; or
- our main competition is coming from this part of the world, and it would be strategically beneficial to move into their territory; or
- we need a presence in this trading bloc in order to be able to compete here without trade restrictions; or
- we need to expand into this territory before our competitors do, to gain first mover advantage in this expanding market.

Or any one of a multiplicity of good strategic reasons for overseas expansion or acquisitions.

Overseas expansion need not take the form of a full acquisition. It might be more prudent for a company to reduce risk by starting with a joint venture or strategic alliance, or even just an international sales office. However, in this chapter we will focus mostly on international finance in the form of acquisitions, rather than start-up greenfield sites or joint ventures. Having said that, much of what we say is relevant to all international situations, including instances where a company is seeking foreign investment in itself.

So, why is 'international' different?

Why is 'international corporate finance' different to the domestic variety? Well, other than the fact that it's harder and riskier, the answer is 'it isn't'. All of the principles set out in this book will apply to your international business in the same way as to your domestic business: the financial strategy should be tailored to the business strategy; levels of gearing and dividend payment should reflect the business risks; etc. However, on top of that there are various other issues to consider, such as the currency implications for the deal itself and for ongoing ownership of the subsidiary; different legal and tax regimes; and divergent cultural values which may affect the success of a transaction.

The rest of this chapter sets out these issues in the context of making an overseas acquisition – and making a success of it.

Finding an acquisition target

Once a company's strategic priorities are determined, the requirements for an acquisition target are known. But knowing what you want and knowing where to find it are two different matters. In some countries, such as the UK, company information is widely available and there are many different ways to conduct an acquisition search. However, in other jurisdictions, different norms apply.

When conducting an acquisition search in a foreign territory a company will almost certainly need to find trusted local advisers who understand the market, and who can find their way around the particularities of local regulations and relationships. Publicly available information on targets may be limited, which makes the dynamics of pre-bid due diligence more complex (particularly in a hostile bid situation). Corporate governance rules, codes, and practices will be different. There may also be local regulations and cultural norms which would restrict an outsider from outright purchase of a local business, even if one could be found. All these issues need to be addressed by experts who understand the local corporate and market environments.

Doing the deal

Once a target has been identified, the acquisition must be completed. Specific 'international' issues to consider during this process include:

- Negotiation strategies.
- Legal context.
- Availability and interpretation of information.
- Pricing difficulties.
- Competition regulations.

Global deals are inevitably more complex than local ones. Entering into negotiations with someone from a different culture involves understanding their stance on the negotiating process; appreciating their cultural norms; and preferably knowing something of their language. (Although unless you have the fluency of a native speaker, negotiations will require a trusted interpreter.) It sounds self-evident, but business people sometimes overlook the fact that, for example, transactions with North Americans must be handled in a very different way to those with the Japanese, who are different again to Thais or to Chinese business people. And of course individuals will have their own stances: a Chinese national who has never left China will have a totally different approach to one with an MBA from a university in Canada.

The legal context in which the acquisition takes place must also be fully understood. For example, when buying a business in one's own country one generally understands, to some extent, the issues surrounding intellectual property rights, environmental liabilities, or employee consultation practices. In a foreign environment, each of these – and a thousand other things – could differ widely from preconceptions. The norms of preparing and presenting accounting information could differ significantly in different countries (with two sets of books being common practice in some parts of the world). Furthermore, takeover regulations differ widely among countries, and hostile bids in particular might be difficult or impossible in some parts of the world. And once a deal is agreed in principle, the decision has to be made as to whether the governing law of the transaction will be your own, or that of the vendor.

Information sources too could be a problem. As already stated, in some jurisdictions access to public information may be limited. But even if the information is published, or if private access is given, the information needs to be understandable. Just as an example, accounting regulations in Japan are very different to those in the USA: what does the profit reported by your Japanese target actually represent? It is always useful in these circumstances to employ professionals to restate the target's financial information using the accounting policies acceptable in the acquirer's home territory – to see if the deal is actually worth doing.

Problems in understanding the financial information will obviously affect the deal pricing, but other issues too will be relevant here. In making local acquisitions, companies generally understand their local market and, in the UK and USA at least, can find a lot of comparative information about previous deals, so that they can price their proposals comparative to the market. In some countries, markets have low liquidity and are not efficient, so market comparisons may be misleading. Furthermore, data on private company deals might not be available, so the potential acquirer is left operating in an information vacuum.

A further issue, of major concern, is the attitude of regulators and competition authorities. Making a major acquisition in their territory may trigger an investigation which could delay the transaction for months or years, or change its form. The *Financial Times*[1] quoted a lawyer involved in the merger of Pechiney (a French company) and Algroup (Swiss) as follows: 'Alcan looked at 43 jurisdictions where they had overlaps, filed in 16 of those, in eight different languages, employed 35 different firms of solicitors and had to respond to a variety of different information requests, one of which alone led to the provision of 1 million e-mails from a single office in one agency.'

Of course, we should point out that these problems can occur even in an apparently domestic transaction. In 2008 the $12.5bn acquisition of US company Motorola Mobility Inc. by US company Google was delayed by several months awaiting approval from China's Ministry of Commerce, based on their antitrust law which caught companies with sale of more than $60m in China.[2]

International transactions will also result in problems for companies in managing the inevitable exposure that arises from foreign currency(ies). Accordingly, before we discuss how deals can be financed we will consider the sources of foreign exchange risk, and how such risks can be mitigated.

Foreign exchange risk

Foreign exchange risks relate to the potential for currency movements to impact on the firm. The issues we need to consider are:

- What foreign exchange risks arise due to overseas acquisitions?
- How can these risks be mitigated? and
- Is it worthwhile to mitigate the risks?

Two matters need to be addressed in dealing with currency issues in an international acquisition: the exposure relating to the deal funding, and the exposure relating to the ongoing operation of a foreign subsidiary. These are both considered in the paragraphs below.

To put it simply,[3] foreign exchange risk can come in one of three flavours: transaction risk, translation risk, and economic risk.

---

1   Ward, S. (2001), 'Staying the Course against Red Tape', *Financial Times*, 2 July.
2   Miller, S. (2012), 'Scaling China's M&A Wall', *Deal Magazine*, 13 July.
3   This is a very basic introduction to a complex subject. Readers who wish to know more should invest in one of the specialist books in this area.

Working Insight 19.1

Example of transaction risk

UKCo enters into a contract to sell services to FrenchCo for €12,000. The current exchange rate is £1 = €1.20. By the time the debt comes to be paid, the rate has become £1 = €1.30.

The original value of the sale to UKCo was	€12,000/1.2 = £10,000
However, the depreciation of the euro means that the sterling amount finally received by UKCo is	€12,000/1.3 = £9,231

By pricing its deal in euros the company has accepted the transaction risk, and has lost £769 on the exchange rate movement, reducing its profit by 7.7% of the expected sales value.

Transaction risk is the risk that arises from undertaking transactions in a foreign currency. It is most easily explained by example, as in Working Insight 19.1.

Translation risk arises from the need to translate all transactions and balance sheet items into domestic currency in order to prepare the holding company's financial statements. Translation risk, sometimes known as 'accounting risk', does not have an immediate cash effect. However, its impact on the financial statements can be considerable, and, for example, this could affect a company's ability to meet banking covenants. Accordingly, companies may wish to structure transactions so that the balance sheet asset of, say, a dollar investment in a subsidiary, is at least partially hedged by the dollar liability of funds raised to make that investment. In such an instance, any appreciation or depreciation in the £/$ rate would affect each side of the balance sheet, reducing to some extent the impact on the financial statements.

Economic risk relates to how a company's value (the present value of its future cash flows) might change due to exchange rate movements. This can occur directly or indirectly. An example of a direct risk would be a change in the currency value of sales remittances or a dividend stream receivable from an overseas subsidiary. But indirect economic risks are also relevant, as shown in Case Study 19.1.

Foreign currency movements can be hedged in several ways, for example, by taking out a forward contract or by using a foreign currency option.

Case Study 19.1

Volvo Cars: natural hedging

In 2012 a *Financial Times* story stated that Volvo Cars, a Swedish company owned by a Chinese company, was considering building an American factory, seeking to counter adverse currency effects from the strengthening of the Swedish krona against the US dollar, which had made its prices uncompetitive. Volvo Cars' CEO was quoted in the article as saying, 'We need natural hedging in US dollars. That could be production [a factory] or sourcing or exports out of China.'

Source: Milne, R. (2012), 'Volvo to build krona hedges', *Financial Times*, 9 September

A *forward contract* fixes the rate of exchange for a future delivery of a specified sum of money. Such a contract is binding on both parties, which limits the company's flexibility: as well as removing the downside risk of the exchange rate moving against the company, any upside potential is also lost.

This contrasts with the purchase of a *foreign currency option* which, as with any option, gives the buyer the choice as to whether to exercise the option when the actual payment/receipt becomes due. The option contract can be used to establish a minimum rate which will apply to the foreign exchange transaction, so that the option premium (the purchase price of the option contract) should be regarded as a kind of insurance cost. If the actual rate of exchange is better than the option exercise rate, the option can simply be allowed to lapse and the foreign currency can be traded in the normal spot market.

Thus exchange rate movements can be financially managed, but how relevant is this to an overseas acquisition? There are several problems in practically applying the hedging possibilities:

1   The future cash flows that are going to be generated by the foreign acquisition are not known with certainty, so it is not obvious what levels of hedging cover should be purchased.

2   Some at least of these future cash flows may be reinvested in the acquired business and therefore will not actually be converted into the buyer's local currency. This highlights a real problem because for reporting purposes it is not the cash flows which should be hedged but the profits of the overseas business, since these will be consolidated into the group's home currency-based published financial statements. It is by no means unusual to find that an overseas subsidiary may have increased its local currency-denominated profits compared to the previous year but, if exchange rates have moved adversely between the two years, the impact on the group's consolidated results may be to show a decline in performance.

3   Forward exchange rates, at which these fixed future contracts would be agreed, are not designed to be forecasts of where the actual spot rate of exchange will be on that future specified date. Because of the way international financial markets work, the forward rate of exchange is always the current rate of exchange adjusted by the difference in interest rates between the two countries. As illustrated in Working Insight 19.2, if this were not the case an arbitrageur could make a guaranteed profit by borrowing in one currency and investing in the other. Such investment actions would force the forward rates of exchange to change in order to close off such arbitrage profit opportunities.

However, the most important problem in trying to manage the currency risk is that it is hoped that the acquisition will continue to produce foreign currency inflows for the foreseeable future, and, quite clearly, trying to hedge uncertain amounts of foreign currencies for an unknown period will become both practically difficult and increasingly expensive.

Because it is effectively impossible to hedge operating cash flows using forward or option contracts, companies may consider other forms of hedge. They may examine whether an alternative financing strategy can be used. As suggested earlier, some companies try to reduce the currency risk by using a source of financing for the acquisition in the same currency as the ensuing income stream. For example, if debt funding were appropriate for the particular deal, the borrowings could be raised in the same currency so that only the remaining profit stream of the foreign acquisition would need to be converted into the parent company's own currency.

Working Insight 19.2

The arbitrage view of forward exchange rates

Using an extreme example to illustrate the point, suppose that the spot rate of exchange is £1 equals $2 and the annual rate of interest is 15% in £s and 5% in $s. An arbitrageur could borrow funds in US dollars, convert them into £s sterling and deposit them at the higher rate. In order to guarantee the repayment of the US-based loan, the £s sterling receipts could be sold forward at a guaranteed rate to produce US dollars. Unless the forward rate reflects the difference in interest rates, the arbitrageur could generate a guaranteed profit! The forward rate should be $2 \times 1.05 \div 1.15$, i.e. $1.826:£1.

> Arbitrageur borrows $100m @ 5% for one year.
> This is converted into £50m at spot rate of $2:£1 and deposited @ 15% for one year.
> The interest income on the deposit will be £7.5m.
> Therefore in one year's time £57.5m will be held but a liability is also outstanding of $105m (principal plus interest on the loan).
> If the forward rate of exchange is $1.826:£1, the proceeds of the deposit just repay the loan and no arbitrage profit is available.

At first glance this would appear to reduce the financial risk associated with the overseas acquisition but this is not so obvious when the driving forces of exchange rate movements are taken into consideration. Over time, exchange rates must reflect the relative purchasing powers of the respective currencies. If this were not true it would be possible to make long-term profits by the physical movement of goods between countries. In the short term, this stable equilibrium position may be disturbed by government interference in interest rates or trade flows, but in the long term this concept, known as *purchasing power parity*, will hold.

Purchasing power parity means that over the long term, exchange rates will move to adjust for differences in inflation rates between any two countries, since this differential inflation will distort the nominal prices of comparable goods. However, interest rates and equity funding costs also include inflation, and so the costs of funding should also be different in these countries if the inflation rates differ. This should result in the source of funding for an international acquisition making no difference to the long-term financial return, as is illustrated in Figure 19.1.

The example in Figure 19.1 shows a UK-based investment opportunity spotted by a USA-based company many years ago (when the rate of exchange was $4 to £1). The investment needed is £250 million and it was expected to generate a return of 20 per cent, which showed a good super-profit as the risk-adjusted cost of funds to the USA-based investor was 10 per cent.

This project could be funded by converting $1 billion into £s sterling at the spot rate of exchange and then repatriating the actual profit streams as dividends. However, during the life of the project, the rate of exchange moves steadily to $2:£1 from its initial point of $4:£1. If purchasing power parity were performing properly, this would not affect the return to the investor because, as is shown, the UK-based profits should have increased due to the higher inflation which has caused the decline in the rate of exchange. In other words, as the rate of exchange halved, prices should have doubled in the UK, relative to the USA. As long as the company had maintained its UK profit margins, it should have achieved double the expected

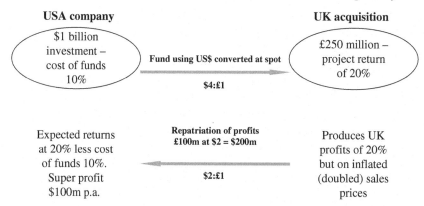

Figure 19.1 Long-term exchange rate movements (purchasing power parity).

sterling profits (£100 million rather than £50 million) and this would convert into the originally expected $200 million. Hence the expected super-profit is achieved despite the change in exchange rate, as long as the exchange rate movement is caused by inflation differences and the locally based business maintains its profit margins.

However, instead of using US dollars to fund the whole investment, part of the financing could be raised locally. This would hedge some of the translation (accounting) exposure, but would it affect the economic risk? Figure 19.2 illustrates what happens if 50 per cent of the funding is injected locally and the other 50 per cent by converting $500 million at the spot rate of exchange.

In Figure 19.2, the changed source of funding does not affect the operating profits produced by the UK business, but the business now has to bear financing costs on the locally sourced funding. As inflation in the UK is much higher (in this example) than in the USA, these funding costs will also be higher (20 per cent, rather than the 10 per cent in the USA). Therefore the £100 million operating profits will be reduced by £25 million (representing a 20 per cent financing cost on the local funding of £125 million). This leaves £75 million which is available for repatriation by converting it at $2:£1 into $150 million. Since the

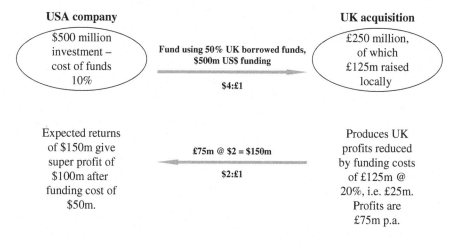

Figure 19.2 Long-term exchange rate movements (purchasing power parity).

USA-based funding is now only $500 million this only absorbs $50 million of financing cost, so that there is still a super-profit of $100 million on the project even though the financing structure has changed significantly.

The example illustrated in Figures 19.1 and 19.2 shows that if exchange rates do move to reflect differences in inflation rates, which must happen in the long term, the international sourcing of finance does not affect the return achieved on any cross-border investment. However, purchasing power parity is a long-term issue. In the real world (the one not inhabited by theoretical economists) there will be long time lags in exchange rate adjustment. As costs of funding and exchange rate movements do not necessarily always reflect differences in inflation rates in the short term, there will be many occasions when the source of financing can make a difference to the performance of the cross-border investment. Thus hedging these potential differences can make sense for a company if it is particularly concerned about its short-term perceived (i.e. accounting) performance.

This helps to explain why many companies operate sophisticated hedging strategies for their short-term international trading cash flows, but do not take out any hedges relating to the longer-term balance sheet exposures which they create by holding overseas assets.

Financing the deal

In Chapter 16 we discussed acquisition finance and stated that there were two basic methods: offer the target's shareholders an equity stake in the acquirer, or offer them cash. In an international transaction, it might not be possible to offer an all share deal, or even a deal for which only part of the consideration is in equity.

There are two potential reasons for equity-based deals to present problems in an international transaction. The first is that regulations may prevent it; in some jurisdictions, nationals are forbidden from owning shares in foreign companies. The second reason is that the shareholders themselves may be uneasy with the idea of exchanging the 'paper' in a domestic company they know for paper in a company with foreign domicile, whose laws and tax regulations are unclear to them, denominated in a foreign currency, and in which dealing in the shares, on a foreign stock exchange, will be unfamiliar, and possibly expensive.

Thus the financing for international acquisitions can be carried out by:

1   raising equity on the home market, and using the proceeds to pay cash to acquire the target;
2   raising debt, and using the proceeds to pay cash to acquire the target; or
3   issuing shares tradable in the target's country, which will be an acceptable currency for shareholders.

The first of these possibilities, financing the transaction by raising equity on the home market, has been considered at various times through this book. The decision as to whether to finance the acquisition through raising debt or equity is similar to any investment financing decision, and is not pursued further in this chapter. (Although we would point out that, almost by definition, expansion into a foreign territory will increase business risk, and companies may wish to strengthen their equity base to compensate.)

The second possibility we suggested was to raise debt and use the proceeds to acquire the target. Again, the question of whether or not to raise debt is addressed elsewhere in this book; what is of interest here is *where* to raise the debt. Although companies always have a choice of markets and currencies for their debt finance, the decision becomes more immediate in an international transaction, as discussed earlier in this chapter.

Raising loans in a foreign currency

The discussion of foreign exchange risks did, we hope, give you some idea as to why companies might wish to raise acquisition funds in a currency other than their own. Should they choose so to do, it is important to understand that entering into such a transaction itself creates a currency exposure.

For example, if a UK company raises funds in dollars, it will need to make interest and capital repayments in that currency. If the company has a dollar income stream from its subsidiary, that is fine; the currency is available, and any currency movements will affect both its income and outgoings. However, if the income stream is insufficient to meet the debt cash flows, the company will face a transaction risk similar to that described in Working Insight 19.1, possibly leading to an unexpectedly high drain on its cash flows. This might be particularly relevant for acquisitions undertaken at a high P/E ratio, for which the finance raised (and thus the servicing charges) will be substantial in relation to the income stream acquired. (Of course, this should only be a problem in the early years after the deal: the whole objective of a high P/E deal is that the target is expected to grow rapidly, and thus generate the required income streams.)

Companies wishing to raise funds in a particular currency will find that today's financial markets provide a variety of mechanisms to effect such transactions, for example, the Eurobond markets.

Eurobonds are bonds which are denominated in currencies other than that of the country in which they are sold. For example, a $-denominated bond issued in London, or a ¥ bond sold in the USA are both Eurobonds; the 'Euro' part of the name has nothing to do with the European currency. These international bonds are widely traded on the markets, and give companies access to a more extensive range of financing sources than they would have were they to restrict their activities to their local currency.

Also, companies have the ability to enter into currency swaps (which operate in a similar manner to the interest rate swaps discussed in Chapter 11), so that the currency in which the loan is first raised need not be the currency finally adopted. For example, it might be the case that an acquisition made in the USA is initially financed in US dollars, but, when the target's main income sources are understood more fully, part of that $ liability is swapped into another more appropriate currency, to hedge trading exposures.

Issuing shares acceptable to foreign shareholders

The third financing possibility we suggested was for the acquirer to issue shares that would be acceptable to the overseas shareholders. This could be done, for example, by listing its shares on the overseas exchange, or by issuing depository receipts.

Secondary listing

If a company makes a major acquisition in an overseas territory, it may choose to take a secondary listing on one of that country's stock markets. Doing this would mean that shareholders in some jurisdictions would legally be able to own the shares, and all shareholders would more easily be able to deal in them. This could make the deal more attractive to the target's shareholders, who might not want to own shares on a foreign exchange.

Companies might choose to list on a second exchange for other reasons. For example, a large company in a relatively small country would have to list on its home market for reasons of prestige, but might also choose to list on a larger exchange to gain access to a wider market of potential investors and more liquidity. Market considerations might also drive a secondary listing to attract a different investor clientele, or to achieve a higher profile in its customer markets. Or a secondary listing might be driven by a desire to demonstrate that a company has adopted the more rigorous governance standards of another exchange, in a desire to reduce its perceived risk and therefore lower its cost of capital. Maintaining a secondary listing can also provide a useful mechanism to reward overseas employees with equity. However, against these possible advantages have to be set the not-insignificant costs of maintaining a secondary listing.

Companies can take secondary listings in two ways, either through a cross-listing, where the company's shares are issued on two or more exchanges, or by being dual-listed, where there are two separate companies, listed on their separate exchanges, but working as one company.

Dual listing is a complex operation and tends to have arisen from the merger of two significant entities from different parts of the world. For example, mining group BHP Billiton was formed from the Australian BHP and the British Billiton. The individual companies form a single operating business, with profits being shared according to a formula. Their shares trade separately on the two exchanges and are not interchangeable.

A cross-listing is simpler and much more common than dual listing. When a company cross-lists, its shares or depository receipts (see later) trade on two or more exchanges and are fungible assets – i.e. they are completely interchangeable and can be bought on one exchange and sold on the other. For example, shares in Brazilian mining giant Vale are listed in São Paulo, NYSE Euronext, Hong Kong, and NYSE.

A possible problem with cross-listing is that shareholders, by and large, just prefer their own territories. When DaimlerChrysler was formed, the company was listed jointly in the USA and Germany, and about 50 per cent of its shareholders were based in the USA. In May 2001 the *Financial Times* reported that only about 20 per cent of the shares remained US owned, the rest having been sold into the German market (a process known as 'flowback'). It seems that many US shareholders preferred not to invest in what is seen as a German company.

Depository receipts

Although cross-listing can be done by through shares traded on another market, the most common method is through the use of depository receipts: either American depository receipts (ADRs) traded in the USA, or global depository receipts (GDRs) traded outside the USA. DRs are certificates which represent the rights of share ownership, but not the ownership itself, and as traded capital instruments they are subject to the requirements of the relevant stock exchange. DRs are sometimes issued in an introduction to a market, but more often used in a fundraising exercise.

Using an ADR/GDR facility a company will deposit some of its shares (existing or newly created) with a depository bank in the relevant country. The bank will then issue investors with bearer certificates confirming that the bank owns a certain number of shares, and the bearer is entitled to the proceeds of those shares. ADR might represent an underlying investment of one share in the company, or 10 or 100 – whatever ratio seems appropriate in the market. The depository bank will pay the underlying dividend entitlement to the bearers, who will be able to trade the DRs. The market price of DRs generally follows that of the underlying shares, although supply and demand may at any time lead to a pricing discount or premium.

The advantage to the company of using DRs is that the administrative burden and cost are considerably lower than those of maintaining a secondary listing. For the investor, DRs give a chance to invest in an overseas company, making a home-currency investment which they can buy and sell far more easily than they could the underlying shares.

Tax considerations

The area of global tax management is complex and ever changing, and not one for this book. Having said that, two aspects are worth mentioning in the context of corporate financial strategy and tax minimization.

The thesis of corporate finance is that debt is cheaper than equity, so it is worthwhile to gear up responsibly and reduce the cost of capital. However, the balance sheets of many US companies currently show them to be holding significant amounts of cash. One reason for this is that the profits which generated that cash were earned outside the USA and so have not been subject to US tax. If the profits were repatriated, the tax would be charged. Because of this, the companies are holding the cash outside the USA and seeking non-US investments. This needs to be understood in any financial analysis of such multinationals.

The other point regarding tax planning is slightly different. One of the seven drivers of value is to reduce the cash tax rate, minimizing cash outflows. Multinational companies have far more opportunities to do this than do companies that operate in only one market, as global operations provide the chance to locate facilities and operations in lower-tax jurisdictions. However, another of the drivers of value is to sustain a competitive advantage. These two can be in conflict. Companies should never let tax planning drive commercial considerations, and while low-tax environments might have short-term advantages, they can have strategic disadvantages. This has been seen particularly in recent years, for example, consumer boycotts of multinationals which make profits in the United Kingdom but which have structured their affairs to pay no UK corporation tax. While legal, this has hit a nerve with customers, and damaged the business brands.

Post-deal management of international acquisitions

In Chapter 16 we pointed out that research indicates that many acquisitions fail. International acquisitions are harder, and the causes of failure more varied. In addition to the 'normal' integration issues, the following should be considered.

1 The global structure of the new organization needs to be determined strategically, and issues such as the location of head offices and operating centres must be addressed.
2 The management resource required to integrate an international acquisition is considerably greater than for a domestic one. Further, integration managers must be based full time in the acquired company's country, and must have relevant language skills as well as fully understanding the business and strategy of the acquirer.
3 Cultural barriers may make integration very difficult. For example, the level of formality between workers and between management levels may differ between countries; employee rights and expectations can be diverse; ethical and governance issues may be seen in very different ways, as may the balance between risks and opportunities. In a more extreme example, if the takeover was hostile, it may be deeply resented by the target company's employees. See, for example, Case Study 19.2 on Vodafone and Mannesmann. Other cultural issues can arise when a global company tries to implement its home language as the official corporate tongue.

4   Without full integration of the new subsidiary, it may be impossible to achieve the planned synergies.

5   Legal differences may cause problems. For example, the divergence in data protection legislation between the UK and USA might mean that a UK subsidiary could not send certain customer information to its US parent; again reducing the opportunities for synergistic expansion.

Taxation issues and repatriation of profits need also to be considered. These are often linked, and a company should not consider making an overseas acquisition unless it understands how the profits of its acquired subsidiary (and maybe even its worldwide profits from other countries) will be taxed. And the issue of whether, and how, profit can be repatriated, should also be addressed in advance; it is not always automatic that dividend distributions can be made as and when desired.

Case Study 19.2

Vodafone and Mannesmann: cultural barriers

The hostile takeover of Mannesmann by Vodafone in 2000 was unusual, in that the regulatory environment means that successful hostile bids for German companies are very rare (although German companies are very adept at acquiring businesses in other countries). Accordingly, the very fact of the deal came as a culture shock to the employees of the long-established German company.

During the initial period of ownership, Vodafone did the following:

- Sold off the prestigious Mannesmann fine art collection.
- Sold off the century-old wood panels in the board room.
- Stopped the practice of sending employees cards and wine on their birthdays.
- Promoted its charitable donations in order to benefit from the publicity (Mannesmann had always given anonymously).

These actions, which would have been seen as reasonable in shareholder value-based Anglo-American cultures, were totally alien to the German employees and caused deep resentment.

Source: Financial Times, 5 June 2001

Conclusion: does the 'global company' exist?

International corporate finance is different to the domestic variety, as companies face far more barriers to success at all stages of the transaction and in its ongoing management.

It is interesting that overseas investment risks and foreign currency exposures still take up so much time of senior managers in many multinational or transnational corporations. The development of global brands, global products, and, to a lesser extent, global customers, has driven expansion, and yet there is no really global company. A global company would not need to hedge foreign currency exposures because they would not exist.

If a company were truly global, it would have balanced its business exposures (in terms of profits and cash flows) to the relative economic size of the countries and currencies around the world. However, it would have gone one stage further and balanced its ownership and funding sources on the same basis as its profits and cash flows so that its investors were not all expecting a return denominated in a particular currency, such as the US dollar. At present, even though investors in very large companies may be located all over the world, they will still view each such investment as being based in a particular currency.

Key messages

- The same principles of finance apply to international deals as apply to all other transactions.
- International corporate finance is more complex than operating within the home country's boundaries. As well as currency issues, management has to understand cultural and legal differences. Post-deal integration will also be more difficult.
- Currency risk takes three forms: transaction, translation, and economic. Companies can choose to take action to reduce each of these risks.
- Funding an overseas acquisition is more difficult than funding one in the same territory, as the target's shareholders might not wish to hold shares in a foreign country.
- Raising debt in a currency in which you have no assets or income streams leaves you exposed to movements in exchange rates which would wipe out any temporary benefit of rate differentials.
- Companies can choose to take a secondary listing through depository receipts, broadening their shareholder base.

Suggested further reading

A Guide to Listing on the London Stock Exchange (2010), London Stock Exchange (and others). www.londonstockexchange.com/home/guide-to-listing.pdf
This book comprises chapters written by lawyers, investment bankers, and other professionals. It contains chapters on establishing a depository receipt programme, and preparing to list depository receipts.
Guide to Public ADR Offerings in the United States (2012), Cleary Gottlieb, www.cgsh.com/fr/guide_to_public_adr_offerings_in_the_united_states_2012
This detailed document is issued by the legal firm Cleary Gottlieb, and explains the legal and practical considerations involved in issuing ADRs.

20 Strategic working capital management

Learning objectives

After reading this chapter you should be able to:

1   Identify the components of working capital generated from a company's business model, and understand the impact of this on its growth and value potential.
2   Select appropriate financing strategies for a company's working capital needs.

Introduction

Working capital, the investment in inventories and receivables net of trade creditors, is the only investment a company makes on which it doesn't expect a defined return. The investment is needed in order to oil the wheels of business rather than to produce something itself. Because of this, many companies have over-invested in working capital, leading to cash-flow problems and to a diminution of shareholder value.

For many businesses, the components of working capital represent the largest items on the balance sheet. Despite this, they tend not to be seen as issues demanding strategic consideration or top management attention. Companies that have detailed procedures for evaluation and approval of even trivial capital expenditure will often leave the management of inventories and receivables (debtors) to junior employees.

We established in Chapter 1 that reductions in the level of working capital can enhance shareholder value. Accordingly, in this chapter we consider why companies hold working capital; how it can be financed; and how the management of working capital should form part of the overall business and financial strategy.

Shareholder value management

In Chapter 1 we considered the seven drivers of shareholder value, and noted that one of these was a reduction in the incremental need for working capital. Reducing working capital means that a business has lower cash requirements (inventories and receivables) as it expands, and the resultant increase in cash flows adds to the value of the business. Other factors also drive shareholder value, for example, increases in profitable sales growth, but for many businesses it is easier to make improvements in the levels of working capital than it is to generate and sustain an improvement in profit. Furthermore, by working on both the profitability and the underlying investment, companies can leverage any improvements they make.

Sustainable growth

The level of working capital in a business has a direct effect on the amount of growth the company can sustain organically from its own internal resources. Growth in sales requires that the business takes on additional inventories and has more receivables. Even if no further capital expenditure is required to achieve the growth, the underlying capital invested in a business will still need to increase.

The amount of growth that a business can sustain out of its own resources, before issuing new capital, is constrained both by its anticipated rate of profitability and by the underlying asset requirement. Thus, if a company is to grow without borrowing or issuing further capital it needs either to increase its profitability or to make better use of its assets. In Appendix 1 the growth assumptions underlying the dividend growth model are established, so growth can be calculated as:

$$g = \text{return on investment} \times \text{retention ratio}$$

Increasing the company's return on investment – for example, making the same return on a lower (working capital) investment – will increase the funds available for reinvestment and thus increase the sustainable growth level.

Factors affecting the working capital cycle

The working capital cycle (the time taken to convert orders to cash received, net of creditors) is illustrated in Figure 20.1. The cycle commences when the company receives an order from its customer (or decides to make for stock). Inventories are acquired, which may be converted through the stages of work in progress and finished goods. These stocks are held as current assets until the customer buys them. However, at that point, no money has changed hands, and the asset of inventory is merely replaced by an asset of trade receivables. It is not

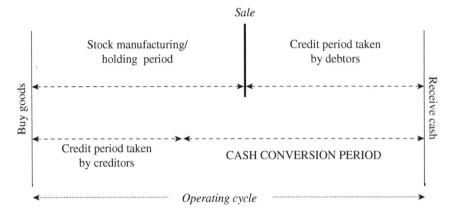

Figure 20.1 The working capital cycle.

until the cash is actually received that the cycle is complete. The level of working capital is shown as the 'cash conversion period'.

The company has to finance the business for the whole of the operating cycle. However, it does not need to do so out of its own resources; some of those inventories will have been bought on credit, and trade creditors finance part of the working capital investment. Thus, the company's cash requirement is limited to the net of inventories and receivables less creditors.

The working capital cycle for any company is a function of several variables: the country; the industry; the company's business strategy and attitude to risk; and the effectiveness of its systems.

Country impact

Cultural norms and logistical factors impact upon working capital policies. For example, in countries in which the transport system is unreliable, larger inventories have to be held to compensate for possible extended lead times. Also, terms of trade vary considerably between countries; at the time of writing, the countries of southern Europe have a payment norm for receivables substantially more than that for, say, the Scandinavian countries.

Industry impact

It is self-evident that the investment in working capital will differ across industries. Business-to-business transactions are generally done on credit; manufacturers will have more inventories than will some service industries; professional service firms will have proportionately less reliance on trade creditors than will most other businesses. Figure 20.2 is an illustrative representation of the working capital cycles of some different types of business.

In Figure 20.2, the manufacturing company has a heavy investment in stock and receivables, offset by significant trade credit. The picture is reversed for supermarkets. These are retail businesses selling to end customers, so there are no receivables; and they operate on minimal inventories. Further, they have the buying power to take long credit periods from their suppliers – accordingly, their net working capital investment is actually negative; the more they grow, the more finance they obtain out of their working capital. Finally, we illustrate the working capital investment for some consultancies and other service firms. Although they have no physical inventories, they can have large sums tied up in work in progress, which

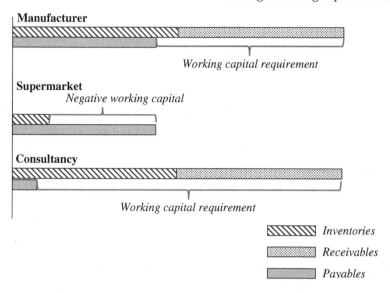

Figure 20.2 Working capital in different industries.

cannot be invoiced until milestones are achieved. Once they have been invoiced, clients are often slow to pay. But consultancy firms, whose main cost is their people, have no trade creditors against which to offset the working capital investment: they can hardly delay paying staff wages in order to mitigate operating needs.

When moving into an industry it is important to understand why its working capital patterns are as they are. Only with this understanding can the accepted norms start to be changed, for example, to reduce stockholdings or manage receivables more effectively.[1]

Risk and return

At the individual company level where financial strategy tends to operate, one of the main factors influencing working capital levels is the business's strategy and its attitude to risk. Each element of the working capital equation can be regarded as taking a particular position on the risk–return continuum, and companies will adopt differing commercial strategies, putting them in different categories.

The trade-off between investing in working capital (reducing returns) and not making the investment (taking risks) is illustrated in Working Insight 20.1.

This can be used to ensure that the chosen working capital strategy ties in with the business strategy. For example:

- A business which sees its competitive advantage as lying in the full service it provides to customers may need to maintain much higher levels of inventory than a discount house with limited ranges and service.

---

1 On principle, we never give advice about managing the third element of the working capital cycle: trade creditors. One business's trade creditors are another's receivables, and taking extended credit just moves the problem along the supply chain. Accordingly, when we work with companies in this area we focus on managing the assets down, rather than increasing liabilities.

Working Insight 20.1

Risk and return in working capital

	Risk avoided by holding working capital	Cost of the working capital investment
Inventories	• Stock outs delaying the manufacturing process. • Loss of customers who cannot wait for delivery.	• Cash tied up in stock. • Costs of holding stock (incl. warehousing, insurance, damage, obsolescence, pilfering, as well as the financial cost).
Receivables	• Loss of customers due to more attractive opportunities elsewhere.	• Credit control costs and bad debts. • Cash tied up in receivables.
Creditors	• Too heavy reliance on bank finance.	• Poor name in the industry. • Charged higher prices.

- Setting a tight credit policy to control receivables could well counteract other marketing initiatives the company is taking; these activities need to be coordinated and controlled.
- A business which has a policy of working closely with its suppliers may decide to pay far more quickly than one which has determined a more combative stance.

Case Study 20.1 illustrates a situation where a large company took a strategic decision for the benefit of its overall supply chain.

It is interesting to contrast actions set out in Case Study 20.1 with the behaviour of some organizations in other sectors, which compromised their competitive positions by simply extending payment terms on all suppliers. Such action led to some critical suppliers failing, and the organizations being unable to sustain their supply chains when demand returned.

Case Study 20.1

Supporting the supply chain

The economic crash of 2008 had a massive effect on the UK construction industry; over a period of just three weeks, building projects were put on hold and work cancelled, which led to cash-flow problems throughout the supply chain.

Although the knee-jerk response for companies might have been to extend their supplier payment time, one large company recognized that this would just pass on the pain, which could result in smaller suppliers going into liquidation. That in turn would have damaged their supply chain, affecting their own business and many others. Their response was to shorten the payment terms on some smaller, more vulnerable businesses (i.e. pay them quicker), but to extend payment terms for the stronger businesses.

This intervention, although unpopular with some, sustained the supply chain and enabled the businesses in that supply chain to survive the downturn.

Other working capital issues relating directly to the chosen business strategy include:

- The need to hold additional inventories for each new outlet (retail or manufacturing) opened.
- Synergies created by reducing overall working capital through horizontal or vertical acquisition strategies.
- Credit terms for suppliers and customers will be dependent on the balance of power within the industry.
- The risk of short business cycles leading to excess stocks of items that are no longer in fashion.
- Decisions to sell into segments with a traditionally poor payment record. (This may be a value-creating strategy if the company can make enough incremental profit out of the customer before the eventual bad debt arises.)

Effectiveness of systems

The ways in which a particular business processes its transactions can have a significant effect on the levels of working capital maintained. This can be investigated using the components of, for example, the order-to-receipt cycle illustrated in Figure 20.3. This sets out, for a typical company, the processes that are undertaken in order to service the customer and, ultimately, to bank their payment. Analysis of what happens at each stage can help to evaluate where improvements can be made, and the cycle can be shortened. For example, a company that only raises invoices once a month might find it beneficial to invoice more often; a business with chaotic collection processes can improve cash management by implementing a structured procedure. Again, it is worth pointing out that such improvements have to be in line with the business strategy of the unit.

Figure 20.3 The order-to-receipt cycle.

Financing working capital

The working capital investment, which will vary from day to day as trading progresses, needs to be funded, and companies have several strategic options in managing this financing requirement. Some businesses choose to have sufficient cash funds available to meet their day-to-day needs; some have overdrafts or borrowing facilities; others use a form of asset finance. Each of these is considered below.

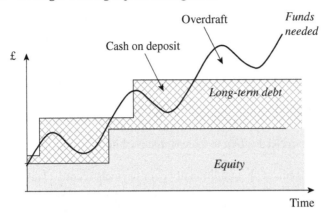

Figure 20.4 Funding requirements over time.

Cash and overdrafts

The advantage of holding cash balances (which in some organizations are viewed as part of the working capital investment) is that the business can always meet demand. The disadvantage of holding cash is that cash itself is an investment which generates a very poor return. Funds on deposit with the bank are unlikely, by definition, to produce a return which will satisfy shareholders.

As mentioned in Chapter 4, for private businesses this latter point need not be a consideration. We know of several small private companies in which considerable amounts of money are kept on deposit, instantly available should they be required. As financiers, we understand that this is an inefficient use of funds; as risk-averse individuals we appreciate the attraction of being able to sleep easy at night, knowing that a cash crisis is unlikely. For a private company, in which 'shareholder value' means meeting the needs of the owner/directors, this is a reasonable attitude.

However, companies with a broader shareholder base need to be more focused in their use of funds, and having excessive cash deposits is a poor strategic decision.

As a general rule, a company should finance itself with a mixture of short- and long-term funds, of which cash plays a part. Figure 20.4 illustrates this.

In Figure 20.4, the business has a mixture of long-term debt and equity, determined in accordance with the principles we have been presenting throughout this book. As it grows, it needs further cash. However, the cash needs are not uniform – either seasonality or a business cycle could mean that the cash requirement varies. This company has chosen to operate with an initially low proportion of debt, increasing gearing over time. It has increased equity over the period,[2] and has also raised long-term loans. The quantum of loans raised is such that cash is sometimes on deposit, but that sometimes an overdraft is required.

The decision as to how much short-term finance will be used, and how it will be structured, should be made in the light of the business requirements and the preferred attitude to financial risk. It will in practice also reflect the state of the banking market, and whether long-term loans are available, either in general or to particular, riskier customers.

---

2 In practice of course, equity will change each period as profits are retained.

Two final points should be noted as regards the use of short-term borrowing facilities. The first is that, in our opinion, it is always useful to have negotiated a borrowing facility even if it is not immediately required, as this gives financial flexibility.[3] The second issue is that, in the UK, overdraft facilities are repayable to the bank on demand. No breach of covenants is needed for the bank to change its mind about the funding, and require repayment. Thus overdraft finance is not nearly as low-risk for companies as would be a negotiated loan.

Asset-based finance

Banks will lend short-term finance against the business generally. However, there are also specialist financial institutions which will advance monies against specific elements of working capital. Inventory finance is available from some, but debtor finance is far more common, and so it is this on which we focus.

Debtor finance (invoice finance) has been in common use for many decades. It is interesting to note that accountants and professional advisers tend to fall into two camps about the use of invoice finance: they either hate it and see it as a sign of the imminent demise of the business, or they appreciate its flexibility.

Invoice finance takes two main forms: factoring and invoice discounting.

In factoring, the company effectively sells its receivables to the factor (often a bank subsidiary that specializes in this type of transaction). When it raises an invoice, it sends one copy to the customer and, at the same time, a copy to the factoring company. The factoring company will then advance to the company a proportion (generally about 80 to 95 per cent) of the invoice value. Thus the business has access to funds immediately, rather than waiting for the debtor to pay. When the debtor does eventually pay, they are instructed to pay the factor rather than their supplier. Once the factor has received the funds, the balance of the invoice amount is credited to the business's bank account. (Commission and interest are of course deducted – nothing is for free in this world.)

The cash flows in factoring are illustrated in Figure 20.5.

Factoring is often used by smaller companies, where credit management can be less sophisticated. Larger companies might prefer the other main invoice finance technique: confidential invoice discounting. Although similar in effect (the company still obtains a proportion of its debtors ledger instantly), invoice discounting differs from factoring in three ways:

- The receivables remain the legal property of the company, which maintains its own debtors ledger.
- The customer is not aware of the financing transaction, as payment is made direct to the supplier; and
- Costs are lower, because the financing firm is providing fewer services.

Factoring and invoice discounting have several advantages as a form of finance. The funds are available immediately, rather than waiting for the customers to pay, and so the finance available is linked directly to the growth needs of the business. Also, companies providing factoring and invoice discounting tend to advance a higher percentage against receivables than

---

3   Although we should point out that if a company's circumstances change such that it does require the financial facility, this change itself is often sufficient to breach banking covenants so that the funds are no longer available. It's not for nothing that there is a saying about bankers only offering to lend you an umbrella when it's not raining!

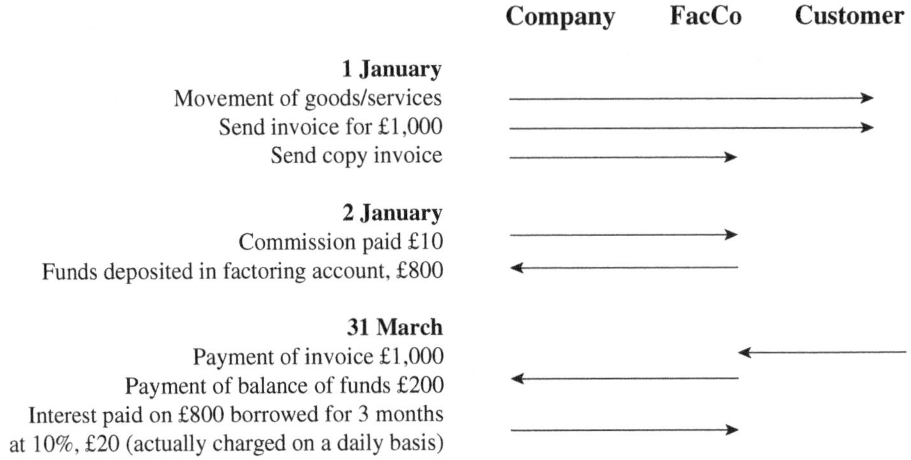

	Company	FacCo	Customer

1 January
Movement of goods/services
Send invoice for £1,000
Send copy invoice

2 January
Commission paid £10
Funds deposited in factoring account, £800

31 March
Payment of invoice £1,000
Payment of balance of funds £200
Interest paid on £800 borrowed for 3 months
at 10%, £20 (actually charged on a daily basis)

Figure 20.5 Cash flows in factoring.

would traditional bankers, because they understand and manage the risks better. Furthermore, the finance company can advise on the creditworthiness of certain customers (and indeed, might decline to fund some customers' invoices). Related to this, some companies choose to have asset finance just for certain parts of their customer list. For example, a small company with export sales but no infrastructure outside its home country might choose to factor those debts to take advantage of the factoring company's expertise.

Factoring and invoice discounting are generally *non-recourse*, which means that if a customer does not pay the debt, the financing company can recover the amount that had been advanced. A *with-recourse* agreement can be arranged; this is riskier for the financing company as they will bear the bad debts, and so the fees are higher.

For small companies, there are further advantages to factoring, in that the debtors ledger is outsourced to the factoring company, which can generally collect receivables promptly due to experience and efficient management.

There is, however, no free lunch, and it is also true to say that there are many disadvantages compared to, say, bank borrowing in a more traditional form. Factoring and invoice discounting are more expensive than traditional borrowing, with commission being paid, as well as higher interest charges. And for factoring in particular there are two further issues to consider. The first is that inserting the factor into the customer–supplier relationship might damage that relationship, particularly if the factor is aggressive in chasing debts. Second, many accountants and business people do not like factoring – it developed a poor reputation in the 1970s as 'lender of last resort', and so the use of factors may send unwelcome (and false) signals about the business's financial stability.

While on the subject of asset-based finance, we need to consider a relatively new form – supply chain finance, or *reverse-factoring*. Whereas the techniques discussed above are supplier centric, in that the supplier of the goods arranges finance for all their receivables, reverse-factoring is a buyer-centric process.

In a situation where a relatively small supplier is selling to a large and financially sound buyer, the funding can relate to a specific buyer. This customer drives the process, which starts with them raising a purchase order to the supplier, copied in to the financing company. The transaction proceeds as usual, but when the supplier raises their invoice it is copied to the finance company, which deposits the requisite funds into their account, in a similar manner to normal factoring. On the due date for payment of the invoice, the financing company automatically debits the buyer's account.

Key messages

- Working capital comprises the net of inventories and trade receivables less trade creditors.
- Working capital represents a substantial investment for most companies, and needs to be managed strategically, to be maintained at the lowest level consistent with value creation.
- Long-term financial needs, including the core element of working capital, should be funded with long-term finance. Short-term needs should be funded with short-term funding.
- Factoring and invoice discounting are types of asset finance which can be used to fund working capital (receivables).

Suggested further reading

Centre for Logistics and Supply Chain Management.
 The Centre is part of Cranfield School of Management, and is Europe's largest grouping of faculty specializing in the management of logistics and supply chains. From their website, accessed via www.cranfield.ac.uk/som, are available academic papers and practitioner articles on various matters relating to inventories and supply chain.

Appendix 1

Review of theories
of finance

Overview

This appendix sets out an explanation of financial theory sufficient to give the reader a background to the issues discussed in the rest of the book. The topics covered are:

- Discounting and calculating the value of bonds.
- The cost of capital:

  - calculating the cost of equity using the dividend growth model;
  - calculating the cost of equity using the Capital Asset Pricing Model;
  - calculating a weighted average cost of capital and designing an appropriate capital structure.

- The efficient market hypothesis.
- Dividend theory.

Introduction

It would be a very daunting prospect to try to review the mass of developments in the theory of finance in one brief appendix of a book. Not surprisingly therefore, this review is both very selective and very concise on each topic, concentrating only on the key elements of the theories and highlighting, where relevant, the essential underlying assumptions on which the theory or model is based. In writing the book we have assumed that our readers already have some familiarity with financial theory, and seek from us only an aide memoire to remind them of the key points. Accordingly, in this appendix we cover the theories of finance only insofar as they are necessary to set a context for the rest of the book, and in summary rather than in depth.

In most cases the theories are referred to by their inventors' or discoverers' names but no attempt, due to constraints of space, has been made to be academically rigorous in giving copious references to the derivation of the formulae, etc. This is also partially because the theories are comprehensively covered in most of the basic existing finance textbooks and it was never our intention to try to reproduce that type of book.

Discounting and the value of bonds

An appreciation of the time value of money is fundamental to financial theory and practice. Money now is worth more than money in the future; accordingly, if we lend or invest money we expect to receive a return on that investment. This return compensates us for not being able to spend the funds immediately, for the risk of non-return of the funds, and for the fact that inflation might erode the value of the funds over the investment period.

Although in practice the return on an investment means that a greater sum is available at the end of the investment period than the beginning, financial convention dictates that when comparing investments we determine the equivalent sum that they would be worth at the start of the period – the *net present value* (NPV) – rather than the total to be received by the end of the period – the *terminal value*. This facilitates comparisons between investments.

We evaluate the net present value of an investment (be it an investment in financial instruments or in real assets of a business) by discounting the cash flows expected from that investment. *Discounted cash flow* (DCF) analysis applies discounting factors (the inverse of compounding factors) – to each future period's expected cash flows. Working Insight A1.1 illustrates an example whereby DCF analysis is used to determine the value of a bond.

In Working Insight A1.1, the bond traded at a discount to its face value. This is because the bond only pays an interest rate of 7 per cent, which is lower than the 8 per cent paid by other similar bonds and so the instrument is worth less.

Working Insight A1.1

Bond valuation (part 1)

A £1m 5-year bond offers a 7% rate of interest, payable annually in arrears. The current required market rate of return for this investment is 8%. What is the value of the bond on the market?

Year	Cash flow	Discount factor @ 8%	Present value
1 – 5 (interest)	£70k p.a.	3.993	£279.5k
5 (repayment)	£1,000k	0.681	£681.0k
			£960.5k

The present value of the cash flows from the bond is £960.5k, therefore that is what a rational investor would be prepared to pay for it.

Working Insight A1.2

Bond valuation (part 2)

The £1m bond offers a 7% rate of interest, payable annually in arrears, and has 3 years to run. The current required market rate of return for this investment is 5%.

Year	Cash flow	Discount factor @ 5%	Present value
1 – 3 (interest)	£70k p.a.	2.723	£190.6k
3 (repayment)	£1,000k	0.864	£864.0k
			£1,054.6k

The present value of the cash flows from the bond is now £1,054.6k.

Working Insight A1.2 shows what would happen to the value of the same bond if, two years later, market interest rates had fallen to 5 per cent.

The fall in market interest rates means that the bond in Working Insight A1.2 is relatively more valuable, and so it is trading at a premium to the £1 million face value.

The principles of discounted cash flow underlie much of the theory of finance and are fundamental in understanding the valuation of all types of financial instrument. In order to apply DCF techniques a discount rate is needed, and the derivation of this discount rate, based on a company's cost of capital, is explored in the next section.

The cost of capital

Companies can raise money using two basic forms of instrument – debt and equity. We established in Chapter 1 that the return that the investors demand from their investment is directly related to their perception of the risk of that investment. For the investor, debt is a much lower-risk investment than is equity (there is less volatility in the expected returns) and therefore lenders require a lower return than shareholders.

In this section we consider the cost of debt (K_d), two different ways of calculating the cost of equity (K_e), and the calculation of the weighted average cost of capital (WACC), which often forms the basis for the discount factor applied in DCF analysis.

The cost of debt

We have seen from the example in Working Insight A1.1 that the cost of debt is based on the current market rate for debt of that risk level. The fact that a business raised debt at 7 per cent some years ago is irrelevant to its cost of debt; what is significant is that lenders now are demanding an 8 per cent return on their money – that must be the basis for the company's K_d calculations.

However, the cost of debt to the company is actually less than 8 per cent, as governments subsidize debt by allowing interest to be tax-deductible. If a company borrows £1 million at 8 per cent, the interest charge of £80,000 is allowable as an expense for tax purposes. Accordingly, if tax rates are 30 per cent, the company's tax liability is reduced by £24,000 (£80,000 × 30%). This means that the net cost to the company is only

£56,000. Thus, provided that a company is paying tax, this *tax shield* reduces the cost of the debt.

$$K_d = i(1 - t) \tag{1}$$

where i is the interest rate to be applied, and t is the tax rate.

This means that debt is doubly cheaper than equity: not only is it inherently cheaper as a low-risk financial instrument for the lender, but the additional tax subsidy reduces its cost still further. One begins to see why companies like to use debt as a source of finance.

The cost of equity

Two separate ways of calculating the cost of equity will be considered: the dividend growth model and the Capital Asset Pricing Model.

Simple dividend growth model

Shareholders achieve their return through a mixture of dividends and capital gain. Assume an investor, let us call him A, buys a share to hold for three years. At the end of each of those three years he receives a dividend on the share, then he sells it on to investor B. Investor B will only buy the share if she too believes that it will be a good investment, generating dividends and a capital gain. She too holds it for three years, selling on to C. And investor C too … well, you get the picture.

We could run through the whole alphabet with investors receiving dividends and then selling on the share, but the basic principle is clear:

1 investors receive a dividend and capital gain;
2 the reason that they can sell the share to other investors is because those buyers also expect to receive a dividend, and to be able to sell it on at some future point.

We all know of shares which do not pay out dividends (indeed, they are discussed in Chapter 5). However, this in no way invalidates the model: profits reinvested by the company will lead to larger profits and greater dividends in the future. Ultimately, the company has to pay out all of its profits by way of dividend – otherwise there is no point in being an investor.

So, investor A paid price P_0 for the share, and received dividends D_1, D_2 and D_3. He then sold for price P_1.

Investor B bought for price P_1, received dividends D_4, D_5 and D_6 and then sold for price P_2.

Investor C paid price P_2, received dividends D_7, D_8 and D_9 and then sold on for price P_3.

If we eliminate the share prices paid between investors, we are left with a stream of cash flows from the company: D_1, D_2, D_3, ... D_t. It is this stream of cash flows that we can value to value the share.

If we assume that the shareholder requires a return of K_e, the cost of equity, then the value to the shareholder of the share (i.e. its price) is

$$P = D_1 \div (1 + K_e) + D_2 \div (1 + K_e)^2 + D_3 \div (1 + K_e)^3 + \ldots + D_t \div (1 + K_e)^t \tag{2}$$

Working Insight A1.3

Calculation of growth for the dividend growth model

Assumptions:
1 Dividend pay-out ratio is constant over time, and so therefore is the retention ratio.
2 Return on reinvestment is constant over time.

The combination of these assumptions means that profits growth (and therefore dividend growth) is constant over time:

 g = retention ratio × return on reinvestment.

If we assume a compounding relationship between the dividends from each year, with dividends growing at the rate of g per annum such that $D_2 = D_1(1 + g)$ and $D_3 = D_2(1 + g)$,[1] equation 2 can be simplified to give the standard dividend growth model as developed by Gordon and Shapiro:[2]

$$P = D_1 \div (Ke - g) \tag{3}$$

This equation sets out the price of the share (or of the company) in terms of its forthcoming dividend, growth assumptions and the cost of equity. It can be rewritten to calculate the cost of equity based on a knowledge of the share price, as follows:

$$K_e = (D_1 \div P) + g \tag{4}$$

It is obvious that a key driver of the functions in equations 3 and 4 is the growth assumption. Technically, this represents growth in dividends, and assumes a constant pay-out ratio over the company's future life (which those of us who have read Chapter 5 will realize is an unlikely situation). We also assume that the amount reinvested (one minus the pay-out ratio) can be reinvested at a constant rate of return. Thus, we can calculate what g might be, as shown in Working Insight A1.3.

The formula in Working Insight A1.3 is illustrated numerically in Working Insight A1.4.

We must point out that although a formula-based approach to determining g is common, the results can be very misleading, not least because balance sheet values under current accounting standards may understate the 'true' position. Also, using a simple formula implies no efficiency in the use of capital as the business grows. In practice, we often prefer to look at historic trends in growth of profit or dividends, or to take directors' estimates of future growth as a more realistic representation.

---

1 We do appreciate the absurdity of the assumption of compound dividend growth to infinity. It is one of the restrictions of the dividend growth model. There are several more complex versions of the model available, which assume staged growth. However, the basic model is widely used and is essential to financial understanding.
2 Gordon, M. J. and Shapiro, E. (1956), 'Capital Equipment Analysis: The Required Rate of Profit', *Management Science*, 3 (October): 102–10.

Working Insight A1.4

Example of growth calculations

Company Z started the year with equity of £1,000 and made profits after tax of £100. Of this £100, £20 was paid out to shareholders by way of dividend, and £80 was reinvested in the business.

Return on opening equity = 100 ÷ 1,000 = 10%.
Closing equity = £1,000 + £80 = £1,080

If the return on reinvestment is constant, the company will make profits of 10% of opening capital next year: 10% × £1,080 = £108.

This represents a growth rate in profits of 8 ÷ 100 = 8%.

Which could also be calculated as:

    g = retention ratio × return on reinvestment
       = 80% × 10%
       = 8%.

Capital Asset Pricing Model (CAPM)

The positive relationship between risk and return has been consistently emphasized in this book; we now examine the theoretical framework for assessing the relevant level of risk. This is one area of finance which has been the subject of massive empirical research because, in the major capital markets at least, there are detailed records of the actual returns achieved by a wide range of alternative financial investments going back decades. Some of these major research studies have compared the levels of average total return (including yield and capital gains) for different investment portfolios over almost this entire period. These analyses confirm the intuitive logic that investors receive a higher return on investments which have a higher risk. (Whether the historic data indicate what the investors *wanted* or *expected* rather than what they *received* is a separate issue, nevertheless, we tend to use these results to predict the future.)

Risk in a financial instrument is defined as the volatility in the expected return. An investor buying a government bond can be reasonably assured that the government will be around in the next few years to honour its interest and repayment commitments; consequently the required return is low. An investor in shares is reliant on the directors' intentions to pay a dividend, and on the company's performance and market conditions for her capital gain – this high volatility in expected results translates into a high required return.

The risk of any particular investment can be split into two components – unique risk (also known as company risk or diversifiable risk) and market (systemic) risk.

Unique risk relates to the particular company. It would include the risk of product failures, of the CEO dying, of product–market changes – anything company-specific that affects the operating results. However, because it relates only to that company, bad news (or indeed good news) here should have no impact on the other shares in an investor's portfolio. Market risk on the other hand relates to the market as a whole – for example, to the economic cycle which would impact all companies. Market risk cannot be diversified. Figure A1.1 illustrates this.

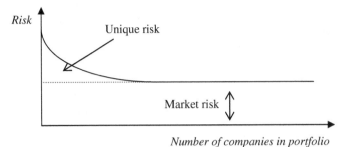

Figure A1.1 Diversification of risk.

If I own just one share, then my financial fortune is geared to how well that share performs. If I buy a second share, in a company whose results are not correlated to the first, then my portfolio is diversified and my overall level of risk is reduced. (This can be shown mathematically, as the average return from the two shares will be the sum of their two average returns, but the volatility of the two, as measured by standard deviation, will be the square root of the sum of their squares, which is lower than merely averaging their individual standard deviations.)

It can be shown that an investor who has a diversified portfolio of about twenty shares can eliminate the unique company risk. However, market risk cannot be eliminated in this way, as all companies, to some extent or another, will be affected by general market movements.

As rational investors can diversify away the unique risk associated with any particular company, they do not need, and should not receive, any additional return to compensate for taking on this unnecessary risk. Therefore shareholders should only be compensated for taking the market risk, which is an inevitable consequence of investing in shares. This is a key principle underlying the Capital Asset Pricing Model (CAPM). In order to use it in practice, we need to understand how individual companies are affected by overall market movements.

The measure we use to determine how sensitive individual shares are to the return of the total stock market is known as beta (β). If, when overall stock market returns increase by 5 per cent, the returns on a particular share rise by 10 per cent, the share is said to have a beta of 2.0. Similarly, a less sensitive company may have a beta of 0.75 which means that if returns on the stock market fall by 10 per cent, this company's return will only fall by 7.5 per cent. Clearly, the stock market as a whole has a beta of one, because the stock market is a weighted average of all shares.

From this analysis we obtain the CAPM developed in the 1960s by various economists.[3]

From Figure A1.2 we can see that if a share has a beta of one, i.e. its movements exactly mirror those of the stock market as a whole, the return that investors require from the share will be the same as the market return. Shares with $\beta > 1$ will demand a higher return than the market; the converse is true for those shares with $\beta < 1$.

The CAPM is elegantly simple, and easy to use. The risk-free rate (R_f) can be obtained from the yield to redemption on government bonds. Companies' betas are calculated by investment services, using regression analysis over (say) five years to determine how that company's

3 For example, Sharpe, W. F. (1964), 'Capital Asset Prices: A Theory of Market Equilibrium under Conditions of Risk', *Journal of Finance*, 19(3): 425–42.

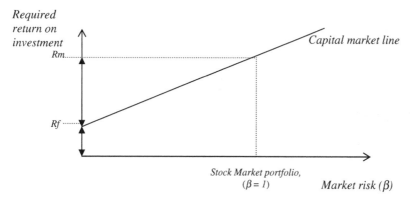

Figure A1.2 Capital Asset Pricing Model.

The cost of equity, Ke, can be represented by the equation:

$$Ke = Rf + \beta\,(Rm - Rf)$$

Where Rf is the risk-free rate, β is the market risk factor of a particular share, and Rm is the required return on the stock market as a whole; (Rm − Rf) is the market risk premium.

share price has moved compared to the market as a whole. And the market risk premium $(R_m - R_f)$ has been determined by various academics and practitioners, often by examining forty or sixty years of data as to how share returns have compared with bond returns.

However, in practice the data are not as straightforward as they may seem. R_f is the yield on government bonds: should this be three month bills, or thirty-year bonds – each has a different yield to redemption. (This is known as the *term structure of interest rates*, or the *yield curve*.) Beta is calculated by regression, but selecting different regression periods, or even carrying out the calculations for different days of the week, can give very different results. The market risk premium has been derived from historic data, but different calculation methods give varying outcomes, and there are also some sources who state that past market returns are no guide to what investors actually require in the future. CAPM, although extensively used in practice, is fraught with problems.

We need to explore one further point on CAPM. As described, the CAPM formula can be used to calculate the cost of equity for a company. The beta we have discussed is the company beta, and reflects the company risk profile. But companies incur two main types of risk – business risk and financial risk. The beta of a company, which reflects its historical volatility against the market, incorporates both of these.

It is possible to deconstruct company betas (which are also known as equity betas) in order to establish the beta of the underlying assets – a reflection of the business risk. This can be done using the following equation:

$$\beta_{\text{asset}} = \beta_{\text{debt}} \times [\text{Debt/(Debt + Equity)}] + \beta_{\text{equity}} \times [\text{Equity/(Debt + Equity)}] \tag{5}$$

where 'Debt' and 'Equity' represent the market values of those instruments.

However, it is more common to adjust the equation to allow for the tax advantage of debt (the existence of the tax shield dampens the volatility related to debt financing), by multiplying the Debt factors in the equation by (1–t) where t is the tax rate. Furthermore, for convenience it is generally assumed that the beta of debt approximates to zero. If we add in the tax factors and take debt as zero, then equation 5 becomes:

$$\beta_{asset} = \beta_{equity} \div (1 + (Debt\ (1-t)/Equity))^4 \tag{6}$$

The difference between the equity beta and the asset beta reflects the financial risk caused by the funding strategy of the company; were the company to be financed totally by equity, the equity beta and the asset beta would be the same.

Asset betas can be used to determine an appropriate discount rate to use on a project which is of a different risk level to the company as a whole, or can be used to determine the appropriate beta to use for evaluating an unquoted business (which, by definition, does not have a share price and so does not have a directly calculated beta).

Weighted average cost of capital

Companies will be funded with a variety of financial instruments, but for the purpose of this section we will simplify matters so that they have a choice only of debt and equity. As established earlier, debt is a cheaper form of finance, being intrinsically safer for the investor, and subsidized by the tax system. However, it would be unrealistic for a company to finance itself solely by debt; although less risky for the investor, debt carries a significant risk to the company, and too much could drive it into liquidation. Accordingly, we need to establish how to determine an appropriate capital structure for a company, and be able to derive its overall cost of capital at that capital structure.

We should point out that much of financial theory derives from the work of Modigliani and Miller[5] who, in a seminal paper, demonstrated that capital structure is irrelevant to the value of a company. The value of the company is determined by the net present value of its future cash flows, and they argued that this total value is not changed by changing the sources of funding. If the total value is fixed, then an increase to one provider will be counterbalanced by a decrease to another provider. Modigliani and Miller's work, set in the conditions of a perfect market with restrictive assumptions about tax and other variables, provided an important foundation for financial theory, but in practice most companies and analysts believe that capital structure does have an impact on the cost of capital.

It is a simple matter to determine the weighted average cost of capital (WACC) for a company. The costs of the individual capital components are averaged based on their weights in terms of market value. Working Insight A1.5 illustrates this.

Based on the above calculation, it might seem that the greater the proportion of debt in the capital structure the lower the WACC of the company. However, this is not the case. As stated earlier, too much debt will increase the company's risk to unacceptable levels, and both the lenders and shareholders will demand increased returns to compensate for this risk. Further, at very high levels of debt the company may suffer the loss of its tax shield

4   Hamada, R. S. (1972), 'The Effect of the Firm's Capital Structure on the Systematic Risk of Common Stocks', *Journal of Finance*, 27(2): 435–52.
5   Modigliani, F. and Miller, M. H. (1958), 'The Cost of Capital, Corporation Finance and the Theory of Investment', *American Economic Review*, 48(3): 261–97.

Working Insight A1.5

Determining the weighted average cost of capital

Company W has established (using CAPM or the DGM) that its cost of equity is 11%. Its pre-tax cost of debt is 6%, and tax rates are 30%. The market capitalization of W's equity is £1m, and its debt is valued at £300,000.

The weighted average cost of capital is calculated as:

$$WACC\ [Ke \times E \div (E + D)] + [Kd \times D \div (E + D)]$$

where E and D are the market values of debt and equity respectively.

For Company W

$$WACC = (0.11 \times 1 \div 1.3) + [(0.06 \times 0.7) \times 0.3 \div 1.3]$$
$$= 9.4\%$$

Note: If market values are unavailable, or unrepresentative, the weights can be based on the company's target capital structure if it has one.

(if interest charges turn profits into losses there is no further tax advantage) and business may experience loss of confidence due to bankruptcy risk.

The trend in the WACC as debt levels change is illustrated in Figure A1.3.

In Figure A1.3, at a gearing level of zero the company is totally equity financed, so the average finance cost is the same as the cost of equity. As the company begins to substitute cheap debt for expensive equity, the WACC reduces. However, this substitution, increasing the gearing of the company, makes both debt and equity more expensive. Accordingly, although the debt is still cheaper than the equity, both rise in cost and the curve flattens. At the extreme right of the curve, investors and lenders realize their somewhat precarious position and demand very high returns to compensate for the risk.

As we use the company's cost of capital as a discount factor to apply to its future cash flows, Figure A1.3 can be mirrored in Figure A1.4, which reflects how the value of equity changes with gearing.

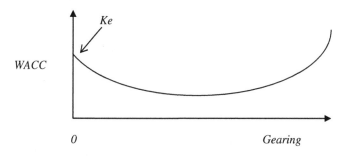

Figure A1.3 The effect of changes in gearing on weighted average cost of capital.

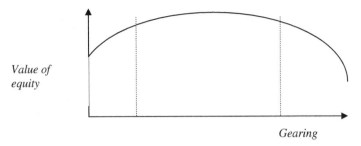

Figure A1.4 The effect of changes in gearing on the value of equity.

It can be seen from Figure A1.4 that ideally a company would wish to position its capital structure somewhere between the dotted lines – minimizing the cost of capital in order to maximize company value. Alas, this theoretical model gives little mathematical indication of where the 'correct' capital structure would lie for any company – hence Chapter 5 of this book, which sets out factors to consider.

The efficient market hypothesis

This one sub-section of this appendix has, itself, been the subject of innumerable books, journal articles, and other academic treatises; consequently only some of the key elements of the continuing debate can even be alluded to. An initial assumption is one already used right at the beginning of the book but in different words. It is much more difficult to find sources of finance (often referred to as financing decisions so as to separate them from the investment decisions made by the company) which by themselves generate positive net present values than it is to find similarly attractive investment opportunities.

Indeed, if capital markets are truly efficient, it should be impossible for financing transactions to generate consistent positive net present values; such a transaction represents a zero sum game so that any gain to one party (the issuer or seller of the financial instrument) must equal a loss to the other party (the purchaser of the same investment).

It is important to be precise about what is meant by the word 'efficient'. This is not intended to mean that asset prices are always 'right' in the sense that expectations are always exactly, but only exactly, fulfilled. It simply means that today's prices incorporate all the information which is currently available to potential buyers and sellers. If this is true then price movements are caused by new information and as the nature of this new information is, by definition, unknown the impact on prices cannot be predicted. Logically this would suggest no correlation between the direction and size of tomorrow's price movement and today's.

The theory of efficient markets was quite neatly broken down into three stages by Roberts in 1967[6] so that interested parties can now select how efficient they think markets are.

- The *weak form* of the efficient market hypothesis is that all historical price information is incorporated into current share prices. This means that price movements are random

---

6 Roberts, H. V. (1967), 'Statistical versus clinical prediction of the stock market', paper presented at Seminar on the Analysis of Security Prices, University of Chicago.

and are not controlled by past trends. Commonly referred to as the 'random walk' theory, this implies that technical analysis of past price movements (such as is done by 'chartists') cannot give investors a competitive advantage.

- The *semi-strong form* argues that all published financial information is already included in the current share price; consequently detailed analysis of a company's published financial statements should not give a consistently superior return.
- The *strong form* of efficient markets says that current prices reflect all the available information which could be known; in other words, even insider and privileged information would not enable investors regularly to make a better than normal return.

These hypotheses have been tested extensively and most research studies have been unable to demonstrate consistently superior performance by investors, which would disprove the theory. However, it is much more difficult to prove such a theory than it is to disprove it, and other researchers have argued that most of the large studies have been flawed, pointing to particular studies which indicate consistent superior performance for certain investor groups (such as managers of the companies) or classes of investment (such as small companies in the 1980s and low P/E multiple large companies). In other words, despite massive research efforts there is not universal agreement on whether financial markets are efficient; even among those who believe they are, there is disagreement as to how efficient.

It is also important to remember that these arguments must be applied to specific financial markets. Just because the intense level of analysis and high degree of competition among research brokers, fund managers, and other professional investors may make the stock markets of New York or London quite efficient, say at the semi-strong level, this does not mean that all the other stock markets around the world automatically function in the same way.

The implications of an efficient market are quite substantial. If future price movements are random, it is fair to say that share prices have no memory; thus talk of the market reaching record levels is irrelevant: share prices merely move to reflect the new information which has become available. Also if markets are efficient so that current prices are always 'as right as they can be', the most logical investment portfolio is the stock market index. No consistent gain can be achieved by active trading, i.e. moving from one share to another, and increased costs will be incurred.

However, another implication for this book is that the theory, even if true, is always applied statistically, i.e. to large samples or to the market 'on average'. Thus it may be impossible to identify superior returns for a significant group of investors but such returns may be achieved by a particular investor. All such specific illustrations of excess return or consistently good financing decisions by particular companies are dismissed by efficient market advocates as 'anecdotal and statistically irrelevant'. (Oh to be such an anecdotal irrelevance!)

Another fundamental conclusion of the efficient market hypothesis is that all financially viable projects (those generating a positive net present value using an appropriately risk-adjusted discount rate) will be able to raise the required funding. This is because investors are intelligent, rational, and objective and can use the available information which is known to the promoters of the project to assess properly its expected risk. Accordingly, their views of the project's financial viability should coincide given this same information which is the essential assumption of an efficient market. Years of experience of trying to raise venture capital for new businesses lead us to doubt the universal truth of this.

Dividend theory

Earlier in this appendix, share values were established as being driven by the present value of future dividends. Yet a fundamental theory of finance argues that dividend policy is irrelevant to share values; an apparent contradiction which requires resolution. Dividends form one part of the total return expected by investors; consequently, if a change in dividend policy is to have no effect on share value this change must cause an equal but opposite change in the expected capital gain component of total return. The only other alternative explanation would be that although the change in dividend policy did alter the return, it also affected the investors' perceived risk by a corresponding amount so that share values were still constant.

The theoretical framework was laid out in 1961 by Modigliani and Miller[7] when they demonstrated that, under the conditions of perfect competition (including no taxes and no transaction costs), dividend policy is irrelevant. Not only do they require the conditions of perfect competition but dividends are defined as being the residual cash-flow item after the company has decided on its investment and borrowing plans. In other words, investment and capital structure decisions are completely independent of the decision of whether or not to pay dividends.

Clearly if dividends are to be increased but investment and borrowing plans are kept constant, there is a financing gap. This financing gap can only be filled by raising equity (issuing new shares). Those new shares must be worth their issue price (under perfect competition, if this were not true no one would buy them) but, in total, this is equal to the total additional dividends being paid. However, the total value of the company has not been altered because its investment policy is still the same, so that the expected present value of its future cash flow has not changed. The value of these new shares can only be produced from a reduction in the value of the existing shares, on which the extra dividend is being declared. The reduction in value of the existing shares is, therefore, exactly equal to the extra dividend being paid to the holders of these existing shares. Hence they should be indifferent as to whether they receive the extra dividend or not; the first alternative condition outlined above has been satisfied. The extra dividends do, of course, provide a cash inflow to the shareholders but, in a perfectly competitive market, they could generate the same cash flow by selling the appropriate proportion of their existing shares in the market. Their remaining fewer shares, which have not been reduced in value by the issue of new shares, will have the same value as the larger number of lower priced shares held following the increased dividend declaration.

The logic of this analysis is self-evident but it does, of course, hinge on some very restrictive assumptions regarding the external market environment and investors' reactions to changes in the mix of their returns. However, the most critical restriction is caused by the total separation of dividend policy from investment and financing policies. Clearly in an environment of no taxes and transaction costs there will be no value change in paying a dividend if the amount of the dividend has to be reinvested, either by the existing investors or by new investors with the same risk perception. This same risk perception is also a key assumption of perfectly competitive and even efficient markets. Indeed this argument of dividend

---

7 Modigliani, F. and Miller, M. H. (1961), 'Dividend Policy, Growth and the Valuation of Shares', *Journal of Business*, 34 (October): 411–33.

irrelevance holds for efficient rather than perfectly competitive markets (the key difference being that perfectly competitive markets require perfect foresight, i.e. no risk regarding future cash flows) as long as the investment and financing policies are kept totally independent of the dividend policy.

This does not contradict the logic of Chapter 5 because an increasing dividend policy was driven by the reducing opportunities for profitable reinvestment during a period of increasing positive cash flow. In other words, the financial strategy is interrelated rather than compartmentalized and abstracted.

There are, as usual, many differing views regarding the relevance of dividend policies to share values in the real world where not only taxes and transaction costs exist but dividends may also provide information signals to investors. Although investors are actually interested in future cash flows, they receive primarily historic accounting-based earnings information from the company. If increased current accounting earnings are followed by an increased dividend payment, investors may become more confident that these earnings are both real, in that they represent current or future increases in cash inflows (i.e. they are not achieved by creative accounting), and are expected by the company's managers to be maintained or further improved in the future. This increased confidence reduces the investors' perceived risk and can therefore increase the share price; but, of course, advocates of the efficient market theory argue that this information is already built into the existing share price. If it is not already incorporated, the counter-argument is that this information flow represents a one-off movement in the share price caused by a change in the dividend payment, hence the actual level of dividends is still irrelevant.

Taxation policies in many economies treat dividends differently to capital gains and hence may create distorted incentives for companies either to pay out or retain profits purely due to the particular taxation environment. Normally dividends are taxed heavily for the average individual investor, thus giving companies an incentive to pay lower dividends. However, in many cases different classes of investors are also taxed differently with some being completely tax exempt, some being more highly taxed on dividends (high-income individuals) and some more highly taxed on capital gains (companies). This further complicates the picture because it makes high dividend-paying stocks less attractive to some investors but more attractive to others.

The good news is that many governments do seem to be trying to reduce some of the distortions but, if capital markets are functioning efficiently, these different groups of investors will buy and sell shares as their attractiveness changes. Thus, as mentioned in Chapter 5, the composition of the shareholder body of a company may change as the financial strategy unfolds; the more predictable this strategy is, the easier it is for the investors to buy and sell at a fair price. Such distortions also encourage companies to find ways around the tax disincentives of paying cash dividends: this may be achieved by offering stock (or scrip) dividends, where instead of cash the investor receives extra free shares in the company, or by repurchasing an equivalent value of existing shares from shareholders. These methods are considered in more detail in Chapter 13.

A very important issue in assessing the theory on dividend policy is to see how companies actually set their dividend policies. Based on the evidence, the most common policies seem to be to pay out a constant proportion of post-tax profits (to give the shareholders their share of the returns achieved by the company), to attempt to maintain, or grow at a steady rate, the value (sometimes in nominal and sometimes in real terms) of the dividend stream, or preferably to do both of these.

Research by Lintner[8] indicated that companies have a target dividend pay-out ratio, but that they never actually pay that full amount. He suggested that companies determine their annual dividend based on the following formula:

$$DIV_1 - DIV_0 = a \times (r \times eps_1) - DIV_0 \qquad (7)$$

where

> DIV_0 is the dividend paid last year
> DIV_1 is the dividend to be paid this year
> eps_1 is the earnings per share this year
> r is the target dividend pay-out ratio
> a is an adjustment factor.

Equation 7 shows how the dividend changes from one year to the next. With a target pay-out ratio of r, the company would pay a dividend of $(r \times eps_1)$. However, it does not pay this full amount, as the directors try to 'smooth' the trend in dividend payments over time. Accordingly, the 'ideal' pay-out is adjusted based on how different it is from the dividend in the previous year. The adjustment factor of 'a' is company specific, and would depend, *inter alia*, on the directors' confidence in the sustainability of future profits.

---

8 Lintner, J. (1956), 'Distribution of Incomes of Corporations among Dividends, Retained Earnings and Taxes', *American Economic Review*, 46(2): 97–113.

Appendix 2

Valuing options
and convertibles

Introduction

In this appendix we explain the different types of option and the terminology used in discussing options, and review the principles behind option valuation. Because convertible financial instruments, as discussed in Chapter 12, include an option component, we then go on to examine the valuation of convertibles.

Options terminology

An option is a contractual right to buy or sell something at a particular time in the future, or during a given future period, at a fixed or specified price. Options can be divided into two basic types; a *call option* gives its owner the future right to buy, while a *put option* provides the future right to sell. The key to the value of options is that ownership conveys the 'right' to do something, i.e. the choice of whether to exercise the option is left to the owner, who can instead choose to do nothing, letting the option lapse.

Sellers of options have to meet their contractual obligations. The seller of a call option must deliver the asset in exchange for the agreed payment (known as the *exercise* or *strike price*) if required to do so by the buyer of the call option. The seller of a put option must pay the agreed price to the buyer of the put option if the asset is offered (put) to the seller.

All options contracts are made for a specified time period but there are two ways in which the contract may be determined. Under what is known as an *American option*, the owner can exercise the option at any time during the period of the contract; whereas under a *European option* exercise is only allowed at the maturity of the contract. An American option is worth more, because of the flexibility, but in most cases, because remaining time to expiry has a positive impact on the value of an option, the differences do not have a major impact on the prices of option contracts. Theoretically, European options are much easier to value.

Valuing options

The factors relevant to option pricing are: the exercise price, the volatility of the underlying asset, the current price of that asset, interest rates, and the time to expiry. Each of these terms will now be explained, together with a discussion of how and why they affect the option value. All of the explanations of value that follow relate to call options, the right to buy an asset. A moment's reflection will tell you how put options – the right to sell – would differ.

The *exercise price*, also known as the strike price is the price that will be paid to exercise the option to acquire the asset. Working Insight A2.1 illustrates this.

Working Insight A2.1

Impact of the exercise price on call option valuation

Shares in Company A are trading at £10 per share.

1   You are offered the option to buy the share two years in the future at £11.
2   You are offered the option to buy the share two years in the future at £15.

Option 1 is obviously more valuable. So, the exercise price is an influence on the value of the call option – the lower it is, the more the option is worth.

Volatility is the variability in the asset price. Its impact on option valuation is illustrated in Working Insight A2.2.

The *asset price* is the current price of the asset over which the option has been granted. Working Insight A2.3 illustrates how this impacts the price of a call option.

Working Insight A2.2

Impact of volatility on call option valuation

Shares in Company B and Company C are both trading at £10 per share, and you are offered an option to buy them at some point in the future at £11.

1   In the past three years Company B shares have traded between £5 and £15.
2   In the past three years Company C shares have traded between £9.90 and £10.10.

The option over Company B is more valuable. There's little point in having an option to buy an asset if the volatility is so low that its price is unlikely ever to reach that level. With Company B, there's a good chance that you'll be able to make a profit on exercise.

On the other hand, the downside volatility is irrelevant: whether the share price falls to £10 or down as far as £1, the option holder will not exercise an out-of-the-money option. Options are a one-way bet.

So, the greater the volatility, the more the option is worth.

Working Insight A2.3

Impact of the asset price on call option valuation

You are offered the option to buy a share in Company D or Company E at £11.

1   The current share price of Company D is £6.
2   The current share price of E is £10.

The option over Company E is more valuable – you have the option to buy a more valuable asset. So, the price of the underlying asset is a factor in valuing the option.

Later in this section we will introduce the Black–Scholes formula for valuing options. However, at this point it is worth noting another piece of terminology relating to option values. The *intrinsic value* is the difference between the asset price and the exercise price. This could be at one of three states. If the intrinsic value is positive (for example, a call option at £10 to buy an asset currently trading at £11) then the option is said to be *in-the-money*. If option price and asset price are the same, the intrinsic value is nil and the option is referred to as *at-the-money*. Finally, the asset price could be lower than the option price – you would not wish to exercise the call option at £10 if you could buy the share for say £8. Such options are known as *out-of-the-money* or colloquially as *underwater*.

Continuing with our discussion of factors that affect value, the level of the *risk-free interest rate* also needs to be taken into account in option valuation, as shown in Working Insight A2.4.

One final factor affects option valuation – the *time to expiry*. This is illustrated in Working Insight A2.5.

Working Insight A2.6 summarizes the five factors affecting call option valuation, and also demonstrates how these same factors affect the value of put options.

Working Insight A2.4

Impact of interest rates on call option valuation

For some unspecified reason, you know that you are going to need to own a share in Company F in two years' time. You have the funds available to buy it now, but if you delay the purchase you will invest the funds in government gilts. You are offered the option to buy a share in Company F for £11 in two years' time.

1   If interest rates are currently 4%, then you could set aside £10.17 now, which will attract interest to compound to £11 in two years' time, when you need to buy the share.
2   If interest rates are currently 10% then you could set aside £9.09 now, and the compounded interest will take this to the required £11 in two years' time.

Accordingly, the interest rate is an important factor in valuing call options – the higher it is, the more the option is worth. (Many people find this counter-intuitive, but it does make sense once you follow the logic through.)

Working Insight A2.5

Impact of time to expiry on call option valuation

Shares in Company G are trading at £10 per share.

1   You are offered the option to buy the share in a month's time at £11.
2   You are offered the option to buy the share in two years' time at £11.

Obviously the two-year option is more valuable – there's more chance that the share price will exceed £11 in two years than in one month. So, time to expiry is another influence on option price: the longer the time to expiry, the greater the value.

One further factor affects the value of options over shares. Shares pay dividends, so the shareholder will receive the dividend, but the owner of a call option over the share will not. So, the higher the dividends a company is paying, the less the value of a call option over its shares (and obviously the opposite applies to a put option).

Option pricing models

These valuation characteristics were brought together in the famous option pricing model developed by Fischer Black and Myron Scholes in 1973.[1] They used some sophisticated mathematics which is deliberately not reproduced in detail here. They produced a continuous time (i.e. using integration calculus rather than discrete binomial models) option pricing valuation model which showed:

Call option value = $[N(d_1) \times P] - [N(d_2) \times EX \times e^{-tr}]$

Where P is the current share price, and $[EX \times e^{-tr}]$ is the present value (PV) of the exercise price, discounted at rate r (the continuously compounded risk-free rate) for period t, the time to maturity of the option.

$$d_1 = \frac{\log\left[P / PV\left(EX\right)\right]}{\sigma\sqrt{t}} + \frac{\sigma\sqrt{t}}{2}$$
$$d_2 = d_1 - \sigma\sqrt{t}$$

σ is the volatility, the annualized standard deviation of daily returns.

N(d) is the probability that a normally distributed random variable x will be less than or equal to $N(d_1)$ is the option delta.

This formula looks fairly mind-blowing and yet its application is relatively straightforward, particularly using tailored computer software. It is even easier when using sets of call option valuation tables; these give the call option value as a percentage of the current asset price.

---

1   Black, F. and Scholes, M. (1973), 'The Pricing of Options and Corporate Liabilities', *Journal of Political Economy*, 81(3): 637–54.

Working Insight A2.6

Factors increasing option valuation

	Call options	*Put options*
Exercise price	Lower	Higher
Volatility	Higher	Higher
Asset price	Higher	Lower
Interest rates	Higher	Lower
Time to expiry	Longer	*

*For a put option, the effect of time is slightly complicated. Although option value increases with time to expiry, the present value of the sum to be received decreases with time, so the net result is uncertain.

Not surprisingly given the earlier discussions, the tables utilize two factors; the time value represented by $\sigma\sqrt{t}$ and the asset value ratio, which is the current asset value divided by the present value of the option exercise price.

The problem with the Black–Scholes formula is not that it is complicated but that it is, as with many financial formulae, based on a series of restrictive assumptions. It represents the value of a simple call option on an asset which produces no income stream during the life of the option (such as a non-dividend paying share in an equity-financed company). However, many real-life options are actually complex options on options; for example, a share in a leveraged company could be described as a call option on the underlying assets and future cash flows of the business, so that an option on a share is really an option on an option. The Black–Scholes model does not handle complex options.

A further complication is that the standard deviation of the return on the asset can itself change over time and can only really be measured historically, when it is the *expected* future volatility that is required. Empirically it has been found that this model tends to price options wrongly where the exercise price is a long way away (either way) from the current asset price, undervaluing deep in-the-money options and overvaluing deep out-of-the-money options.

(It should be noted that another model was subsequently developed in 1979 by Cox, Ross, and Rubinstein[2] and independently by Rendleman and Bartter,[3] which encompasses the Black–Scholes model as a particular continuous-time case. This is known as the binomial option pricing model, not surprisingly because it uses multi-period binomial distributions to drive the option valuation.)

Structuring and valuing convertibles

As explained in Chapter 12, convertibles are financial instruments that start out as debt (or preference shares) but give the holder the option to convert into ordinary shares of the company.

---

2   Cox, J., Ross, S., and Rubinstein, M. (1979), 'Option Pricing: A Simplified Approach', *Journal of Financial Economics*, September: 229–63.
3   Rendleman, R. J. Jr. and Bartter, B. J. (1979), 'Two-State Option Pricing', *Journal of Finance*, 34: 1093–1110.

Working Insight A2.7

COSMIC plc – using a convertible

COSMIC plc wants to raise £100m in long-term financing for a project which will take some time to become significantly profitable and cash positive. Accordingly, the company prefers not to raise either debt or equity and is considering using a convertible.

The current post-tax cost of debt for COSMIC is 6% compared to the risk-free rate of interest at 4%. At present COSMIC has a total of 1,000m issued shares with a market price of 50p per share. Its forthcoming results are expected to show eps of 4p and dividends per share of 1p; in addition to the current dividend yield it is known that shareholders expect capital growth of 12% p.a.

Using Gordon's dividend growth model, the company's cost of equity capital can be calculated as 14% as follows:

$$Ke = (D_1 \div P) + g$$
$$= 1p \div 50p + 12\%$$
$$= 14\%$$

Because of this, we value convertibles based on both their bond value and their option value. In this section we show how the variables of yield and potential capital gain can be combined to produce a convertible bond that is attractive to the markets.

In Working Insight A2.7 we set out the parameters for COSMIC plc, a growth company which seeks to raise £100 million using convertible debt.

It can be seen from Working Insight A2.7 that the majority of the investors' expected return in COSMIC plc comes from the capital growth of 12 per cent p.a. This implies that current shareholders expect the price of the shares to have doubled to 100p in six years' time ($1.12^6 = 2$), provided that the current 75 per cent retention policy is maintained during this period.

The future expected share price is important as it determines, from the existing shareholders' perspective, the level at which the conversion price should be set. Any conversion price below 100p in six years' time should represent an expected gain to the option holder, because that level of increase in value is already effectively expected by current investors.

The company is considering issuing a six-year convertible and the first alternative is to issue £100 million of a 7 per cent six-year convertible unsecured loan stock. At the end of the six-year period, the loan stock can either be redeemed at par or it can be converted into ordinary shares at a price per share of 85p; i.e. a total of 117.65 million new shares will be issued.

The company has an effective tax rate of 30 per cent which is the same as its major investors, so that for both parties the post-tax return on the debt portion of the convertible is 4.9 per cent. However, from Working Insight A2.7 we know that investors require a 6 per cent yield after tax on debt issued by COSMIC plc. This enables the present value of the debt component to be valued by applying this rate of discount to the expected cash flows from the potentially redeemable bond, as is done in Working Insight A2.8.

From Working Insight A2.8 we can see that the bond portion of the convertible should be valued by the market at £94.6 million. However, the company wishes to raise £100 million.

Working Insight A2.8

Valuing the bond part of a convertible

The redeemable bond portion is simply valued at the present value of its expected future cash flows, assuming redemption at maturity, but using the appropriate full cost of debt as the discount rate rather than the yield actually offered on the bond. For COSMIC plc this gives:

$K_d = 6\%$

Year	Cash flow	Discount factor	Present value
1–6	£4.9m	4.917	£24.1m
6	£100m	0.705	£70.5m
		Net present value	£94.6m

Thus the conversion option must be designed to have a present value of at least £5.4 million in order to fill the gap.

The equity option can be valued by the investors in a number of different ways but its exercise has an opportunity cost of £100 million in total because, by exercising their conversion option, the investors forgo their right to redeem their bonds at par. Thus the option will not be exercised unless the share price increases above 85p. Remember, however, that the share price is expected to increase to 100p during this period; this would leave the convertible holder with a capital gain upon conversion into equity.

Technically, the Black–Scholes option pricing formula does not work properly for options on options, which is what a convertible is (remember that a share represents a call option on the assets of the company), particularly when dividends are paid on the shares. However, developments and variations of the formula are widely used in financial markets so that this practice will be followed here. The option valuation can be simplified by employing the key value drivers and call option valuation tables; this requires calculating the intrinsic value of the option and the time value.

The time value of the option depends on the time to maturity (note that this is a simple European option as it can only be exercised at maturity) and the expected volatility of the share price during the option period. We will assume that the standard deviation of the return of COSMIC plc is 0.25. Based on these parameters, the calculation of the option value is shown in Working Insight A2.9. This demonstrates that the option value should have a present value of £8.1 million which can be added to the bond's present value of £94.6 million.

If we add the £8.1m option value calculated in Working Insight A2.9 to the £94.6m bond value shown in Working Insight A2.8, we arrive at a total value for the convertible of £102.7 million. In practice, this would enable the company to raise its required £100 million and pay the expenses of the issue.

By now, it should be clear that in corporate finance there are, at best, usually only zero-sum games, so where does the extra value of 2.7 million come from?

Looked at from the current investors' point of view there is a saving created by the reduced rate of interest for the six-year life of the bond element of the convertible; this has a

---

Working Insight A2.9

Valuing the option part of a convertible

Time value

Standard deviation (σ) of COSMIC plc	= 0.25 p.a.
Time to maturity	= 6 years
Time value factor	$= \sigma\sqrt{t}$
	$= 0.25 \times \sqrt{6}$
	= 0.61

Intrinsic value

Risk-free rate of interest	= 4%
Present value of exercise price	$= 85p \div (1.04)^6$
	= 67.18
Asset value ratio (current price ÷ PV of exercise price)	= 50 ÷ 67.18
	= 74.4%

Using the call option tables at the end of this book, the closest we can come to these parameters is an asset value ratio of 0.75 and $\sqrt{t}$ of 0.6, which gives a factor of 13.8%.

Thus the value of each option is 13.8% of the current	= 13.8% × 50p
share price	= 6.9p

In total, 117.65m options are created at an exercise price of 85p per share.

The present value of these options is	= 117.65m × 6.9p
	= £8.1m

---

present value of £5.4 million. Therefore the current investor can afford to give away an equity option with a present value of £5.4 million and be made no worse off as a result of this financing structure.

In order to keep the rational convertible investor happy, this £5.4m present value of the option has to increase by at least 14 per cent per annum (the full cost of equity must be used because no dividends are received on the option). As shown in Working Insight A2.10, this gives a required Year 6 value of £11.9 million for the equity option. This can be added to the redemption value of the bond which is the convertible investor's opportunity cost, i.e. if the value of the equity offered at the time of conversion is less than £100 million, redemption will take place in preference to conversion.

From the shareholders' perspective, this can all be achieved by offering to issue 111.9 million new shares in Year 6, which implies a conversion exercise price of 89.4p per share (Working Insight A2.10). This price would leave current investors indifferent, and should make the convertible bond just attractive to the new investor.

If more attractive investment terms than 89.4p are offered, the transaction becomes less than break-even from the current shareholders' viewpoint unless the issue generates greater

Working Insight A2.10

Break-even equity option value – viewed from existing shareholders' perspective

Saving from lower interest rate on bond portion of convertible – present value of £5.4m. This present value can be given away in the equity option without making current shareholders worse off; it also keeps convertible holders at break-even.

However, the option will be exercised in Year 6 so, in order to have a present value of £5.4m, it should have a Year 6 expected value of £5.4m × $(1.14)^6$ or £11.9m.

(*Note*: The expected return on options may be slightly higher than the normal cost of equity to allow for the higher risk perception of investors in the option.)

Desired equity total value at end of Year 6	
Redemption value of bond	£100.0m
Expected value of equity option	£11.9m
Equity value to be issued	£111.9m

Current shareholders expect share price to be 100p in Year 6. So, from their perspective, £111.9m of equity value in Year 6 can be satisfied by offering to issue 111.9m shares. This gives an option exercise price of

£100m ÷ 111.9m = 89.4p

from the perspective of the convertible holder.

Note: Strictly speaking, existing shareholders could still be marginally worse off after granting this option; they want the share price after the option exercise to be kept at the 100p which they are currently expecting in Year 6. Allowing 111.9m new shares to be issued at 89.4p would reduce the average share price below this desired level; however, in an efficient market the earlier saving in financing costs should have boosted share prices above their expected levels.

proceeds. In other words the £2.7 million in the first structure has been achieved at the expense of existing shareholders, as the equity conversion option has been made more attractive (85p rather than 89.4p) but only £100 million has been received by the company. However, this is not unreasonable – the shareholders always end up paying the effective cost of new fund raising.

The basic valuation model has made a number of simplifying assumptions, several of which have been mentioned in the above discussion. However, one important issue has not yet been considered. The equity conversion option, if exercised, automatically will lead to an increase in the total issued shares of the company in five years' time, but no new funding will be made available to the company at that time. It has been assumed that the exercise of the equity option does not lead to a decline in the value of all the existing shares; such a decline would also decrease the capital gain achieved by the conversion. If the financial market can properly value the convertible (through its component parts) prior to its conversion, there should be no such change – but this is a big 'if'. Remember, the valuation of traded equity options is different to the situation of a convertible, as the exercise of a traded option does not result in an increase in the total number of shares in existence; the shares required under the option contract are either already owned or must be bought in the market.

Another way to value convertibles

In the above discussion, the convertible in the example was kept very simple and restrictive; a six-year fixed term with the exercise of the conversion option only being allowed at the end of the term. In practice companies issuing convertibles like to offer potential investors more alternatives, as they see this as making the investment more attractive. One way of making any investment involving an option more attractive is to extend the life of the option: for example, a fifteen-year convertible might appear better than a six-year time period. However, the other part of the convertible is a bond which carries a below-market rate of interest; thus the longer the life of the bond, the lower its present value.

Normally it is uneconomic for the company to increase the value of the option at the expense of an equal decline in the bond value, due to the different effective costs of capital used by investors to value each element. Therefore companies are constantly looking for ways to increase the value of the option without an offsetting decline in the value of the bond, or vice versa. One common way of increasing investor flexibility is to allow conversion of the bond into equity within the life of the convertible; an American option, of course, has this ability to exercise the option at any time already built in. In many convertible issues, conversion is allowed on a specified date each year or for a stated number of years prior to the expiry of the convertible when, if conversion has not been requested, redemption takes place.

In theory for a normal option, this extra flexibility should have no real impact because an unexpired option always has a time value; thus it should be financially more attractive to sell the option rather than to exercise it before maturity date. However, convertibles have a complication because shares can receive a dividend yield, while the unexercised options do not. This means that there may be an opportunity cost associated with not exercising the option within its lifetime. There is an offsetting cost associated with exercising the option because the yield on the convertible bond or preference share will be lost once the conversion option is exercised.

This trade-off has led to the development of a different method of valuing certain convertibles, which is commonly described as the 'dividend cross-over model'. The model basically assumes that, as long as the market price of the share is above the exercise price of the option, conversion will take place when the opportunity cost of the foregone dividend exceeds the yield on the bond or preference share. Thus the value of the convertible can be calculated as the present value of the equivalent equity investment made now, plus differential cash flows received in this period up to conversion, plus the value of the put redemption option should conversion never take place.

This is at first sight a complex issue, but can be made much clearer using an example. The case of COSMIC plc is not appropriate to this situation, as it would not be expected that the dividend in that high growth company would exceed the interest yield during its six-year life. Accordingly a new, more appropriate example is given in Working Insight A2.11.

The logic of the cross-over valuation model is to consider the investment in the convertible as an investment in a deferred equity, in that the investor could, as an alternative investment, buy an equivalent number of shares today. If the shares are bought now, the investors receive

Working Insight A2.11

Example of use of a dividend cross-over model

The current share price of Slowing Growth Inc. is 100p. Its expected dividend yield is 4%; the dividend and capital value are expected to grow at 8% per annum. The company has recently issued a 10-year convertible redeemable preference share which has a 5% fixed dividend yield and the right to convert into ordinary shares at any time at a price of 125p per share.

Thus £100 of convertible preference shares can convert into 80 ordinary shares. The company wishes to use a dividend cross-over model to value these convertible preference shares. The full company rate for debt is 6% and for equity 12%. (Tax is ignored in this example.)

Assuming conversion of £100 of convertibles into 80 shares, the equivalent alternative equity investment today is to buy 80 shares (i.e. an investment of £80).

		Equivalent 80 shares investment			*£100 nominal convertible investment*		
Year	Expected dividend payment per share	Dividend on 80 shares	Discount factor @ 12%	Present value	Preference dividend	Discount factor @ 6%	Present value
1	4.0p	320p	.893	285.7p	500p	.943	471.7p
2	4.3p	346p	.797	275.5p	500p	.890	445.0p
3	4.7p	373p	.712	265.7p	500p	.840	419.8p
4	5.0p	403p	.636	256.2p	500p	.792	396.0p
5	5.4p	435p	.567	247.0p	500p	.747	373.6p
6	5.9p	470p	.507	238.2p	500p	.705	352.5p
7*	6.3p	*508p	N/A	N/A	*500p	N/A	N/A
8	6.9p	548p	N/A	N/A	500p	N/A	N/A
9	7.4p	592p	N/A	N/A	500p	N/A	N/A
10	8.0p	640p	N/A	N/A	500p	N/A	N/A
		Total present value		1,568.3p	Total present value		2,458.7p

Shows where conversion becomes logical.

Difference in present value	£8.90
Plus equivalent investment cost at present value	£80.00
	£88.90
Deemed minimum value of redemption put option (balancing figure)	£11.10
Total value of convertibles	£100.00

dividends and make capital gains from 100p (or make losses if the value falls). These dividends are discretionary and should therefore be discounted to their present values using the equity cost of capital. Once these equity dividends exceed the convertible preference yield, which is fixed, investors will exercise their right to convert (the option should be 'in-the-money' from Year 3 onwards using an 8 per cent p.a. rate of capital growth); this conversion is expected to occur at the end of Year 6. After conversion, the two investments are exactly the same so there is no need to continue the comparison.

During the life of the convertible, the fixed preference dividend would be received and its present value can be assessed using the debt-based rate of discount (6 per cent) due to its non-discretionary nature. The convertible also has the added attraction that the bond can be redeemed at the end of its ten-year life if the share price has not risen above 125p. This shows how this method of valuation looks at the convertible in the opposite way to the earlier method; the convertible is regarded as being equivalent to buying the shares today and having a put option on the bond back to the company.

Glossary of selected financial terms

A

Agency theory   Theory which considers the divergence of goals between shareholders (principals of the company) and directors (their agents, who run the company).

Anchoring   Behavioural bias whereby we estimate numbers based on a stimulus number perceived earlier, whether or not this is relevant.

Annuity   Receipt or payment of the same sum of money each year for a given number of years.

Anti-dilution clause   Clause in a venture capital term sheet which provides that the VC investor cannot be diluted by a *down-round*.

B

Basis point   0.01 per cent.

Beta   Measure of volatility compared to the market. The equity beta is the beta of the company's share. The asset beta reflects the business risk.

Bond   Long-term negotiable debt.

Bonus issue   Issue of shares to existing shareholders made by capitalizing retained profits. No cash is transferred, and shareholders end up holding the same proportions of the company as they did before the issue.

Business angel   An individual investing venture capital.

Business risk   Risks related to the volatility of operating results, before financing.

Buy-back   Also known as a share repurchase, this is where the company acquires its own shares.

C

CAPM (Capital Asset Pricing Model)   Method of calculating a company's cost of equity by using the risk-free rate, the company's beta and the market premium.

Carried interest   A way of rewarding private equity and venture capital general partners, entitling them to a percentage of the investment returns above a certain level.

Carve-out   Where a listed company restructures by floating part of a subsidiary and retaining the rest.

Convertible   Financial instrument that starts as a debt or preference security, but gives the holder an option to convert into ordinary shares instead of being repaid.

Corporate venturing   Venture capital investment done by a commercial company rather than an investment fund, generally with a strategic business aim.

Cost of capital   An average of a company's costs of equity and debt (and other forms of finance such as preference shares), weighted in accordance with their relative values in the capital structure.

Coupon   Stated yield of a debt, calculated based on its nominal value.

Covenant   Clause in a loan agreement giving the lender the right to call in the loan if conditions are breached.

D

Delisting   Opposite of flotation – when a listed company goes private.

Depository Receipt   Certificate representing the rights to share ownership, but not the ownership itself. An American Depository Receipt (ADR) represents a non-US company and is traded in the USA; a Global Depository Receipt (GDR) is traded outside the USA, representing any company trading not in its home exchange country.

Discounted cash flow (DCF)   A way of evaluating a stream of future cash flows as if they all took place immediately – it allows for the fact that money in the future is worth less than money now.

Discount rate   Rate used to discount future cash flows. Often a company's cost of capital, suitably risk-adjusted, used as the discount rate.

Dividend growth model (DGM) Method of calculating a company's cost of equity capital by taking the dividend yield and the expected future growth in dividends.

Down-round   Where later venture capital investments are done at a lower price than earlier investments, because the company has lost value.

Due diligence   Investigatory work undertaken by a prospective acquirer or lender prior to an investment being made.

E

Earn-out   Mechanism for rewarding the vendor of a business with additional consideration if the acquired business meets stated targets in the initial period after the sale.

EBIT, EBITDA   Earnings Before Interest and Tax [and Depreciation and Amortization]. EBIT is the operating profit of the business, before finance charges. Depreciation and amortization are non-cash expenses, based on a company's accounting policies, and EBITDA is often used as a proxy for cash profit.

EBIT multiple   Enterprise value divided by the EBIT. The EBIT multiple is used in valuation on multiples.

Economic profit   Surplus earned after deducting all expenses, including the cost of capital.

Enterprise value   Total value of a company, represented by the market values of its debt and equity (and other forms of finance).

Envy ratio   In a leveraged transaction, the ratio of the private equity capitalization to the management's capitalization of the company. Capitalizations are calculated as the amount invested by each party, divided by their percentage share of the equity.

Eps (earnings per share)   Profits available to the ordinary shareholders divided by the number of ordinary shares outstanding. If calculated using the number of shares that could ultimately be issued, it is known as diluted eps.

Exercise price   Price at which an option may be exercised. Also known as the strike price.

F

Financial risk   Risks related to a company's financial structure. (See *gearing*.)

Flotation   Listing a company on a public stock market. Also known as an *Initial Public Offering* (IPO).

Fundamental value   Value of a share calculated based on its fundamentals: projected cash flows discounted at a risk-adjusted cost of capital.

G

GAAP (Generally Accepted Accounting Principles)   Accepted set of rules and standards for preparing financial statements in the USA.

Gearing   Relationship between a company's debt and equity. Also known as Leverage.

H

High-yield debt   Also known as 'junk bonds', this is debt which is rated below investment grade.

I

IFRS (International Financial Reporting Standards)   Accepted set of rules and standards for preparing financial statements in many countries around the world.

Intrinsic value Difference between an option's exercise price and the price of the underlying security. Could be 'in-the-money', 'at-the-money', or 'out-of-the-money' depending on whether the exercise price is below, the same as, or above the asset price.

IPO (Initial Public Offering)   Another term for flotation.

IRR (internal rate of return)   Discount rate which when applied to all of the cash flows to be generated by a project results in a net present value of zero. If the IRR exceeds the company's criterion discount rate, this is an indication that the company is returning greater than its target rate.

J

Junk bonds   High-yield bonds, with a credit rating lower than BBB– (Standard & Poor's rating) or Baa (Moody's rating).

L

LBO (leveraged buyout)   Private equity acquisition of a company, financed with a significant element of debt.

Leverage   Gearing.

LIBOR (London Inter Bank Offered Rate)   Benchmark rate used in determining corporate interest rates.

Liquidation preference   Mechanism whereby venture capital investors can obtain repayment of their initial investment (or a multiple thereof) in precedence to other investors.

M

Market capitalization   The market value of a company's equity, calculated as the current share price multiplied by the number of shares outstanding.

MBO (management buyout)   Transaction in which the company's management acquire the company, often financed by private equity.

N

Nominal   Including inflation.

NPV (net present value)   Sum of the present values of all positive and negative cash flows associated with a project. A positive NPV implies that the project is making a return in excess of the discount rate used, and so is worth undertaking.

O

Operating leverage   Ratio of fixed costs to total costs in a business.

Option The right, but not the obligation, to do something. A *call option* gives the holder the right to buy a given security at an agreed price at a specific time; a *put option* gives the right to sell. Options which have a specific date on which they can be exercised are known as *European options*; those which can be exercised over a given period are known as *American options*.

P

Pay-out ratio Dividend paid to ordinary shareholders as a proportion of the profits available for ordinary shareholders. (Pay-out ratio = 1 − retention ratio.)

P/E Price/earnings ratio is the company's current share price divided by its earnings per share. If calculated on past earnings it is the *historic* P/E; on anticipated earnings it is the *prospective* P/E.

Perpetuity Receipt or payment of the same sum every year for ever.

Perpetuity value of a share Value justified by the current level of earnings per share.

Poison pill Specific bid defence tactic which makes the target company less attractive to the bidder.

Post-money valuation Value of a venture capital-backed company after the venture capital investment has been made.

Pre-emption rights Where a company issuing new shares is obliged to offer those shares first to the existing shareholders (see *rights issue*).

Preference gearing Use of preference shares in a private equity transaction in order to increase management's proportion of the equity.

Pre-money valuation Value of a venture capital-based company just before the venture capital investment has been made. Generally calculated as the *post-money valuation* less the sum invested.

Present value Equivalent in today's money of a sum due to be paid or received in the future. Calculated by discounting, generally at the cost of capital.

PVGO (present value of growth opportunities) Amount of the current share price that is not supported by existing earnings.

R

Ratchet A means to increase or decrease management's proportion of the equity in a private equity transaction based on the achievement of certain results.

Real Excluding inflation; at constant prices.

Retention ratio The retained profits of a company as a proportion of the profits earned for ordinary shareholders. (Retention ratio = 1 − pay-out ratio.)

Return on equity (RoE) Profits available for ordinary shareholders divided by the company's equity.

Return on investment Profits before financing charges (and often before tax) divided by the total funds (debt and equity) invested in the business.

Rights issue An issue of shares to existing shareholders, generally at a price below current market value.

Risk Volatility in the expected return.

S

Securitization Process of converting assets or future cash flows into a marketable security.

Security (1) A financial instrument.

Security (2) Lenders can gain security by taking a charge over assets such that the assets can be used to repay their loan if the company fails.

Spin-off   Company reconstruction whereby the shares in a subsidiary business are distributed to the shareholders of the holding company.

Steady state   A company in steady state is neither growing nor contracting. This is a theoretical construct, unlikely ever to occur in practice.

T

Tax shield   Reduction in the company's tax burden due to debt interest being tax-deductible. Calculated as the interest charge multiplied by the tax rate.

Term sheet   Document setting out the terms of a venture capital deal, from which the final deal documentation will be derived.

Total shareholder return (TSR)   Percentage return to shareholders in a period based on the dividends received and the increase in the share price over the period.

U

Underwriting   Arrangement whereby a financial services company agrees to acquire the shares in a listing if they are not taken up by other shareholders.

Up-round   Where later venture capital investments are done at a higher price than earlier investments, because the company has gained in value.

V

Value driver   The seven value drivers suggested by Alfred Rappaport are: increase sales growth; increase operating profit margin; decrease cash tax rate; decrease fixed assets as a percentage of sales; decrease working capital as a percentage of sales; increase timescale of competitive advantage; decrease cost of capital.

Value multiple   Market value of a share divided by its fundamental value.

W

WACC (weighted average cost of capital)   See *Cost of Capital*.

Y

Yield   Payment received from an investment which do not reducing the capital balance.

Discount table: present value of £1

Discount rate

Years	1%	2%	4%	5%	6%	8%	10%	12%	14%	15%	16%	18%	20%	22%	24%	25%	26%	28%	30%	35%	40%
1	0.990	0.980	0.962	0.952	0.943	0.926	0.909	0.893	0.877	0.870	0.862	0.847	0.833	0.820	0.806	0.800	0.794	0.781	0.769	0.741	0.714
2	0.980	0.961	0.925	0.907	0.890	0.857	0.826	0.797	0.769	0.756	0.743	0.718	0.694	0.672	0.650	0.640	0.630	0.610	0.592	0.549	0.510
3	0.971	0.942	0.889	0.864	0.840	0.794	0.751	0.712	0.675	0.658	0.641	0.609	0.579	0.551	0.524	0.512	0.500	0.477	0.455	0.406	0.364
4	0.961	0.924	0.855	0.823	0.792	0.735	0.683	0.636	0.592	0.572	0.552	0.516	0.482	0.451	0.423	0.410	0.397	0.373	0.350	0.301	0.260
5	0.951	0.906	0.822	0.784	0.747	0.681	0.621	0.567	0.519	0.497	0.476	0.437	0.402	0.370	0.341	0.328	0.315	0.291	0.269	0.223	0.186
6	0.942	0.888	0.790	0.746	0.705	0.630	0.564	0.507	0.456	0.432	0.410	0.370	0.335	0.303	0.275	0.262	0.250	0.227	0.207	0.165	0.133
7	0.933	0.871	0.760	0.711	0.665	0.583	0.513	0.452	0.400	0.376	0.354	0.314	0.279	0.249	0.222	0.210	0.198	0.178	0.159	0.122	0.095
8	0.923	0.853	0.731	0.677	0.627	0.540	0.467	0.404	0.351	0.327	0.305	0.266	0.233	0.204	0.179	0.168	0.157	0.139	0.123	0.091	0.068
9	0.914	0.837	0.703	0.645	0.592	0.500	0.424	0.361	0.308	0.284	0.263	0.225	0.194	0.167	0.144	0.134	0.125	0.108	0.094	0.067	0.048
10	0.905	0.820	0.676	0.614	0.558	0.463	0.386	0.322	0.270	0.247	0.227	0.191	0.162	0.137	0.116	0.107	0.099	0.085	0.073	0.050	0.035
11	0.896	0.804	0.650	0.585	0.527	0.429	0.350	0.287	0.237	0.215	0.195	0.162	0.135	0.112	0.094	0.086	0.079	0.066	0.056	0.037	0.025
12	0.887	0.788	0.625	0.557	0.497	0.397	0.319	0.257	0.208	0.187	0.168	0.137	0.112	0.092	0.076	0.069	0.062	0.052	0.043	0.027	0.018
13	0.879	0.773	0.601	0.530	0.469	0.368	0.290	0.229	0.182	0.163	0.145	0.116	0.093	0.075	0.061	0.055	0.050	0.040	0.033	0.020	0.013
14	0.870	0.758	0.577	0.505	0.442	0.340	0.263	0.205	0.160	0.141	0.125	0.099	0.078	0.062	0.049	0.044	0.039	0.032	0.025	0.015	0.009
15	0.861	0.743	0.555	0.481	0.417	0.315	0.239	0.183	0.140	0.123	0.108	0.084	0.065	0.051	0.040	0.035	0.031	0.025	0.020	0.011	0.006
16	0.853	0.728	0.534	0.458	0.394	0.292	0.218	0.163	0.123	0.107	0.093	0.071	0.054	0.042	0.032	0.028	0.025	0.019	0.015	0.008	0.005
17	0.844	0.714	0.513	0.436	0.371	0.270	0.198	0.146	0.108	0.093	0.080	0.060	0.045	0.034	0.026	0.023	0.020	0.015	0.012	0.006	0.003
18	0.836	0.700	0.494	0.416	0.350	0.250	0.180	0.130	0.095	0.081	0.069	0.051	0.038	0.028	0.021	0.018	0.016	0.012	0.009	0.005	0.002
19	0.828	0.686	0.475	0.396	0.331	0.232	0.164	0.116	0.083	0.070	0.060	0.043	0.031	0.023	0.017	0.014	0.012	0.009	0.007	0.003	0.002
20	0.820	0.673	0.456	0.377	0.312	0.215	0.149	0.104	0.073	0.061	0.051	0.037	0.026	0.019	0.014	0.012	0.010	0.007	0.005	0.002	0.001
21	0.811	0.660	0.439	0.359	0.294	0.199	0.135	0.093	0.064	0.053	0.044	0.031	0.022	0.015	0.011	0.009	0.008	0.006	0.004	0.002	0.001
22	0.803	0.647	0.422	0.342	0.278	0.184	0.123	0.083	0.056	0.046	0.038	0.026	0.018	0.013	0.009	0.007	0.006	0.004	0.003	0.001	0.001
23	0.795	0.634	0.406	0.326	0.262	0.170	0.112	0.074	0.049	0.040	0.033	0.022	0.015	0.010	0.007	0.006	0.005	0.003	0.002	0.001	
24	0.788	0.622	0.390	0.310	0.247	0.158	0.102	0.066	0.043	0.035	0.028	0.019	0.013	0.008	0.006	0.005	0.004	0.003	0.002	0.001	
25	0.780	0.610	0.375	0.295	0.233	0.146	0.092	0.059	0.038	0.030	0.024	0.016	0.010	0.007	0.005	0.004	0.003	0.002	0.001	0.001	
26	0.772	0.598	0.361	0.281	0.220	0.135	0.084	0.053	0.033	0.026	0.021	0.014	0.009	0.006	0.004	0.003	0.002	0.002	0.001	0.001	
27	0.764	0.586	0.347	0.268	0.207	0.125	0.076	0.047	0.029	0.023	0.018	0.011	0.007	0.005	0.003	0.002	0.002	0.001	0.001	0.001	
28	0.757	0.574	0.333	0.255	0.196	0.116	0.069	0.042	0.026	0.020	0.016	0.010	0.006	0.004	0.002	0.002	0.001	0.001	0.001		
29	0.749	0.563	0.321	0.243	0.185	0.107	0.063	0.037	0.022	0.017	0.014	0.008	0.005	0.003	0.002	0.002	0.001	0.001	0.001		
30	0.742	0.552	0.308	0.231	0.174	0.099	0.057	0.033	0.020	0.015	0.012	0.007	0.004	0.003	0.002	0.002	0.001	0.001	0.001		
35	0.706	0.500	0.253	0.181	0.130	0.068	0.036	0.019	0.010	0.008	0.006	0.003	0.002	0.001	0.001	0.001	0.001				
40	0.672	0.453	0.208	0.142	0.097	0.046	0.022	0.011	0.005	0.004	0.003	0.001	0.001								
45	0.639	0.410	0.171	0.111	0.073	0.031	0.014	0.006	0.003	0.002	0.001	0.001	0.001								
50	0.608	0.372	0.141	0.087	0.054	0.021	0.009	0.003	0.001	0.001	0.001										

Discount table: present value of £1 received annually for *N* years

Discount rate

Years	1%	2%	4%	5%	6%	8%	10%	12%	14%	15%	16%	18%	20%	22%	24%	25%	26%	28%	30%	35%	40%
1	0.990	0.980	0.962	0.952	0.943	0.926	0.909	0.893	0.877	0.870	0.862	0.847	0.833	0.820	0.806	0.800	0.794	0.781	0.769	0.741	0.714
2	1.970	1.942	1.886	1.859	1.833	1.783	1.736	1.690	1.647	1.626	1.605	1.566	1.528	1.492	1.457	1.440	1.424	1.392	1.361	1.289	1.224
3	2.941	2.884	2.775	2.723	2.673	2.577	2.487	2.402	2.322	2.283	2.246	2.174	2.106	2.042	1.981	1.952	1.923	1.868	1.816	1.696	1.589
4	3.902	3.808	3.630	3.546	3.465	3.312	3.170	3.037	2.914	2.855	2.798	2.690	2.589	2.494	2.404	2.362	2.320	2.241	2.166	1.997	1.849
5	4.853	4.713	4.452	4.329	4.212	3.993	3.791	3.605	3.433	3.352	3.274	3.127	2.991	2.864	2.745	2.689	2.635	2.532	2.436	2.220	2.035
6	5.795	5.601	5.242	5.076	4.917	4.623	4.355	4.111	3.889	3.784	3.685	3.498	3.326	3.167	3.020	2.951	2.885	2.759	2.643	2.385	2.168
7	6.728	6.472	6.002	5.786	5.582	5.206	4.868	4.564	4.288	4.160	4.039	3.812	3.605	3.416	3.242	3.161	3.083	2.937	2.802	2.508	2.263
8	7.652	7.325	6.733	6.463	6.210	5.747	5.335	4.968	4.639	4.487	4.344	4.078	3.837	3.619	3.421	3.329	3.241	3.076	2.925	2.598	2.331
9	8.566	8.162	7.435	7.108	6.802	6.247	5.759	5.328	4.946	4.772	4.607	4.303	4.031	3.786	3.566	3.463	3.366	3.184	3.019	2.665	2.379
10	9.471	8.983	8.111	7.722	7.360	6.710	6.145	5.650	5.216	5.019	4.833	4.494	4.192	3.923	3.682	3.571	3.465	3.269	3.092	2.715	2.414
11	10.368	9.787	8.760	8.306	7.887	7.139	6.495	5.938	5.453	5.234	5.029	4.656	4.327	4.035	3.776	3.656	3.544	3.335	3.147	2.752	2.438
12	11.255	10.575	9.385	8.863	8.384	7.536	6.814	6.194	5.660	5.421	5.197	4.793	4.439	4.127	3.851	3.725	3.606	3.387	3.190	2.779	2.456
13	12.134	11.348	9.986	9.394	8.853	7.904	7.103	6.424	5.842	5.583	5.342	4.910	4.533	4.203	3.912	3.780	3.656	3.427	3.223	2.799	2.468
14	13.004	12.106	10.563	9.899	9.295	8.244	7.367	6.628	6.002	5.724	5.468	5.008	4.611	4.265	3.962	3.824	3.695	3.459	3.249	2.814	2.477
15	13.865	12.849	11.118	10.380	9.712	8.559	7.606	6.811	6.142	5.847	5.575	5.092	4.675	4.315	4.001	3.859	3.726	3.483	3.268	2.825	2.484
16	14.718	13.578	11.652	10.838	10.106	8.851	7.824	6.974	6.265	5.954	5.669	5.162	4.730	4.357	4.033	3.887	3.751	3.503	3.283	2.834	2.489
17	15.562	14.292	12.166	11.274	10.477	9.122	8.022	7.120	6.373	6.047	5.749	5.222	4.775	4.391	4.059	3.910	3.771	3.518	3.295	2.840	2.492
18	16.398	14.992	12.659	11.690	10.828	9.372	8.201	7.250	6.467	6.128	5.818	5.273	4.812	4.419	4.080	3.928	3.786	3.529	3.304	2.844	2.494
19	17.226	15.678	13.134	12.085	11.158	9.604	8.365	7.366	6.550	6.198	5.877	5.316	4.844	4.442	4.097	3.942	3.799	3.539	3.311	2.848	2.496
20	18.046	16.351	13.590	12.462	11.470	9.818	8.514	7.469	6.623	6.259	5.929	5.353	4.870	4.460	4.110	3.954	3.808	3.546	3.316	2.850	2.497
21	18.857	17.011	14.029	12.821	11.764	10.017	8.649	7.562	6.687	6.313	5.973	5.384	4.891	4.476	4.121	3.963	3.816	3.551	3.320	2.852	2.498
22	19.660	17.658	14.451	13.163	12.042	10.201	8.772	7.645	6.743	6.359	6.011	5.410	4.909	4.488	4.130	3.970	3.822	3.556	3.323	2.853	2.498
23	20.456	18.292	14.857	13.489	12.303	10.371	8.883	7.718	6.792	6.399	6.044	5.432	4.925	4.499	4.137	3.976	3.827	3.559	3.325	2.854	2.499
24	21.243	18.914	15.247	13.799	12.550	10.529	8.985	7.784	6.835	6.434	6.073	5.451	4.937	4.507	4.143	3.981	3.831	3.562	3.327	2.855	2.499
25	22.023	19.523	15.622	14.094	12.783	10.675	9.077	7.843	6.873	6.464	6.097	5.467	4.948	4.514	4.147	3.985	3.834	3.564	3.329	2.856	2.499
26	22.795	20.121	15.983	14.375	13.003	10.810	9.161	7.896	6.906	6.491	6.118	5.480	4.956	4.520	4.151	3.988	3.837	3.566	3.330	2.856	2.500
27	23.560	20.707	16.330	14.643	13.211	10.935	9.237	7.943	6.935	6.514	6.136	5.492	4.964	4.524	4.154	3.990	3.839	3.567	3.331	2.856	2.500
28	24.316	21.281	16.663	14.898	13.406	11.051	9.307	7.984	6.961	6.534	6.152	5.502	4.970	4.528	4.157	3.992	3.840	3.568	3.331	2.857	2.500
29	25.066	21.844	16.984	15.141	13.591	11.158	9.370	8.022	6.983	6.551	6.166	5.510	4.975	4.531	4.159	3.994	3.841	3.569	3.332	2.857	2.500
30	25.808	22.396	17.292	15.372	13.765	11.258	9.427	8.055	7.003	6.566	6.177	5.517	4.979	4.534	4.160	3.995	3.842	3.569	3.332	2.857	2.500
35	29.409	24.999	18.665	16.374	14.498	11.655	9.644	8.176	7.070	6.617	6.215	5.539	4.992	4.541	4.164	3.998	3.845	3.571	3.333	2.857	2.500
40	32.835	27.356	19.793	17.159	15.046	11.925	9.779	8.244	7.105	6.642	6.234	5.548	4.997	4.544	4.166	3.999	3.846	3.571	3.333	2.857	2.500
45	36.095	29.490	20.720	17.774	15.456	12.108	9.863	8.283	7.123	6.654	6.242	5.552	4.999	4.545	4.166	4.000	3.846	3.571	3.333	2.857	2.500
50	39.196	31.424	21.482	18.256	15.762	12.234	9.915	8.305	7.133	6.661	6.246	5.554	4.999	4.545	4.167	4.000	3.846	3.571	3.333	2.857	2.500

Black–Scholes value of call option expressed as a percentage of the share price

Share price divided by present value of exercise price, that is S/PV(*E*)

Square root of cumulative variance, that is t	0.30	0.35	0.40	0.45	0.50	0.55	0.60	0.65	0.70	0.75	0.80	0.82	0.84	0.86	0.88	0.90	0.92	0.94	0.96	0.98	1.00	1.02	1.04	1.06	1.08	1.10	1.12	1.14	1.16	1.18	1.20	1.25	1.30	1.35	1.40	1.45	1.50	1.75	2.00	2.50	
0.05	0.0	0.0	0.0	0.0	0.0	0.0	0.0	0.0	0.0	0.0	0.0	0.0	0.0	0.0	0.0	0.0	0.1	0.3	0.6	1.2	2.0	3.1	4.5	6.0	7.5	9.1	10.7	12.3	13.8	15.3	16.7	20.0	23.1	25.9	28.6	31.0	33.3	42.9	50.0	60.0	**0.05**
0.10	0.0	0.0	0.0	0.0	0.0	0.0	0.0	0.0	0.0	0.0	0.0	0.1	0.2	0.3	0.5	0.8	1.2	1.7	2.3	3.1	4.0	5.0	6.1	7.3	8.6	10.0	11.3	12.7	14.1	15.4	16.8	20.0	23.1	25.9	28.6	31.0	33.3	42.9	50.0	60.0	**0.10**
0.15	0.0	0.0	0.0	0.0	0.0	0.0	0.0	0.0	0.1	0.2	0.5	0.7	1.0	1.3	1.7	2.2	2.8	3.5	4.2	5.1	6.0	7.0	8.0	9.1	10.2	11.4	12.6	13.8	15.0	16.2	17.4	20.4	23.3	26.0	28.6	31.0	33.3	42.9	50.0	60.0	**0.15**
0.20	0.0	0.0	0.0	0.0	0.0	0.0	0.0	0.1	0.4	0.8	1.5	1.9	2.3	2.8	3.4	4.0	4.7	5.4	6.2	7.1	8.0	8.9	9.9	10.9	11.9	13.0	14.1	15.2	16.3	17.4	18.5	21.2	23.9	26.4	28.9	31.2	33.5	42.9	50.0	60.0	**0.20**
0.25	0.0	0.0	0.0	0.0	0.0	0.1	0.2	0.5	1.0	1.8	2.8	3.3	3.9	4.5	5.2	5.9	6.6	7.4	8.2	9.1	9.9	10.9	11.8	12.8	13.7	14.7	15.7	16.7	17.7	18.7	19.8	22.3	24.7	27.1	29.4	31.7	33.8	42.9	50.0	60.0	**0.25**
0.30	0.0	0.0	0.0	0.0	0.1	0.1	0.3	0.7	1.2	2.0	3.1	4.4	5.0	5.7	6.3	7.0	7.8	8.6	9.4	10.2	11.1	11.9	12.8	13.7	14.6	15.6	16.5	17.4	18.4	19.3	20.3	21.2	23.5	25.8	28.1	30.2	32.3	34.3	43.1	50.1	60.0	**0.30**
0.35	0.0	0.0	0.1	0.2	0.4	0.8	1.4	2.3	3.3	4.6	6.2	6.8	7.5	8.2	9.0	9.8	10.6	11.4	12.2	13.0	13.9	14.8	15.6	16.5	17.4	18.3	19.2	20.1	21.0	21.9	22.7	24.9	27.1	29.2	31.2	33.2	35.1	43.5	50.2	60.0	**0.35**
0.40	0.0	0.1	0.2	0.5	0.9	1.6	2.4	3.5	4.8	6.3	8.0	8.7	9.4	10.2	11.0	11.7	12.5	13.4	14.2	15.0	15.9	16.7	17.5	18.4	19.2	20.1	20.9	21.8	22.6	23.5	24.3	26.4	28.4	30.4	32.3	34.2	36.0	44.0	50.5	60.1	**0.40**
0.45	0.1	0.2	0.5	1.0	1.7	2.6	3.7	5.0	6.5	8.1	9.9	10.6	11.4	12.2	12.9	13.7	14.5	15.3	16.2	17.0	17.8	18.6	19.4	20.3	21.1	21.9	22.7	23.5	24.3	25.1	25.9	27.9	29.8	31.7	33.5	35.3	37.0	44.6	50.8	60.2	**0.45**
0.50	0.2	0.5	1.0	1.7	2.6	3.7	5.1	6.6	8.2	10.0	11.8	12.6	13.4	14.2	14.9	15.7	16.5	17.3	18.1	18.9	19.7	20.5	21.3	22.1	22.9	23.7	24.5	25.3	26.1	26.8	27.6	29.5	31.3	33.1	34.8	36.4	38.1	45.3	51.3	50.4	**0.50**
0.55	0.5	1.0	1.7	2.6	3.8	5.1	6.6	8.3	10.0	11.9	13.8	14.6	15.4	16.1	16.9	17.7	18.5	19.3	20.1	20.9	21.7	22.4	23.2	24.0	24.8	25.5	26.3	27.0	27.8	28.5	29.2	31.0	32.8	34.5	36.1	37.7	39.2	46.1	51.9	60.7	**0.55**
0.60	0.9	1.6	2.5	3.7	5.1	6.6	8.3	10.1	11.9	13.8	15.8	16.6	17.4	18.1	18.9	19.7	20.5	21.3	22.0	22.8	23.6	24.3	25.1	25.8	26.6	27.3	28.1	28.8	29.5	30.2	30.9	32.6	34.3	35.9	37.5	39.0	40.4	47.0	52.5	61.0	**0.60**
0.65	1.4	2.4	3.6	4.9	6.5	8.2	10.0	11.9	13.8	15.8	17.8	18.6	19.3	20.1	20.9	21.7	22.5	23.2	24.0	24.7	25.5	26.2	27.0	27.7	28.4	29.1	29.8	30.5	31.2	31.9	32.6	34.2	35.8	37.4	38.9	40.3	41.7	48.0	53.3	61.4	**0.65**
0.70	2.1	3.3	4.7	6.3	8.1	9.9	11.9	13.8	15.8	17.8	19.8	20.6	21.3	22.1	22.9	23.6	24.4	25.2	25.9	26.6	27.4	28.1	28.8	29.5	30.2	30.9	31.6	32.3	32.9	33.6	34.2	35.8	37.3	38.8	40.3	41.6	43.0	49.0	54.0	61.9	**0.70**
0.75	3.0	4.4	6.1	7.9	9.8	11.7	13.7	15.8	17.8	19.8	21.8	22.5	23.3	24.1	24.8	25.6	26.3	27.1	27.8	28.5	29.2	29.9	30.6	31.3	32.0	32.7	33.3	34.0	34.6	35.3	35.9	37.4	38.9	40.3	41.7	43.0	44.3	50.0	54.9	62.4	**0.75**
0.80	4.0	5.7	7.5	9.5	11.5	13.6	15.7	17.7	19.8	21.8	23.7	24.5	25.3	26.0	26.8	27.5	28.3	29.0	29.7	30.4	31.1	31.8	32.4	33.1	33.8	34.4	35.1	35.7	36.3	36.9	37.5	39.0	40.4	41.8	43.1	44.4	45.6	51.1	55.8	63.0	**0.80**
0.85	5.1	7.1	9.1	11.2	13.3	15.5	17.6	19.7	21.8	23.8	25.7	26.5	27.2	28.0	28.7	29.4	30.2	30.9	31.6	32.2	32.9	33.6	34.2	34.9	35.5	36.2	36.8	37.4	38.0	38.6	39.2	40.6	41.9	43.3	44.5	45.8	46.9	52.2	56.7	63.6	**0.85**
0.90	6.4	8.5	10.7	13.0	15.2	17.4	19.6	21.7	23.8	25.8	27.2	28.4	29.2	29.9	30.6	31.3	32.0	32.7	33.4	34.1	34.7	35.4	36.0	36.6	37.3	37.9	38.5	39.1	39.6	40.2	40.8	42.1	43.5	44.7	46.0	47.1	48.3	53.3	57.6	64.3	**0.90**
0.95	7.8	10.1	12.5	14.8	17.1	19.4	21.6	23.7	25.7	27.7	29.6	30.4	31.1	31.8	32.5	33.2	33.9	34.6	35.2	35.9	36.5	37.2	37.8	38.4	39.0	39.6	40.1	40.7	41.3	41.8	42.4	43.7	45.0	46.2	47.4	48.5	49.6	54.5	58.6	65.0	**0.95**
1.00	9.3	11.8	14.3	16.7	19.1	21.4	23.6	25.7	27.7	29.7	31.6	32.3	33.0	33.7	34.4	35.1	35.7	36.4	37.0	37.7	38.3	38.9	39.5	40.1	40.7	41.2	41.8	42.4	42.9	43.4	44.0	45.2	46.5	47.6	48.8	49.9	50.9	55.6	59.5	65.7	**1.00**
1.05	10.9	13.6	16.1	18.6	21.0	23.3	25.6	27.7	29.7	31.6	33.5	34.2	34.9	35.6	36.2	36.9	37.6	38.2	38.8	39.4	40.0	40.6	41.2	41.8	42.4	42.9	43.5	44.0	44.5	45.0	45.5	46.8	48.0	49.1	50.2	51.2	52.2	56.7	60.5	66.5	**1.05**
1.10	12.6	15.4	18.0	20.6	23.0	25.3	27.5	29.6	31.6	33.5	35.4	36.1	36.7	37.4	38.1	38.7	39.3	40.0	40.6	41.2	41.8	42.3	42.9	43.5	44.0	44.5	45.1	45.6	46.1	46.6	47.1	48.3	49.4	50.5	51.6	52.6	53.5	57.9	61.5	67.2	**1.10**
1.15	14.4	17.2	20.0	22.5	25.0	27.3	29.5	31.6	33.6	35.4	37.2	37.9	38.6	39.2	39.9	40.5	41.1	41.7	42.3	42.9	43.5	44.0	44.6	45.1	45.6	46.2	46.7	47.2	47.7	48.2	48.6	49.8	50.9	51.9	52.9	53.9	54.9	59.0	62.5	68.0	**1.15**
1.20	16.2	19.1	21.9	24.5	27.0	29.3	31.5	33.6	35.5	37.3	39.1	39.7	40.4	41.0	41.7	42.3	42.9	43.5	44.0	44.6	45.1	45.7	46.2	46.7	47.3	47.8	48.3	48.7	49.2	49.7	50.1	51.3	52.3	53.4	54.3	55.2	56.1	60.2	63.5	68.8	**1.20**
1.25	18.1	21.1	23.9	26.5	29.0	31.3	33.5	35.5	37.4	39.2	40.9	41.5	42.2	42.8	43.4	44.0	44.6	45.2	45.7	46.3	46.8	47.3	47.8	48.4	48.8	49.3	49.8	50.3	50.7	51.2	51.6	52.7	53.7	54.7	55.7	56.6	57.4	61.3	64.5	69.6	**1.25**
1.30	20.0	23.0	25.9	28.5	31.0	33.3	35.4	37.4	39.3	41.0	42.7	43.3	43.9	44.5	45.1	45.7	46.3	46.8	47.4	47.9	48.4	48.9	49.4	49.9	50.4	50.9	51.3	51.8	52.2	52.7	53.1	54.1	55.1	56.1	57.0	57.9	58.7	62.4	65.5	70.4	**1.30**
1.35	21.9	25.0	27.9	30.5	33.0	35.2	37.3	39.3	41.1	42.8	44.4	45.1	45.7	46.3	46.8	47.4	47.9	48.5	49.0	49.5	50.0	50.5	51.0	51.5	52.0	52.4	52.9	53.3	53.7	54.1	54.6	55.6	56.5	57.4	58.3	59.1	59.9	63.5	66.5	71.1	**1.35**
1.40	23.9	27.0	29.9	32.5	34.9	37.1	39.2	41.1	42.9	44.6	46.2	46.8	47.4	47.9	48.5	49.0	49.6	50.1	50.6	51.1	51.6	52.1	52.6	53.0	53.5	53.9	54.3	54.8	55.2	55.6	56.0	56.9	57.9	58.7	59.6	60.4	61.2	64.6	67.5	71.9	**1.40**
1.45	25.8	29.0	31.9	34.5	36.9	39.1	41.1	43.0	44.7	46.4	47.9	48.5	49.0	49.6	50.1	50.7	51.2	51.7	52.2	52.7	53.2	53.6	54.1	54.5	55.0	55.4	55.8	56.2	56.6	57.0	57.4	58.3	59.2	60.0	60.9	61.6	62.4	65.7	68.4	72.7	**1.45**
1.50	27.8	31.0	33.8	36.4	38.8	40.9	42.9	44.8	46.5	48.1	49.6	50.1	50.7	51.2	51.8	52.3	52.8	53.3	53.7	54.2	54.7	55.1	55.6	56.0	56.4	56.8	57.2	57.6	58.0	58.4	58.8	59.7	60.5	61.3	62.1	62.9	63.6	66.8	69.4	73.5	**1.50**
1.55	29.8	33.0	35.8	38.4	40.7	42.8	44.8	46.6	48.2	49.8	51.2	51.8	52.3	52.8	53.3	53.8	54.3	54.8	55.3	55.7	56.2	56.6	57.0	57.4	57.8	58.2	58.6	59.0	59.4	59.7	60.1	61.0	61.8	62.6	63.3	64.1	64.7	67.8	70.3	74.3	**1.55**
1.60	31.8	35.0	37.8	40.3	42.6	44.6	46.5	48.3	49.9	51.4	52.8	53.4	53.9	54.4	54.9	55.4	55.9	56.3	56.8	57.2	57.6	58.0	58.5	58.9	59.2	59.6	60.0	60.4	60.7	61.1	61.4	62.3	63.1	63.8	64.5	65.2	65.9	68.8	71.3	75.1	**1.60**
1.65	33.8	36.9	39.7	42.2	44.4	46.4	48.3	50.0	51.6	53.1	54.4	54.9	55.4	55.9	56.4	56.9	57.3	57.8	58.2	58.6	59.1	59.5	59.9	60.2	60.6	61.0	61.4	61.7	62.1	62.4	62.7	63.5	64.3	65.0	65.7	66.4	67.0	69.9	72.2	75.9	**1.65**
1.70	35.8	38.9	41.6	44.0	46.2	48.2	50.0	51.7	53.2	54.7	56.0	56.5	57.0	57.5	57.9	58.4	58.8	59.2	59.7	60.1	60.5	60.9	61.2	61.6	62.0	62.3	62.7	63.0	63.4	63.7	64.0	64.8	65.5	66.2	66.9	67.5	68.2	70.9	73.1	76.6	**1.70**
1.75	37.7	40.8	43.5	45.9	48.0	50.0	51.7	53.4	54.8	56.2	57.5	58.0	58.5	58.9	59.4	59.8	60.2	60.7	61.1	61.5	61.8	62.2	62.6	62.9	63.3	63.6	64.0	64.3	64.6	64.9	65.3	66.0	66.7	67.4	68.0	68.7	69.2	71.9	74.0	77.4	**1.75**
2.00	47.3	50.1	52.5	54.6	56.5	58.2	59.7	61.1	62.4	63.6	64.6	65.0	65.4	65.8	66.2	66.6	66.9	67.3	67.6	67.9	68.3	68.6	68.9	69.2	69.5	69.8	70.0	70.3	70.6	70.8	71.1	71.7	72.3	72.9	73.4	73.9	74.4	76.5	78.3	81.0	**2.00**
2.25	56.1	58.6	60.7	62.5	64.1	65.6	66.8	68.0	69.1	70.0	70.9	71.5	71.6	71.9	72.2	72.5	72.8	73.1	73.4	73.7	73.9	74.2	74.4	74.7	74.9	75.2	75.4	75.6	75.8	76.0	76.3	76.8	77.2	77.7	78.1	78.5	78.9	80.6	82.1	84.3	**2.25**
2.50	64.0	66.1	67.9	69.4	70.8	72.0	73.1	74.0	74.9	75.7	76.4	76.7	77.0	77.2	77.5	77.7	78.0	78.2	78.4	78.7	78.9	79.1	79.3	79.5	79.7	79.9	80.0	80.2	80.4	80.6	80.7	81.1	81.5	81.9	82.2	82.6	82.9	84.3	85.4	87.2	**2.50**
2.75	70.9	72.7	74.2	75.4	76.6	77.5	78.4	79.2	79.9	80.5	81.1	81.4	81.6	81.8	82.0	82.2	82.4	82.6	82.7	82.9	83.1	83.3	83.4	83.6	83.7	83.9	84.0	84.2	84.3	84.4	84.6	84.9	85.2	85.5	85.8	86.0	86.3	87.4	88.3	89.7	**2.75**
3.00	76.9	78.3	79.5	80.5	81.4	82.2	82.9	83.5	84.1	84.6	85.1	85.3	85.4	85.6	85.8	85.9	86.1	86.2	86.4	86.5	86.6	86.8	86.9	87.0	87.1	87.3	87.4	87.5	87.6	87.7	87.8	88.1	88.3	88.5	88.8	89.0	89.2	90.0	90.7	91.8	**3.00**
3.50	86.0	86.9	87.6	88.3	88.8	89.3	89.7	90.1	90.5	90.8	91.1	91.2	91.3	91.4	91.5	91.6	91.6	91.7	91.8	91.9	92.0	92.1	92.1	92.2	92.3	92.4	92.4	92.5	92.6	92.6	92.7	92.8	93.0	93.1	93.3	93.4	93.5	94.0	94.4	95.1	**3.50**
4.00	92.0	92.5	92.9	93.3	93.6	93.9	94.2	94.4	94.6	94.8	94.9	95.0	95.0	95.1	95.2	95.2	95.3	95.3	95.4	95.4	95.4	95.5	95.5	95.6	95.6	95.7	95.7	95.7	95.8	95.8	95.8	95.9	96.0	96.1	96.2	96.2	96.3	96.6	96.8	97.2	**4.00**
4.50	95.7	96.0	96.2	96.4	96.6	96.7	96.9	97.0	97.1	97.2	97.3	97.3	97.3	97.4	97.4	97.4	97.5	97.5	97.5	97.5	97.6	97.6	97.6	97.6	97.6	97.7	97.7	97.7	97.7	97.8	97.8	97.8	97.9	97.9	97.9	98.0	98.0	98.2	98.3	98.5	**4.50**
5.00	97.8	97.9	98.1	98.2	98.3	98.3	98.4	98.5	98.5	98.6	98.6	98.6	98.6	98.7	98.7	98.7	98.7	98.7	98.7	98.7	98.8	98.8	98.8	98.8	98.8	98.8	98.8	98.8	98.8	98.9	98.9	98.9	98.9	98.9	99.0	99.0	99.0	99.1	99.1	99.2	**5.00**
6.00	99.5	99.5	99.6	99.6	99.6	99.6	99.7	99.7	99.7	99.7	99.7	99.7	99.7	99.7	99.7	99.7	99.7	99.7	99.7	99.7	99.7	99.7	99.7	99.7	99.7	99.7	99.7	99.7	99.7	99.8	99.8	99.8	99.8	99.8	99.8	99.8	99.8	99.8	99.8	99.8	**6.00**

Note: Values in the table represent percentages of the underlying share price: for example, 40.4 denotes a call option worth 40.4 per cent of the underlying share price.

Values in the table were computed from the Black–Scholes option pricing model. Reprinted with permission from *Corporate Finance Europe*, by Buckley, Ross, Westerfield, and Jaffe (Maidenhead, UK: McGraw-Hill, 1998).

Companies' Index

Index

Note: Page numbers in **bold** type refer to **figures**; page numbers in *italic* type refer to *tables*; page numbers followed by 'n' refer to notes